Cinema 2 *The Time-Image*

Cinema 2
The Time-Image

Gilles Deleuze
*Translated by Hugh Tomlinson
and Robert Galeta*

 University of Minnesota Press
Minneapolis

Library of Congress Number 85-28898

ISBN 0-8166-1676-0 (v. 2)
ISBN 0-8166-1677-9 (pbk.; v. 2)

Contents

Chapter 4   *The crystals of time*

Chapter 5   *Peaks of present and sheets of past: fourth commentary on Bergson*

Chapter 6 *The powers of the false*

Chapter 7 *Thought and cinema*

Chapter 8 *Cinema, body and brain, thought*

Chapter 9 *The components of the image*

Chapter 10 *Conclusions*

Preface to the English edition

Over several centuries, from the Greeks to Kant, a revolution took place in philosophy: the subordination of time to movement was reversed, time ceases to be the measurement of normal movement, it increasingly appears for itself and creates paradoxical movements. Time is out of joint: Hamlet's words signify that time is no longer subordinated to movement, but rather movement to time. It could be said that, in its own sphere, cinema has repeated the same experience, the same reversal, in more fast-moving circumstances. The movement-image of the so-called classical cinema gave way, in the post-war period, to a direct time-image. Such a general idea must of course be qualified, corrected, adapted to concrete examples.

Why is the Second World War taken as a break? The fact is that, in Europe, the post-war period has greatly increased the situations which we no longer know how to react to, in spaces which we no longer know how to describe. These were 'any spaces whatever', deserted but inhabited, disused warehouses, waste ground, cities in the course of demolition or reconstruction. And in these any-spaces-whatever a new race of characters was stirring, kind of mutant: they saw rather than acted, they were seers. Hence Rossellini's great trilogy, *Europe 51*, *Stromboli*, *Germany Year 0*: a child in the destroyed city, a foreign woman on the island, a bourgeoise woman who starts to 'see' what is around her. Situations could be extremes, or, on the contrary, those of everyday banality, or both at once: what tends to collapse, or at least to lose its position, is the sensory-motor schema which constituted the action-image of the old cinema. And thanks to this loosening of the sensory-motor linkage, it is time, 'a little time in the pure state', which rises up to the surface of the screen. Time ceases to be derived from the movement, it appears in itself and itself gives rise to *false movements*. Hence the importance of *false continuity* in modern cinema: the images are no longer linked by rational cuts and continuity, but are relinked by means of false continuity and irrational cuts. Even the body is no longer exactly what moves; subject of movement or the instrument of action, it becomes rather the developer [*révélateur*] of time, it shows time through its tirednesses and waitings (Antonioni).

It is not quite right to say that the cinematographic image is in the present. What is in the present is what the image .'represents', but not the image itself, which, in cinema as in painting, is never to be confused with what it represents. The image itself is the system of the relationships between its elements, that is, a set of relationships of time from which the variable present only flows. It is in this sense, I think, that Tarkovsky challenges the distinction between montage and shot when he defines cinema by the 'pressure of time' in the shot. What is specific to the image, as soon as it is creative, is to make perceptible, to make visible, relationships of time which cannot be seen in the represented object and do not allow themselves to be reduced to the present. Take, for example, a depth of field in Welles, a tracking shot in Visconti: we are plunged into time rather than crossing space. Sandra's car, at the beginning of Visconti's film, is already moving in time, and Welles's characters occupy a giant-sized place in time rather than changing place in space.

This is to say that the time-image has nothing to do with a flashback, or even with a recollection. Recollection is only a former present, whilst the characters who have lost their memories in modern cinema literally sink back into the past, or emerge from it, to make visible what is concealed even from recollection. Flashback is only a signpost and, when it is used by great authors, it is there only to show much more complex temporal structures (for example, in Mankiewicz, 'forking' time: recapturing the moment when time could have taken a different course . . .) In any case, what we call temporal structure, or direct time-image, clearly goes beyond the purely empirical succession of time – past-present-future. It is, for example, a coexistence of distinct durations, or of levels of duration; a single event can belong to several levels: the sheets of past coexist in a non-chronological order. We see this in Welles with his powerful intuition of the earth, then in Resnais with his characters who return from the land of the dead.

There are yet more temporal structures: the whole aim of this book is to release those that the cinematographic image has been able to grasp and reveal, and which can echo the teachings of science, what the other arts uncover for us, or what philosophy makes understandable for us, each in their respective ways. It is foolish to talk about the death of the cinema because cinema is still at the beginning of its investigations: making visible these relationships of time which can only appear in a creation of the image. It is not cinema which needs television – whose image remains so regrettably in the present unless it is enriched by the art of cinema. The relations and disjunctions between visual and sound, between what is seen and what is said, revitalize the problem and endow cinema with new powers for capturing time in the image (in quite different ways, Pierre Perrault, Straub, Syberberg . . .). Yes, if cinema does not die a violent death, it retains the power of a beginning. Conversely, we must look in pre-war cinema, and even in silent cinema, for the workings of a very pure time-image which has always been breaking through, holding back or encompassing the movement-image: an Ozu still life as unchanging form of time?

I would like to thank Robert Galeta and Hugh Tomlinson for the care which they have put into translating this adventure of movement and time.

Gilles Deleuze
July 1988

Translators' introduction

This is a translation of *L'image-temps*, the second and final volume
of Deleuze's work on the cinema, which was first published in
France in 1985. The first volume, *L'image-mouvement* was translated in 1986 as *Cinema I*.[1] Each volume can be read on its own as
dealing with a separate aspect of the cinema, classical and modern,
pre-and post-war, movement and time. Together, they constitute
what has been called 'one of the finest contemporary reflections on
the liveliness and grandeur of the modern cinema'.[2]

But Deleuze does not set out to provide another theory *of* the
cinema. His project is a philosophical one. Philosophy itself is not
a reflection on an autonomous object but a practice of creation of
concepts, a constructive pragmatism. This is a book of philosophical invention, a theory of cinema as conceptual practice. It is not a
question of 'applying' philosophical concepts to the cinema.
Philosophy works with the concepts which the cinema itself gives
rise to.

For Deleuze, the philosopher 'works alongside' the cinema,
producing a classification of its images and signs but reordering
them for new purposes. What makes cinema of special interest is
that, as with painting[3], it gives conceptual construction new
dimensions, those of the percept and affect – which should not be
confused with perception and feeling. 'Affect, percept and
concept are three inseparable powers, going from art to philosophy and the reverse'.[4] Cinema and philosophy are brought
together in a continuing process of intercutting. This is philosophy as assemblage, a kind of provoked becoming of thought.

The book's first aim is descriptive. Deleuze sets out to describe
the two fundamental images of the cinema – the movement-
image and the time-image – and their corresponding signs. The
first volume dealt with the various movement-images of the
classical cinema: perception-image, affect-image and action-
image. The present one deals with the forms of the direct
time-image of the modern cinema.

The point of transition between the two volumes, and the two
images, is the crisis of the 'action-image' after the Second World
War. The unities of situation and action can no longer be
maintained in the disjointed post-war world. This gives rise to
pure optical and sound situations from which the 'direct time-

image' emerges. *Cinema II* is concerned with the taxonomy of the
time-image and its signs, which are called 'chronosigns'. These are
signs of the order of time, of its internal relations and signs of time
as series. Both types of signs bring the notion of truth into question
and the book culminates in powerful discussions of the powers of
the false in cinema, thought in the cinema and the body and the
brain.

But this simple summary gives little impression of the extraordinary range and richness of the book. The time-image which
Deleuze releases from modern cinema gives him a new line of
approach to a number of important problems of modern thought:
the undecidability of truth and falsity, the relation of inside and
outside, the nature of 'the people', the relation between brain and
body.

Modern cinema recreates the concepts of modern philosophy,
but in a new way. In particular, the cinematic reversal of the
subordination of time to movement repeats a philosophical
revolution which took place over several centuries. Deleuze draws
a number of consequences from this reversal in the cinema. His
analysis begins with the break up of the classical notion of the image
which was defined in relation to external world and self-aware
subject. This notion was adequate to the movement-image of
pre-war cinema but is also a victim of its post-war disintegration.

The modern world and the modern image operate in the realm
of 'incommensurability'. The films of Welles, Resnais or Marguerite Duras no longer rely on world or subject. The modern
image cannot be integrated into a totality, it is connected through
'irrational cuts' between the non-linked, a confrontation takes
place between 'outside' and 'inside'.

From this confrontation 'thought' appears. Deleuze sees the
modern cinema as exploring a thought outside itself and an
unthought within thought. And it is 'thought' which remains his
concern throughout. The construction of concepts is guided by a
secret 'image of thought' which

> inspires by its developments, forkings and mutations the
> necessity of always creating new concepts, not as a function of
> external determinism, but as a function of a becoming which
> carries along the problems themselves.[5]

The creation of concepts in the cinema is guided by a powerful
'image of thought' which is central to our 'modernity'. As Deleuze

says in a recent interview, what interested him about the cinema was that

> in the screen there can be a brain, as in Resnais or Syberberg's cinema. Cinema does not operate only with linkages by rational cuts, but by re-linkages on irrational cuts: this is not the same image of thought.[6]

This image of thought through re-linkage by 'irrational cuts' inspires Deleuze's own constructive pluralism. He is engaged in the creation, the constant re-creation, of a philosophy of immanence, a constructive pragmatism. This book shows such a philosophy at work in the post-war cinema.

A whole range of new terminology is introduced in this volume. In general, these terms gain their sense through the roles they play in the assemblage of the text and we have not sought to provide further explanations. The reader is referred to the glossary of terms in *Cinema I*. However, the translation of a number of terms have presented additional difficulties.

The word 'auteur' is a problem for all translators of French writings about the cinema. Its usual sense is 'author', but it was applied to film makers to indicate a view of the director as author of the film. The word has sometimes been left untranslated but this turns an ordinary French word into a technical term. We have, in general, rendered 'auteur' as 'author'. It should be borne in mind that, when this word is used of film makers, it carries the sense of 'director' as well as 'author'.

Deleuze uses the word 'bal(l)ade' to convey both 'balade' (trip) and 'ballade' (ballad). We have been unable to retain this dual sense in English and have rendered this terms as 'trip/ballad'. In this volume, as in *Cinema I*, Deleuze uses the term 'englobant' as a noun. The verb 'englober' has the sense of 'to include, embody, bring together into a whole'. We have translated this term as 'encompasser'.

The word 'récit' is commonly translated as 'story', 'account' or even 'narrative' but is often used in conjunction with 'histoire' which is also translated as 'story', but also has the sense, 'history'. We have rendered 'récit' as 'story' with the French word in brackets when appropriate. The word 'fabulation' has been translated as 'story-telling'.

As always, Gilles Deleuze provided prompt and clear answers to all our questions and we would like to express our thanks for this and for the opportunity to take part in this adventure of time and movement. We owe a large debt of gratitude to Denise Cole for the word processing of a manuscript that always lived dangerously on the margins of legibility. Tippin Beesley did the same for a part of the manuscript. Simon Beesley provided support and assistance when it seemed it would never end. Martin Joughlin was constructive. Caroline Davidson is always told that this is the last one but continues to be tolerant. The translation is dedicated to Michael Galeta and Dorothy Thompson who have seen a lot of films.

Hugh Tomlinson
Robert Galeta

Notes

1 Cinema I: The Movement-Image, translated Hugh Tomlinson and Barbara Habberjam, London: The Athlone Press, 1986.
2 Reda Bensmaia, *Magazine littéraire*, No. 257, septembre, 1988, p. 57.
3 See Gilles Deleuze, *Francis Bacon: Logique de la Sensation*, 2 volumes, Paris: Edition de la Différence, 1981.
4 See 'Signes et événements', *Magazine littéraire*, No. 257, septembre 1988, p. 17.
5 *ibid.*, p. 23.
6 *loc cit.*

1 Beyond the movement-image

1

Against those who defined Italian neo-realism by its social content, Bazin put forward the fundamental requirement of formal aesthetic criteria. According to him, it was a matter of a new form of reality, said to be dispersive, elliptical, errant or wavering, working in blocs, with deliberately weak connections and floating events. The real was no longer represented or reproduced but 'aimed at'. Instead of representing an already deciphered real, neo-realism aimed at an always ambiguous, to be deciphered, real; this is why the sequence shot tended to replace the montage of representations. Neo-realism therefore invented a new type of image, which Bazin suggested calling 'fact-image'.[1] This thesis of Bazin's was infinitely richer than the one that he was challenging, and showed that neo-realism did not limit itself to the content of its earliest examples. But what the two theses had in common was the posing of the problem at the level of reality: neo-realism produced a formal or material 'additional reality'. However, we are not sure that the problem arises at the level of the real, whether in relation to form or content. Is it not rather at the level of the 'mental', in terms of thought? If all the movement-images, perceptions, actions and affects underwent such an upheaval, was this not first of all because a new element burst on to the scene which was to prevent perception being extended into action in order to put it in contact with thought, and, gradually, was to subordinate the image to the demands of new signs which would take it beyond movement?

When Zavattini defines neo-realism as an art of encounter – fragmentary, ephemeral, piecemeal, missed encounters – what does he mean? It is true of encounters in Rossellini's *Paisà*, or De Sica's *Bicycle Thief*. And in *Umberto D*, De Sica constructs the famous sequence quoted as an example by Bazin: the young maid going into the kitchen in the morning, making a series of mechanical, weary gestures, cleaning a bit, driving the ants away from a water fountain, picking up the coffee grinder, stretching out her foot to close the door with her toe. And her eyes meet her pregnant woman's belly, and it is as though all the misery in the

perception → action

world were going to be born. This is how, in an ordinary or everyday situation, in the course of a series of gestures, which are insignificant but all the more obedient to simple sensory-motor schemata, what has suddenly been brought about is a *pure optical situation* to which the little maid has no response or reaction. The eyes, the belly, that is what an encounter is . . . Of course, encounters can take very different forms, even achieving the exceptional, but they follow the same formula. Take, for example, Rossellini's great quartet, which, far from marking an abandonment of neo-realism, on the contrary, perfects it. *Germany Year 0* presents a child who visits a foreign country (this is why the film was criticized for not maintaining the social mooring which was held to be a condition of neo-realism), and who dies from what he sees. *Stromboli* presents a foreign woman whose revelation of the island will be all the more profound because she cannot react in a way that softens or compensates for the violence of what she sees, the intensity and the enormity of the tunny-fishing ('It was awful . . .'), the panic-inducing power of the eruption ('I am finished, I am afraid, what mystery, what beauty, my God . . .'). *Europe 51* shows a bourgeoise woman who, following the death of her child, crosses various spaces and experiences the tenement, the slum and the factory ('I thought I was seeing convicts'). Her glances relinquish the practical function of a mistress of a house who arranges things and beings, and pass through every state of an internal vision, affliction, compassion, love, happiness, acceptance, extending to the psychiatric hospital where she is locked up at the end of a new trial of Joan of Arc: she sees, she has learnt to see. *The Lonely Woman [Viaggio in Italia]* follows a female tourist struck to the core by the simple unfolding of images or visual clichés in which she discovers something unbearable, beyond the limit of what she can personally bear.[2] This is a cinema of the seer and no longer of the agent *[de voyant, non plus d'actant]*.

What defines neo-realism is this build-up of purely optical situations (and sound ones, although there was no synchronized sound at the start of neo-realism), which are fundamentally distinct from the sensory-motor situations of the action-image in the old realism. It is perhaps as important as the conquering of a purely optical space in painting, with impressionism. It may be objected that the viewer has always found himself in front of 'descriptions', in front of optical and sound-images, and nothing more. But this is not the point. For the characters themselves reacted to situations; even when one of them found himself reduced to helplessness, bound and gagged, as a result of the ups and downs of the action. What the viewer perceived therefore was a sensory-motor image in which he took a greater or lesser part by identification with the characters. Hitchcock had begun the inversion of this point of view by including the viewer in the film. But it is now that the identification is actually inverted: the character has become a kind of viewer. He shifts, runs and becomes animated in vain, the situation he is in outstrips his motor capacities on all sides, and makes him see and hear what is no longer subject to the rules of a response or an action. He records rather than reacts. He is prey to a vision, pursued by it or pursuing it, rather than engaged in an action. Visconti's *Obsession* rightly stands as the forerunner of neo-realism; and what first strikes the viewer is the way in which the black-clad heroine is possessed by an almost hallucinatory sensuality. She is closer to a visionary, a sleepwalker, than to a seductress or a lover (similarly, later, the Countess in *Senso*).

In Volume 1 the crisis of the action-image was defined by a number of characteristics: the form of the trip/ballad,[3]* the multiplication of clichés, the events that hardly concern those they happen to, in short the slackening of the sensory-motor connections. All these characteristics were important but only in the sense of preliminary conditions. They made possible, but did not yet constitute, the new image. What constitutes this is the purely optical and sound situation which takes the place of the faltering sensory-motor situations. The role of the child in neo-realism has been pointed out, notably in De Sica (and later in France with Truffaut); this is because, in the adult world, the child is affected by a certain motor helplessness, but one which makes him all the more capable of seeing and hearing. Similarly, if everyday banality is so important, it is because, being subject to sensory-motor schemata which are automatic and pre-established, it is all the more liable, on the least disturbance of equilibrium between stimulus and response (as in the scene with the little maid in *Umberto D*), suddenly to free itself from the laws of this schema and reveal itself in a visual and sound nakedness, crudeness and brutality which make it unbearable, giving it the pace of a dream or a nightmare. There is, therefore, a necessary passage from the crisis of image-action to the pure optical-sound image. Sometimes it is an evolution from one aspect to the other: beginning with trip/ballad films [*films de bal(1)ade*] with the

sensory-motor connections slackened, and then reaching purely
optical and sound situations. Sometimes the two coexist in the
same film like two levels, the first of which serves merely as a
melodic line for the second.

It is in this sense that Visconti, Antonioni and Fellini are
definitely part of neo-realism, in spite of all their differences.
Obsession, the forerunner, is not merely one of the versions of a
famous American thriller, or the transposition of this novel to the
plain of the Po.[4] In Visconti's film, we witness a very subtle
change, the beginnings of a mutation of the general notion of
situation. In the old realism or on the model of the action-image,
objects and settings already had a reality of their own, but it was a
functional reality, strictly determined by the demands of the
situation, even if these demands were as much poetic as dramatic
(for instance, the emotional value of objects in Kazan). The
situation was, then, directly extended into action and passion.
After *Obsession*, however, something appears that continues to
develop in Visconti: objects and settings [*milieux*] take on an
autonomous, material reality which gives them an importance in
themselves. It is therefore essential that not only the viewer but
the protagonists invest the settings and the objects with their gaze,
that they see and hear the things and the people, in order for
action or passion to be born, erupting in a pre-existing daily life.
Hence the arrival of the hero of *Obsession*, who takes a kind of
visual possession of the inn, or, in *Rocco and his Brothers*, the arrival
of the family who, with all their eyes and ears, try to take in the
huge station and the unknown city: this will be a constant theme
in Visconti's work, this 'inventory' of a setting – its objects,
furniture, tools, etc. So the situation is not extended directly into
action: it is no longer sensory-motor, as in realism, but primarily
optical and of sound, invested by the senses, before action takes
shape in it, and uses or confronts its elements. Everything
remains real in this neo-realism (whether it is film set or exteriors)
but, between the reality of the setting and that of the action, it is
no longer a motor extension which is established, but rather a
dreamlike connection through the intermediary of the liberated
sense organs.[5] It is as if the action floats in the situation, rather
than bringing it to a conclusion or strengthening it. This is the
source of Visconti's visionary aestheticism. And *The Earth Trembles*
confirms these new parameters in a singular way. Of course the
fishermen's situation, the struggle they are engaged in, and the
birth of a class conciousness are revealed in this first episode, the

only one that Visconti completed. But this embryonic 'communist consciousness' here depends less on a struggle with nature and between men than on a grand vision of man and nature, of their perceptible and sensual unity, from which the 'rich' are excluded and which constitutes the hope of the revolution, beyond the setbacks of the floating action: a Marxist romanticism.[6]

In Antonioni, from his first great work, *Story of a Love Affair*, the police investigation, instead of proceeding by flashback, transforms the actions into optical and sound descriptions, whilst the tale itself is transformed into actions which are dislocated in time (the episode where the maid talks while repeating her tired gestures, or the famous scene with the lifts).[7] And Antonioni's art will continue to evolve in two directions: an astonishing development of the idle periods of everyday banality; then, starting with *The Eclipse*, a treatment of limit-situations which pushes them to the point of dehumanized landscapes, of emptied spaces that might be seen as having absorbed characters and actions, retaining only a geophysical description, an abstract inventory of them. As for Fellini, from his earliest films, it is not simply the spectacle which tends to overflow the real, it is the everyday which continually organizes itself into a travelling spectacle, and the sensory-motor linkages which give way to a succession of *varieties* subject to their own laws of passage. Barthélemy Amengual produces a formula which is true for the first half of this work: 'The real becomes spectacle or spectacular, and fascinates for being the real thing . . . The everyday is identified with the spectacular . . . Fellini achieves the deliberate confusion of the real and the spectacle' by denying the heterogeneity of the two worlds, by effacing not only distance, but the distinction between the spectator and the spectacle.[8]

The optical and sound situations of neo-realism contrast with the strong sensory-motor situations of traditional realism. The space of a sensory-motor situation is a setting which is already specified and presupposes an action which discloses it, or prompts a reaction which adapts to or modifies it. But a purely optical or sound situation becomes established in what we might call 'any-space-whatever', whether disconnected, or emptied (we find the passage from one to the other in *The Eclipse*, where the disconnected bits of space lived by the heroine – stock exchange, Africa, air terminal – are reunited at the end in an empty space which blends into the white surface). In neo-realism, the sensory-motor connections are now valid only by virtue of the upsets that

affect, loosen, unbalance, or uncouple them: the crisis of the
action-image. No longer being induced by an action, any more
than it is extended into one, the optical and sound situation is,
therefore, neither an index nor a synsign. There is a new breed of
signs, *opsigns* and *sonsigns*. And clearly these new signs refer to
very varied images – sometimes everyday banality, sometimes
exceptional or limit-circumstances – but, above all, subjective
images, memories of childhood, sound and visual dreams or
fantasies, where the character does not act without seeing himself
acting, complicit viewer of the role he himself is playing, in the
style of Fellini. Sometimes, as in Antonioni, they are objective
images, in the manner of a *report*, even if this is a report of an
accident, defined by a geometrical frame which now allows only
the existence of relations of measurement and distance between
its elements, persons and objects, this time transforming the
action into displacement of figures in space (for instance, the
search for the vanished woman in *The Adventure*).[9] It is in this
sense that the critical objectivism of Antonioni may be contrasted
with the knowing subjectivism of Fellini. There would be, then,
two kinds of opsigns, reports [*constats*] and 'instats',[10]* the former
giving a vision with depth, at a distance, tending towards
abstraction, the other a close, flat-on vision inducing involvement.
This opposition corresponds in some respects to the alternative as
defined by Worringer: abstraction or *Einfühlung*. Antonioni's
aesthetic visions are inseparable from an objective critique (we are
sick with Eros, because Eros is himself objectively sick: what has
love become that a man or a woman should emerge from it so
disabled, pitiful and suffering, and act and react as badly at the
beginning as at the end, in a corrupt society?), whilst Fellini's
visions are inseparable from an 'empathy', a subjective sympathy
(embrace even that decadence which means that one loves only in
dreams or in recollection, sympathize with those kinds of love, be
an accomplice of decadence, and even provoke it, in order to save
something, perhaps, as far as is possible . . .).[11] On both sides
these are higher, more important, problems than commonplaces
about solitude and incommunicability.

The distinctions, on one hand between the banal and the
extreme, and on the other between the subjective and the
objective, have some value, but only relatively. They are valid for
an image or a sequence, but not for the whole. They are still valid
in relation to the action-image, which they bring into question,
but already they are no longer wholly valid in relation to the new

image that is coming into being. They mark poles between which there is continual passage. In fact, the most banal or everyday situations release accumulated 'dead forces' equal to the life force of a limit-situation (thus, in De Sica's *Umberto D*, the sequence where the old man examines himself and thinks he has fever). In addition, the idle periods in Antonioni do not merely show the banalities of daily life, they reap the consequences or the effect of a remarkable event which is reported only through itself without being explained (the break-up of a couple, the sudden disappearance of a woman . . .). The method of report in Antonioni always has this function of bringing idle periods and empty spaces together: drawing all the consequences from a decisive past experience, once it is done and everything has been said. 'When everything has been said, when the main scene seems over, there is what comes afterwards . . .'[12]

As for the distinction between subjective and objective, it also tends to lose its importance, to the extent that the optical situation or visual description replaces the motor action. We run in fact into a principle of indeterminability, of indiscernibility: we no longer know what is imaginary or real, physical or mental, in the situation, not because they are confused, but because we do not have to know and there is no longer even a place from which to ask. It is as if the real and the imaginary were running after each other, as if each was being reflected in the other, around a point of indiscernibility. We will return to this point, but, already, when Robbe-Grillet provides his great theory of descriptions, he begins by defining a traditional 'realist' description: it is that which presupposes the independence of its object, and hence proposes a discernibility of the real and the imaginary (they can become confused, but none the less by right they remain distinct). Neo-realist description in the *nouveau roman* is completely different: since it *replaces* its own object, on the one hand it erases or *destroys* its reality which passes into the imaginary, but on the other hand it powerfully brings out all the reality which the imaginary or the mental *create* through speech and vision.[13] The imaginary and the real became indiscernible. Robbe-Grillet will become more and more conscious of this in his reflection on the *nouveau roman* and the cinema: the most objectivist determinants do not prevent their realizing a 'total subjectivity'. This is what was embryonic from the start of Italian neo-realism, and what makes Labarthe remark that *Last Year in Marienbad* is the last of the great neo-realist films.[14]

We can already see in Fellini that a particular image is clearly subjective, mental, a recollection or fantasy – but it is not organized into a spectacle without becoming objective, without going behind the scenes, into 'the reality of the spectacle, of those who make it, who live from it, who are absorbed in it': the mental world of a character is so filled up by other proliferating characters that it becomes inter-mental, and through flattening of perspectives ends 'in a neutral, impersonal vision . . . all our world' (hence the importance of the telepath in *8½*).[15] Conversely, in Antonioni, it is as if the most objective images are not formed without becoming mental, and going into a strange, invisible subjectivity. It is not merely that the method of report has to be applied to feelings as they exist in a society, and to draw from them such consequences as are internally developed in characters: Eros sick is a story of feelings which go from the objective to the subjective, and are internalized in everyone. In this respect, Antonioni is much closer to Nietzsche than to Marx; he is the only contemporary author to have taken up the Nietzschean project of a real critique of morality, and this thanks to a 'symptomatologist' method. But, from yet another point of view, it is noticeable that Antonioni's objective images, which impersonally follow a becoming, that is, a development of consequences in a story [*récit*], none the less are subject to rapid breaks, interpolations and 'infinitesimal injections of a-temporality': for example, the lift scene in *Story of a Love Affair*. We are returned once more to the first form of the any-space-whatever: disconnected space. The connection of the parts of space is not given, because it can come about only from the subjective point of view of a character who is, nevertheless, absent, or has even disappeared, not simply out of frame, but passed into the void. In *The Outcry*, Irma is not only the obsessive, subjective thought of the hero who runs away to forget, but the imaginary gaze under which this flight takes place and connects its own segments: a gaze which becomes real again at the moment of death. And above all in *The Adventure*, the vanished woman causes an indeterminable gaze to weigh on the couple – which gives them the continual feeling of being spied on, and which explains the lack of co-ordination of their objective movements, when they flee whilst pretending to look for her. Again in *Identification of a Woman*, the whole quest or investigation takes place under the presumed gaze of the departed woman, concerning whom we will not know, in the marvellous images at the end, whether or not she has seen the hero curled up in the lift cage. The imaginary gaze makes the real something imaginary, at the same time as it in turn becomes real and gives us back some reality. It is like a circuit which exchanges, corrects, selects and sends us off again. From *The Eclipse* onwards, the any-space-whatever had achieved a second form: empty or deserted space. What happened is that, from one result to the next, the characters were objectively emptied: they are suffering less from the absence of another than from their absence from themselves (for example, *The Passenger*). Hence, this space refers back again to the lost gaze of the being who is absent from the world as much as from himself, and, as Ollier says in a phrase which is true for the whole of Antonioni's work, replaces 'traditional drama with a kind of *optical drama* lived by the character'.[16]

In short, pure optical and sound situations can have two poles – objective and subjective, real and imaginary, physical and mental. But they give rise to opsigns and sonsigns, which bring the poles into continual contact, and which, in one direction or the other, guarantee passages and conversions, tending towards a point of indiscernibility (and not of confusion). Such a system of exchange between the imaginary and the real appears fully in Visconti's *White Nights*.[17]

The French new wave cannot be defined unless we try to see how it has retraced the path of Italian neo-realism for its own purposes – even if it meant going in other directions as well. In fact, the new wave, on a first approximation, takes up the previous route again: from a loosening of the sensory-motor link (the stroll or wandering, the ballad, the events which concern no one, etc.), to the rise of optical and sound situations. Here again, a cinema of seeing replaces action. If Tati belongs to the new wave, it is because, after two ballad-films, he fully isolates what was taking shape in these – a burlesque whose impetus comes from purely optical and, in particular, sound, situations. Godard begins with some extraordinary ballads, from *Breathless* to *Pierrot le fou*, and tends to draw out of them a whole world of opsigns and sonsigns which already constitute the new image (in *Pierrot le fou*, the passage from the sensory-motor loosening, 'I dunno what to do', to the pure poem sung and danced, 'the line of your hips'). And these images, touching or terrible, take on an ever greater autonomy after *Made in USA*; which may be summed up as follows: 'A witness providing us with a series of reports with neither conclusion nor logical connection ... without really

effective reactions.'[18] Claude Ollier says that, with *Made in USA*,
the violently hallucinatory character of Godard's work is affirmed
for itself, in an art of description which is always being renewed
and always replacing its object.[19] This descriptive objectivism is
just as critical and even didactic, sustaining a series of films, from
Two or Three Things I Know about Her, to *Slow Motion*, where
reflection is not simply focused on the content of the image but on
its form, its means and functions, its falsifications and creativities,
on the relations within it between the sound dimension and the
optical. Godard has little patience with or sympathy for fantasies:
Slow Motion will show us the decomposition of a sexual fantasy
into its separate, objective elements, visual, and then of sound.
But this objectivism never loses its aesthetic force. Initially serving
a politics of the image, the aesthetic force is powerfully brought
out for its own sake in *Passion*: the free build-up of pictorial and
musical images as *tableaux vivants*, whilst at the other end the
sensory-motor linkages are beset by inhibitions (the stuttering of
the female worker and the boss's cough). *Passion*, in this sense,
brings to its greatest intensity what was already taking shape in *Le
Mépris*, when we witnessed the sensory-motor failure of the
couple in the traditional drama, at the same time as the optical
representation of the drama of Ulysses and the gaze of the gods,
with Fritz Lang as the intercessor, was soaring upwards.
Throughout all these films, there is a creative evolution which is
that of a visionary Godard.

For Rivette, *Le pont du Nord* has exactly the same perfection of
provisional summary as *Passion* for Godard. It is the ballad of two
strange women strollers to whom a grand vision of the stone lions
of Paris will present pure optical and sound situations, in a kind of
malicious snakes and ladders where they replay the hallucinatory
drama of Don Quixote. But, from the same starting-point,
Rivette and Godard seem to mark out the two contrasting sides.
This is because, with Rivette, the break in the sensory-motor
situations – to the benefit of optical and sound situations – is
connected to a knowing subjectivism, an empathy, which most
frequently works through fantasies, memories, or pseudo-
memories, and finds in them a unique gaiety and lightness (*Celine
and Julie Go Boating* is certainly one of the greatest French comic
films, along with the work of Tati). Whilst Godard drew inspiration from the strip cartoon at its most cruel and cutting, Rivette
clothes his unchanging theme of an international conspiracy in an
atmosphere of fable and children's games. Already in *Paris*

Belongs to Us, the stroll culminates in a twilight fantasy where the cityscape has no reality or connections other than those given by our dream. And *Celine and Julie Go Boating*, after the stroll-pursuit of the girl with a double, has us witness the pure spectacle of her fantasy, a young girl whose life is threatened in a family novel. The double, or rather the woman double [*la double*], is herself present with the aid of magic sweets; then, thanks to the alchemical potion, she introduces herself into the spectacle which no longer has viewers, but only behind the scenes, and finally saves the child from her appointed fate as a little boat takes her off into the distance: there is no more cheerful a fairy-tale. *Twilight* does not even have to get us into the spectacle; the heroines of the spectacle, the solar woman and the lunar woman, who have already passed into the real, under the sign of the magic stone track down, make disappear or kill the surviving characters who would still be capable of being witnesses.

Rivette could be said to be the most French of the new wave authors. But 'French' here has nothing to do with what has been called the French quality. It is rather in the sense of the pre-war French school, when it discovers, following the painter Delaunay, that there is no struggle between light and darkness (expressionism), but an alternation and duel of the sun and the moon, which are both light, one constituting a circular, continuous movement of complementary colours, the other a faster and uneven movement of jarring, iridescent colours, the two together making up and projecting an eternal mirage on to the earth.[20] This is the case with *Twilight*. This is the case with *Merry-go-round*, where the description made of light and colours constantly begins again in order to obliterate its objects. Rivette takes this to the highest level in his art of light. All his heroines are daughters of fire, all his work is under this sign. In the end, if he is the most French of film-makers, it is in the sense that Gérard de Nerval could be called the supreme French poet, could even be called the 'Good Gerard', singer of the Ile de France, just like Rivette, singer of Paris and its rustic streets. When Proust asks himself what there is behind all these names that were applied to Nerval, he replies that in fact it is some of the greatest poetry that there has been in the world, and madness itself or the mirage to which Nerval succumbed. For, if Nerval needs to see, and to walk in the Valois, he needs this like some reality which has to 'verify' his hallucinatory vision, to the point where we no longer have any idea what is present or past, mental or physical. He needs the Ile de France as the real that his speech and his vision create, as the objective in his pure subjectivity: a 'dream lightning', a 'bluish and purple atmosphere', solar and lunar.[21] The same goes for Rivette and his need of Paris. Here again, we have to conclude that the difference between the objective and the subjective has only a provisional, relative value, from the point of view of the optical-sound image. The most subjective, the knowing subjectivism of Rivette, is utterly objective, because it creates the real through the force of visual description. And conversely what is most objective, Godard's critical objectivism, was already completely subjective, because in place of the real object it put visual description, and made it go 'inside' the person or object (*Two or Three Things I Know about Her*).[22] On both sides, description tends towards a point of indiscernibility of the real and the imaginary.

A final question: why does the collapse of traditional sensory-motor situations, in the form these had in the old realism or in the action-image, allow only pure optical and sound situations, opsigns and sonsigns, to emerge? It will be noted that Robbe-Grillet, at least at the beginning of his reflections, was even harsher: he renounced not merely the tactile, but even sounds and colours as inept for the report, too tied to emotions and reactions, and he kept only visual descriptions which operated through lines, surfaces and sizes.[23] The cinema was one of the causes of his evolution, because it made him discover the descriptive power of colour and sounds, as these replace, obliterate and re-create the object itself. But, even more, it is the tactile which can constitute a pure sensory image, on condition that the hand relinquishes its prehensile and motor functions to content itself with a pure touching. In Herzog, we witness an extraordinary effort to present to the view specifically tactile images which characterize the situation of 'defenceless' beings, and unite with the grand visions of those suffering from hallucinations.[24] But it is Bresson, in a quite different way, who makes touch an object of view in itself. Bresson's visual space is fragmented and disconnected, but its parts have, step by step, a manual continuity. The hand, then, takes on a role in the image which goes infinitely beyond the sensory-motor demands of the action, which takes the place of the face itself for the purpose of affects, and which, in the area of perception, becomes the mode of construction of a space which is adequate to the decisions of the spirit. Thus, in *Pickpocket*, it is the hands of the three accomplices which connect the parts of space in the Gare de Lyon, not exactly through their seizing an object, but through brushing it, arresting it in its movement, giving it another direction, passing it on and making it circulate in this space. The hand doubles its prehensile function (of object) by a connective function (of space); but, from that moment, it is the whole eye which doubles its optical function by a specifically 'grabbing' [*haptique*] one, if we follow Riegl's formula for indicating a touching which is specific to the gaze. In Bresson, opsigns and sonsigns cannot be separated from genuine tactisigns which perhaps regulate their relations (this is the originality of Bresson's any-space-whatevers).

2

Although he was subject, from the outset, to the influence of certain American authors, Ozu built up in a Japanese context a body of work which was the first to develop pure optical and sound situations (even so he came quite late to the talkie, in 1936). The Europeans did not imitate him, but came back to him later via their own methods. He none the less remains the inventor of opsigns and sonsigns. The work borrows a trip/ballad [*bal(l)ade*] form, train journey, taxi ride, bus trip, a journey by bicycle or on foot: the grandparents' return journey from the provinces to Tokyo, the girl's last holiday with her mother, an old man's jaunt . . . But the object is everyday banality taken as family life in the Japanese house. Camera movements take place less and less frequently; tracking shots are slow, low 'blocs of movement'; the always low camera is usually fixed, frontal or at an unchanging angle: dissolves are abandoned in favour of the simple *cut*.[25] What might appear to be a return to 'primitive cinema' is just as much the elaboration of an astonishingly temperate modern style: the montage-cut which will dominate modern cinema, is a purely optical passage or punctuation between images, working directly, sacrificing all synthetic effects. The sound is also affected, since the montage-cut may culminate in the 'one shot, one line' procedure borrowed from American cinema. But there, for instance, in Lubitsch, it was a matter of an action-image functioning as an index, whereas Ozu modifies the meaning of the procedure, which now shows the absence of plot: the action-image disappears in favour of the purely visual image of what a character *is*, and the sound image of what he *says*, completely

banal nature and conservation constituting the essentials of the
script (this is why the only things that count are the choice of
actors according to their physical and moral appearance, and the
establishment of any dialogue whatever, apparently without a
precise subject-matter.[26]

It is clear that this method immediately presents idle periods,
and leads to their increase in the course of the film. Of course, as
the film proceeds, it might be thought that the idle periods are no
longer important simply for themselves but recoup the effect of
something important: the shot or the line would, on this view, be
extended by a quite long silence or emptiness. But it is definitely
not the case, with Ozu, that we get the remarkable *and* the
ordinary, limit-situations *and* banal ones, the former having an
effect on, or purposely insinuating themselves into, the latter. We
cannot follow Paul Schrader when he contrasts, like two phases,
'the everyday' on one hand, and, on the other, 'the moment of
decision', 'the disparity', which introduce an inexplicable break or
emotion into daily banality.[27] This distinction would seem strictly
more valid for neo-realism. In Ozu, everything is ordinary or
banal, even death and the dead who are the object of a natural
forgetting. The famous scenes of sudden tears (that of the father
in *An Autumn Afternoon* who starts to weep silently after his
daughter's wedding, that of the daughter in *Late Spring* who half
smiles as she looks at her sleeping father, then finds herself on the
verge of tears, that of the daughter in *Dernier caprice* who makes a
sharp comment about her dead father, then bursts into tears) do
not mark out a strong period which might be contrasted with the
weak periods in the flow of life, and there is no reason to suggest
the emergence of a repressed emotion as 'decisive action'.

The philosopher Leibniz (who was not unaware of the existence of the Chinese philosophers) showed that the world is made
up of series which are composed and which converge in a very
regular way, according to ordinary laws. However, the series and
sequences are apparent to us only in small sections, and in a
disrupted or mixed-up order, so that we believe in breaks,
disparities and discrepancies as in things that are out of the
ordinary. Maurice Leblanc wrote a very good serial which comes
close to a Zen kind of wisdom: the hero, Balthazar, 'professor of
everyday philosophy', teaches that there is nothing remarkable or
exceptional in life, that the oddest adventures are easily
explained, and that everything is made up of ordinary things.[28] It
is just that we have to admit that, because the linkages of the terms

in the series are naturally weak, they are constantly upset and do not appear in order. An ordinary term goes out of sequence, and emerges in the middle of another sequence of ordinary things in relation to which it takes on the appearance of a strong moment, a remarkable or complex point. It is men who upset the regularity of series, the continuity of the universe. There is a time for life, a time for death, a time for the mother, a time for the daughter, but men mix them up, make them appear in disorder, set them up in conflicts. This is Ozu's thinking: life is simple, and man never stops complicating it by 'disturbing still water' (as in the three companions in *Late Autumn*). And if, after the war, Ozu's work does not at all fall into the decline that has sometimes been suggested, it is because the post-war period helps confirm this thinking, but by renewing it, by reinforcing and going beyond the theme of conflicting generations: American ordinariness helps break down what is ordinary about Japan, a clash of two everyday realities which is even expressed in colour, when Coca-Cola red or plastic yellow violently interrupt the series of washed-out, unemphatic tones of Japanese life.[29] And, as the character says in *The Flavour of Green Tea over Rice*: what if the opposite had occurred, if saki, samisen and geisha wigs had suddenly been introduced into the everyday banality of Americans . . .? On this point it seems to us that nature does not, as Schrader believes, intervene in a decisive moment or in a clear break with everyday man. The splendour of nature, of a snow-covered mountain, tells us one thing only: everything is ordinary and regular, everything is everyday! Nature is happy to renew what man has broken, she restores what man sees shattered. And, when a character emerges for a moment from a family conflict or a wake to contemplate the snow-covered mountain, it is as if he were seeking to restore to order the series upset in his house but reinstated by an unchanging, regular nature, as in an equation that provides us with the reason for apparent breaks, 'for the turns and returns, the highs and the lows', as Leibniz puts it.

Daily life allows only weak sensory-motor connections to survive, and replaces the action-image by pure optical and sound images, opsigns and sonsigns. In Ozu, there is no universal line which connects moments of decision, and links the dead to the living, as in Mizoguchi; nor is there any breathing space or encompasser to contain a profound question, as in Kurosawa. Ozu's spaces are raised to the state of any-space-whatevers, whether by disconnection, or vacuity (here again Ozu may be

considered one of the first inventors). The false continuity of
gaze, of direction and even of the position of objects are constant
and systematic. One case of camera movement gives a good
example of disconnection: in *Early Summer*, the heroine goes
forward on tiptoe to surprise someone in a restaurant, the camera
drawing back in order to keep her in the centre of the frame; then
the camera goes foward to a corridor, but this corridor is no
longer in the restaurant, it is in the house of the heroine who has
already returned home. As for the empty spaces, without
characters or movement, they are interiors emptied of their
occupants, deserted exteriors or landscapes in nature. In Ozu
they take on an autonomy which they do not immediately possess
even in neo-realism, which accords them an apparent value which
is relative (in relation to a story) or consequential (once the action
is done with). They reach the absolute, as instances of pure
contemplation, and immediately bring about the identity of the
mental and the physical, the real and the imaginary, the subject
and the object, the world and the I. They correspond in part to
what Schrader calls 'cases of stasis', Noël Burch 'pillow-shots',
Richie 'still lifes'. The question is to know whether there is not all
the same a distinction to be made at the centre of this category
itself.[30]

Between an empty space or landscape and a still life properly so
called there are certainly many similarities, shared functions and
imperceptible transitions. But it is not the same thing; a still life
cannot be confused with a landscape. An empty space owes its
importance above all to the absence of a possible content, whilst
the still life is defined by the presence and composition of objects
which are wrapped up in themselves or become their own
container: as in the long shot of the vase almost at the end of *Late
Spring*. Such objects are not necessarily surrounded by a void, but
may allow characters to live and speak in a certain soft focus, like
the still life with vase and fruit in *The Woman of Tokyo*, or the one
with fruit and golf-clubs in *What Did the Lady Forget?* It is like
Cézanne, the landscapes – empty or with gaps – do not have the
same principles of composition as the full still lifes. There comes a
point when one hesitates between the two, so completely can their
functions overlap each other and so subtle are the transitions that
can be made: for instance, in Ozu, the marvellous composition
with the bottle and the lighthouse, at the beginning of *A Story of
Floating Weeds*. The distinction is none the less that of the empty
and the full, which brings into play all the nuances or relations in

Chinese and Japanese thought, as two aspects of contemplation. If empty spaces, interiors or exteriors, constitute purely optical (and sound) situations, still lifes are the reverse, the correlate.

The vase in *Late Spring* is interposed between the daughter's half smile and the beginning of her tears. There is becoming, change, passage. But the form of what changes does not itself change, does not pass on. This is time, time itself, 'a little time in its pure state': a direct time-image, which gives what changes the unchanging form in which the change is produced. The night that changes into day, or the reverse, recalls a still life on which light falls, either fading or getting stronger (*That Night's Wife, Passing Fancy*). The still life is time, for everything that changes is in time, but time does not itself change, it could itself change only in another time, indefinitely. At the point where the cinematographic image most directly confronts the photo, it also becomes most radically distinct from it. Ozu's still lifes endure, have a duration, over ten seconds of the vase: this duration of the vase is precisely the representation of that which endures, through the succession of changing states. A bicycle may also endure; that is, represent the unchanging form of that which moves, so long as it is at rest, motionless, stood against the wall (*A Story of Floating Weeds*). The bicycle, the vase and the still lifes are the pure and direct images of time. Each is time, on each occasion, under various conditions of that which changes in time. Time is the full, that is, the unalterable form filled by change. Time is 'the visual reserve of events in their appropriateness'.[31] Antonioni spoke of 'the horizon of events', but noted that in the West the word has a double meaning, man's banal horizon and an inaccessible and always receding cosmological horizon. Hence the division of western cinema into European humanism and American science fiction.[32] He suggested that it is not the same for the Japanese, who are hardly interested in science fiction: one and the same horizon links the cosmic to the everyday, the durable to the changing, one single and identical time as the unchanging form of that which changes. It is in this way that nature or stasis was defined, according to Schrader, as the form that links the everyday in 'something unified and permanent'. There is no need at all to call on a transcendence. In everyday banality, the action-image and even the movement-image tend to disappear in favour of pure optical situations, but these reveal connections of a new type, which are no longer sensory-motor and which bring the emancipated senses into direct relation with time and thought.

This is the very special extension of the opsign: to make time and thought perceptible, to make them visible and of sound.

3

A purely optical and sound situation does not extend into action, any more than it is induced by an action. It makes us grasp, it is supposed to make us grasp, something intolerable and unbearable. Not a brutality as nervous aggression, an exaggerated violence that can always be extracted from the sensory-motor relations in the action-image. Nor is it a matter of scenes of terror, although there are sometimes corpses and blood. It is a matter of something too powerful, or too unjust, but sometimes also too beautiful, and which henceforth outstrips our sensory-motor capacities. *Stromboli*: a beauty which is too great for us, like too strong a pain. It can be a limit-situation, the eruption of the volcano, but also the most banal, a plain factory, a wasteland. In Godard's *Les carabiniers* the girl militant recites a few revolutionary slogans, so many clichés; but she is so beautiful, of a beauty which is unbearable for her torturers who have to cover up her face with a handkerchief. And this handkerchief, lifted again by breath and whisper ('Brothers, brothers, brothers . . .'), itself becomes unbearable for us the viewers. In any event something has become too strong in the image. Romanticism had already set out this aim for itself: grasping the intolerable or the unbearable, the empire of poverty, and thereby becoming visionary, to produce a means of knowledge and action out of pure vision.[33]

Nevertheless, are there not equal amounts of fantasy and dreaming in what we claim to see as there are of objective apprehending? Moreover, do we not have a subjective sympathy for the unbearable, an empathy which permeates what we see? But this means that the unbearable itself is inseparable from a revelation or an illumination, as from a third eye. Fellini has strong sympathies with decadence, only in so far as he prolongs it, extends its range, 'to the intolerable', and reveals beneath the movements, faces and gestures a subterranean or extra-terrestrial world, 'the tracking shot becoming a means of peeling away, proof of the unreality of movement', and the cinema becoming, no longer an undertaking of recognition [*reconnaisance*], but of knowledge [*connaisance*], 'a science of visual impressions, forcing us to forget our own logic and retinal habits'.[34] Ozu himself is not the guardian of traditional or reactionary values, he is the greatest critic of daily life. He picks out the intolerable from the insignificant itself, provided that he can extend the force of a contemplation that is full of sympathy or pity across daily life. The important thing is always that the character or the viewer, and the two together, become visionaries. The purely optical and sound situation gives rise to a seeing function, at once fantasy and report, criticism and compassion, whilst sensory-motor situations, no matter how violent, are directed to a pragmatic visual function which 'tolerates' or 'puts up with' practically anything, from the moment it becomes involved in a system of actions and reactions.

In Japan and Europe, Marxist critics have attacked these films and their characters for being too passive and negative, in turn bourgeois, neurotic or marginal, and for having replaced modifying action with a 'confused' vision.[35] And it is true that, in cinema, characters of the trip/ballad are unconcerned, even by what happens to them: whether in the style of Rossellini, the foreign woman who discovers the island, the bourgeoise woman who discovers the factory; or in the style of Godard, the Pierrot-le-fou generation. But it is precisely the weakness of the motor-linkages, the weak connections, that are capable of releasing huge forces of disintegration. These are the characters with a strange vibrance in Rossellini, strangely well-informed in Godard and Rivette. In the west as in Japan, they are in the grip of a mutation, they are themselves mutants. On the subject of *Two or Three Things . . .*, Godard says that *to describe* is to observe mutations.[36] Mutation of Europe after the war, mutation of an Americanized Japan, mutation of France in '68: it is not the cinema that turns away from politics, it becomes completely political, but in another way. One of the two women strollers in Rivette's *Pont du Nord* has all the characteristics of an unforeseeable mutant: she has at first the capacity of detecting the Maxes, the members of the organization for enslaving the world, before going through a metamorphosis inside a cocoon, then being drafted into their ranks. Similarly with the ambiguity of the *Petit soldat*. A new type of character for a new cinema. It is because what happens to them does not belong to them and only half concerns them, because they know how to extract from the event the part that cannot be reduced to what happens: that part of inexhaustible possibility that constitutes the unbearable, the intolerable, the visionary's part. A new type of actor was needed: not simply the non-professional actors that neo-realism had revived at the beginning, but what might be called professional non-actors, or, better, 'actor-mediums', capable of seeing and showing rather than acting, and either remaining dumb or undertaking some never-ending conversation, rather than of replying or following a dialogue (such as, in France, Bulle Ogier or Jean-Pierre Léaud).[37]

Neither everyday nor limit-situations are marked by anything rare or extraordinary. It is just a volcanic island of poor fishermen. It is just a factory, a school . . . We mix with all that, even death, even accidents, in our normal life or on holidays. We see, and we more or less experience, a powerful organization of poverty and oppression. And we are precisely not without sensory-motor schemata for recognizing such things, for putting up with and approving of them and for behaving ourselves subsequently, taking into account our situation, our capabilities and our tastes. We have schemata for turning away when it is too unpleasant, for prompting resignation when it is terrible and for assimilating when it is too beautiful. It should be pointed out here that even metaphors are sensory-motor evasions, and furnish us with something to say when we no longer know what do to: they are specific schemata of an affective nature. Now this is what a cliché is. A cliché is a sensory-motor image of the thing. As Bergson says, we do not perceive the thing or the image in its entirety, we always perceive less of it, we perceive only what we are interested in perceiving, or rather what it is in our interest to perceive, by virtue of our economic interests, ideological beliefs and psychological demands. We therefore normally perceive only clichés. But, if our sensory-motor schemata jam or break, then a different type of image can appear: a pure optical-sound image, the whole image without metaphor, brings out the thing in itself, literally, in its excess of horror or beauty, in its radical or unjustifiable character, because it no longer has to be 'justified', for better or for worse . . . The factory creature gets up, and we can no longer say 'Well, people have to work . . .' *I thought I was seeing convicts*: the factory is a prison, school is a prison, literally, not metaphorically. You do not have the image of a prison following one of a school: that would simply be pointing out a resemblance, a confused relation between two clear images. On the contrary, it is necessary to discover the separate elements and relations that elude us at the heart of an unclear image: to show

how and in what sense school is a prison, housing estates are examples of prostitution, bankers killers, photographs tricks – literally, without metaphor.[38] This is the method of Godard's *Comment ça va*: not being content to enquire if 'things are OK' or if 'things are not OK' between two photos, but 'how are things' [*comment ça va*] for each one and for the two together. This was the problem with which Volume 1 ended: tearing a real iamge from clichés,

On the one hand, the image constantly sinks to the state of cliché: because it is introduced into sensory-motor linkages, because it itself organizes or induces these linkages, because we never perceive everything that is in the image, because it is made for that purpose (so that we do not perceive everything, so that the cliché hides the image from us . . .). Civilization of the image? In fact, it is a civilization of the cliché where all the powers have an interest in hiding images from us, not necessarily in hiding the same thing from us, but in hiding something in the image. On the other hand, at the same time, the image constantly attempts to break through the cliché, to get out of the cliché. There is no knowing how far a real image may lead: the importance of becoming visionary or seer. A change of conscience or of heart is not enough (although there is some of this, as in the heroine's heart in *Europe 51*, but, if there were nothing more, everything would quickly return to the state of cliché, other clichés would simply have been added on). Sometimes it is necessary to restore the lost parts, to rediscover everything that cannot be seen in the image, everything that has been removed to make it 'interesting'. But sometimes, on the contrary, it is necessary to make holes, to introduce voids and white spaces, to rarify the image, by suppressing many things that have been added to make us believe that we were seeing everything. It is necessary to make a division or make emptiness in order to find the whole again.

What is difficult is to know in what respect an optical and sound image is not itself a cliché, at best a photo. We are not thinking simply of the way in which these images provide more cliché as soon as they are repeated by authors who use them as formulas. But is it not the case that the creators themselves sometimes have the idea that the new image has to stand up against the cliché on its own ground, make a higher bid than the postcard, add to it and parody it, as a better way of getting over the problem (Robbe-Grillet, Daniel Schmid)? The creators invent obsessive framings, empty or disconnected spaces, even still lifes: in a certain sense they stop movement and rediscover the power of the fixed shot, but is this not to resuscitate the cliché that they aim to challenge? Enough, for victory, to parody the cliché, not to make holes in it and empty it. It is not enough to disturb the sensory-motor connections. It is necessary to *combine* the optical-sound image with the enormous forces that are not those of a simply intellectual consciousness, nor of the social one, but of a profound, vital intution.[39]

Pure optical and sound images, the fixed shot and the montage-cut, do define and imply a beyond of movement. But they do not strictly stop it, neither in the characters nor even in the camera. They mean that movement should not be perceived in a sensory-motor image, but grasped and thought in another type of image. The movement-image has not disappeared, but now exists only as the first dimension of an image that never stops growing in dimensions. We are not talking about dimensions of space, since the image may be flat, without depth, and through this very fact assumes all the more dimensions or powers which go beyond space. Three of these growing powers can be briefly summarized. First, while the movement-image and its sensory-motor signs were in a relationship only with an indirect image *of* time (dependent on montage), the pure optical and sound image, its opsigns and sonsigns, are directly connected to a time-image which has subordinated movement. It is this reversal which means that time is no longer the measure of movement but movement is the perspective of time: it constitutes a whole cinema of time, with a new conception and new forms of montage (Welles, Resnais). In the second place, at the same time as the eye takes up a clairvoyant function, the sound as well as visual elements of the image enter into internal relations which means that the whole image has to be 'read', no less than seen, readable as well as visible. For the eye of the seer as of the soothsayer, it is the 'literalness' of the perceptible world which constitutes it like a book. Here again all reference of the image of description to an object assumed to be independent does not disappear, but is now subordinated to the internal elements and relations which tend to replace the object and to delete it where it does appear, continually displacing it. Godard's formula, 'it isn't blood, it's some red', stops being only pictural and takes on a sense specific to the cinema. The cinema is going to become an analytic of the image, implying a new conception of cutting, a whole 'pedagogy' which will operate in different ways; for instance, in Ozu's work, in Rossellini's late period, in Godard's middle period, or in the Straubs. Finally, the fixity of the camera does not represent the only alternative to movement. Even when it is mobile, the camera is no longer content sometimes to follow the characters' movement, sometimes itself to undertake movements of which they are merely the object, but in every case it subordinates description of a space to the functions of thought. This is not the simple distinction between the subjective and the objective, the real and the imaginary, it is on the contrary their indiscernibility which will endow the camera with a rich array of functions, and entail a new conception of the frame and reframings. Hitchcock's premonition will come true: a camera-consciousness which would no longer be defined by the movements it is able to follow or make, but by the mental connections it is able to enter into. And it becomes questioning, responding, objecting, provoking, theorematizing, hypothesizing, experimenting, in accordance with the open list of logical conjunctions ('or', 'therefore', 'if', 'because', 'actually', 'although . . .'), or in accordance with the functions of thought in a *cinéma-vérité*, which, as Rouch says, means rather truth of cinema [*vérité du cinéma*].

This is the triple reversal which defines a beyond of movement. The image had to free itself from sensory-motor links; it had to stop being action-image in order to become a pure optical, sound (and tactile) image. But the latter was not enough: it had to enter into relations with yet other forces, so that it could itself escape from a world of clichés. It had to open up to powerful and direct revelations, those of the time-image, of the readable image and the thinking image. It is in this way that opsigns and sonsigns refer back to 'chronosigns', 'lectosigns' and 'noosigns'.[40]

Antonioni, considering the evolution of neo-realism in relation to *Outcry*, said that he was tending to do without a bicycle – De Sica's bicycle, naturally. Bicycle-less neo-realism replaces the last quest involving movement (the trip) with a specific weight of time operating inside characters and excavating them from within (the chronicle).[41] Antonioni's art is like the intertwining of consequences, of temporal sequences and effects which flow from events out-of-field. Already in *Story of a Love Affair* the investigation has the result, of itself, of provoking the outcome of a first love affair, and the effect of making two oaths of murder ring out in the future and in the past. It is a whole world of chronosigns, which would be enough to cast doubt on the false evidence according to which the cinematographic image is necessarily in

the present. If we are sick with Eros, Antonioni said, it is because
Eros is himself sick; and he is sick not just because he is old and
worn out in his content, but because he is caught in the pure form
of a time which is torn between an already determined past and a
dead-end future. For Antonioni, there is no other sickness than
the chronic. Chronos is sickness itself. This is why chronosigns are
inseparable from lectosigns, which force us to read so many
symptoms in the image, that is, to treat the optical and sound
image like something that is also readable. Not only the optical
and the sound, but the present and the past, and the here and the
elsewhere, constitute internal elements and relations which must
be deciphered, and can be understood only in a progression
analogous to that of a reading: from *Story of a Love Affair*,
indeterminate spaces are given a scale only later on, in which
Burch calls a 'continuity grasped through discrepancy' [*raccord à
appréhension décalée*], closer to a reading than to a perception.[42]
And later, Antonioni the colourist would be able to treat
variations of colours as symptoms, and monochrome as the
chronic sign which wins a world, thanks to a whole play of
deliberate modifications. But *Story of a Love Affair* already exhibits
a 'camera autonomy' when it stops following the movement of the
characters or directing its own movement at them, to carry out
constant reframings as functions of thought, noosigns expressing
the logical conjunctions of sequel, consequence, or even intention.

2 Recapitulation of images and signs

1

It is necessary to carry out a recapitulation of the images and signs in the cinema at this point. This is not merely a pause between the movement-image and another kind of image, but an opportunity to deal with the most pressing problem, that of the relations between cinema and language. In fact, the possibility of a semiology of the cinema seems to be dependent on these relations. Christian Metz has taken a number of precautions on this point. Instead of asking 'In what way is the cinema a language (the famous universal language of humanity)?', he poses the question 'Under what conditions should cinema be considered as a language?' And his reply is a double one, since it points first to a fact, and then to an approximation. The historical fact is that cinema was constituted as such by becoming narrative, by presenting a story, and by rejecting its other possible directions. The approximation which follows is that, from that point, the sequences of images and even each image, a single shot, are assimilated to propositions or rather oral utterances: the shot will be considered as the smallest narrative utterance. Metz himself underlines the hypothetical character of this assimilation. But it could be said that he takes more precautions only to allow himself a decisive recklessness. He posed a very rigorous question of right (*quid juris?*), and he replies with a fact and an evaluation. Substituting an utterance for the image, he can and must apply to it certain determinations which do not belong exclusively to the language system [*langue*], but condition the utterances of a language [*langage*], even if this language is not verbal and operates independently of a language system. The principle according to which linguistics is only a part of semiology is thus realized in the definition of languages without a language system (semes), which includes the cinema as well as the languages of gestures, clothing or music. There is therefore no reason to look for features in cinema that only belong to a language system, like double articulation. On the other hand, language features which necessarily apply to utterances will be found in the cinema, as rules of use, in the language system and outside of it: the syntagm (conjunction of present relative units) and the paradigm (disjunction of present units with comparable absent units). The semiology of cinema will be the discipline that applies linguistic models, especially syntagmatic ones, to images as constituting one of their principal 'codes'. We are moving in a strange circle here, because syntagmatics assumes that the image can in fact be assimilated to an utterance, but it is also what makes the image by right assimilable to the utterance. It is a typically Kantian vicious circle: syntagmatics applies because the image is an utterance, but the image is an utterance because it is subject to syntagmatics. The double of utterances and 'grand syntagmatics' has been substituted for that of images and signs, to the point where the very notion of sign tends to disappear from this semiology. It obviously disappears, clearly, to the benefit of the signifier. The film appears as a text, with a distinction comparable to that made by Julia Kristeva, between a 'phenotext' of utterances which actually appear and a 'genotext' of structuring, constitutive or productive syntagms and paradigms.[1]

The first difficulty concerns narration: this is not an evident [*apparent*] given in cinematographic images in general, even ones which are historically established. There can certainly be no quarrel with the passages in which Metz analyses the historical fact of the American model which was constituted as cinema of narration.[2] And he recognizes that this narration itself indirectly presupposes montage: the fact is that there are many linguistic codes that interfere with the narrative code or the syntagmatics (not only montages, but punctuations, audio-visual connections, camera movements . . .). Similarly, Christian Metz has no insurmountable difficulty in accounting for the deliberate disturbances of narration in modern cinema: it is enough to point to changes of structure in the syntagmatics.[3] The difficulty is therefore elsewhere: it is that, for Metz, narration refers to one or several codes as underlying linguistic determinants from which it flows into the image in the shape of an evident given. On the contrary, it seems to us that narration is only a consequence of the visible [*apparent*] images themselves and their direct combinations – it is never a given. So-called classical narration derives directly from the organic composition of movement-images [*montage*], or from their specification as perception-images, affection-images and action-images, according to the laws of a sensory-motor schema. We shall see that the modern forms of narration derive from the compositions and types of the time-image: even 'readability'. Narration is never an evident [*apparent*] given of images, or the effect of a structure which underlies them; it is a consequence of the visible [*apparent*] images themselves, of the perceptible images in themselves, as they are initially defined for themselves.

The root of the difficulty is the assimilation of the cinematographic image to an utterance. From that point on, this narrative utterance necessarily operates through resemblance or analogy, and, in as much as it proceeds through signs, these are 'analogical signs'. Semiology thus needs to have a double transformation: on the one hand the reduction of the image to an analogical sign belonging to an utterance; on the other hand, the codification of these signs in order to discover the (non-analogical) linguistic structure underlying these utterances. Everything will take place between the utterance by analogy, and the 'digital' or digitalized structure of the utterance.[4]

But at the very point that the image is replaced by an utterance, the image is given a false appearance, and its most authentically visible characteristic, movement, is taken away from it.[5] For the movement-image is not analogical in the sense of resemblance: it does not resemble an object that it would represent. This is what Bergson showed from the first chapter of *Matter and Memory*: if movement is taken from the moving body, there is no longer any distinction between image and object, because the distinction is valid only through immobilization of the object. The movement-image is the object; the thing itself caught in movement as continuous function. The movement-image is the modulation of the object itself. We encounter 'analogical' again here, but in a sense which now has nothing to do with resemblance, and which indicates modulation, as in so-called analogical machines. It may be objected that modulation in turn refers on the one hand to resemblance, even if only to evaluate degrees in a continuum, and on the other hand to a code which is able to 'digitalize' analogy. But, here again, this is true only if movement is immobilized. The similar and the digital, resemblance and code, at least have in common the fact that they are *moulds*, one by perceptible form, the other by intelligible structure: that is why they can so easily have links with each other.[6] But *modulation* is completely different; it is a putting into variation of the mould, a transformation of the mould at each moment of the operation. If it refers to one or several codes, it is by grafts, code-grafts that multiply its power (as in the electronic image). By themselves, resemblances and codifications are poor methods; not a great deal can be done with codes, even when they are multiplied, as semiology endeavours to do. It is modulation that nourishes the two moulds and makes them into subordinate means, even if this involves drawing a new power from them. For modulation is the operation of the Real, in so far as it constitutes and never stops reconstituting the identity of image and object.[7]

In this respect, Pasolini's highly complex thesis is in danger of being misunderstood. Umberto Eco reproached him for his 'semiological naïveté'. This incensed Pasolini. It is the fate of the trick to appear too naive to those who are naive but over-clever. Pasolini seems to want to go still further than the semiologists: he wants cinema to be a language system, to be provided with a double articulation (the shot, equivalent to the moneme, but also the objects appearing in the frame, 'cinemes' equivalent to phonemes). It is as if he wants to return to the theme of a universal language system. Except that he adds: it is the language system . . . of reality. 'Descriptive science of reality', this is the misunderstood nature of semiotics, beyond 'existing languages', verbal or otherwise. Does he not mean that the movement-image (the shot) consists of a first articulation in relation to a change or becoming which the movement expresses, but also a second articulation in relation to the objects between which it is established, which have become at the same time integral parts of the image (cinemes)? It would, therefore, be pointless to object to Pasolini that the object is only a referent, and the image a portion of the signified: the objects of reality have become units of the image, at the same time as the movement-image has become a reality which 'speaks' through its objects.[8] The cinema, in this sense, has constantly achieved a language of objects, in very varied ways; in Kazan the object is behavioural function; in Resnais it is mental function; in Ozu formal function or still life; in Dovzhenko first, then in Paradjanov, material function, ponderous matter roused by the spirit (*Sayat Nova* is definitely the masterpiece of a material language of object).

In fact, this language system of reality is not at all a language. It is the system of the movement-image, which, as we saw in Volume 1, was defined on vertical and horizontal axes which have nothing to do with paradigm and syntagm, but constitute two 'processes'. On the one hand, the movement-image expresses a whole which changes, and becomes established between objects: this is a process of *differentiation*. The movement-image (the shot) thus has two sides, depending on the whole that it expresses and depending on the objects between which it passes. The whole constantly divides depending on the objects, and constantly combines the objects into a whole [*tout*]: 'everything' [*tout*] changes from one to the other. On the other hand, the movement-image includes intervals: if it is referred to an interval, distinct kinds of image appear, with signs through which they are made up, each in itself and all of them together (thus the perception-image is at one end of the interval, the action-image at the other end and the affection-image in the interval itself). This is a process of *specification*. These components of the movement-image, from the dual point of view of specification and differentiation, constitute a *signaletic material* which includes all kinds of modulation features, sensory (visual and sound), kinetic, intensive, affective, rhythmic, tonal, and even verbal (oral and written). Eisenstein compared them first to ideograms, then, more profoundly, to the internal monologue as proto-language or primitive language system. But, even with its verbal elements, this is neither a language system nor a language. It is a plastic mass, an a-signifying and a-syntaxic material, a material not formed linguistically even though it is not amorphous and is formed semiotically, aesthetically and pragmatically.[9] It is a condition, anterior by right to what it conditions. It is not an enunciation, and these are not utterances. It is an *utterable*. We mean that, when language gets hold of this material (and it necessarily does so), then it gives rise to utterances which come to dominate or even replace the images and signs, and which refer in turn to pertinent features of the language system, syntagms and paradigms, completely different from those we started with. We therefore have to define, not semiology, but 'semiotics', as the system of images and signs independent of language in general. When we recall that linguistics is only a part of semiotics, we no longer mean, as for semiology, that there are languages without a language system, but that the language system only exists in its reaction to a *non-language-material* that it transforms. This is why utterances and narrations are not a given of visible images, but a consequence which flows from this reaction. Narration is grounded in the image itself, but it is not given. As for the question of knowing if there are specific and intrinsic cinematographic utterances – written in silent cinema, oral in talking cinema – it is a completely different question, which has to do with

the specificity of these utterances, and with the conditions on
which they belong to the system of images and signs, in short, on
the reverse reaction.

2

Peirce's strength, when he invented semiotics, was to conceive of
signs on the basis of images and their combinations, not as a
function of determinants which were already lingusitic. This led
him to the most extraordinary classification of images and signs,
of which we offer only a brief summary. Peirce begins with the
image, from the phenomenon or from what appears. The image
seems to him to be of three kinds, no more: firstness (something
that only refers to itself, quality or power, pure possibility; for
instance, the red that we find identical to itself in the proposition
'You have not put on your red dress' or 'You are in red');
secondness (something that refers to itself only through something else, existence, action-reaction, effort-resistance); thirdness
(something that refers to itself only by comparing one thing to
another, relation, the law, the necessary). It will be noted that the
three kinds of images are not simply ordinal – first, second, third
– but cardinal: there are two in the second, to the point where
there is a firstness in the secondness, and there are three in the
third. If the third marks the culmination, it is because it cannot be
made up with dyads, but also because combinations of triads on
their own or with the other modes can produce any multiplicity.
This said, the sign in Peirce apparently combines the three kinds
of image, but not in any kind of way: the sign is an image which
stands for another image (its object), through the relation of a
third image which constitutes 'its interpretant', this in turn being
a sign, and so on to infinity. Hence Peirce, by combining the three
modes of the image and the three aspects of the sign, produces
nine sign elements, and ten corresponding signs (because all the
combinations of elements are not logically possible).[10] If we ask
what the function of the sign is in relation to the image, it seems to
be a cognitive one: not that the sign makes it object known; on the
contrary, it presupposes knowledge of the object in another sign,
but adds new elements of knowledge to it as a function of the
interpretant. It is like two processes to infinity. Or rather, what
amounts to the same thing, the sign's function must be said to

'make relations efficient': not that relations and laws lack actuality *qua* images, but they still lack that efficiency which makes them act 'when necessary', and that only knowledge gives them.[11] But, on this basis, Peirce can sometimes find himself as much a linguist as the semiologists. For, if the sign elements still imply no privilege for language, this is no longer the case with the sign, and linguistic signs are perhaps the only ones to constitute a pure knowledge, that is, to absorb and reabsorb the whole content of the image as consciousness or appearance. They do not let any material that cannot be reduced to an utterance survive, and hence reintroduce a subordination of semiotics to a language system. Peirce would thus not have maintained his original position for very long; he would have given up trying to make semiotics a 'descriptive science of reality' (logic).

This is because, in his phenomenology, he claims the three types of image as a fact, instead of deducing them. We saw in Volume 1 that firstness, secondness and thirdness corresponded to the affection-image, the action-image and the relation-image. But all three are deduced from the movement-image as material, as soon as it is related to the interval of movement. Now this deduction is possible only if we first assume a perception-image. Of course, perception is strictly identical to every image, in so far as every image acts and reacts on all the others, on all their sides and in all their parts. But, when they are related to the interval of movement which separates, within *one* image, a received and an executed movement, they now vary only in relation to this one image, which will be called 'perceiving' the movement received, on one of its sides, and 'carrying out' the movement executed, on another side or in other parts. A special perception-image is therefore formed, an image which no longer simply expresses movement, but the relation between movement and the interval of movement. If the movement-image is already perception, the perception-image will be perception of perception, and perception will have two poles, depending on whether it is identified with movement or with its interval (variation of all the images in their relations with each other, *or* variation of all the images in relation to one of them). And perception will not constitute a first type of image in the movement-image without being extended into the other types, if there are any: perception of action, of affection, of relation, etc. The perception-image will therefore be like a degree zero in the deduction which is carried out as a function of the movement-image: there will be a 'zeroness' before

Peirce's firstness. As for the question: are there types of image in the movement-image other than the perception-image?, it is resolved by the various aspects of the interval: the perception-image received movement on one side, but the affection-image is what occupies the interval (firstness), the action-image what executes the movement on the other side (secondness), and the relation-image what reconstitutes the whole of the movement with all the aspects of the interval (thirdness functioning as closure of the deduction). Thus the movement-image gives rise to a sensory-motor whole which grounds narration in the image.

Between the perception-image and the others, there is no intermediary, because perception extends by itself into the other images. But, in the other cases, there is necessarily an intermediary which indicates the extension as passage.[12] This is why, in the end, we find ourselves faced with six types of perceptible visible images that we see, not three: *perception-image, affection-image, impulse-image* (intermediates between affection and action), *action-image, reflection-image* (intermediate between action and relation), *relation-image.* And since, on the one hand, deduction constitutes a genesis of types, and, on the other, its degree zero, the perception-image, gives the others a bipolar composition appropriate to each case, we shall find ourselves with at least two signs of composition, and at least one sign of genesis for each type of image. We therefore take the term 'sign' in a completely different way from Peirce: it is a particular image that refers to a type of image, whether from the point of view of its bipolar composition, or from the point of view of its genesis. It is clear that all this involves the discussion in Volume 1: the reader may, then, skip it, as long as he keeps in mind the recapitulation of signs set out earlier, where we borrowed from Peirce a certain number of terms whilst changing their meaning. Thus the signs of composition for the perception-image are the *dicisign* and the *reume*. The dicisign refers to a perception of perception, and usually appears in cinema when the camera 'sees' a character who is seeing; it implies a firm frame, and so constitutes a kind of solid state of perception. But the reume refers to a fluid or liquid perception which passes continuously through the frame. The *engramme*, finally, is the genetic sign or the gaseous state of perception, molecular perception, which the two others presuppose. The affection-image has the *icon* as sign of composition, which can be of quality or of power; it is a quality or a power which are only expressed (for example, a face) without being actualized.

But it is the *qualisign* or the *potisign* which constitute the genetic element because they construct quality or power in an any-space-whatever, that is, in a space that does not yet appear as a real setting. The impulse-image, intermediate between affection and action, is composed of *fetishes*, fetishes of Good or Evil: these are fragments torn from a derived setting, but which refer genetically to the *symptom* of an originary world operating below the setting. The action-image implies a real actualized setting which has become sufficient, so that a global situation will provoke an action, or on the contrary an action will disclose a part of the situation: the two signs of composition, therefore, are the *synsign* and the *index*. The internal link between situation and action, in any case, constitutes the genetic element or the *imprint*. The reflection-image, which goes from action to relation, is composed when action and situation enter into indirect relations: the signs are then *figures*, of attraction or inversion. And the genetic sign is *discursive*, that is, a situation or an action of discourse, independent of the question: is the discourse itself realized in a language? Finally, the relation-image relates movement to the whole that it expresses, and makes the whole vary according to the distribution of movement: the two signs of composition will be the *mark*, or the circumstance, through which two images are united, according to a habit ('natural' relation), and the *demark*, the circumstance through which an image finds itself torn from its natural relation or series; the sign of genesis the *symbol*, the circumstance through which we are made to compare two images, even arbitrarily united ('abstract' relation).

The movement-image is matter [*matière*] itself, as Bergson showed. It is a matter that is not linguistically formed, although it is semiotically, and constitutes the first dimension of semiotics. In fact, the different kinds of image which are necessarily deduced from the movement-image, the six kinds, are the elements that make this matter into a signaletic material [*matière signalétique*]. And the signs themselves are the features of expression that compose and combine these images, and constantly re-create them, borne or carted along by matter in movement [*la matière en mouvement*].

A final problem then arises: why does Peirce think that everything ends with thirdness and the relation-image and that there is nothing beyond? This is undoubtedly true from the point of view of the movement-image: this is framed by the relations which relate it to the whole that it expresses, so much so that a logic of relations seems to close the transformations of the movement-image by determining the corresponding changes of the whole. We have seen, in this sense, that a cinema like that of Hitchcock, taking relation as its explicit object, completed the circuit of the movement-image and brought to its logical perfection what could be called classical cinema. But we have encountered signs which, eating away at the action-image, also brought their effect to bear above and below, on perception and relation, and called into question the movement-image as a whole: these are opsigns or sonsigns. The interval of movement was no longer that in relation to which the movement-image was specified as perception-image, at one end of the interval, as action-image at the other end, and as affection-image between the two, so as to constitute a sensory-motor whole. On the contrary the sensory-motor link was broken, and the interval of movement produced the appearance as such of *an image other than the movement-image*. Sign and image thus reversed their relation, because the sign no longer presupposed the movement-image as material that it represented in its specified forms, but set about presenting the other image whose material it was itself to specify, and forms it was to constitute, from sign to sign. This was the second dimension of pure, non-linguistic semiotics. There was to arise a whole series of new signs, constitutive of a transparent material, or of a time-image irreducible to the movement-image, but not without a determinable relationship with it. We could no longer consider Peirce's thirdness as a limit of the system of images and signs, because the opsign (or sonsign) set everything off again, from the inside.

3

The movement-image has two sides, one in relation to objects whose relative position it varies, the other in relation to a whole – of which it expresses an absolute change. The positions are in space, but the whole that changes is in time. If the movement-image is assimilated to the shot, we call framing the first facet of the shot turned towards objects, and montage the other facet turned towards the whole. Hence a first thesis: it is montage itself which constitutes the whole, and thus gives us the image of time. It is therefore the principal act of cinema. Time is necessarily an indirect representation, because it flows from the montage which links one movement-image to another. This is why the connection cannot be a simple juxtaposition: the whole is no more an addition than time is a succession of presents. As Eisenstein said over and over again, montage must proceed by alterations, conflicts, resolutions, and resonances, in short an activity of selection and co-ordination, in order to give time its real dimension, and the whole its consistency. This position of principle implies that movement-image is itself in the present, and nothing else. That the present is the sole direct time of the cinematographic image seems to be almost a truism. Pasolini will again rely on it to maintain a very classical notion of montage: precisely because it selects and co-ordinates 'significant moments', montage has the property of 'making the present past', of transforming our unstable and uncertain present into 'a clear, stable and desirable past', in short of achieving time. It is useless for him to add that this is the operation of death, not a death that is over and done with, but a death in life or a being for death ('death achieves a dazzling montage of our life').[13] This black note reinforces the classic, grandiose concept of the montage king: time as indirect representation that flows from the synthesis of images.

But this thesis has another aspect, which seems to contradict the first: the synthesis of movement-images must rely on characteristics intrinsic to each of them. Each movement-image expresses the whole that changes, as a function of the objects between which movement is established. The shot must therefore already be a potential montage, and the movement-image, a matrix or cell of time. From this point of view, time depends on movement itself and belongs to it: it may be defined, in the style of ancient philosophers, as the number of movement. Montage will therefore be a relation of number, variable according to the intrinsic nature of the movements considered in each image, in each shot. A uniform movement in the shot appeals to a simple measure, but varied and differential movements to a rhythm; intensive movements proper (like light and heat) to a tonality, and the set of all the potentialities of a shot, to a harmony. Hence Eisenstein's distinctions between a metrical, rhythmic, tonal and harmonic montage. Eisenstein himself saw a certain opposition between the synthetic point of view, according to which time flowed from the montage, and the analytic point of view, according to which the time set up was dependent on a movement-image.[14] According to

Pasolini, 'the present is transformed into past' by virtue of montage, but this past 'still appears as a present' by virtue of the nature of the image. Philosophy had already encountered a similar opposition, in the notion of 'number of movement', because number appeared sometimes like an independent instance, sometimes like a simple dependence on what it measured. Should we not, however, maintain both points of view, as the two poles of an indirect representation of time: time depends on movement, but through the intermediary of montage; it flows from montage, but as if subordinate to movement? Classical reflection turns on this kind of alternative, montage *or* shot.

It is still necessary for movement to be normal: movement can only subordinate time, and make it into a number that indirectly measures it, if it fulfils conditions of normality. What we mean by normality is the existence of centres: centres of the revolution of movement itself, of equilibrium of forces, of gravity of moving bodies, and of observation for a viewer able to recognize or perceive the moving body, and to assign movement. A movement that avoids centring, in whatever way, is as such abnormal, aberrant. Antiquity came up against these aberrations of movement, which even affected astronomy, and which became more and more pronounced when one entered the sub-lunar world of men (Aristotle). Now, aberrant movement calls into question the status of time as indirect representation or number of movement, because it evades the relationships of number. But, far from time itself being shaken, it rather finds this the moment to surface directly, to shake off its subordination in relation to movement and to reverse this subordination. Conversely, then, a direct presentation of time does not imply the halting of movement, but rather the promotion of aberrant movement. What makes this problem as much a cinematographic as a philosophical one is that the movement-image seems to be in itself a profoundly aberrant and abnormal movement. Epstein was perhaps the first to focus theoretically on this point, which viewers in the cinema experienced practically: not only speeded up, slowed down and reversed sequences, but the non-distancing of the moving body ('a deserter was going flat out, and yet remained face to face with us'), constant changes in scale and proportion ('with no possible common denominator') and false continuities of movement (what Eisenstein called 'impossible continuity shots').[15]

More recently, Jean-Louis Schefer, in a book in which the theory forms a kind of great poem, showed that the ordinary cinema-viewer, the man without qualities, found his correlate in the movement-image as extraordinary movement. The movement-image does not reproduce a world, but constitutes an autonomous world, made up of breaks and disproportion, deprived of all its centres, addressing itself as such to a viewer who is in himself no longer centre of his own perception. The *percipiens* and the *percipi* have lost their points of gravity. Schefer draws the most rigorous consequence from this: the aberration of movement specific to the cinematographic image sets time free from any linkage; it carries out a direct presentation of time by reversing the relationship of subordination that time maintains with normal movement; 'cinema is the sole experience where time is given to me as a perception'. Certainly Schefer points to a primordial crime with an essential link to this condition of cinema, just as Pasolini invoked a primordial death for the other situation. It is a homage to psychoanalysis, which has only ever given cinema one sole object, one single refrain, the so-called primitive scene. But there is no other crime than time itself. What aberrant movement reveals is time as everything, as 'infinite opening', as anteriority over all normal movement defined by motivity [*motricité*]: time has to be anterior to the controlled flow of every action, there must be 'a birth of the world that is not completely restricted to the experience of our motivity' and 'the most distant recollection of image must be separated from all movement of bodies'.[16] If normal movement subordinates the time of which it gives us an indirect representation, aberrant movement speaks up for an anteriority of time that it presents to us directly, on the basis of the disproportion of scales, the dissipation of centres and the false continuity of the images themselves.

What is in question is the obviousness on the basis of which the cinematographic image is in the present, necessarily in the present. If it is so, time can be represented only indirectly, on the basis of a present movement-image and through the intermediary of montage. But is this not the falsest obviousness, in at least two respects? First, there is no present which is not haunted by a past and a future, by a past which is not reducible to a former present, by a future which does not consist of a present to come. Simple succession affects the presents which pass, but each present coexists with a past and a future without which it would not itself pass on. It is characteristic of cinema to seize this past and this future that coexist with the present image. To film what is

before and what is *after* . . . Perhaps it is necessary to make what is
before and after the film pass inside it in order to get out of the
chain of presents. For example, the characters: Godard says that
it is necessary to know what they were before being placed in the
picture, and will be after. 'That is what cinema is, the present
never exists there, except in bad films.'[17] This is very difficult,
because it is not enough to eliminate fiction, in favour of a crude
reality which would lead us back all the more to presents which
pass. On the contrary, it is necessary to move towards a limit, to
make the limit of before the film and after it pass into the film and
to grasp in the character the limit that he himself steps over in
order to enter the film and leave it, to enter into the fiction as into
a present which is inseparable from its before and after (Rouch,
Perrault). We shall see that this is precisely the aim of *cinéma-vérité*
or of direct cinema: not to achieve a real as it would exist
independently of the image, but to achieve a before and an after
as they coexist with the image, as they are inseparable from the
image. This is what direct cinema must mean, to the point where
it is a component of all cinema: to achieve the direct presentation
of time.

Not only is the image inseparable from a before and an after
which belong to it, which are not to be confused with the
preceding and subsequent images; but in addition it itself tips
over into a past and a future of which the present is now only an
extreme limit, which is never given. Take, for example, the depth
of field in Welles: when Kane is going to catch up with his friend
the journalist for the break, it is in time that he moves, he occupies
a place in time rather than changing place in space. And when the
investigator at the beginning of *Mr Arkadin* emerges into the great
courtyard, he literally emerges from time rather than coming
from another place. Take Visconti's tracking shots: at the
beginning of *Sandra*, when the heroine returns to the house
where she was born, and stops to buy the black headscarf that she
will cover her head with, and the cake that she will eat like magic
food, she does not cover space, she sinks into time. And in a film a
few minutes long, *Appunti su un Fatto di Cronaca*, a slow tracking
shot follows the empty path of the raped and murdered school-
girl, and comes back to the fully present image to load it with a
petrified perfect tense, as well as with an inescapable future
perfect.[18] In Resnais too it is time that we plunge into, not at the
mercy of a psychological memory that would give us only an
indirect representation, nor at the mercy of a recollection-image

that would refer us back to a former present, but following a
deeper memory, a memory of the world directly exploring time,
reaching in the past that which conceals itself from memory. How
feeble the flashback seems beside explorations of time as
powerful as this, such as the silent walk on the thick hotel carpet
which each time puts the image into the past in *Last Year in
Marienbad*. The tracking shots of Resnais and Visconti, and
Welles's depth of field, carry out a temporalization of the image
or form a direct time-image, which realizes the principle: the
cinematographic image is in the present only in bad films. 'Rather
than a physical movement, it is a question above all of a
displacement in time.'[19] And undoubtedly there are many
possible ways of proceeding: it is, on the contrary, the crushing of
depth and the planitude of the image, which, in Dreyer and other
authors, will directly open the image on to time as fourth
dimension. This is, as we shall see, because there are varieties of
the time-image just as there were types of the movement-image.
But the direct time-image always gives us access to that Proustian
dimension where people and things occupy a place in time which
is incommensurable with the one they have in space. Proust
indeed speaks in terms of cinema, time mounting its magic
lantern on bodies and making the shots coexist in depth.[20] It is this
build-up, this emancipation of time, which ensures the rule of
impossible continuity and aberrant movement. The postulate of
'the image in the present' is one of the most destructive for any
understanding of cinema.

But were these characteristics not clear in the cinema at an early
stage (Eisenstein, Epstein)? Is Schefer's theme not valid for the
whole of the cinema? How are we to delineate a modern cinema
which would be distinct from 'classical' cinema or from the
indirect representation of time? We might once more rely on an
analogy in thought: if it is true that aberrations of movement were
recognized at an early stage, they were in some sense corrected,
normalized, 'elevated', and brought into line with laws which
saved movement, extensive movement of the world or intensive
movement of the soul, and which maintained the subordination
of time. In fact we will have to wait for Kant to carry out the great
reversal: aberrant movement became the most everyday kind,
everydayness itself, and it is no longer time that depends on
movement, but the opposite . . . A similar story appears in
cinema. For a long time aberrations of movement were
recognized, but warded off. The intervals of movement first

called its communication into question and introduced a gap or disproportion between a received movement and an executed one. Even so, related to such an interval, the movement-image finds in it the principle of its differentiation into the perception-image (received movement) and the action-image (executed movement). What was aberration in relation to the movement-image cases to be so in relation to these two images: the interval itself now plays the role of centre, and the sensory-motor schema restores the lost proportion, re-establishes it in a new mode, between perception and action. The sensory-motor schema moves forward by selection and co-ordination. Perception is organized in obstacles and distances to be crossed, while action invents the means to cross and surmount them, in a space which sometimes constitutes an 'encompasser', sometimes a 'line of the universe': movement is saved by becoming relative. And this status, of course, does not exhaust the movement-image. As soon as it stops being related to an interval as sensory-motor centre, movement finds its absolute quality again, and every image reacts with every other one, on all their sides and in all their parts. This is the regime of universal variation, which goes beyond the human limits of the sensory-motor schema towards a non-human world where movement equals matter, or else in the direction of a super-human world which speaks for a new spirit. It is here that the movement-image attains the sublime, like the absolute condition of movement, whether in the material sublime of Vertov, in the mathematical sublime of Gance, or in the dynamic sublime of Murnau or Lang. But in any event the movement-image remains primary, and gives rise only indirectly to a representation of time, through the intermediary of montage as organic composition of relative movement, or supra-organic recomposition of absolute movement. Even Vertov, when he carries perception over into matter, and action into universal interaction, peopling the universe with micro-intervals, points to a 'negative of time' as the ultimate product of the movement-image through montage.[21]

Now, from its first appearances, something different happens in what is called modern cinema: not something more beautiful, more profound, or more true, but something different. What has happened is that the sensory-motor schema is no longer in operation, but at the same time it is not overtaken or overcome. It is shattered from the inside. That is, perceptions and actions ceased to be linked together, and spaces are now neither co-ordinated nor filled. Some characters, caught in certain pure optical and sound situations, find themselves condemned to wander about or go off on a trip. These are pure seers, who no longer exist except in the interval of movement, and do not even have the consolation of the sublime, which would connect them to matter or would gain control of the spirit for them. They are rather given over to something intolerable which is simply their everydayness itself. It is here that the reversal is produced: movement is no longer simply aberrant, aberration is now valid in itself and designates time as its direct cause. 'Time is out of joint': it is off the hinges assigned to it by behaviour in the world, but also by movements of world. It is no longer time that depends on movement; it is aberrant movement that depends on time. The relation, *sensory-motor situation* → *indirect image of time* is replaced by a non-localizable relation, *pure optical and sound situation-* → *direct time-image*. Opsigns and sonsigns are direct presentations of time. False continuity shots are the non-localizable relation itself: characters no longer jump across them, they are swallowed up in them. Where has Gertrud gone? Into the false continuity shots . . .[22] Of course they have always been there, in the cinema, like aberrant movements. But what makes them take on a specifically new value, to the point where *Gertrud* was not understood at the time and still offends perception? We can choose between emphasizing the continuity of cinema as a whole, or emphasizing the difference between the classical and the modern. It took the modern cinema to re-read the whole of cinema as already made up of aberrant movements and false continuity shots. The direct time-image is the phantom which has always haunted the cinema, but it took modern cinema to give a body to this phantom. This image is virtual, in opposition to the actuality of the movement-image. But, if virtual is opposed to actual, it is not opposed to real, far from it. Again, this time-image will be said to presuppose montage, just as much as indirect representation did. But montage has changed its meaning, it takes on a new function: instead of being concerned with movement-images from which it extracts an indirect image of time, it is concerned with the time-image, and extracts from it the relations of time on which aberrant movement must now depend. To adopt a word of Lapoujade's, montage has become 'montrage'.[23]*

What seems to be broken is the circle in which we were led from shot to montage and from montage to shot, one constituting the movement-image, the other the indirect image of time. Despite all its efforts (and especially those of Eisenstein), the classical conception had difficulty in getting rid of the idea of a vertical construction going right to the edge in both directions, where montage worked on movement-images. It has often been pointed out, in modern cinema, that the montage was already in the image, or that the components of an image already implied montage. There is no longer an alternative between montage and shot (in Welles, Resnais, or Godard). Sometimes montage occurs in the depth of the image, sometimes it becomes flat: it no longer asks how images are linked, but 'What does the image *show*?'[24] This identity of montage with the image itself can appear only in conditions of the direct time-image. In a text with important implications Tarkovsky says that what is essential is the way time flows in the shot, its tension or rarefaction, 'the pressure of time in the shot'. He appears to subscribe to the classical alternative, shot *or* montage, and to opt strongly for the shot ('the cinematographic figure only exists inside the shot'). But this is only a superficial appearance, because the force or pressure of time goes outside the limits of the shot, and montage itself works and lives in time. What Tarkovsky denies is that cinema is like a language working with units, even if these are relative and of different orders: montage is not a unit of a higher order which exercises power over unit-shots and which would thereby endow movement-images with time as a new quality.[25] The movement-image can be perfect, but it remains amorphous, indifferent and static if it is not already deeply affected by injections of time which put montage into it, and alter movement. 'The time in a shot must flow independently and, so to speak, as its own boss': it is only on this condition that the shot goes beyond the movement-image, and montage goes beyond indirect representation of time, to both share in a direct time-image, the one determining the form or rather force of time in the image, the other the relations of time or of forces in the succession of images (relations that are no more reducible to succession, than the image is to movement). Tarkovsky calls his text 'On the cinematographic figure', because he calls figure that which expresses the 'typical', but expresses it in a pure singularity, something unique. This is the sign, it is the very function of the sign. But, as long as signs find their material in the movement-image, as long as they form the singular expressional features, from a material in movement, they are in danger of evoking another generality which would lead to their being confused with a language. The representation of time can be extracted from this only by association and generalization, or as concept (hence Eisenstein's bringing together of montage and concept). Such is the ambiguity of the sensory-motor schema, agent of abstraction. It is only when the sign opens directly on to time, when time provides the signaletic material itself, that the type, which has become temporal, coincides with the feature of singularity separated from its motor associations. It is here that Tarkovsky's wish comes true: that 'the cinematographer succeeds in fixing time in its indices [in its signs] perceptible by the senses'. And, in a sense, cinema had always done this; but, in another sense, it could only realize that it had in the course of its evolution, thanks to a crisis of the movement-image. To use a formula of Nietzsche's, it is never at the beginning that something new, a new art, is able to reveal its essence; what it was from the outset it can reveal only after a detour in its evolution.

3 From Recollection to Dreams: third commentary on Bergson

1

Bergson distinguishes two kinds of 'recognition'. *Automatic or habitual recognition* (the cow recognizes grass, I recognize my friend Peter) works by extension: perception extends itself into the usual movements; the movements extend perception so as to draw on its useful effects. It is a sensory-motor recognition that comes about above all through movements: motor mechanisms which the sight of the object is enough to trigger are constituted and accumulated. In a certain sense we constantly distance ourselves from the first object: we pass from one object to *another one*, according to a movement that is horizontal or of associations of images, but remaining on *one and the same plane* (the cow moves from one clump of grass to another, and, with my friend Peter, I move from one subject of conversation to another). The second mode of recognition, *attentive recognition*, is very different. Here, I abandon the extending of my perception, I cannot extend it. My movements – which are more subtle and of another kind – revert to the object, return to the object, so as to emphasize certain contours and take 'a few characteristic features' from it. And we begin all over again when we want to identify different features and contours, but each time we have to start from scratch. In this case, instead of an addition of distinct objects on the same plane, we see the object remaining *the same*, but passing through *different planes*.[1] In the first case, we had, we perceived, a sensory-motor image from the thing. In the other case, we constitute a pure optical (and sound) image of the thing, we make a description.

How are the two kinds of images distinguished? It would seem first of all that the sensory-motor image is richer, because it is the thing itself, at least the thing as it extends into the movements by which we make use of it. Whilst the pure optical image seems necessarily poorer and more rarefied: as Robbe-Grillet says, it is not the thing, but a 'description' which tends to replace the thing, which 'erases' the concrete object, which selects only certain features of it, even if this means making way for different descriptions which will pick out different lines or features, which are always provisional, always in question, displaced or replaced. It may be objected that a cinematographic image – even a sensory-motor one – is necessarily a description. But at this point we must contrast two kinds of descriptions: one is organic (as when we say that a chair is made to sit on, or grass to be eaten), while the other is physical-geometrical, inorganic. We have already noted in Rossellini the extent to which the factory seen by the bourgeoise woman, in *Europe 51*, was a visual and sound 'abstract', barely 'concretely denoted', reduced to a few features. And in *Les carabiniers* Godard makes each shot a description which replaces the object, and which will make way for a different description, so that, instead of organically describing an object, we are shown pure descriptions which are unmade at the same time as they are outlined.[2] If the new cinema, like the new novel, is of considerable philosophical and logical importance, it is first of all because of the theory of descriptions which it implies – of which Robbe-Grillet was the pioneer.[3]

At this point everything is reversed. The sensory-motor image effectively retains from the thing only what interests us, or what extends into the reaction of a character. Its richness is thus superficial and comes from the fact that it associates with the thing many different things that resemble it on the same plane, in so far as they provoke all the same movements: it is grass in general that interests the herbivore. It is in this sense that the sensory-motor schema is an agent of abstraction. Conversely, the pure optical image may be only a description, and concern a character who no longer knows how or is no longer able to react to the situation; the restraint of this image, the thinness of what it retains, line or simple point, 'slight fragment without importance', bring the thing each time to an essential singularity, and describe the inexhaustible, endlessly referring to other descriptions. It is, then, the optical image which is really rich, or 'typical'.

At least it would be if we knew what use it was. It was easy to say that the sensory-motor image was useful because it linked a perception-image to an action-image; it already modelled the first on the second and extended the one into the other. But the pure optical image is a completely different matter, not only because it is a different type of image, a different type of perception, but also because its mode of linkage is not the same. There is a simple, provisional answer and it is the one Bergson gives initially: the optical (and sound) image in attentive recognition does not extend into movement, but enters into relation with a 'recollection-image' that it calls up. Perhaps we should also imagine other possible answers, more or less related, more or less distinct: what would enter into relation would be the real and the imaginary, the physical and the mental, the objective and the subjective, description and narration, *the actual and the virtual* . . . The essential point, in any event, is that the two related terms differ in nature, and yet 'run after each other', refer to each other, reflect each other, without it being possible to say which is first, and tend *ultimately* to become confused by slipping into the same point of indiscernibility. A zone of recollections, dreams, or thoughts corresponds to a particular aspect of the thing: each time it is a plane or a circuit, so that the thing passes through an infinite number of planes or circuits which correspond to its own 'layers' or its aspects. A different, virtual mental image would correspond to a different description, and vice versa: a different circuit. The heroine of *Europe 51* sees certain features of the factory, and thinks she is seeing convicts: 'I thought I saw convicts . . .' (it should be noted that she does not evoke a simple recollection, the factory does not remind her of a prison, the heroine calls up a mental vision, almost an hallucination). She could have seized on other features, and had a different vision: the workers' entry, the call of the siren, I thought I saw condemned survivors, running towards dark shelters . . .

How can we say that it is the same object (the factory) which passes through different circuits, because each time description has obliterated the object, at the same time as the mental image has created a different one? Each circuit obliterates and creates an object. But it is precisely in this 'double movement of creation and erasure' that successive planes and independent circuits, cancelling each other out, contradicting each other, joining up with each other, forking, will simultaneously constitute the layers of one and the same physical reality, and the levels of one and the same mental reality, memory or spirit. As Bergson says, 'it will be seen that the progress of attention results in creating anew, not only the object perceived, but also the ever-widening systems with which it may be bound up; so that in the measure in which the circles, B, C, D, represent a higher expansion of memory, their reflection attains in B', C', D' deeper strata of reality'.[4]

Thus, in Rossellini, the island of *Stromboli* passes through ever deeper descriptions, the approaches, the fishing, the storm, the eruption, at the same time as the foreign woman climbs higher and higher on the island, until description is engulfed in depth and the spirit is shattered by a tension which is too strong. From the slopes of the unleashed volcano, the village is seen far below, sparkling above the black waves, while the spirit whispers: 'I am finished, I am afraid, what mystery, what beauty, my God . . .' There are no longer sensory-motor images with their extensions, but much more complex circular links between pure optical and sound images on the one hand, and on the other hand images from time and thought, on planes which all coexist by right, constituting the soul and body of the island.

2

The purely optical and sound situation (description) is an actual image, but one which, instead of extending into movement, links up with a virtual image and forms a circuit with it. The problem is to know more precisely what is capable of playing the role of virtual image. What Bergson calls 'recollection-image' seems at first sight to have the requisite qualities. Of course, recollection-images already intervene in automatic recognition; they insert themselves between stimulation and response, and contribute to the better adjustment to the motor mechanism by reinforcing it with a psychological causality. But, in this sense, they only intervene accidentally and in a secondary way in automatic recognition, whilst they are essential to attentive recognition: this latter comes about *through* them. In other words, with recollection-images, a whole new sense of subjectivity appears. We have seen that subjectivity already emerged in the movement-image; it appears as soon as there is a gap between a received and an executed movement, an action and a reaction, a stimulation and a response, a perception-image and an action-image. And if affection itself is also a dimension of this first subjectivity, it is because it belongs to the gap, it constitutes its 'insides', it in a sense occupies it, but without filling or fulfilling it. Now, on the contrary, the recollection-image comes to fill the gap and really does fulfil it, in such a way that it leads us back individually to perception, instead of extending this into generic movement. It makes full use of the gap, it assumes it, because it lodges itself there, but it is of a different nature. Subjectivity, then, takes on a new sense, which is no longer motor or material, but temporal and spiritual: that which 'is added' to matter, not what distends it; recollection-image, not movement-image.[5]

The relation of the actual image to recollection-images can be
seen in the flashback. This is precisely a closed circuit which goes
from the present to the past, then leads us back to the present. Or
rather, as in Carné's *Daybreak*, it is a multiplicity of circuits each of
which goes through a zone of recollections and returns to an even
deeper, ever more inexorable, state of the present situation.
Carné's hero, at the end of each circuit, finds himself back in his
hotel room besieged by the police, each time closer to the fatal
outcome (the window-panes smashed, the bullet holes in the wall,
the succession of cigarettes . . .). But we know very well that the
flashback is a conventional, extrinsic device: it is generally
indicated by a dissolve-link, and the images that it introduces are
often superimposed or meshed. It is like a sign with the words:
'watch out! recollection'. It can, therefore, indicate, by convention, a causality which is psychological, but still analogous to a
sensory-motor determinism, and, despite its circuits, only confirms the progression of a linear narration. The question of the
flashback is this: it has to be justified from elsewhere, just as
recollection-images must be given the internal mark of the past
from elsewhere. The circumstances must be such that the story
cannot be told in the present. It is therefore necessary for
something else to justify or impose the flashback, and to mark or
authenticate the recollection-image. Carné's response here is very
clear: it is destiny which goes beyond determinism and causality;
it is destiny that sketches out a super-linearity; it is destiny that
both justifies flashback and provides recollection-images with a
mark of the past. Thus, in *Daybreak*, the sound of the obsessive
refrain comes from the depths of time to justify the flashback, and
the 'anger' carries the tragic hero away to the depths of time to
deliver him to the past.[6] But if the flashback and the recollection-
image thus find their foundation in destiny, it is only in a relative
or conditional way. For destiny can be exhibited directly in other
ways, and can affirm a pure power of time which overflows all
memory, an already-past which exceeds all recollections: we are
not just thinking of expressionist figures of blind men or tramps
with which Carné's work is strewn, but of the immobilizings and
petrifications in *Visiteurs du Soir*, or the use of mime in *Les Enfants
du Paradis*, and more generally of light, which Carné uses in the
French style – luminous grey which passes through every
atmospheric nuance and constitutes a great circuit of the sun and
moon.

Mankiewicz is undoubtedly the greatest flashback author. But the use he makes of it is so special that it may be contrasted with that of Carné, as the two extreme poles of the recollection-image. There is no longer any question of an explanation, a causality or a linearity which ought to go beyond themselves in destiny. On the contrary it is a matter of an inexplicable secret, a fragmentation of all linearity, perpetual forks like so many breaks in causality. Time in Mankiewicz is exactly as Borges describes it in 'The Garden of Forking Paths':[7]* it is not space but time which forks, 'web of time which approaches, forks, is cut off or unacknowledged for centuries, embracing every possibility'. It is here that the flashback finds its justification: at each point where time forks. The multiplicity of circuits thus finds a new meaning. It is not simply several people each having a flashback, it is the flashback belonging to several people (three in *The Barefoot Contessa*, three in *A Letter to Three Wives*, two in *All About Eve*). And it is not just the circuits forking between themselves, it is each circuit forking within itself, like a split hair. In the three circuits in *A Letter to Three Wives*, each of the women wonders in her own way when and how her marriage began to go adrift, to take a forking route. And even when there is a single fork, like the taste for mud in a proud and splendid creature (*The Barefoot Contessa*), its repetitions are not accumulations, its manifestations refuse to be aligned, or to reconstitute a destiny, but constantly split up any state of equilibrium and each time impose a new 'meander', a new break in causality, which itself forks from the previous one, in a collection of non-linear relations.[8] One of Mankiewicz's most beautiful forks is in *Whispers in the City*, where the doctor, who has come to tell the father that his daughter is pregnant, finds himself in the middle of talking to the daughter about love and asks to marry her, in a dream-landscape. Two characters are eternal enemies, in a universe of automata; but there is a world where one of the two maltreats the other and forces a clown costume on him, and a world where the other takes on the dress of inspector and becomes master in turn, until the unleashed automata shuffle all the possibilities, all worlds and all times (*The Bloodhound*). Mankiewicz's characters never develop in a linear evolution: the stages passed through by Eve, taking the place of the actress, stealing her lover, seducing the girlfriend's husband, blackmailing the girlfriend, do not take part in a progression but each time constitute a deviation which makes a circuit, allowing a secret to exist in the whole which the new Eve at the end of the film will inherit, point of departure for other forks.

In effect, there is neither straight line nor circle which completes itself. *All About Eve*[9]* is not exactly 'all about Eve', it is rather 'a bit', as a character in the film says: 'She will be able to tell you a bit about this subject . . .' And, in *Suddenly Last Summer*, there is only one flashback, when the girl again encounters at the end the horrible recollection which is eating away at her, because the other flashbacks have been blocked, replaced by stories and hypotheses, without, however, cancelling the corresponding forks which allow an inexplicable secret to exist for ever. In fact, the son's homosexuality explains nothing. The mother's jealousy is a first fork, as soon as she is supplanted by the girl; the homosexuality is a second, when the son uses the girl as he used his mother, as baits for boys; but there is still one more, still another circuit, which takes up the description of the carnivorous flowers and the story of the horrendous fate of the little tortoises which are devoured, when the flashback reveals, beneath the son's homosexuality, an orgiastic mystery, cannibalistic tastes of which he ends up victim, hacked and dismembered by his young, wretched lovers, to the sounds of a barbaric music of the slums. And here again, at the end, it seems that everything starts up again, and the mother 'will devour' the young doctor that she has mistaken for her son. In Mankiewicz, the flashback always reveals its *raison d'être* in these angled accounts which shatter causality and, instead of dispersing the enigma, refer it back to other still deeper ones. Chabrol will rediscover this power and use of the flashback in *Violette Nozière*, when he wants to indicate the heroine's continual forks, the variety of her faces, the irreducible diversity of the hypotheses (did she or did she not want to spare her mother, etc?).[10]

Time's forks thus provide flashback with a necessity, and recollection-images with an authenticity, a weight of past without which they would remain conventional. But why, and how? The answer is simple: the forking points are very often so impercep- tible that they cannot be revealed until after their occurrence, to an attentive memory. It is a story that can be told only in the past. This was already the constant question for Fitzgerald, to whom Mankiewicz is very close: what happened? How have we arrived at this point?[11] This is what governs the three flashbacks of women in *A Letter to Three Wives* and Harry's recollections in *The Barefoot Contessa*. It is perhaps the question of all questions.

The theatrical character of Mankiewicz's work has often been pointed out, but there is also a 'novelistic' element (or more precisely 'a short story' element, for it is the short story that asks: what happened?). What has not been sufficiently analysed, however, is the relation between the two, their original fusion which means that Mankiewicz re-created a complete cinematographic specificity. On one hand, the novelistic element, the story, appears in the memory. The memory in fact, following a formula of Janet's, is story behaviour. In its very essence, memory is voice, which speaks, talks to itself, or whispers, and recounts what happened. Hence the voice-off which accompanies the flashback. In Mankiewicz this spiritual role of memory often gives way to a creature more or less connected with the beyond: the phantom in *Mrs Muir's Adventure*, the ghost in *Whispers in the City*, the automata in *Bloodhound*. In *A Letter to Three Wives*, there is the fourth girlfriend, the one that will never be seen, that is once barely glimpsed, and who has made it known to the three others that she is going off with one of their husbands (but which one?): it is her voice-off which looms over the other three flashbacks. In any event, the voice as memory frames the flashback. But, in another sense, what the latter 'shows', and what the former reports, are more voices: characters and décors which are of course meant to be seen, but are in essence speaking and of sound. This is the theatrical element: the dialogue between the characters who appear, and sometimes even the appearance of the character himself, produces a story (*All About Eve*). In one of the flashbacks in *A Letter to Three Wives* there is the dinner scene where the teacher-husband and the wife in advertising entertain the latter's female boss: all the movements of characters and camera are determined by the mounting violence of their dialogue, and the distribution of two opposed sound-sources, that of the radio programme, and that of the classical music with which the teacher challenges it. The essential point, then, is the intimacy of the relation between the novelistic element in memory as story behaviour, and the theatrical element of the dialogues, words and sounds as conducts of the characters.

Now this internal relation is determined in a very original way in Mankiewicz. What is reported is always a skidding, a detour, a fork. But, although the fork may in principle be discovered only after the event, through flashback, there is one character who has been able to foresee it, or grasp it at the time, whether he uses it later for good or for evil. Mankiewicz is brilliant with these scenes. It is not only Harry's role in *The Barefoot Contessa*; it happens in two important scenes in *All About Eve*. First, the actress's

secretary-dresser has understood straight away Eve's deceit-
fulness, her split personality: at the exact moment that Eve was
producing her false story, she heard everything from the next
room, out of frame, and comes into the frame to give Eve an
intense look and briefly show her doubt. And then, later, the
devilish theatre-critic will surprise another of Eve's forks, when
she strives to seduce the actress's lover. He hears, and perhaps
notices, through the half-open door, as between two fields. He
will know how to use this later, but he has understood at the time
(and it is at different moments that each of the characters
understands, thanks to a new fork). Now, in all these cases, we do
not leave memory. But instead of a constituted memory, as
function of the past which reports a story, we witness the birth of
memory, as function of the future which retains what happens in
order to make it the object to come of the other memory. This is
what Mankiewicz has very clearly understood: memory could
never evoke and report the past if it had not already been
constituted at the moment when the past was still present, hence
in an aim to come. It is in fact for this reason that it is behaviour: it
is in the present that we make a memory, in order to make use of it
in the future when the present will be past.[12] It is this memory of
the present which makes the two elements communicate from the
inside, novelistic memory as it appears in the reporting story, and
the theatrical present as it appears in the reported dialogues. It is
this circulating third which gives the whole a totally cinematographic value. It is this role of spy, or of involuntary witness, which
gives Mankiewicz's cinema its whole force: visual and auditory
birth of memory. Hence the way in which we find in him the two
distinct aspects of the out-of-field: an aside concerning the
character who surprises the fork, and a beyond concerning the
character who relates it to the past (sometimes the same character,
sometimes a different one).

But if it is true that flashback and the recollection-image thus
find a reason for their existence in these forks of time, this reason
– as we have seen in the very different case of Carné – may act
directly, without going through flashback, outside any memory.
This is true in particular of the two great, theatrical, Shake-
spearean films, *Julius Caesar* and *Cleopatra*. It is true that the
historical character of these films already takes the place of
memory (and, in *Cleopatra*, the technique of frescoes which come
to life). It is still the case that, in them, time's forks take on a direct
meaning which confounds flashback. The interpretation of

Shakespeare's *Julius Caesar* by Mankiewicz underlines the psychological opposition between Brutus and Mark Antony. The fact is that Brutus appears to be an absolutely linear character: of course he is torn by his affection for Caesar, of course he is a skilful orator and politician, but his love of the republic sketches a perfectly straight course for him. We said that in Mankiewicz there is no character who develops in a linear way. Yet there is Brutus. But, precisely, after speaking to the people, he allows Mark Antony the chance to speak, without waiting himself or leaving an *observer*: he will find himself proscribed, assured of defeat, alone and backed into suicide, locked in his rectitude before he has been able to understand anything of what has happened. Mark Antony, on the contrary, is a supremely forked being: presenting himself as a soldier, playing on his unskilled speech, rough-spoken, with awkward phrasings, and plebeian accents, he sustains an extraordinary speech wholly in forks, which will make the Roman people turn (Mankiewicz's art and Brando's voice unite here in one of the finest scenes in theatre-cinema). Finally, in *Cleopatra*, it is Cleopatra who has become the eternal forking woman, devious, capricious, while Mark Antony (now played by Burton) is simply a prisoner of his insane passion, trapped between the recollection of Caesar and the proximity of Octavian. Hidden behind a pillar, he will witness one of Cleopatra's forkings before Octavian, and will take refuge in the background, but always to return to her. He too will die without understanding what has actually happened, although he rediscovers Cleopatra's love in a final fork by her. All the pinks intensifying to golds testify to the universal changeability of Cleopatra. Mankiewicz disowned this film, which is no less magnificent for that; perhaps one of his main reasons was that he had been forced into too many rational, oppressive justifications of the forkings of the queen.

We come to the same conclusion again: either the flashback is an unsophisticated, conventional notice or it gets a justification from elsewhere; Carné's destiny, Mankiewicz's forking time. But in these latter cases, what gives flashback a necessity does so only relatively, conditionally, and may be expressed in a different way. For there is not simply an insufficiency in the flashback in relation to the recollection-image; *there is at a deeper level an insufficiency in the recollection-image in relation to the past.* Bergson constantly reminded us that it was not by its own efforts that the recollection-image retained the mark of the past, that is, of 'virtuality' which it represents and embodies, and which distinguishes it from other types of images. If the image becomes 'recollection-image' it is only in so far as it has been to look for a 'pure recollection' in the place where it was, pure virtuality contained in the hidden zones of the past as in oneself . . . 'Pure recollections, summoned from the depths of Memory develop into recollection-images'; 'Imagining is not recollecting. No doubt a recollection, as it becomes actual, tends to live in an image, but the converse is not true, and the image pure and simple will not be referred to the past unless, indeed, it was in the past that I sought it, thus following the continuous progress which brought it from darkness into light.'[13] Contrary to our first hypothesis it is not, then, the recollection-image which is sufficient to define the new dimension of subjectivity. We asked: when a present, actual image has lost its motor extension, with what virtual image does it enter into relation, the two images forming a circuit where they run after each other and each is reflected in the other? Now the recollection-image is not virtual, it actualizes a virtuality (which Bergson calls 'pure recollection') on its own account. This is why the recollection-image does not deliver the past to us, but only represents the former present that the past 'was'. The recollection-image is an image which is actualized or in process of being made actual, which does not form with the actual, present image a circuit of indiscernibility. Is this because the circuit is too broad, or on the contrary not broad enough? In any case, once again, the heroine of *Europe 51* does not evoke a recollection-image. And even when an author proceeds by flashback, he subordinates the flashback to another process which gives it foundation, and the recollection-image to deeper time-images (not only Mankiewicz, but Welles, Resnais, etc.).

There is no doubt that attentive recognition, when it succeeds, comes about *through* recollection-images: it is the man I met last week at such and such a place . . . But it is precisely this success which allows the sensory-motor flux to take up its temporarily interrupted course again. So that Bergson constantly circles around the following conclusion, which will also haunt cinema: attentive recognition informs us to a much greater degree when it fails than when it succeeds. When we cannot remember, sensory-motor extension remains suspended, and the actual image, the present optical perception, does not link up with either a motor image or a recollection-image which would re-establish contact. It rather enters into relation with genuinely virtual elements, feelings of *déjà vu* or past 'in general' (I must have seen that man somewhere . . .), dream-images (I have the feeling that I saw him in a dream . . .), fantasies or theatre scenes (he seems to play a role that I am familiar with . . .). In short, it is not the recollection-image or attentive recognition which gives us the proper equivalent of the optical-sound image, it is rather the disturbances of memory and the failures of recognition.

3

This is why European cinema at an early stage confronted a group of phenomena; amnesia, hypnosis, hallucination, madness, the vision of the dying, and especially nightmare and dream. This was an important aspect of Soviet cinema, and its various alliances with futurism, constructivism and formalism; of German expressionism and its various alliances with psychiatry and psychoanalysis; and of the French school and its various alliances with surrealism. European cinema saw in this a means of breaking with the 'American' limitations of the action-image, and also of reaching a mystery of time, of uniting image, thought and camera in a single 'automatic subjectivity', in contrast to the over-objective conception of the Americans.[14] In fact, the first common factor in all these states is that a character finds himself prey to visual and sound sensations (or tactile ones, cutaneous or coenaesthetic) which have lost their motor extension. This may be a limit-situation, the imminent arrival or consequence of an accident, the nearness of death but also the most ordinary states of sleep, dream, or a disturbance of attention. And, in the second place, these actual sensations and perceptions are as cut off from memory-based recognition as they are from motor recognition: no specific group of recollections comes to correspond to them, and to fit into the optical and sound situation. But, what is very different, it is a whole temporal 'panorama', an unstable set of floating memories, images of a past *in general* which move past at dizzying speed, as if time were achieving a profound freedom. It is as if total and anarchic mobilizing of the past now responds to the character's motor powerlessness. Dissolves and superimpositions arrive with a vengeance. It is in this way that expressionism attempted to restore the 'panoramic vision' of those who feel mortally threatened or lost: images thrown up from the unconscious of a woman being operated on – Alfred Abel's *Narcosis*, from that of an assaulted man – Metzner's *Attack*, from that of a man in the middle of drowning – Fejos' *The Last Moment*. (*Daybreak* moves towards this limit, the hero getting nearer to an inescapable death.) The same may be said of dream-states or states of extreme sensory-motor relaxation: the purely optical or sound perspectives of a divested present which no longer enjoys links with a disconnected past, floating child-hood memories, fantasies, or impressions of *déjà vu*. This is again the most immediate or visible content of Fellini's *8½*: from the hero's overwork and collapse from stress to the final panoramic vision, taking in the nightmare of the underground passage and the kite-man which is used as the film's opening.

The Bergsonian theory of dreams shows that the dreamer is not at all closed to the sensations of the external and internal world. However, he no longer relates them to specific recollec-tion-images, but to fluid, malleable sheets of past which are happy with a very broad or floating adjustment. If we go back to Bergson's previous schema, *the dream represents the largest visible circuit or 'the outermost envelope' of all the circuits.*[15] This is no longer the sensory-motor link of the action-image in habitual recogni-tion, but nor is it the various circuits of perception-recollection which come to supplement it in attentive recognition; it would rather be the weak and dislocatory connection between an optical (or sound) sensation and a panoramic vision; between any sensory image whatever and a total dream-image.

What, more precisely, is the difference between a recollection-image and a dream-image? We start from a perception-image, the nature of which is to be actual. The recollection, in contrast – what Bergson calls 'pure recollection' – is necessarily a virtual image. But, in the first case, it becomes actual in so far as it is summoned by the perception-image. It is actualized in a recollec-tion-image which corresponds to the perception-image. The case of dream brings two important differences to light. On the one hand, the sleeper's perceptions exist, but in the diffuse condition of a dust of actual sensations – external and internal – which are not grasped in themselves, escaping consciousness. On the other hand, the virtual image which becomes actual does not do so directly, but becomes actual in a different image, which itself plays the role of virtual image being actualized in a third, and so on to infinity: the dream is not a metaphor but a series of anamorphoses which sketch out a very large circuit. These two characteristics are linked. When the sleeper is given over to the actual luminous sensation of a green surface broken by white patches, the dreamer who lives in the sleeper may evoke the image of a meadow dotted with flowers, but this image is only actualized by already becoming the image of a billiard table furnished with balls, which in turn does not become actual without becoming something else. These are not metaphors, but a becoming which can by right continue to infinity. In René Clair's *Entr'acte*, the dancer's tutu seen from beneath 'spreads out like a flower', and the flower 'opens and closes its corolla, enlarges its petals, and lengthens its stamens', to turn back into the opening legs of a dancer; the city lights become a 'pile of lighted cigarettes' in the hair of a man playing chess, cigarettes which in turn become 'the columns of a Greek temple, then of a silo, whilst the chessboard becomes transparent to give a view of the Place de la Concorde'.[16] In Buñuel's *Un chien andalou* the image of the thinning cloud which bisects the moon is actualized, but by passing into that of the razor which bisects the eye, thus maintaining the role of virtual image in relation to the next one. A tuft of hairs becomes a sea-urchin, which is transformed into a circular head of hair, to give way to a circle of onlookers. American cinema grasped this state of the dream-image at least once, in the conditions of Buster Keaton's burlesque, due to its natural affinity with surrealism, or rather with Dadaism. In the dream in *Sherlock Junior*, the image of the unbalanced chair in the garden gives way to the somersault in the street, then to the precipice at the edge of which the hero leans, but in the jaws of a lion, then to the desert and the cactus on which he sits down, then to the little hill which gives birth to an island battered by the waves, where he dives into an already snowy expanse, from which he emerges to find himself back in the garden. Sometimes the dream-images are scattered thoughout a film, in such a way that it is possible to reconstitute them in their totality. Thus, with Hitchcock's *Spellbound* the real dream does not appear in the Daliesque paste and cardboard sequence, but is shared between widely separated elements: these are the impressions of a fork on a sheet which will become stripes on pyjamas, to jump to the striations on a white cover, which will produce the widening-out space of a washbasin, itself taken up by an enlarged glass of milk, giving way in turn to a field of snow marked by parallel ski lines. A series of scattered images which form a large circuit, of which each one is like the virtuality of the next that makes it actual, until

all return together to the hidden sensation which has all the time
been actual in the hero's unconscious, that of the lethal toboggan.

Dream-images in turn seem to have two poles, which may be
distinguished according to their technical production. One
proceeds by rich and overloaded means – dissolves, superimpositions, deframings, complex camera movements, special
effects, manipulations in the laboratory – going right to the
abstract, in the direction of abstraction. The other, on the
contrary, is very restrained, working by clear cuts or montage-cut,
making progress simply through a perpetual unhinging which
'looks like' dream, but between objects that remain concrete. The
techniques of the image always refers to a metaphysics of the
imagination: it is like two ways of imagining the passage from one
image to the other. In this respect dreamlike states are, in relation
to the real, a bit like the 'anomalous' states of a language system in
relation to the current language: sometimes addition, compli-
cation, over-saturation, sometimes, in contrast, elimination, ellipse, break, cut, unhinging. If this second pole appears clearly in
Keaton's *Sherlock Junior*, the first is the driving force of the great
dream in Murnau's *The Last Man*, where the uncontrollable
batterers at the door are dissolved and superimposed, and tend
towards infinitely restless abstract angles. The opposition is
especially clear between *Entr'acte* and *Un chien andalou*: René
Clair's film multiplies every technique, taking them in the
direction of cinetic abstraction of the last mad race, whilst Buñel's
film works through more restrained means, and maintains the
dominant circular shape in the consistently concrete objects that
he has following one another through definite cuts.[17] But,
whichever pole is chosen, the dream-image obeys the same law: a
large circuit where each image actualizes the preceding one and is
actualized in the subsequent one, to return in the end to the
situation which set it off. It does not, then, guarantee the
indiscernibility of the real and the imaginary any more than the
recollection-image does. The dream-image is subject to the
condition of attributing the dream to a dreamer, and the
awareness of the dream (the real) to the viewer. Buster Keaton
purposely accentuates the split by making a frame which resembles a screen, in such a way that the hero goes from the
semi-darkness of the room to the completely lit-up world of the
screen . . .

Perhaps there is a way to go beyond this split in the large circuit,
through states of reverie, of waking dream, of strangeness or

enchantment. For the whole group of these states, which differ from the explicit dream, Michel Devillers proposed a very interesting notion, that of 'implied dream'.[18] The optical and sound image is quite cut off from its motor extension, but it no longer compensates for this loss by entering into relation with explicit recollection-images or dream-images. If we likewise attempt to define this state of implied dream, we would say that the optical and sound image extends into *movement of world*. There is definitely return to movement (hence its insufficiency again). But it is no longer the character who reacts to the optical-sound situation, it is a movement of world which supplements the faltering movement of the character. There takes place a kind of worldizing [mondialization] or 'societizing' [mondianization], a depersonalizing, a pronominalizing of the lost or blocked movement.[19] The road is not slippery without sliding on itself. The frightened child faced with danger cannot run away, but the world sets about running away for him and takes him with it, as if on a conveyor belt. Characters do not move, but, as in an animated film, the camera causes the movement of the path on which they change places, 'motionless at a great pace'. The world takes responsibility for the movement that the subject can no longer or cannot make. This is a virtual movement, but it becomes actual at the price of an expansion of the totality of space and of a stretching of time. It is therefore the limit of the largest circuit. Of course, these phenomena already appear in the dream: in Buñuel's *Los Olvidados*, in the dream of the Virgin with the chunk of meat, the child is slowly sucked towards the meat rather than thrusting himself forward; in the nightmare in Murnau's *Phantom*, the dreamer pursues the carriage, but is himself urged on by the shadow of the houses which pursue him. However, it seems to us that the explicit dream contains or retains these movements of world which are, on the contrary, liberated in the implied dream.

One of the first great works in this direction was Epstein's *The Fall of the House of Usher*: the optical perceptions of things, landscapes, or furniture, extend into infinitely stretched gestures which depersonalize movement. Slow motion frees movement from its moving body to make a sliding of world, a sliding of ground, up to the final fall of the house. Hathaway's *Peter Ibbetson* is less an American film of dream than an implied dream, culminating with the avalanche of rocks and the collapse of the castle made of clouds. The only film by Laughton, *Night of the Hunter*, shows us the great pursuit of the children by the preacher; but the latter is dispossessed of his own movement of pursuit in favour of his silhouette as shadow theatre, whilst the whole of nature takes on the responsibility of the children's movement of flight, and the boat where they take refuge seems itself a motionless shelter on a floating island or a conveyor belt. In most of his films Louis Malle has more or less obviously used movement of world, hence the enchantment of this work: the bolt from the blue in *The Lovers* is mixed up with the extensions of the park and the moon in the boat trip; bodily states themselves link up with movements of world. From *Lift to the Scaffold*, it was the halting of the lift which blocked the murderer's movement, to put in its place movements of world involving the other characters. The culmination is *Black Moon*, where the depersonalized movements take the heroine with the unicorn from one world to another and still another: it is by running away from the initial images of violence that the heroine moves from one world to the other, in the sense that Sartre says that each dream is a world, and even each phase or image of dream.[20] Each is marked by animals, and is peopled by inversions (sound-inversion of speech, aberrations of behaviour such as when the old woman talks to the rats and sucks the girl's breast). In Malle, it is always a movement of world which brings the character to incest, prostitution, or disgrace, and makes him capable of a crime like the one dreamed of by the old man who tells tall stories (*Atlantic City*). In the whole cinema of enchantment these universalized, depersonalized and pronominalized movements, with their slow motion or rushing, with their inversions, pass just as much through nature as through artifice and the manufactured object. It was precisely a whole enchantment of artifice and inversion that L'Herbier had exhibited in *The Fantastic Night*, in order to extend the states of an apparent sleeper. Neo-realism does not go back on, but on the contrary remains true to, its aims, when it extends optical and sound situations into artificial, yet cosmic movements which involve characters: not only De Sica's enchantment in *Miracle in Milan*, but all Fellini's fairgrounds, with rides, slides, tunnels, stairways, rockets, or big dippers which 'must lead the visitor-viewer from one particular space-time to another similarly autonomous space-time' (especially *City of Women*).[21]

Musical comedy is the supreme depersonalized and pronominalized movement, the dance which outlines a dreamlike world as it goes. In Berkeley, the multiplied and reflected girls form an enchanted proletariat whose bodies, legs and faces are the parts of a great transformational machine: the 'shapes' are like kaleidoscopic views which contract and dilate in an earthly or watery space, usually shot from above, turning around the vertical axis and changing into each other to end up as pure abstractions.[22] Of course, even in Berkeley, and all the more in musical comedy in general, the dancer or couple retain an individuality as creative source of movement. But what counts is the way in which the dancer's individual genius, his subjectivity, moves from a personal motivity to a supra-personal element, to a movement of world that the dance will outline. This is the moment of truth where the dancer is still going, but already a sleepwalker, who will be taken over by the movement which seems to summon him: this can be seen with Fred Astaire in the walk which imperceptibly becomes dance (Minnelli's *Band Wagon*) as well as with Kelly in the dance which seems to have its origin in the unevenness of the pavement (Donen's *Singing in the Rain*). Between the motor step and the dance step there is sometimes what Alain Masson calls a 'degree zero', like a hesitation, a discrepancy, a making late, a series of preparatory blunders (Sandrich's *Follow the Fleet*), or on the contrary a sudden birth (*Top Hat*). Astaire's style has often been contrasted with Kelly's. And it is true that, in the former, the centre of gravity passes outside his slight body, floats beyond him, and defies verticality, rolls crosswise, and follows a line which is now only that of his silhouette, his shadow or his shadows, to the extent that it is his shadows which dance with him (Stevens's *Swingtime*). Whilst, in the latter, the centre of gravity grounds itself vertically in a compact body, to free and raise up from the inside the mannequin who is the dancer. 'Powerful acrobat's movements often augment the enthusiasm and force of Kelly, the way that he gives himself some spring with a jump is sometimes easy to see. Astaire's gestures, in contrast, link up through a clear will of the intellect, without ever surrendering movement to the body', and define 'successive and perfect shadows'.[23] It is like the two extremes of grace as defined by Kleist, 'in the body of a man entirely deprived of consciousness and of the man who possesses an infinite consciousness', Kelly and Astaire. But, in both cases, musical comedy is not content to get us into the dance, or, what amounts to the same thing, to make us dream. The cinematographic act consists in this: that the dancer himself begins dancing, as one starts to dream. If musical comedy gives us in an explicit way so many scenes which work like dreams or pseudo-dreams with

metamorphoses (*Singing in the Rain, Band Wagon*, and especially
Minnelli's *An American in Paris*), it is because it is entirely a gigantic
dream, but an implied dream, which in turn implies the passage
of a presumed reality in the dream.

However, even presumed, this reality is quite ambiguous. We
might present the case in two ways. On one hand we think that
musical comedy gives us in the first place ordinary sensory-motor
images, where the characters find themselves in situations to
which they will respond through their actions, but that more or
less progressively their personal actions and movements are
transformed by dance into movement of world which goes
beyond the motor situation, only to return to it, etc. Or we
suppose, on the other hand, that the point of departure only gave
the appearance of being a sensory-motor situation: at a deeper
level it was a pure optical and sound situation which had already
lost its motor extension; it was a pure description which had
already replaced its object, a film set pure and simple. In this case
the movement of world responds directly to the call of opsigns
and sonsigns (and the 'degree zero' no longer signals a progressive transformation but the cancelling of the ordinary sensory-
motor links). In the first case, in the words of Masson, we move
from the narrative to the spectacular, we are admitted to the
implied dream; in the other we go from the spectacular to the
spectacle, just as from the film set to the dance, in the whole of an
implied dream which even envelops walking. The two points of
view are superimposed in musical comedy, but it is clear that the
second is more comprehensive. In Stanley Donen, the sensory-
motor situation allows 'flat views' to show through, postcards or
snapshots of landscapes, towns and silhouettes. It gives way to
those purely optical and sound situations where colour takes on a
fundamental value, and the action, itself flattened, is no longer
distinguishable from a moving element of the coloured film set.
So dance arises directly as the dreamlike power which gives depth
and life to these flat views, which makes use of a whole space in the
film set and beyond, which gives a world to the image, surrounds
it with an atmosphere of world (*Pyjama Picnic, Singing in the Rain*,
not just the dance in the street but the Broadway finale). 'Dance
will thus guarantee the transition between the flat view and the
opening up of space.'[24] It will be the movement of the world which
corresponds, in the dream, to the optical and sound image.

It fell to Minnelli to discover that dance does not simply give a
fluid world to images, but that there are as many worlds as

images: 'Every image', Sartre said, 'is surrounded by an atmosphere of world.' The plurality of worlds is Minnelli's first discovery, his very great position in cinema. But how, then, do we pass from one world to the other? This is the second discovery; dance is no longer simply movement of world, but passage from one world to another, entry into another world, breaking in and exploring. It is no longer a matter of going from a world which is real in general to particular dream-worlds, since the real world would presuppose those links that the worlds of dreams seem to disallow us, as in the inversion in *Brigadoon*, where the reality, from which we are separated by the immortal and isolated village, is now visible only in a vast high-angle shot. In Minnelli, every world and every dream is shut in on itself, closed up around everything it contains, including the dreamer. He has his prisoner-sleepwalkers, his women-panthers, his women-warders and his sirens. Each set attains its fullest power, and becomes pure description of world which replaces the situation.[25] Colour is dream, not because the dream is in colour, but because colours in Minnelli are given a highly absorbent, almost devouring, value. This means that we have to insinuate ourselves, to let ourselves become absorbed, without at the same time losing ourselves or being snatched away. Dance is no longer the movement of dream which outlines a world, but now acquires depth, grows stronger as it becomes the sole means of entering into another world, that is, into another's world, into another's dream or past. *Yolande* and *The Pirate* will be the two great successes where Astaire and then Kelly introduce themselves respectively into a girl's dreams, and not without mortal danger.[26] And, in all the works that are not musical comedy, but just comedies or dramas, Minnelli has to have an equivalent of dance and song which always introduces the character into the other's dream. In *Undercurrent*, the young wife will go to the very heart of her husband's nightmare, on a Brahms tune, to reach the dream and love of the unknown brother, so passing from one world to another. It is an escalator as movement of world which, in *The Clock*, breaks the heel on the girl's shoe and carries her away into the waking dream of the soldier on leave. With the grandiose *Four Horsemen of the Apocalypse* it takes the heavy gallop of the knights and the horrible recollection of the stricken father to snatch the aesthete from his own dream and get him into the generalized nightmare of the war. Reality from this point on will necessarily be conceived sometimes as the heart of a nightmare, when the hero dies of being in this way a prisoner of the dream of the Other (not only *The Four Horsemen*, but in *Brigadoon* the death of the man attempting to escape), sometimes as a harmony of dreams with each other, in a happy ending where each person finds himself again by being absorbed into the opposite (thus, in *The Perfect Wife*, the dancer who reconciles the two worlds in conflict). The relation between set-description and movement-dance is no longer as with Donen, that between a flat view and an organization of space, but that between an absorbent world and a passage between worlds, for better or for worse. Musical comedy has never come as close to a mystery of memory, of dream and of time, as a point of indiscernibility of the real and the imaginary, as in Minnelli. A strange and fascinating conception of dream, where the dream is all the more implied because it always refers to the dream of another, or else – as in the masterpiece *Madame Bovary* – constitutes itself a devouring, merciless power, for its real subject.

Perhaps the renewal of burlesque by Jerry Lewis owes many of its elements to musical comedy. We can briefly summarize the succeeding ages of burlesque: it all began with an enormous exaltation of sensory-motor situations, where the links of each of them were enlarged and brought forward, indefinitely extended; where the junctures and shocks between their independent causal series were multiplied, forming a proliferating whole. And in the second age this element would survive, with enrichments and purifications (Keaton's trajectories, Lloyd's ascending series, the dismantled series of Laurel and Hardy). But what characterizes this second age is the introduction of a very strong emotive, affective element into the sensory-motor scheme: this is embodied, for example, in the pure quality of Buster Keaton's impassive, reflective face, and also in the power of Chaplin's intense and variable face, in accordance with the two poles of the action-image; however, in both cases, it is inserted and spreads into the form of the action, whether it opens the 'small form' of Chaplin or envelops and transforms the 'large form' of Keaton. This affective element is found in the moonstruck pierrots [*pierrots lunaires*] of burlesque: Laurel is lunatic, but so is Langdon with his irresistible sleeps and waking dreams, and Harpo Marx's dumb character in the violence of his drives and the peace of his harp. But even with Langdon, the affective element always remains caught up in the mazes of the sensory-motor schema or of the movement-image, giving the shocks and encounters of causal series a new dimension which was lacking in the first age.

The third age of burlesque implies the talkie, but the talkie comes in here only as the support or condition of a new image: it is the mental image which takes a sensory-motor texture to its limit, this time regulating the detours, encounters and shocks by a chain of logical relations as irrefutable as they are absurd or provocative. This mental image is the discursive image as it appears in the big speeches in Chaplin's talking films; it is also the argument-image in the nonsense of Groucho Marx or of Fields. Brief as this analysis is, it may lead us to foresee how a fourth stage or age is going to arise: a breaking of sensory-motor links, an inauguration of pure optical and sound situations which, instead of extending into action, enter into a circuit which turns back on them, then launch another circuit. This is what we see in Jerry Lewis. The set has its own importance, pure description having replaced its object, as in the famous girls' house seen in its entirety in section in *Ladies' Man*, whilst the action gives way to the grand ballet of the Devouring Woman and the hero become dancer. It is in this sense that Jerry Lewis's burlesque finds its source in musical comedy.[27] And even the way he walks seems like so many misperformed dance steps, an extended and recommenced 'degree zero', with every possible variation, until the perfect dance is born (*The Patsy*).

The sets present an intensification of forms, colours and sounds. Jerry Lewis's character, more involuted than infantile, is such that everything resonates in his head and soul; but, conversely, his smallest sketched or inhibited gestures, and the inarticulate sounds he comes out with, in turn resonate, because they set off a movement of world which goes as far as catastrophe (the destruction of the set at the music professor's in *The Patsy*), or which travels from one world to another, in a pulverizing of colours, a metamorphosis of forms and a mutation of sounds (*The Nutty Professor*). Lewis takes up a classic figure of American cinema, that of the *Loser*,[28]* of the born loser, whose definition is: he 'goes too far'. But it is precisely in the burlesque dimension that this 'too far' becomes movement of world which saves him and will make him a winner. His body is shaken by spasms and various currents, successive waves, as when he is going to throw the dice (*Hollywood or Bust*). This is no longer the age of the tool or machine, as they appear in the earlier stages, notably in the machines of Keaton that we have described. This is a new age of electronics, and the remote controlled object which substitutes optical and sound signs for sensory-motor ones. It is no longer the machine that goes wrong and goes mad, like the feeding-machine in *Modern Times*, it is the cold rationality of the autonomous technical object which reacts on the situation and ravages the set: not just the electronic house and the lawn-mowers in *It's Only Money*, but the caddies who destroy the self-service (*The Disorderly Orderly*) and the Hoover that devours everything in the shop, goods, clothes, customers and wallpaper (*Who's Minding the Store*).[29] The new burlesque no longer originates in an output of energy by the character, who spreads and grows as before. It arises from the fact that the character places himself (involuntarily) on an energy band which carries him along and which is precisely movement of world, a new way of dancing, of modulating: 'the low frequency wave-action takes the place of heavy duty mechanics and the full blownness of gestures'.[30] It is here for once, that it can be said that Bergson is outstripped: the comic is no longer something mechanical stuck on to something living, but movement of world carrying away and sucking up the living. Jerry Lewis's use of modern techniques taken to extremes (particularly the electronic circuit which he invented) is only of interest because it corresponds to the form and content of this new burlesque image. Pure optical and sound situations, which are no longer extended into action, but are connected back to a wave. And it is this wave, movement of world on which the character is placed as if in orbit, which will provoke the finest of Jerry Lewis's themes, in that very special fantasizing or that state of implied dream: the 'proliferations' by which the burlesque character makes others swarm together (the six uncles in *Family Jewels*), or implicates others who are absorbed (the three in *Three on a Couch*); the cases of 'spontaneous generation' of faces, bodies, or crowds; the 'agglutinations' of characters who meet, join together and separate (*The Big Mouth*).[31]

This new age of burlesque was invented by Tati in his own way, without there being a resemblance but with a lot of correspondences between the two authors. In Tati, the pane, the 'shop window', became the supreme optical and sound situation. The waiting-room in *Playtime*, the exhibition park in *Traffic* (as essential as the fairground in Fellini) were so many set-descriptions, opsigns and sonsigns which made up burlesque's new substance.[32] Sound, as we shall see, enters into profoundly creative relations with the visual, because both cease to be integrated into simple sensory-motor schemata. It is enough for Mr Hulot to appear, with his walk which at each step gives birth to a dancer which it takes up and sets off again: a cosmic wave enters, like the wind and storm in the little beach hotel in *Mr Hulot's Holiday*; the electronic house in *Mon oncle* breaks down in a depersonalized, pronominalized movement; the restaurant in *Playtime* goes to pieces in a flourish which suppresses one description in order to give rise to a different one. Mr Hulot is always ready to be carried away by the movements of world to which he gives rise or rather which themselves wait for him to be born. The whole genius of Tati is a low-frequency wave-action, but one which spreads Mr Hulots everywhere, forms and breaks up groups, joins and separates characters, in a kind of modern ballet, like that of the little cobbles in the garden in *Mon oncle*, or the scene of the mechanics' weightlessness in *Traffic*. The awaited fireworks in *Mr Hulot's Holiday* are already, as Daney says of *Parade*, the luminous trail of colours in an electronic landscape.

Tati hid away his own fantasizing and restrained any movement of musical comedy which could come from it, in favour of sound and visual configurations capable of making up a new op'art, a new son'art. It is Jacques Demy who takes up the thread, not with musical comedy, but a sung opera, a popular opera, as he calls it. He perhaps takes up the thread with what was most original in René Clair, when the situation became pure set valid for itself, whilst the action gave way to a popular sung ballet where the groups and characters chased each other, crossed in front of each other, played pass the slipper and the four corners game.[33]*
In Demy we witness optical and sound situations realized by coloured set-descriptions, which no longer extend into actions but into songs, producing in some sense an 'unhooking', a 'discrepancy' of the action. We find both levels: on one hand sensory-motor situations defined by the city, its people, its classes, the relations, actions and passions of the characters. But, in another way, and at a deeper level, the city merges with what provides the set in it, Pommeraye passage; and the sung action becomes a movement of city and classes, where the characters pass without recognizing each other, or on the contrary find each other, take up opposite positions, unite, stir each other up and separate in a purely optical and sound situation which traces an implied dream around them, 'charmed circle' or real 'enchantment'.[34] As with Lewis and Tati, it is set which replaces situation, and the to-and-fro which replaces action.

4 The crystals of time

1

The cinema does not just present images, it surrounds them with a world. This is why, very early on, it looked for bigger and bigger circuits which would unite an actual image with recollection-images, dream-images and world-images. This is surely the extension that Godard calls into question in *Slow Motion*, when he takes issue with the vision of the dying ('I'm not dead, because my life hasn't passed before me'). Should not the opposite direction have been pursued? Contracting the image instead of dilating it. Searching for the smallest circuit that functions as internal limit for all the others and that puts the actual image beside a kind of immediate, symmetrical, consecutive or even simultaneous double. The broad circuits of recollection in dream assume this narrow base, this extreme point, and not the other way round. This sort of direction already appears in links through flashback: in Mankiewicz, a short circuit is produced between the character who tells a story 'in the past' and the same person in so far as he has surprised something in order to be able to relate it; in Carné, in *Daybreak*, all the circuits of recollection which bring us back each time to the hotel room, rest on a small circuit, the recent recollection of the murder which has just taken place in this very same room. If we take this direction to its limit, we can say that the actual image itself has a virtual image which corresponds to it like a double or a reflection. In Bergsonian terms, the real object is reflected in a mirror-image as in the virtual object which, from its side and simultaneously, envelops or reflects the real: there is 'coalescence' between the two.[1] There is a formation of an image with two sides, actual *and* virtual. It is as if an image in a mirror, a photo or a postcard came to life, assumed independence and passed into the actual, even if this meant that the actual image returned into the mirror and resumed its place in the postcard or photo, following a double movement of liberation and capture.

We recognize here the very specific genre of *description* which, according to Robbe-Grillet's requirement, instead of being concerned with a supposedly distinct object constantly both absorbs and creates its own object.[2] Ever vaster circuits will be able to develop, corresponding to deeper and deeper layers of reality and higher and higher levels of memory or thought. But it is this most restricted circuit of the actual image and *its* virtual image which carries everything, and serves as internal limit. We have seen how, on the broader trajectories, perception and recollection, the real and the imaginary, the physical and the mental, or rather their images, continually followed each other, running behind each other and referring back to each other around a point of indiscernibility. But this point of indiscernibility is precisely constituted by the smallest circle, that is, the coalescence of the actual image and the virtual image, the image with two sides, actual and virtual at the same time. We gave the name opsign (and sonsign) to the actual image cut off from its motor extension: it then formed large circuits, and entered into communication with what could appear as recollection-images, dream-images and world-images. But here we see that the opsign finds its true genetic element when the actual optical image crystallizes with *its own* virtual image, on the small internal circuit. This is a crystal-image, which gives us the key, or rather the 'heart', of opsigns and their compositions. The latter are nothing other than slivers of crystal-images.

The crystal-image, or crystalline description, has two definite sides which are not to be confused. For the confusion of the real and the imaginary is a simple error of fact, and does not affect their discernibility: the confusion is produced solely 'in someone's head'. But indiscernibility constitutes an objective illusion; it does not suppress the distinction between the two sides, but makes it unattributable, each side taking the other's role in a relation which we must describe as reciprocal presupposition, or reversibility.[3] In fact, there is no virtual which does not become actual in relation to the actual, the latter becoming virtual through the same relation: it is a place and its obverse which are totally reversible. These are 'mutual images' as Bachelard puts it, where an exchange is carried out.[4] The indiscernibility of the real and the imaginary, or of the present and the past, of the actual and the virtual, is definitely not produced in the head or the mind, it is the objective characteristic of certain existing images which are by nature double. Hence two orders of problems arise, one of structure, the other of genesis. First, what are these consolidates of actual and virtual which define a crystalline structure (in a general, aesthetic, rather than a scientific, sense)? And, later on, what is the genetic process which appears in these structures?

The most familiar case is the mirror. Oblique mirrors, concave and convex mirrors and Venetian mirrors are inseparable from a circuit, as can be seen throughout Ophüls's work, and in Losey, especially in *Eve* and *The Servant*.[5] This circuit itself is an exchange: the mirror-image is virtual in relation to the actual character that the mirror catches, but it is actual in the mirror which now leaves the character with only a virtuality and pushes him back out-of-field. The exchange is all the more active when the circuit refers to a polygon with a growing number of sides: as in a face reflected on the facets of a ring, an actor seen in an infinity of twins. When virtual images proliferate like this, all together they absorb the entire actuality of the character, at the same time as the character is no more than one virtuality among others. This situation was prefigured in Welles's *Citizen Kane*, when Kane passes between two facing mirrors; but it comes to the fore in its pure state in the famous palace of mirrors in *The Lady from Shanghai*, where the principle of indiscernibility reaches its peak: a perfect crystal-image where the multiple mirrors have assumed the actuality of the two characters who will only be able to win it back by smashing them all, finding themselves side by side and each killing the other.

The actual image and *its* virtual image thus constitute the smallest internal circuit, ultimately a peak or point, but a physical point which has distinct elements (a bit like the epicurean atom). Distinct, but indiscernible, such are the actual and the virtual which are in continual exchange. When the virtual image becomes actual, it is then visible and limpid, as in the mirror or the solidity of finished crystal. But the actual image becomes virtual in its turn, referred elsewhere, invisible, opaque and shadowy, like a crystal barely dislodged from the earth. The actual-virtual couple thus immediately extends into the opaque-limpid, the expression of their exchange. But it needs only a modification of conditions (notably of temperature) for the limpid face to darken, and for the opaque face to acquire or rediscover its limpidity. The exchange is started again. So long as the conditions are not made precise there is definitely a distinction between the two sides, but they are indiscernible. This situation seems to bring us close to science. And it is no accident that it is developed in Zanussi as a result of a scientific inspiration. What interests Zanussi, however, is the 'power' of science, its relation to life, and first of all its projection into the life of men of science themselves.[6] *The Structure of Crystals* clearly shows two men of science, one of whom shines and already possesses all the light of official science, pure science, whilst the other has withdrawn into an opaque life and obscure tasks. But, from another point of view, is it not the obscure face which becomes luminous, even if this light is no longer that of science, even if it becomes more like faith as in an Augustinian 'illumination', whilst the representatives of pure science become peculiarly opaque and pursue projects with a shameful will to power (*Camouflage, The Imperative*)? Zanussi is one of those authors who, since Dreyer, have known how to enrich dialogue with a religious, metaphysical, or scientific content, while still keeping it as the most everyday and trivial determination. And this success comes precisely from a principle of indiscernibility. Which is luminous, the clear scientific schema of a brain section, or the opaque cranial dome of a monk at prayer (*Illumination*)? Between the two distinct sides, a doubt will always remain, preventing us from knowing which is limpid and which is dark, considering the conditions. In *A Woman's Decision*, the two protagonists 'stay in the middle [*milieu*] of their fight, frozen and covered in mud, while the sun rises'.[7] This is because the conditions echo the environment [*milieu*] too, like the weather conditions that we see again and again in Zanussi. The crystal is no longer reducible to the external position of two mirrors face to face, but to the internal disposition of a seed in relation to the environment. What will be the seed with which we can sow the environment, this desert-like and snowy expanse which is opened out in Zanussi's films? Or else, despite men's efforts, will the environment remain amorphous, at the same time as the crystal is emptied of its interiority, and as the seed is only a seed of death, fatal illness, or suicide (*Spiral*)? Exchange or indiscernibility thus follow each other in three ways in the crystalline circuit: the actual and the virtual (or the two mirrors face to face); the limpid and the opaque; the seed and the environment. Zanussi attempts to bring the whole cinema under the influence of these various aspects of an uncertainty principle.

Zanussi has made an actor out of the man of science; that is, a dramatic being *par excellence*. But this was already the situation of the actor in himself: the crystal is a stage, or rather a track [*piste*], before being an amphitheatre. The actor is bracketed with his public role: he makes the virtual image of the role actual, so that the role becomes visible and luminous. The actor is a 'monster', or rather monsters are born actors – Siamese twin, limbless man – because they find a role in the excess or shortcoming that affects them. But the more the virtual image of the role becomes actual and limpid, the more the actual image of the actor moves into the shadows and becomes opaque: there will be a private project of the actor, a dark vengeance, a strangely obscure criminal or justice-bringing activity. And this underground activity will detach itself and become visible in turn, as the interrupted role falls back into opacity. We can already recognize the dominant theme of Tod Browning's work, in silent film. A fake limbless man takes to his role and has his arms really cut off, for the love of the woman who could not bear men's hands, but tries to recover his dignity by organizing the murder of a rival who is whole (*The Unknown*). In *The Unholy Three*, the ventriloquist Echo can no longer speak except through his dummy, but regains control of himself in the criminal project he pursues disguised as an old woman, even though he confesses his crime through the mouth of the man who was wrongly accused. The monsters in *Freaks* are monsters only because they have been forced to move into their explicit role, and it is through a dark vengeance that they find themselves again and regain a strange clarity which arrives in the lightning to interrupt their role.[8] In *The Black Bird* it is in the course of a transformation that 'the actor' is struck by paralysis, when he was going to use his role of bishop in a criminal intent: as if the monstrous exchange suddenly froze. An abnormal, suffocating slowness permeates Browning's characters in general, in the crystal. What we see in Browning is not a reflection on the theatre or the circus, as we will see in others, but a double face of the actor, that only the cinema could capture by instituting its own circuit. The virtual image of the public role becomes actual, but in relation to the virtual image of a private crime, which becomes actual in turn and replaces the first image. We no longer know which is the role and which is the crime. Perhaps it needed an extraordinary understanding between an actor and an author: Browning and Lon Chaney. This crystalline circuit of the actor, its transparent face and its opaque face, is travesty. If Browning achieved a poetry of the unassignable in this way, it seems that two great films of travesty have inherited his inspiration: Hitchcock's *Murder*, and Ichikawa's *An Actor's Revenge*, with its marvellous black backgrounds.

To such a varied list we should add the ship. It too is a track, a circuit. It is as if, as in Turner's paintings, splitting in two is not an accident, but a power which is part of the ship. It is Herman Melville who, in his novels, fixed this structure for all time. Seed impregnating the sea, the ship is caught between its two crystal-line faces: a limpid face which is the ship from above, where everything should be visible, according to order; an opaque face which is the ship from below, and which occurs underwater, the black face of the engine-room stokers. But it is as if the limpid face actualizes a kind of theatre or dramaturgy which takes hold of the passengers themselves, whilst the virtual passes into the opaque face, and is actualized in turn in the settling of scores between engineers, in the demonic perversity of a boatswain, in a captain's obsession, in the secret revenge of insurgent blacks.[9] This is the circuit of two virtual images which continually become actual in relation to each other, and are continually revived. It is not so much Huston's *Moby Dick* which gives the cinematographic version of the ship, but rather Welles's *The Lady from Shanghai*, in which the majority of the forms of the crystal-image are un-doubtedly to be found: the yacht called 'The Circe' reveals a visible face and an invisible face, a limpid face that for a moment the naive hero allows himself to be caught by, while the other face, the opaque one, the great dark stage of the aquarium of monsters, rises in silence and grows as the first one becomes vague or blurred. And, in a different way, it is Fellini who discovers, beyond the circus-track, a circuit of the ship as ultimate fate. The ship in *Amarcord* already presented itself as a vast seed of death or life on the sea of plastic. But, in *The Ship Sails On*, the ship makes the face of a growing polygon proliferate. It initially splits in two according to the division of bottom and top: the entire visible order of the ship and its sailors is at the service of the grand dramaturgical project of the singer-passengers; but, when these passengers from the top come to see the proletariat at the bottom, it is the latter who become in turn spectators, and listeners to the singing competition which they impose on those at the top, or to the musical competition in the kitchens. Then the split changes its orientation and now divides the singer-passengers and the proletarian-shipwrecked on the bridge: here again the exchange is made between the actual and the virtual, the limpid and the opaque, in a Bartok-like musical device. Then, later, the split has become almost a splitting in two: the dark warship, blind and closed-up, terrifying, which arrives to reclaim the fugitives, is actualized all the better because the transparent ship carried out its funerary dramaturgy in a marvellous circuit of faster and faster images where the two ships end up exploding and sinking, giving back to the sea what ends up as the sea, an eternally amorphous environment, a melancholy rhinoceros which stands for Moby Dick. This is the mutual image, this is the cycle of the crystal ship in a pictorial and musical end of the world, and, among the final gestures, the young maniacal terrorist who cannot stop himself throwing a final bomb into the dark ship's narrow porthole.

The ship can also be the ship of the dead, the nave of a simple chapel as place of an exchange. The virtual survival of the dead can be actualized, but is this not at the price of our existence, which becomes virtual in turn? Is it the dead who belong to us, or we who belong to the dead? And do we love them against the living, or for and with life? Truffaut's fine film, *The Green Room*, arranges the four faces which form a strange green crystal, an emerald. At one point, the hero hides in a little shelter with dulled windows with green reflections, where he seems to have a glaucous existence, where it is impossible to tell whether he is living or dead. And in the chapel's crystal can be seen a thousand candles, a bush of fire which is always missing a branch to make it into the 'perfect figure'. The final candle of he or she who has been able to light only the last-but-one will always be missing, in an irreducible persistence of life which makes the crystal infinite.

The crystal is expression. Expression moves from the mirror to the seed. It is the same circuit which passes through three figures, the actual and the virtual, the limpid and the opaque, the seed and the environment. In fact, the seed is on the one hand the virtual image which will crystallize an environment which is at present [*actuellement*] amorphous; but on the other hand the latter must have a structure which is virtually crystallizable, in relation to which the seed now plays the role of actual image. Once again the actual and the virtual are exchanged in an indiscernibility which on each occasion allows distinction to survive. In a famous sequence in *Citizen Kane*, the little glass ball breaks apart when it falls from the hands of the dying man, but the snow that it contained seems to come towards us in gusts to impregnate the environment [*milieux*] that we will discover. We do not know in advance if the virtual seed ('Rosebud') will be actualized, because we do not know in advance if the actual environment enjoys the corresponding virtuality. Perhaps this is also the perspective from which to understand the splendour of the images in Herzog's *Heart of Glass*, and the film's double aspect. The search for the alchemical heart and secret, for the red crystal, is inseparable from the search for cosmic limits, as the highest tension of the spirit and the deepest level of reality. But the crystal's fire will have to connect with the whole range of manufacturing for the world, for its part to stop being a flat, amorphous environment which ends at the edge of a gulf, and to reveal infinite crystalline potentialities in itself ('the earth rises up from the waters, I see a new earth . . .').[10] In this film Herzog has set out the greatest crystal-images in the history of the cinema. There is an analogous attempt in Tarkovsky, continued from one film to the next, but always closed again: *Mirror* is a turning crystal, with two sides if we relate it to the invisible adult character (his mother, his wife), with four sides if we relate it to two visible couples (his mother and the child he was, his wife and the child he has). And the crystal turns on itself, like a homing device that searches an opaque environment: what is Russia, what is Russia . . .? The seed seems to be frozen in these sodden, washed and heavily translucent images, with their sometimes bluish, sometimes brown surfaces, while the green environment seems, in the rain, to be unable to go beyond the condition of a liquid crystal which keeps its secret. Are we to believe that the soft planet Solaris gives a reply, and that it will reconcile the ocean and thought, the environment and the seed, at once designating the transparent face of the crystal (the rediscovered woman) and the crystallizable form of the universe (the rediscovered dwelling)? *Solaris* does not open up this optimism, and *Stalker* returns the environment to the opacity of an indeterminate zone, and the seed to the morbidity of something aborting, a closed door. Tarkovsky's wash[11]* (the woman also washes her hair against a wet wall in *Mirror*), the rains that provide rhythm for each film, as intense as in Antonioni or Kurosawa, but with different functions, constantly bring us back to the question: what burning bush, what fire, what soul, what sponge will staunch this earth? Serge Daney observed that, after Dovzhenko, certain Soviet film-makers (or those from eastern Europe like Zanussi) kept the taste for heavy materials and dense still lifes which were, in constrast, removed by the movement-image in western cinema.[12] In the crystal-image there is this mutual search – blind and halting – of matter and spirit: beyond the movement-image, 'in which we are still pious'.

The seed and the mirror are taken up yet again, the one in the work in process of being made, the other in the work reflected in the work. These two themes, which had run through all the other arts, had to affect cinema as well. Sometimes it is the film which is reflected in a theatre play, a show, a painting, or, better, a film within the film; sometimes it is the film which takes itself as its object in the process of its making or of its setbacks in being made. And sometimes the two themes are quite distinct: in Eisenstein, the *montage of attractions* already produced images in the mirror; in *Last Year in Marienbad* by Resnais and Robbe-Grillet, the two big theatre scenes are images in a mirror (and the entire Marienbad hotel is a pure crystal, with its transparent side, its opaque side and their exchange).[13] In contrast, Fellini's *8½* is a seed-image, in process of being produced, which feeds on its setbacks (except perhaps in the big scene with the telepath which introduces a mirror-image). Wenders's *The State of Things* is all the more in seed-form because it aborts, becomes dispersed and can be reflected only in the reasons which block it. Buster Keaton, who is sometimes presented as a genius without reflection, is perhaps the first along with Vertov to have introduced the film within the film. In *Sherlock Junior*, this is in the form of a mirror-image; on another occasion, in *The Cameraman*, it is in the form of a seed which arrives directly via the cinema, even though manipulated by a monkey or a reporter, and constitutes the film in process of being made. Sometimes, on the other hand, in the manner of Gide's *Counterfeiters*, the two themes or the two cases cross and join up, becoming indistinguishable.[14] In Godard's *Passion*, the pictorial and musical *tableaux vivants* are in the process of being produced; at the same time the female worker, the wife and the boss are the mirror-image of what, nevertheless, reflects them themselves. In Rivette, theatrical representation is a mirror-image but, precisely because it is constantly failing, is the seed of that which does not manage to come to completion or to be reflected, hence the very odd role of the rehearsals of Pericles in *Paris Belongs to Us*, or Phaedra in *L'amour fou*. Yet another form appears in Welles's *Immortal Story*: the whole film was the mirror-image of a legend staged again by the old man, but at the same time stood on its own terms as the initial occasion which would make the legend itself germinate and give it back to the sea.[15]

It was inevitable that the cinema, in the crises of the action-image, went through melancholic Hegelian reflections on its own death: having no more stories to tell, it would take itself as object and would be able to tell only its own story (Wenders). But, in fact, the work in the mirror and the work in the seed have always accompanied art without ever exhausting it, because art found in them a means of creation for certain special images. By the same token, the film within the film does not signal an end of history, and is no more self-sufficient than is the flashback or the dream: it is just a method of working, which must be justified from elsewhere. In fact, it is a mode of the crystal-image. If this mode is used, then it has to be grounded on considerations capable of giving it a higher justification. It will be observed that, in all the arts, the work within the work has often been linked to the consideration of a surveillance, an investigation, a revenge, a conspiracy, or a plot. This was already true for the theatre in the theatre of Hamlet, but also for the novel of Gide. We have seen the importance that this theme of the conspiracy takes on in the cinema, with the crisis of the action-image; and it is not only in Rivette – an irresistible atmosphere of conspiracy spreads through *Last Year in Marienbad*. Yet all this would only constitute a perspective of very secondary importance if the cinema did not have the most powerful reasons for giving it new and specific depth. The cinema as art itself lives in a direct relation with a permanent plot [*complot*], an international conspiracy which conditions it from within, as the most intimate and most indispensable enemy. This conspiracy is that of money; what defines industrial art is not mechanical reproduction but the internalized relation with money. The only rejoinder to the harsh law of cinema – a minute of image which costs a day of collective work – is Fellini's: 'When there is no more money left, the film will be finished.' Money is the obverse of all the images that the cinema shows and sets in place, so that films about money are already, if implicitly, films within the film or about the film.[16] This is the true 'state of things': it is not in a goal of cinema, as Wenders says, but rather, as he shows, in a constitutive relation between the film in process of being made and money as the totality of the film. Wenders, in *The State of Things*, shows the deserted, run-down hotel, and the film crew, each of whom returns to his solitude, victim of a plot whose key is elsewhere; and this key is revealed in the second half of the film as the other side, the mobile home of the producer on the run who is going to get himself murdered, causing the death of the film-maker, in such a way as to make plain that there is not, and there never will be, equivalence or equality in the mutual camera-money exchange.

This is the old curse which undermines the cinema: time is money. If it is true that movement maintains a set of exchanges or an equivalence, a symmetry as an invariant, time is by nature the conspiracy of unequal change or the impossibility of an equivalence. It is in this sense that it is money: in Marx's two formulations, C-M-C is that of equivalence, but M-C-M is that of impossible equivalence or tricked, dissymmetrical exchange. Godard presented *Passion* as posing precisely this problem of exchange. And if Wenders, as we saw in the case of his first films, treated the camera as the general equivalent of all movement of translation, he discovers in *The State of Things* the impossibility of a camera-time equivalence, time being money or the circulation of money. L'Herbier had said it all, in an astonishing and mocking lecture: space and time becoming more and more expensive in the modern world, art had to make itself international industrial art, that is, cinema, in order to *buy* space and time as 'imaginary warrants of human capital'.[17] This was not the explicit theme of the masterpiece *Money*, but it was its implicit theme (and in a film of the same title, inspired by Tolstoy, Bresson shows that money, because it is of the order of time, makes impossible any reparation for evil done, any equivalence or just retribution, except of course through grace). In short, *the cinema confronts its most internal presupposition, money, and the movement-image makes way for the time-image in one and the same operation.* What the film within the film expresses is this infernal circuit between the image and money, this inflation which time puts into the exchange, this 'overwhelming rise'. The film is movement, but the film within the film is money, is time. The crystal-image thus receives the principle which is its foundation: endlessly relaunching exchange which is dissymmetrical, unequal and without equivalence, giving image for money, giving time for images, converting time, the transparent side, and money, the opaque side, like a spinning top on its end. And the film will be finished when there is no more money left . . .

2

The crystal-image may well have many distinct elements, but its irreducibility consists in the indivisible unity of an actual image and 'its' virtual image. But what is this virtual image in coalescence with the actual one? What is a mutual image? Bergson constantly posed the question and sought the reply in time's abyss. What is actual is always a present. But then, precisely, the present changes or passes. We can always say that it becomes past when it no longer is, when a new present replaces it. But this is meaningless.[18] It is clearly necessary for it to pass on for the new present to arrive, and it is clearly necessary for it to pass at the same time as it is present, at the moment that it is the present. Thus the image has to be present and past, still present and already past, at once and at the same time. If it was not already past at the same time as present, the present would never pass on. The past does not follow the present that it is no longer, it coexists with the present it was. The present is the actual image, and *its* contemporaneous past is the virtual image, the image in a mirror. According to Bergson, 'paramnesia' (the illusion of *déjà-vu* or already having been there) simply makes this obvious point perceptible: there is a recollection of the present, contemporaneous with the present itself, as closely coupled as a role to an actor. 'Our actual existence, then, whilst it is unrolled in time, duplicates itself along with a virtual existence, a mirror-image. Every moment of our life presents the two aspects, it is actual and virtual, perception on the one side and recollection on the other . . . Whoever becomes conscious of the continual duplicating of his present into perception and recollection . . . will compare himself to an actor playing his part automatically, listening to himself and beholding himself playing.'[19]

Bergson calls the virtual image 'pure recollection', the better to distinguish it from mental images – recollection-images, dream or dreaming – with which it might be readily confused. In fact, the latter are certainly virtual images, but actualized or in the course of actualization in consciousnesses or psychological states. And they are necessarily actualized in relation to a new present, in relation to a different present from the one that they have been: hence these more or less broad circuits, evoking mental images in accordance with the requirements of the new present which is defined as later than the former one, and which defines the former one as earlier according to a law of chronological succession (the recollection-image will thus be dated). In contrast, the virtual image in the pure state is defined, not in accordance with a new present in relation to which it would be (relatively) past, but in accordance with the actual present *of which* it is the past, absolutely and simultaneously: although it is specific it is none the less part of 'the past in general', in the sense that it has not yet received a date.[20] As pure virtuality, it does not have to be actualized, since it is strictly correlative with the actual image with which it forms the smallest circuit which serves as base or point for all the others. It is the virtual image which corresponds to a particular actual image, instead of being actualized, of having to be actualized in a *different* actual image. It is an actual-virtual circuit on the spot, and not an actualization of the virtual in accordance with a shifting actual. It is a crystal-image, and not an organic image.

The virtual image (pure recollection) is not a psychological state or a consciousness: it exists outside of consciousness, in time, and we should have no more difficulty in admitting the virtual insistence of pure recollections in time than we do for the actual existence of non-perceived objects in space. What causes our mistake is that recollection-images, and even dream-images or dreaming, haunt a consciousness which necessarily accords them a capricious or intermittent allure, since they are actualized according to the momentary needs of this consciousness. But, if we ask *where* consciousness is going to look for these recollection-images and these dream-images or this reverie that it evokes, according to its states, we are led back to pure virtual images of which the latter are only modes or degrees of actualization. Just as we perceive things in the place where they are, and have to place ourselves among things in order to perceive them, we go to look for recollection in the place where it is, we have to place ourselves with a leap into the past in general, into these purely virtual images which have been constantly preserved through time. It is in the past as it is in itself, as it is preserved in itself, that we go to look for our dreams or our recollections, and not the opposite.[21] It is only on this condition that the recollection-image will carry the sign of the past which distinguishes it from a different image, or the dream-image, the distinctive sign of a temporal perspective: they exhaust the sign in an 'original virtuality'. This is why, earlier, we were able to assimilate virtual images to mental images, recollection-images, dream or dreaming: these were so many incomplete solutions, but on the track of the right solution. The more or less broad, always relative, circuits, between the present and the past, refer back, on the one hand, to a small internal circuit between a present and *its own* past, between an actual image and *its* virtual image; on the other hand, they refer to deeper and deeper circuits which are themselves virtual, which each time mobilize the whole of the past, but in which the relative circuits bathe or plunge to trace an actual shape and bring in their provisional harvest.[22] The crystal-image has these two aspects: internal limit of all the relative circuits, but also outer-most, variable and reshapable envelope, at the edges of the world, beyond even moments of world. The little crystalline seed and the vast crystallizable universe: everything is included in the capacity for expansion of the collection constituted by the seed and the universe. Memories, dreams, even worlds are only apparent relative circuits which depend on the variations of this Whole. They are degrees or modes of actualization which are spread out between these two extremes of the actual and the virtual: the actual and *its* virtual on the small circuit, expanding virtualities in the deep circuits. And it is from the inside that the small internal circuit makes contact with the deep ones, directly, through the merely relative circuits.

What constitutes the crystal-image is the most fundamental operation of time: since the past is constituted not after the present that it was but at the same time, time has to split itself in two at each moment as present and past, which differ from each other in nature, or, what amounts to the same thing, it has to split the present in two heterogeneous directions, one of which is launched towards the future while the other falls into the past.[23] Time has to split at the same time as it sets itself out or unrolls itself: it splits in two dissymmetrical jets, one of which makes all the present pass on, while the other preserves all the past. Time consists of this split, and it is this, it is time, that we *see in the crystal*. The crystal-image was not time, but we see time in the crystal. We see in the crystal the perpetual foundation of time, non-chronological time, Cronos and not Chronos. This is the power-ful, non-organic Life which grips the world. The visionary, the seer, is the one who sees in the crystal, and what he sees is the gushing of time as dividing in two, as splitting. Except, Bergson adds, this splitting never goes right to the end. In fact the crystal constantly exchanges the two distinct images which constitute it, the actual image of the present which passes and the virtual image of the past which is preserved: distinct and yet indiscernible, and all the more indiscernible because distinct, because we do not know which is one and which is the other. This is unequal exchange, or the point of indiscernibility, the mutual image. The crystal always lives at the limit, it is itself the 'vanishing limit between the immediate past which is already no longer and the immediate future which is not yet . . . mobile mirror which endlessly reflects perception in recollection'. What we see in the crystal is therefore a dividing in two that the crystal itself constantly causes to turn on itself, that it prevents from reaching

completion, because it is a perpetual *self-distinguishing*, a distinction in the process of being produced; which always resumes the
distinct terms in itself, in order constantly to relaunch them. 'The
putting into abyss [*mise-en-abyme*] does not redouble the unit, as an
external reflection might do; in so far as it is an internal
mirroring, it can only ever split it in two', and subject it 'to the
infinite relaunch of endlessly new splitting'.[24] The crystal-image
is, then, the point of indiscernibility of the two distinct images, the
actual and the virtual, while what we see in the crystal is time itself,
a bit of time in the pure state, the very distinction between the two
images which keeps on reconstituting itself. So there will be
different states of the crystal, depending on the acts of its
formation and the figures of what we see in it. We analysed earlier
the elements of the crystal, but not the crystalline states; each of
these states we can now call *crystal of time*.[25]

Bergson's major theses on time are as follows: the past coexists
with the present that it has been; the past is preserved in itself, as
past in general (non-chronological); at each moment time splits
itself into present and past, present that passes and past which is
preserved. Bergsonism has often been reduced to the following
idea: duration is subjective, and constitutes our internal life. And
it is true that Bergson had to express himself in this way, at least at
the outset. But, increasingly, he came to say something quite
different: the only subjectivity is time, non-chronological time
grasped in its foundation, and it is we who are internal to time, not
the other way round. That we are in time looks like a common-
place, yet it is the highest paradox. Time is not the interior in us,
but just the opposite, the interiority in which we are, in which we
move, live and change. Bergson is much closer to Kant than he
himself thinks: Kant defined time as the form of interiority, in the
sense that we are internal to time (but Bergson conceives this
form quite differently from Kant). In the novel, it is Proust who
says that time is not internal to us, but that we are internal to time,
which divides itself in two, which loses itself and discovers itself in
itself, which makes the present pass and the past be preserved. In
the cinema, there are perhaps three films which show how we
inhabit time, how we move in it, in this form which carries us
away, picks us up and enlarges us: Dovzhenko's *Zvenigora*,
Hitchcock's *Vertigo* and Resnais' *Je t'aime je t'aime*. In Resnais' film,
the opaque hyper-sphere is one of the most beautiful crystal-
images, while what we see in the crystal is time itself, the gushing
forth of time. Subjectivity is never ours, it is time, that is, the soul

or the spirit, the virtual. The actual is always objective, but the
virtual is subjective: it was initially the affect, that which we
experience in time; then time itself, pure virtuality which divides
itself in two as affector and affected, 'the affection of self by self'
as definition of time.

3

Let us suppose an ideal state which would be the perfect,
completed crystal. Ophüls's images are perfect crystals. Their
facets are oblique mirrors, as in *Madame de . . .* And the mirrors
are not content with reflecting the actual image, but constitute the
prism, the lens where the split image constantly runs after itself to
connect up with itself, as on the circus-track in *Lola Montez*. On the
track or in the crystal, the imprisoned characters bustle, acting
and acted on, a bit like Raymond Roussel's heroes exercising their
prowess at the heart of a diamond or a glass cage, under an
iridescent light (*The Tender Enemy*). One can only just turn in the
crystal: hence the round of episodes, and also of colours (*Lola
Montez*), of waltzes and also of earrings (*Madame de . . .*), of the
master of ceremonies' visions in the round in *La ronde*. Crystalline
perfection lets no outside subsist: there is no outside of the mirror
or the film set, but only an obverse where the characters who
disappear or die go, abandoned by life which thrusts itself back
into the film set. In *House of Pleasure*, the tearing-off of the old
dancer's mask reveals no outside but an obverse which sends and
guides the busy doctor back to the ball.[26] And, even in his tender
and familiar asides, the pitiless M. Loyal in *Lola Montez* keeps on
thrusting the failing heroine back on the stage. If we consider the
relations between theatre and cinema in general, we no longer
find ourselves in the classical situation where the two arts are two
different ways of actualizing the same virtual image, but neither
do we find ourselves in the situation of a 'montage of attraction',
where a theatrical spectacle (or a circus, etc.), being filmed, itself
plays the role of a virtual image which would serve to extend the
actual images by succeeding them for a time, during a sequence.
The situation is quite different: the actual image and the virtual
image coexist and crystallize; they enter into a circuit which
brings us constantly back from one to the other; they form one
and the same 'scene' where the characters belong to the real and

yet play a role. In short, it is the whole of the real, life in its entirety, which has become spectacle, in accordance with the demands of a pure optical and sound perception. The scene, then, is not restricted to providing a sequence but becomes the cinematographic unity which replaces the shot or itself consti- tutes a sequence shot. It is a properly cinematographic theatri- cality, the 'excess of theatricality' that Bazin spoke of, and that only cinema can give to theatre.

Its origin would perhaps be Tod Browning's masterpieces. At any event, Ophüls's monsters do not really need a monstrous appearance. They pursue their round in frozen and iced images. And what do we see in the perfect crystal? Time, but time which has already rolled up, rounded itself, at the same time as it was splitting. *Lola Montez* can include flashbacks: the film would be enough to confirm, if it were necessary, the degree to which the flashback is a secondary procedure whose value arises only from serving a deeper move. For what counts is not the link between the actual and miserable present (the circus) and the recollection- image of former magnificent presents. The evocation is certainly there; but what it reveals at a deeper level is the dividing in two of time, which makes all the presents pass and makes them tend towards the circus as if towards their future, but also preserves all the pasts and puts them into the circus as so many virtual images in pure recollections. Lola Montez herself experiences the vertigo of this dividing in two when, drunk and feverish, she is about to throw herself from the top of the marquee into the tiny net which is waiting for her below: the whole scene is seen as in the lens of the pen-holder dear to Raymond Roussel. The dividing in two, the differentiation of the two images, actual and virtual, does not go to the limit, because the resulting circuit repeatedly takes us back from one kind to the other. There is only a vertigo, an oscillation.

In Renoir too, from *The Little Match-Girl* where the Christmas tree appears adorned with crystals, automata and living beings, objects and reflections enter into a circuit of coexistence and exchange which constitutes a 'theatricality in the pure state'. And it is in *The Golden Coach* that this coexistence and exchange will be taken to their highest point, with the two sides of the camera or the image, the actual image and the virtual image. But what are we to say when the image ceases to be flat or double-faced, and depth of field adds a third side to it? It is depth of field, for example in *La règle du jeu*, which ensures a nesting of frames, a waterfall of mirrors, a system of rhymes between masters and valets, living beings and automata, theatre and reality, actual and virtual. It is depth of field which substitutes the scene for the shot. We will be all the more hesitant to give it the role intended by Bazin, namely a pure function of reality. The function of depth is rather to constitute the image in crystal, and to absorb the real which thus passes as much into the virtual as into the actual.[27] There is, however, a great difference between the crystals of Renoir and those of Ophüls. In Renoir, the crystal is never pure and perfect; it has a failing, a point of flight, a 'flaw'. It is always cracked. And this is what depth of field reveals: there is not simply a rolling-up of a round in the crystal; something is going to slip away in the background, in depth, through the third side or third dimension, through the crack. This was already true of the mirror in the flat image, as in *The Golden Coach*, but it was less visible, whilst depth makes it clear that the crystal is there so something can escape in it, in the background, through the background. *La règle du jeu* produces a coexistence of the actual image of men and the virtual image of beasts, the actual image of living beings and the virtual image of automata, the actual image of characters and the virtual image of their roles during the party, the actual image of the masters ʾnd their virtual image in the servants, the actual image of the servants and their virtual image in the masters. Everything is mirror-images, distributed in depth. But depth of field always arranges a background in the circuit through which something can flee: the crack. It is interesting that a number of answers have been given to the question, who does not play the rules of the game? Truffaut, for instance, says that it is the airman. Yet the airman remains locked into the crystal, prisoner of his role, and hides when the woman proposes that he should escape with her. As Bamberger observed, the only character who is out of line [*hors règle*], not allowed in the château and yet belonging to it, neither outside nor inside, but always in the background, is the gamekeeper, the only person who does not have a double or reflection. Bursting in, despite the prohibition, in pursuit of the poaching valet, mistakenly killing the airman, he is the one who breaks the circuit, who shatters the cracked crystal with rifle shots and causes its contents to escape.

La règle du jeu is one of Renoir's finest films, but it does not give us the key to the others. For it is pessimistic, and proceeds by violence. And it does violence first of all to Renoir's complete idea. This complete idea is that the crystal or the scene is not restricted to putting into circuit the actual image and the virtual image, and absorbing the real into a generalized theatre. Without recourse to violence, and through the development of an experimentation, something will come out of the crystal, a new Real will come out beyond the actual and virtual. Everything happens as if the circuit served to try out roles, as if roles were being tried in it until the right one were found, the one with which we escape to enter a clarified reality. In short, the circuit, the round, are not closed because they are selective, and produce a winner each time. Renoir has sometimes been criticized for his taste for the makeshift and improvisation, both in his direction in general, and in his directing of the actors. This is in fact a creative virtue, linked to the substitution of the scene for the shot. According to Renoir, theatre is inseparable – for both characters and actors – from the enterprise of experimenting with and selecting roles, until you find the one which goes beyond theatre and enters life.[28] In his pessimistic moments, Renoir is doubtful that there can be a winner: in that case there are only the keeper's shots which make the crystal explode, as in *La règle du jeu*, or the turbulence of the river swollen by the storm and stung by the rain in *A Day in the Country*. But, following his temperament, Renoir bets on a win: something takes shape inside the crystal which will succeed in leaving through the crack and spreading freely. This was already the case with Boudu, who rediscovers the thread of water when he comes out of the intimate, closed-in theatre of the bookshop where he has tried many roles. It will be the case with Harriet in the grandiose film *The River*, where the children, sheltered in a kind of crystal or Hindu pavilion, try roles, some of which take a tragic turn, as a result of which the younger brother dies tragically, but in which the girl will serve her apprenticeship, until she finds in it the powerful will for life which becomes identified with the river and joins it again on the outside. A film strangely close to Lawrence. For Renoir, theatre is primary, but because life must emerge from it. Theatre is valuable only as a search for an art of living; this is what the disparate couple in *Little Theatre* learn. 'Where then, does theatre finish and life begin?' remains the question always asked by Renoir. We are born in a crystal, but the crystal retains only death, and life must come out of it, after trying itself out. Even as an adult, the teacher in *Picnic on the Grass* will experience this adventure. The wild dance at the end of *French Cancan* is not a round, a flowing-back of life into the circuit, into the theatrical scene, as in Ophüls, but, on the contrary, a gallop, a means by which theatre opens into life, pours out into life, carrying Nini along in a troubled stream. At the end of *The Golden Coach*, three characters will have found their living role, while Camilla will remain in the crystal, to try still other roles in it, one of which will perhaps make her discover the true Camilla.[29]

This is why, although he fully shares the general taste of the French school for water, Renoir makes such a special use of it. There are, according to him, two states of water, the frozen water of the glass pane, the flat mirror, or the deep crystal, and the fast, flowing water (or the wind, which plays the same role in *Picnic on the Grass*). Rather than being naturalism, this is much closer to Maupassant, who often sees things through a pane, before following their course on a river. In *A Day in the Country* it is through the window that the two men observe the family arriving, each of the two playing his role, one that of the cynic, the other that of the scrupulous sentimentalist. But, when the action develops on the river, the test of life causes the roles to be dropped, and shows a good sort in the cynic, while the sentimental one is revealed as an unscrupulous seducer.

What we see through the pane or in the crystal is time, in its double movement of making presents pass, replacing one by the next while going towards the future, but also of preserving all the past, dropping it into an obscure depth. This dividing in two, this differentiation, did not achieve completion in Ophüls because time rolled itself up, and its two aspects relaunched themselves into the circuit whose poles they recharged while blocking up the future. Now, in contrast, the dividing in two can come to completion, but precisely on condition that one of the two tendencies leaves the crystal, through the point of flight. From the indiscernibility of the actual and the virtual, a new distinction must emerge, like a new reality which was not pre-existent. Everything that has happened falls back into the crystal and stays there: this is all the frozen, fixed, finished-with and over-conforming roles that the characters have tried in turn, dead roles or roles of death, the macabre dance of recollections that Bergson speaks of, as in the château in *La règle du jeu* or the fortress in *Grand Illusion*. Some of these roles may be heroic, like the two enemy officers in pursuit of rites which are already outmoded, or charming, like the test of first love: they are none the less condemned, because already destined for recollection. And yet the trying out of roles is indispensable. It is indispensable so that the other tendency, that of presents which pass and are replaced, emerges from the scene and launches itself towards a future, creates this future as a bursting forth of life. The two fugitives will be saved by the sacrifice of the other. Harriet will be saved because she will be able to renounce the role of her first love. Saved from the waters, Boudu will also be saved by the waters, abandoning the successive roles granted him by the too intimate dreams of the bookshop and his wife. One leaves the theatre to get to life, but one leaves it imperceptibly, on the thread of the stream, that is, of time. It is by leaving it that time gives itself a future. Hence the importance of the question: where does life begin? Time in the crystal is differentiated into two movements, but one of them takes charge of the future and freedom, provided that it leaves the crystal. Then the real will be created; at the same time as it escapes the eternal referral back of the actual and the virtual, the present and the past. When Sartre criticized Welles (and *Citizen Kane*) for having reconstituted time on the basis of the past, instead of understanding it in terms of a dimension of the future, he was perhaps unaware that the film-maker closest to his wishes was Renoir. It was Renoir who had a lively awareness of the identity of freedom with a collective or individual future, with a leap towards the future, an opening of the future. This is even Renoir's political consciousness, the way in which he conceives the French Revolution or the Popular Front.

There is perhaps yet a third state: the crystal caught in its formation and growth, related to the 'seeds' which make it up. In fact there is never a completed crystal; each crystal is infinite by right, in the process of being made, and is made with a seed which incorporates the environment and forces it to crystallize. The question is no longer that of knowing what comes out of the crystal and how, but, on the contrary, how to get into it. For each entrance is itself a crystalline seed, a component element. We recognize the method that will be increasingly adopted by Fellini. He began with films of wandering, which relaxed the sensory-motor connections, and made pure sound-and-optical images rise up – photo-novel, investigation-photo, music-hall, party. But the concerns were still those of escaping, leaving and going away. He became increasingly concerned with entering into a new element, and multiplying the entrances. There are geographical entrances, psychic ones, historical, archaelogical, etc: all the entrances into Rome, or into the world of clowns. Sometimes an entrance is explicitly double; thus the crossing of the Rubicon in

Fellini's Roma is a historical evocation, but a comical one, through the intermediary of a school memory. One could, for example, make a count of these entrances as so many types of image in *8½*: the childhood recollection, the nightmare, the distraction, the dreaming, the fantasy, the feeling of already having been there.[30] Hence the honeycomb-presentation, the cubicled images, the huts, niches, cabins and windows which mark *Satyricon*, *Juliet of the Spirits*, and *City of Women*. Two things happen at once. On the one hand, purely optical and sound-images crystallize: they attract their contents, make them crystallize and compose them from an actual image and its virtual image, its mirror-image. These are so many seeds or entrances: in Fellini, numbers and amusements have replaced the scene, and made the depth of field redundant. But, on the other hand, by entering into coalescence the images constitute one and the same crystal in the course of infinite growth. For the crystal as a whole is only the ordered set of its seeds or the transversal of all its entrances.

Fellini has fully grasped the economic principle which says that only admission [*entrée*] pays. The only unity of Rome is that of the spectacle which connects all its entrances. The spectacle becomes universal, and keeps on growing, precisely because it has no object other than entrances into the spectacle, which are so many seeds in this respect. Amengual has given a profound definition of this originality of spectacle in Fellini, with no distinction between watching and watched, without spectators, without exit, without wings or stage: less a theatre than a kind of giant Luna Park, where movement, which has become movement of world, makes us pass from one shop-window to another, from one entrance to another through all the cubicles.[31] Thus, we can see from this the difference between Fellini and Renoir or Ophüls: Fellini's crystal does not include any crack through which we could, we should, leave to reach life; but neither has it the perfection of an established and cut crystal which would hold life to freeze it. It is a crystal which is always in the process of formation, expansion, which makes everything it touches crystallize, and to which its seeds give a capacity for indefinite growth. It is life as spectacle, and yet in its spontaneity.

Does this mean that all entrances are equal? Yes, certainly, in so far as they are seeds. Of course seeds maintain the distinction that there was between the types of sound and optical images that they make crystallize – perceptions, recollections, dreams, fantasies . . . But these distinctions become indiscernible, because there is a homogeneity of seed and crystal, the whole of the latter being no more than a greater seed in the process of growth. But other differences are introduced, in so far as the crystal is an ordered set: certain seeds abort and others are successful; certain entrances open while others close again, as in the frescoes of Rome which turn blank on being looked at and become opaque. It is not possible to predict this, even if one has premonitions; nevertheless, a selection is made (although in a completely different way from in Renoir). Let us take the entrances or successive seeds in one of Fellini's masterpieces, *The Clowns*. The first, as often in Fellini, is the childhood memory; but it will crystallize with impressions of nightmare and poverty (the imbecile clown). The second entrance is the historical and sociological investigation with an interview of clowns: the clowns and the filmed locations enter into resonance with the crew in process of filming, and form another impasse. The third, the worst, is more archaeological, in the television archives. At least, it persuades us, at this point in our classification, that the imaginary counts for more than the archive (only the imaginary can develop the seed). Then the fourth entrance is kinesthic: but it is not a movement-image which represents a circus spectacle, it is a mirror-image which represents a movement of world, a de-personalized movement, and reflects the death of the circus in the death of the clown. It is the hallucinatory perception of the clown's death, the funeral gallop ('faster, faster') where the funeral carriage is transformed into a champagne bottle from which the clown pops. And this fourth entrance is in turn replugged, in the emptiness and silence, like at the end of a party. But an old clown, left behind at the fourth entrance (he was out of breath, the movement was going too fast), is going to open a fifth, purely of sound and music: with his trumpet he invoked his vanished companion, and the other trumpet replied. Across death it was like a 'beginning of world', a sound-crystal, the two trumpets each alone, and yet each a mirror, an echo . . .[32]

The organization of the crystal is bipolar, or rather two-sided. In surrounding the seed, it sometimes passes on an acceleration, a hurrying, sometimes a hopping or fragmenting, which will constitute the opaque side of the crystal; and sometimes it gives it a limpidity which is like the test of the eternal. On one side would be written 'Saved!', and on the other 'Doomed!', in an apocalyptic landscape like the desert in *Satyricon*.[33] But we cannot tell in advance; an opaque side may even become limpid through imperceptible transformation, and a limpid side be revealed as deceptive and become dark like Claudia in *8½*. Will everything be saved, as the final round in *8½* leads us to believe, carrying along all the seeds around the white child? Will everything be lost, as in the mechancial starts and funerary fragmentations which lead to the woman-automaton in *Casanova*? It is never wholly one or wholly the other, and the opaque side of the crystal, for instance, the ship of death on the sea of plastic in *Amarcord*, also points to the other side which extricates itself and does not die, whilst the limpid side, like the rocket of the future in *8½*, waits for the seeds to come out of their honeycomb or their funerary haste to carry them off. In fact, the selection is so complex, and the imbrication so tight, that Fellini created a word, something like 'procadence', to indicate both the inexorable course of decadence and the possibility of freshness or creation which must accompany it (it is in this sense that he calls himself fully an 'accomplice' of decadence and ruination).

What we see in the crystal is always the bursting forth of life, of time, in its dividing in two or differentiation. However, in opposition to Renoir, not only does nothing leave the crystal – since it keeps on and on growing – but it is as if the signs of selection are reversed. In Fellini, it is the present, the parade of presents that pass, which constitutes the *danse macabre*. They run, but to the tomb, not towards the future. Fellini is the author who was able to produce the most prodigious galleries of monsters: a tracking shot surveys them, stopping at one or another, but they are always caught in the present, birds of prey disturbed by the camera, diving into it for a moment. Salvation can come only from the other side, from the side of the pasts which are preserved: there, a fixed shot isolates a character, takes him out of the line, and gives him, even if it is only for an instant, a chance which is in itself eternal, a virtuality which will be valid for ever even if it is not actualized. It is not that Fellini has a particular taste for memory and recollection-images: there is no cult of former presents in his work. It is in fact like in Péguy, where the horizontal succession of presents which pass outlines a route to death, whilst for every present there corresponds a vertical line which unites it at a deep level with its own past, as well as to the past of the other presents, constituting between them all one and the same coexistence, one and the same contemporaneity, the 'in-ternal' [*internel*] rather than the eternal. It is not in the recollection-image but in pure recollection that we remain contemporary with the child that we were as the believer feels himself contemporary with Christ. The child in us, says Fellini, is contemporary with the adult, the old man and the adolescent. Thus it is that the past which is preserved takes on all the virtues of beginning and beginning again: it is what holds in its depths or in its sides the surge of the new reality, the bursting forth of life. One of the finest images in *Amarcord* shows the group of schoolboys, the timid one, the prankster, the dreamer, the good pupil, etc., who meet in front of the big hotel as soon as the season is over; and, while the snow crystals fall, each on his own and yet all of them together sketch a clumsy dance-step or an imitation of a musical instrument, one going in a straight line, another tracing circles, another turning round on the spot . . . There is in this image a science of precisely measured distance which separates each of them from the others, and yet an organization which connects them. They lodge themselves in a depth which is no longer that of memory, but that of a coexistence where we become their contemporaries, as they become the contemporaries of all the 'seasons' past and to come. The two aspects, the present that passes and goes to death, the past which is preserved and retains the seed of life, repeatedly interfere and cut into each other. It is the line of those taking the waters in a nightmare in *8½*, but interrupted by the dream-image of the luminous girl, the white nurse who gives out the tumblers. Whatever the speed or the slowness, the line, the tracking shot is a race, a cavalcade, a gallop. But safety comes from a ritornello which is placed or unrolls round a face, and extracts it from the line. *La Strada* was already the quest for the moment when the wandering ritornello could settle on the man who is finally at peace. And on whom will the ritornello place itself, calming the anxiety in *8½*, on Claudia, on the wife, or even on the mistress, or only on the white child, the internal [*internel*] or contemporary of all the pasts, who saves everything that can be saved?

The crystal-image is as much a matter of sound as it is optical, and Félix Guattari was right to define the crystal of time as being a 'ritornello' par excellence.[34] Or, perhaps, the melodic ritornello is only a musical component which contrasts and is mixed with another, rhythmic component: the gallop. The horse and the bird would be two great figures, one of which carries away and speeds up the other, but the other of which is reborn from itself up to the final destruction or extinction (in many dances, an accelerated gallop comes as the conclusion of figures of rounds).

The gallop and the ritornello are what we hear in the crystal, as the two dimensions of musical time, the one being the hastening of the presents which are passing, the other the raising or falling back of pasts which are preserved. Now, if we consider the problem of a specificity of cinema music, it seems to us that this specificity cannot simply be defined by a dialectic of the sound and the optical which would enter into a new synthesis (Eisenstein, Adorno). Cinema music, through itself, tends towards releasing the ritornello and the gallop as two pure and self-sufficient elements, while many other components necessarily intervene in music in general, except in exceptional cases such as the Bolero. This is already true in the Western, where the little melodic phrase comes as the interruption of galloping rhythms (*Blowing Wild* by Zinnemann and Tiomkin); it is even more obvious in musical comedy, where the rhythmic stepping and walking, which is sometimes military even for the girls, come up against the melodic song. But the two elements are also combined as in *Daybreak* by Carné and Jaubert, where the basses and the percussion give the rhythm while the little flute launches the melody. In Gremillon, one of the cinema's most musician-like authors, the gallop of the farandoles returns us back to the repeat of the ritornellos, the two separated or brought together (Roland-Manuel). It is these tendencies that achieve perfect expression when the cinematographic image becomes crystal-image. In Ophüls, the two elements fuse in the identification of the round with the gallop, while in Renoir and Fellini they are distinct, one of them taking on to itself the force of life, the other the power of death. But, for Renoir, the force of life is on the side of the presents which are launched towards the future, on the side of the gallop, whether this is that of the French cancan or the Marseillaise, whilst the ritornello has the melancholy of that which is already falling back into the past. For Fellini, it seems to be the opposite: the gallop accompanies the world which runs to its end, the earthquake, the incredible entropy, the hearse, but the ritornello immortalizes a beginning of world and removes it from passing time. The galloping of the circus clowns[35*] and the ritornello of the ordinary clowns. Again things are never that simple, and there is something unascribable in the distinction of ritornellos from gallops. It is this that makes the collaboration between Fellini and the musician Nino Rota extraordinary. At the end of *Orchestra Rehearsals*, we first hear the purest gallop from the violins, but a ritornello rises imperceptibly to succeed it, until the two intertwine with one another more and more closely, throttling themselves like wrestlers, lost-saved, lost-saved . . . The two musical movements become the object of the film, and time itself becomes a thing of sound.

The final state to be considered would be the crystal in the process of decomposition. The work of Visconti shows this. This work reached its perfection when Visconti was able both to distinguish and put into play, in varying combinations, four fundamental elements which haunted him. In the first place, the aristocratic world of the rich, the aristocratic former-rich: this is what is crystalline, but like a synthetic crystal, because it is outside history and nature, outside divine creation. The abbot in *The Leopard* will explain it: we do not understand these rich, because they have created a world to themselves, whose laws we are unable to grasp, and where what seems to us secondary or even inopportune takes on an extraordinary urgency and importance; their motives always escape us like rites whose religion is not known (as in the old prince who gets his country back and orders a picnic). This world is not that of the creative artist, even though *Death in Venice* presents a musician, but precisely one whose work has been too intellectual and cerebral. Nor is it a world of simple art enthusiasts. Rather, they are surrounded by art; they are profoundly 'knowledgeable about' art both as works and as life, but it is this knowledge which separates them from life and creation, as in the teacher in *Conversation Piece*. They demand freedom, but a freedom which they enjoy like an empty privilege which could come to them from elsewhere, from the forebears from whom they are descended, and from the art by which they are surrounded. Ludwig II wants 'to prove his freedom', whilst the true creator, Wagner, is of another race, much more prosaic and less abstract in reality. Ludwig II wants roles and more roles, like those that he tears from the exhausted actor. The king orders his deserted castles, as the prince his picnic, in a movement which empties art and life of all interiority. Visconti's genius culminates in the great scenes or 'compositions', often in red and gold: opera in *Senso*, reception rooms in *The Leopard*, Munich castle in *Ludwig*, grand hotel rooms in Venice and music-room in *The Innocent*: crystalline images of an aristocratic world. But, in the second place, these crystalline environments are inseparable from a process of decomposition which eats away at them from within, and makes them dark and opaque: the rotting of Ludwig II's teeth, family rot which takes over the teacher in *Conversation Piece*, the debasement of Ludwig II's love-affairs; and incest every-where as in the Bavarian family, the return of *Sandra*, the abomination of *The Damned*; everywhere the thirst for murder and suicide, or the need for forgetting and death, as the old prince says on behalf of the whole of Sicily. It is not just that these aristocrats are on the brink of being ruined; the approaching ruin is only a consequence. For it is a vanished past, but one which survives in the artificial crystal, which is waiting for them, absorbing them and snapping them up, taking away all their power at the same time as they become lodged in it. Thus the famous tracking shot with which *Sandra* opens: this is not displacement in space but sinking into time without exit. Vis-conti's great compositions have a saturation which determines their darkening. Everything becomes confused, to the point of indiscernibility of the two women in *The Innocent*. In *Ludwig*, in *The Damned*, the crystal is inseparable from a process of making opaque which now makes triumphant the bluish, violet and sepulchral shades, those of the moon as twilight of the gods or lost kingdom of heroes (the sun-moon movement thus has a com-pletely different value than in German expressionism, and especially in the French school).

The third element in Visconti is history. Because, of course, it doubles decomposition, accelerates or even explains it: wars, assumption of power by new forces, the rise of the new rich, who are not interested in penetrating the secret laws of the old world, but aim to make it disappear. However, history is not identical with the internal decomposition of the crystal; it is an autono-mous factor which stands on its own, and to which Visconti sometimes dedicates marvellous images and sometimes grants a presence which is all the more intense for being elliptical and out-of-field. In *Ludwig*, very little history will be seen; we know about the horrors of war and Prussia's assumption of power only indirectly, all the more so, perhaps, because Ludwig II wants to know nothing about it. History growls at the door. In *Senso*, in contrast, history is present, with the Italian movement, the famous battle and the abrupt elimination of Garibaldi's sup-porters; or, in *The Damned*, with the rise of Hitler, the organiz-ation of the SS, and the exterminations of the SA. But, present or out-of-field, history is never scenery. It is caught obliquely in a low-angled perspective in a rising or setting ray, a kind of laser which comes and cuts into the crystal, disorganizes its substance, hastens its darkening and disperses its sides, under a pressure that is all the more powerful for being external, like the plague in Venice, or the silent arrival of the SS at dawn . . .

And then there is the fourth element, the most important in Visconti, because it ensures the unity and circulation of the others. This is the idea, or rather the revelation, that *something* arrives too late. Caught in time, this could perhaps have avoided the natural decomposition and historical dismantling of the crystal-image. But it is history, and nature itself, the structure of the crystal, which make it impossible for this to arrive in time. Already in *Senso*, the distraught lover cried 'Too late, too late', too late in relation to the history that divides us, but also because of our nature, as rotten in you as in me. The prince, in *The Leopard*, hears the 'too late' which spreads through the whole of Sicily: the island, whose sea Visconti never shows, is so completely embedded in the past of its nature and history that even the new regime will be powerless to do anything for it. 'Too late' will constantly be the rhythm of the images in *Ludwig*, because it is his fate. This something that comes too late is always the perceptual and sensual revelation of a unity of nature and man. Thus it is not a simple lack; it is the mode of being of this grandiose revelation. The 'too-late' is not an accident that takes place in time but a dimension of time itself. As a dimension of time, it is, through the crystal, the one which is opposed to the static dimension of the past as this survives and weighs in the interior of the crystal. It is a sublime clarity which is opposed to the opaque, but it has the property of arriving too late, dynamically. As perceptible revelation, the too-late is a matter of unity of nature and man, as world or milieu. But, as sensual revelation, the unity becomes personal. Thus the shattering revelation of the musician in *Death in Venice*, when through the young boy he has a vision of what has been lacking in his work: sensual beauty. It is the unbearable revelation of the teacher in *Conversation Piece*, when he discovers a petty criminal in the young man, his lover in nature and his son in culture. Already in *Obsession*, Visconti's first film, the possibility of homosexuality arose as the chance of salvation, of escaping from a stifling past, but too late. However, let us not think that homosexuality is Visconti's obsession. Amongst the finest of the *The Leopard*'s images is the one where the old prince, having given approval for the love-match between his nephew and the daughter of the *nouveau riche*, to save what can be saved, has a revelation in a dance with the girl: their glances embrace; they are for each other and at each other, while the nephew is pushed into the background, himself fascinated and nullified by the grandeur of this couple, but it is too late for the old man and the girl alike.

Visconti is not in control of the four elements right from the beginning of his work: often they are still difficult to distinguish, or encroach on each other. But Visconti is searching and has a foreboding. It has often been observed that the fishermen in *The Earth Trembles* present a slowness, a hieratic quality which was the sign of a natural aristocracy, in contrast to the *nouveaux riches*; and, if the fishermen's attempt fails, it is not just because of the wholesalers, but because of the weight of an archaic past which ensures that their project is too late.[36] Rocco himself is not just a 'saint'; he is an aristocrat by nature, in his family of poor peasants: but too late to come back to the village, because the city is already totally corrupt, because everything has become opaque and because history has already brought change to the village . . . But it seems to us that it is in *The Leopard* that Visconti achieves complete control, as it were the harmony of his four elements. The searing too-late becomes as intense as the 'Nevermore' of Edgar Allan Poe; it also explains the direction Visconti would have been able to take in translating Proust.[37] And Visconti's pleas cannot be reduced to his apparent aristocratic pessimism: the work of art will be made from this plea, as with the pain and suffering from which we make a statue. The too-late conditions the work of art, and conditions its success, since the perceptible and sensual unity of nature and man is the essence of art *par excellence*, in so far as it is characteristic of it to arrive too late in all other respects except precisely this one: time regained. As Baroncelli put it, the Beautiful truly becomes a dimension in Visconti; it 'plays the role of the fourth dimension'.[38]

5 Peaks of present and sheets of past: fourth commentary on Bergson

1

The crystal reveals a direct time-image, and no longer an indirect image of time deriving from movement. It does not abstract time; it does better: it reverses its subordination in relation to movement. The crystal is like a *ratio cognoscendi* of time, while time, conversely, is *ratio essendi*.[1]* What the crystal reveals or makes visible is the hidden ground of time, that is, its differentiation into two flows, that of presents which pass and that of pasts which are preserved. Time simultaneously makes the present pass and preserves the past in itself. There are, therefore, already, two possible time-images, one grounded in the past, the other in the present. Each is complex and is valid for time as a whole.

We have seen that Bergson gave an assured status to the first image. This is the model of the inverse cone. The past is not to be confused with the mental existence of recollection-images which actualize it in us. It is preserved in time: it is the virtual element into which we penetrate to look for the 'pure recollection' which will become actual in a 'recollection-image'. The latter would have no trace of the past if we had not been to look for its seed in the past. It is the same as with perception: just as we perceive things where they are present, in space, we remember where they have passed, in time, and we go out of ourselves just as much in each case. Memory is not in us; it is we who move in a Being-memory, a world-memory. In short, the past appears as the most general form of an already-there, a pre-existence in general, which our recollections presuppose, even our first recollection if there was one, and which our perceptions, even the first, make use of. From this point of view the present itself exists only as an infinitely contracted past which is constituted at the extreme point of the already-there. The present would not pass on without this condition. It would not pass on if it was not the most contracted degree of the past. In fact it is striking that the successive is not the past but the present which is passing. The past appears, in contrast, as the coexistence of circles which are more or less dilated or contracted, each one of which contains everything at the same time and the present of which is the extreme limit (the smallest circuit that contains all the past). Between the past as pre-existence in general and the present as infinitely contracted past there are, therefore, all the circles of the past constituting so many stretched or shrunk *regions, strata,* and *sheets*: each region with its own characteristics, its 'tones', its 'aspects', its 'singularities', its 'shining points' and its 'dominant' themes. Depending on the nature of the recollection that we are looking for, we have to jump into a particular circle. It is true that these regions (my childhood, my adolescence, my adult life, etc.), appear to succeed each other. But they succeed each other only from the point of view of former presents which marked the limit of each of them. They coexist, in contrast, from the point of view of the actual present which each time represents their common limit or the most contracted of them. What Fellini says is Bergsonian: 'We are constructed in memory; we are *simultaneously* childhood, adolescence, old age and maturity.' What happens when we search for a recollection? We have to put ourselves intò the past in general, then we have to choose between the regions: in which one do we think that the recollection is hidden, huddled up waiting for us and evading us? (It is a friend from childhood or youth, from school or the army. . . ?) We have to jump into a chosen region, even if we have to return to the present in order to make another jump, if the recollection sought for gives no response and does not realize itself in a recollection-image. These are the paradoxical characteristics of a non-chronological time: the pre-existence of a past in general; the coexistence of all the sheets of past; and the existence of a most contracted degree.[2] It is a conception that can be found in the first great film of a cinema of time, Welles's *Citizen Kane.*

And, with Bergson, this time-image extends naturally into a language-image, and a thought-image. What the past is to time, sense is to language and idea to thought. Sense as past of language is the form of its pre-existence, that which we place ourselves in at once in order to understand images of sentences, to distinguish the images of words and even phonemes that we hear. It is therefore organized in coexisting circles, sheets, or regions, between which we choose according to actual auditory signs which are grasped in a confused way. Similarly, we place ourselves initially in the idea; we jump into one of its circles in order to form images which correspond to the actual quest. Thus chronosigns are continually extended into lectosigns and noo-signs.

But, to approach it in a different way, can the present in turn stand for the whole of time? Yes, perhaps, if we manage to separate it from its own actual quality, in the same way that we distinguish the past from the recollection-image which actualized it. If the present is actually distinguishable from the future and the past, it is because it is presence of something, which precisely stops being present when it is replaced by *something else*. It is in relation to the present of something else that the past and future are said of a thing. We are, then, passing along different events, in accordance with an explicit time or a form of succession which entails that a variety of things fill the present one after another. It is quite different if we are established inside one single event; if we plunge into an event that is in preparation, arrives and is over; if for a longitudinal, pragmatic view we substitute a vision which is purely optical, vertical, or, rather, one in depth. The event is no longer confused with the space which serves as its place, nor with the actual present which is passing: 'the time of the event comes to an end before the event does, so the event will start again at another time . . . the whole event is as it were in the time where nothing happens', and it is in empty time that we anticipate recollection, break up what is actual and locate the recollection once it is formed.[3] On this occasion there is no longer a future, present and past in succession, in accordance with the explicit passage of presents which we make out. Adopting St Augustine's fine formulation, there is *a present of the future, a present of the present and a present of the past*, all implicated in the event, rolled up in the event, and thus simultaneous and inexplicable. From affect to time: a time is revealed inside the event, which is made from the simultaneity of these three implicated presents, from these de-actualized *peaks of present*. It is the possibility of treating the world or life, or simply a life or an episode, as one single event which provides the basis for the implication of presents. An accident is about to happen, it happens, it has happened; but equally it is at the same time that it will take place, has already taken place and is in the process of taking place; so that, before taking place, it has not taken place, and, taking place, will not take place . . . etc. This is the paradox of Josephine the mouse in Kafka: is she singing, did she sing, will she sing, or none of these, even though it all produces inexplicable differences in the collective present of mice?[4] At the same time someone no longer has the key (that is, used to have it), still has it (had not lost it), and finds it (that is, will have it and did not have it). Two people know each other, but already knew each other and do not yet know each other. Betrayal happens, it never happened, and yet has happened and will happen, sometimes one betraying the other and sometimes the other betraying the first – all at the same time. We find ourselves here in a direct time-image of a different kind from the previous one: no longer the coexistence of sheets of past, but the simultaneity of peaks of present. We therefore have two kinds of chronosigns: the first are *aspects* (regions, layers), the second *accents* (peaks of view [*pointes de vue*]).

This second type of time-image is to be found in Robbe-Grillet, in a kind of Augustinianism. In his work there is never a succession of passing presents, but a simultaneity of a present of past, a present of present and a present of future, which make time frightening and inexplicable. The encounter in *Last Year in Marienbad*, the accident in *L'immortelle*, the key in *Trans-Europe Express*, the betrayal in *The Man Who Lies*: the three implicated presents are constantly revived, contradicted, obliterated, substituted, re-created, fork and return. This is a powerful time-image. This does not mean to say, however, that it suppresses all narration. But, much more importantly, it gives narration a new value, because it abstracts it from all successive action, as far as it replaces the movement-image with a genuine time-image. Thus narration will consist of the distribution of different presents to different characters, so that each forms a combination that is plausible and possible in itself, but where all of them together are 'incompossible', and where the inexplicable is thereby maintained and created. In *Last Year . . .*, it is X who knew A (so A does not remember or is lying), and it is A who does not know X (so X is mistaken or playing a trick on her). Ultimately, the three characters correspond to the three different presents, but in such a way as to 'complicate' the inexplicable instead of throwing light on it; in such a way as to bring about its existence instead of suppressing it: what X lives in a present of past, A lives in a present of future, so that the difference exudes or assumes a present of present (the third, the husband), all implicated in each other. The repetition distributes its variations on the three presents. In *The Man Who Lies*, the two characters are not simply the same: their difference arises only in making the betrayal inexplicable, because this is attributed differently, but simultaneously, to each of them as identical to the other. In _Le jeu avec le feu_ the kidnapping of the girl has to be the means of warding it off but equally the means of warding it off must be the kidnapping itself, so that she has never been kidnapped at the moment when she is and will be, and kidnaps herself at the moment when she has not been. However, this new mode of narration still remains human, even though it constitutes a lofty form of non-sense. It does not yet tell us the essential point. The essential point rather appears if we think of an earthly event which is assumed to be transmitted to different planets, one of which would receive it at the same time (at the speed of light), but the second more quickly, and the third less quickly, hence before it happened and after. The latter would not yet have received it, the second would already have received it, the first would be receiving it, in three simultaneous presents bound into the same universe. This would be a sidereal time, a system of relativity, where the characters would be not so much human as planetary, and the accents not so much subjective as astronomical, in a plurality of worlds constituting the universe.[5] It would be a pluralist cosmology, where there are not only different worlds (as in Minnelli), but where one and the same event is played out in these different worlds, in incompatible versions.

Subjecting the image to a power of repetition-variation was already Buñuel's contribution, and a way of setting time free, of reversing its subordination to movement. Although we have seen that in most of Buñuel's work time remained a cyclical time, where sometimes forgetfulness (_The Devil and the Flesh_), sometimes exact repetition (_The Exterminating Angel_), marked the end of one cycle and the possible beginning of another, in a cosmos which was still unique. Influence, then, perhaps reversed in Buñuel's last period, where he adapts an inspiration which has come from Robbe-Grillet for his own ends. It has been noted that the regime of dream or fantasy was changing in this last period.[6]* But is is less a question of a state of the imaginary than of a deepening of the problem of time. In _Belle de jour_, the husband's final paralysis does and does not take place (he suddenly gets up to talk about holidays with his wife); _The Discreet Charm of the Bourgeoisie_ shows less a cycle of interrupted meals than different versions of the same meal in irreducible modes and worlds. In _The Phantom of Liberty_, the postcards are truly pornographic, even though they represent only monuments stripped of all ambiguity; and the little girl is lost, even though she has never stopped being there and will be found again. And in *That Obscure Object of Desire* there blossoms one of Buñuel's finest inventions: instead of having one character play different roles, casting two characters, and two actresses, as one person. It is as if Buñuel's naturalist cosmology, based on the cycle and the succession of cycles, gives way to a plurality of simultaneous worlds; to a simultaneity of presents in different worlds. These are not subjective (imaginary) points of view in one and the same world, but one and the same event in different objective worlds, all implicated in the event, inexplicable universe. Buñuel achieves here a direct time-image which was previously impossible for him because of his naturalist and cyclical point of view.

Still more instructive is the confrontation between Robbe-Grillet and Resnais in *Last Year in Marienbad*. What seems extraordinary in this collaboration is that two authors (for Robbe-Grillet was not just scriptwriter) produced so coherent a work while approaching it in such different and almost opposite ways. They perhaps reveal in this way the truth about all real collaboration, where the work is not simply understood but constructed according to quite different creative procedures which marry to make a success that is repeatable but each time unique. This confrontation between Resnais and Robbe-Grillet is complex, blurred by their extremely amicable statements, and may be considered on three different levels. First, there is a level of 'modern' cinema, marked by the crises of the action-image. *Last Year . . .* was itself an important point in this crisis: the failure of sensory-motor models, the wandering of characters, the rise of clichés and postcards were a constant inspiration in Robbe-Grillet's work. And in his work the bonds of the captive woman do not just have erotic and sadistic value, they are the simplest way to stop the movement.[7] But in Resnais too, wanderings, immobilizings, petrifications and repetitions are constant evidence of a general dissolution of the action-image. The second level is that of the real and the imaginary: it has been noted that, for Resnais, there is always something real which persists, and notably spatio-temporal co-ordinates maintaining their reality, even though they come into conflict with the imaginary. It is in this way that Resnais maintains that something actually did happen 'Last Year . . .', and, in his subsequent films, establishes a topography and a chronology which are all the more rigorous because what happens in them is imaginary or mental.[8] While in Robbe-Grillet everything happens 'in the head' of the characters, or, better, of the viewer himself. Yet this difference exhibited by Robbe-Grillet is hardly the point. Nothing happens in the viewer's head which does not derive from the character of the image. We have seen that, in the image, a distinction is always made between the real and the imaginary, the objective and the subjective, the physical and the mental, and the actual and the virtual, but that this distinction becomes reversible, and in that sense indiscernible. *Distinct and yet indiscernible* – these are the characteristics of the imaginary and the real in each of the two authors. So that the difference between the two can only appear in other ways. It would present itself rather in the manner identified by Mireille Latil: large continuums of real and imaginary in Resnais, in contrast to Robbe-Grillet's discontinous blocs or 'shocks'. But this new criterion seems incapable of development at the level of the imaginary-real pair; a third level must necessarily intervene – this is time.[9]

Robbe-Grillet himself suggests that the difference between himself and Resnais must ultimately be sought at the level of time. The dissolution of the action-image, and the indiscernibility which results, sometimes take place in favour of an 'architecture of time' (this would be the case with Resnais), sometimes in favour of a 'perpetual present' cut off from its temporality, that is, of a structure stripped of time (the case of Robbe-Grillet himself).[10] Nevertheless, here again we should not rush into thinking that a perpetual present implies less time-image than an eternal past. The present belongs no less to time than the pure past. The difference is thus in the nature of the time-image, which is plastic in one case and architectural in the other. For Resnais conceived *Last Year* . . . like his other films, in the form of sheets or regions of past, while Robbe-Grillet sees time in the form of points of present. If *Last Year* . . . could be divided, the man X might be said to be closer to Resnais, and the woman A closer to Robbe-Grillet. The man basically tries to envelop the woman with continuous sheets of which the present is the narrowest, like the advance of a wave, whilst the woman, at times wary, at times stiff, at times almost convinced, jumps from one bloc to another, continually crossing an abyss between two points, two simultaneous presents. In any event, the two authors, we shall see, are no longer in the domain of the real and the imaginary but in time, in the even more alarming domain of the true and the false. Of course the real and the imaginary continue their circuit, but only as the base of a higher figure. This is no longer, or no longer only, the *indiscernible becoming* of distinct images; it is *undecidable alternatives* between circles of past, *inextricable differences* between peaks of present. With Resnais and Robbe-Grillet, an understanding occurs, all the stronger for being based on two opposed conceptions of time which crashed into each other. The coexistence of sheets of virtual past, and the simultaneity of peaks of de-actualized present, are the two direct signs of time itself.

In an animated film, *Chronopolis*, Piotr Kamler *fashioned* time out of two elements, small balls manipulated with pointed instruments, and supple sheets covering the balls. The two elements formed moments, polished and crystal spheres, but these quickly darkened, unless . . . (we shall see the sequel of this animated story later).

2

It is a mistake to think of the cinematographic image as being by nature in the present. Yet Robbe-Grillet on occasion assumes this attitude for his own purposes, in a strategic or mocking way: after all, why would he devote so much care to achieving present-images if this were a given of the image? And the first occasion on which a direct time-image was seen in the cinema was not in the (even implicit) mode of the present but, on the contrary, in the form of sheets of past, with Welles's *Citizen Kane*. Here time became out of joint and reversed its dependent relation to movement; temporality showed itself as it really was for the first time, but in the form of a coexistence of large regions to be explored. The scheme of *Citizen Kane* may appear simple: Kane being dead, witnesses who offer their recollection-images in a series of subjective flashbacks are questioned. But it is more complex than this. The investigation is focused on 'Rosebud' (what is it? or what does this word mean?). And the investigator carries out soundings; each of the witnesses questioned will be equivalent to a slice of Kane's life, a circle or sheet of virtual past, a continuum. And each time the question is: is it in this continuum, is it in this sheet, that lies the thing (the being) called Rosebud? It is true that these regions of past have a chronological course which is that of the former presents to which they refer. But if this course can easily be upset it is precisely because in themselves, and in relation to the actual present where the quest begins (Kane dead), they are all coexistent, each containing the whole of Kane's life in one form or another. Each has what Bergson calls 'shining points', singularities, but each collects around these points the totality of Kane or his life as a whole as a 'vague nebulosity'.[11] Of course, it is on these sheets that the witnesses will draw to evoke the recollection-images, that is, to reconstitute the former presents. But they are themselves as different from the recollection-images which actualize them as the pure past may be from the former present which it was. Each witness jumps into the past in general and at once installs himself in one or another coexisting region, before embodying certain points of the region in a recollection-image.

What shows that unity does not lie in the recollection-image is that the latter bursts out in two directions. It induces two kinds of very distinct images, and *Citizen Kane's* famous montage determines the continuity of the relations between the two (rhythm). The first kind of image reconstitutes motor-series of former presents, 'events' [*actualités*] or habits. These are the cross-cutting *shot-reaction shots*, the succession of which shows Kane's habits as a married man, bleak days and idle periods. It is the short overall shots whose superimpression shows the cumulative effect of a desire on Kane's part (to make Susan a singer). Sartre saw in this the equivalent of the frequentative in English, the tense of habit or the passing present. But what happens when Susan's accumulated efforts emerge into a scene in long shot and depth of field, her suicide attempt? This time, the image moves to a true exploration of a sheet of past. The images in depth express regions of past as such, each with its own accents or potentials, and mark critical moments in Kane's will to power. The hero acts, walks and moves; but it is the past that he plunges himself into and moves in: time is no longer subordinated to movement, but movement to time. Hence in the great scene where Kane catches up in depth with the friend he will break with, it is in the past that he himself moves; this movement *was* the break with the friend. And, at the beginning of *Mr Arkadin*, the adventurer who advances in the great court re-emerges from a past whose zones he will make us explore.[12] In short, in the second case the recollection-image does not pass on in a succession of former presents which it reconstitutes but goes beyond itself into regions of coexisting past which make it possible. This is the function of depth of field: to explore each time a region of past, a continuum.

Do we have to reconsider the problems of depth of field that

Bazin was able to propose and resolve by inventing the notion of 'sequence shot'? The first problem concerned the novelty of the process. And it seems true, in this respect, that depth reigned supreme in the image from the beginning of the cinema, as long as there was neither montage nor cutting, nor camera mobility, and while the different spatial shots were necessarily given all together. Nor does it come to an end even when shots become really distinct but can be joined together in a new whole which relates each to itself. There are already two forms of depth here which do not allow themselves to become confused in the cinema, any more than in painting. They have in common, however, the fact that they constitute a depth in the image or field and not yet a depth *of* field, or a depth *of* image. If we think of sixteenth-century painting, we can see a clear distinction, but one which takes place in parallel and successive planes [*plans*], each autonomous, defined by characters or elements side by side, while they all contribute to the whole. But each plane, especially the first, performs its own task and stands only for itself in the grand business of the painting which harmonizes them. It will be a novel change, and crucial, in the seventeenth century, when an element of a plane refers directly to an element of a different plane, when characters address each other directly from one plane to another, in an organization of the picture along the diagonal, or through a gap which thus privileges the background and brings it into immediate touch with the foreground. The picture 'is internally hollowed out'. At this moment, depth becomes depth *of* field, whilst the dimensions of the foreground take on an abnormal size, and those of the background are reduced, in a violent perspective which does even more to unite the near and the faraway.[13]

The same story runs through the cinema. For a long time, depth was produced by a simple juxtaposition of independent shots [*plans*], a succession of parallel planes [*plans*] in the image: the conquest of Babylon in Griffith's *Intolerance*, for instance, shows the lines of defence of the besieged in depth, from foreground to background, each with its own importance and connecting neighbouring elements into a harmonious whole. Welles invents a depth of field, in a very different way, along a diagonal or gap crossing all planes, making elements from each interact with the rest, and in particular having the background in direct contact with the foreground (as in the suicide scene where Kane bursts in through the door at the back, tiny, while Susan is

dying in the shadow in mid-shot and the large mirror is seen in
close-up. Diagonals like this will be seen in Wyler, as in *The Best
Years of Our Life*, when a character is busy in a secondary, but
picturesque, scene in the foreground while another character
makes a crucial telephone call in the background: the first
watches the second along a diagonal which joins the back to the
front, and makes them react. Before Welles, the only precursors
in depth of field seem to have been Renoir, with *La règle du jeu*,
and Stroheim, particularly in *Greed*. Increasing depth by the use
of wide angles, Welles obtains gigantic dimensions in the foreground connected to reductions of size in the background, which
becomes all the more powerful; the light-centre is at the back,
while masses of shadow are allowed to take up the foreground
and the whole is scored with stark contrasts; ceilings inevitably
become apparent, whether in the placing of a height which is
itself enormous, or, in contrast, in a crushing which follows the
perspective. The volume of each body overflows any given plane
[*plan*], plunging into or emerging from shadow and expressing
the relationship of this body with the others located in front or
behind: an art of masses. The term 'baroque' or neo-expressionism is literally appropriate. In this freeing of depth which now
subordinates all other dimensions we should see not only the
conquest of a continuum but the temporal nature of this
continuum: it is a continuity of duration which means that the
unbridled depth is of time and no longer of space.[14] It is
irreducible to the dimensions of space. As long as depth remained
caught in the simple succession of parallel planes, it already
represented time, but in an indirect way which kept it subordinate
to space and movement. The new depth, in contrast, directly
forms a region of time, a region of past which is defined by *optical*
aspects or elements borrowed from interacting planes.[15] It is a set
of non-localizable connections, always from one plane to another,
which constitutes the region of past or the continuum of
duration.

The second problem concerns the function of this depth of
field. We know that Bazin gave it a function of reality, since the
viewer had to organize his perception himself in the image
instead of receiving it ready-made. Mitry denied this, seeing in
depth of field a no less restrictive organization which forces the
viewer to follow the diagonal or gap. Bazin's position was
nevertheless complex: he showed that this gain in reality could be
achieved only through an 'excess of theatricality' as we saw in *La*

règle du jeu.[16] But neither a function of theatricality nor one of reality seems to exhaust this complicated problem. We suggest that depth of field has many functions, and that they all come together in a direct time-image. The special quality of depth of field would be to reverse time's subordination to movement and show time for itself. We are not saying that depth of field has the exclusive rights to the time-image. For there are many other kinds of direct time-images. There are time-images which are formed through suppression of depth (depth in the field as well as depth of field) and this case of the planitude of the image itself has a number of forms; it is a varied concept of time since the processes are not the same in Dreyer, Robbe-Grillet, Syberberg . . . Our point is that depth of field creates a certain type of direct time-image that can be defined by memory, virtual regions of past, the aspects of each region. This would be less a function of reality than a function of remembering, of temporalization: not exactly a recollection but 'an invitation to recollect . . .'

We must note the fact before trying to explain it: most of the occasions where depth of field appears wholly necessary are in connection with memory. And here again cinema is Bergsonian: it is not a case of a psychological memory, made up of recollection-images, as the flashback can conventionally represent it. It is not a case of a succession of presents passing according to chronological time. It is a case *either* of an attempt to evoke, produced in an actual present, and preceding the formation of recollection-images, *or* of the exploration of a sheet of past from which these recollection-images will later arise. It is an on-this-side-of and a beyond of psychological memory: the two poles of a metaphysics of memory. These two extremes of memory are presented by Bergson as follows: the extension of sheets of past and the contraction of the actual present.[17] And the two are connected, since to evoke recollection is to jump into a region of past where one assumes that it is lying in a virtual state, all the sheets or regions coexisting in relation to the contracted actual present from which the evocation proceeds (whilst they follow each other psychologically in relation to the presents that they were). What must be noted is that depth of field sometimes shows us evocation in the act of occurring and sometimes virtual sheets of past that we explore in order to find the recollection sought. The first case, contraction, often appears in *Citizen Kane*: a high-angle shot, for instance, bears down on an alcoholic Susan lost in the big room at the club in such a way as to force her to evoke. In another case, in *The Magnificient Ambersons*, a whole scene maintained in depth is justified because the young boy wants, without appearing to want, to force his aunt to remember a recollection that is crucial for him.[18] And similarly, in *The Trial*, the low-angle shot at the beginning marks the starting-point of the hero's efforts as he searches at all costs for what the law is charging him with. The second case can be seen in most of the scenes in transverse depth in *Citizen Kane*, where each corresponds to a sheet of past of which it is asked: is it here that the virtual secret, Rosebud, is lying? And in *Mr Arkadin*, where the successive characters are sheets of past, stages towards other sheets, all coexisting in relation to the contracted initial effort. It is quite clear that the recollection-image is of little interest in itself, but that it presupposes two things which go beyond it: a variation in the sheets of pure past where it can be found and a contraction of the actual present which is the starting-point of the continually renewed search. Depth of field will go from one to the other, from extreme contraction to large sheets and vice versa. Welles 'deforms space and time simultaneously; dilating and contracting them in turn, he dominates or gets deep inside a situation'.[19] The high- and low-angle shots form contractions, just as oblique and lateral tracking shots form sheets. Depth of field feeds on these two sources of memory. Not the recollection-image (or flashback) but the actual effort of evocation, to summon this up, and the exploration of virtual zones of past, to find, choose and bring it back.

Many critics today consider depth of field to be a technical procedure which is in danger of hiding from us still more important innovations on Welles's part. These innovations indeed exist. But depth retains its full importance, beyond a technique, if we take it as a function of remembering, that is, a figure of temporalization. It then gives rise to all kinds of adventures of the memory, which are not so much psychological accidents as misadventures of time, disturbances of its constitution. Welles's films develop these problems according to a rigorous progression. Bergson distinguished two main instances: the past recollection may still be evoked in an image, but the latter is now useless, because the present from which the evocation set off has lost its motor-extension which would make the image usable; or, secondly, the recollection can no longer be evoked in an image, although it persists in a region of past, but the actual present can no longer reach it. In one case recollections 'are still evoked but can no longer be applied to corresponding perceptions', in the other 'evocation of recollections is itself prevented'.[20] We find the dramatic equivalent of these instances in Welles's films where temporalization operates through memory.

It all begins with *Citizen Kane*. It has often been said that depth internalized montage in the scene, in the *mise-en-scène*, but this is only partly correct. The sequence shot is clearly a sheet of past, with its nebulae and shining points which will feed the recollection-image and determine what it retains from a former present. But montage persists in its own right under three other aspects: the relation between the sequence shots or sheets of past and the short shots of passing presents; the relation of the sheets between themselves, each with the others (as Burch remarked, the longer a shot is, the more important it is to know where and how to end it); the relation of the sheets to the contracted actual present which evokes them. In this respect, each witness in *Citizen Kane* makes his effort to evoke, which corresponds to the sheet of past to which he is committed. But all of these efforts coincide in the actuality of 'Kane has just died, Kane is dead' which constitutes a kind of given, fixed point from the outset (similarly in *Mr Arkadin* and *Othello*). And it is in relation to death as a fixed point where all the sheets of past coexist; childhood, youth, the adult and the old man. If montage, therefore, remains the cinematographic act *par excellence* in Welles it none the less changes its meaning: instead of producing an indirect image of time on the basis of movement, it will organize the order of non-chronological coexistences or relations in the direct time-image. Diverse sheets of past will be evoked and will embody their aspects in recollection-images. And, on each occasion, it is on the theme: is it here that the pure recollection 'Rosebud' lies? Rosebud will not be found in any of the regions explored, even though it is in one of them, in that of childhood, but so deeply buried that it is overlooked. Moreover, when Rosebud becomes embodied from its own movement in an image it is strictly *for nobody*, in the hearth where the discarded sledge burns. Not only could Rosebud have been anything; in so far as it is something, it goes down into an image which burns independently, is totally pointless and of interest to no one.[21] It thereby casts suspicion on all the sheets of past which have been evoked by the various characters, even the ones who were interested: the images to which they gave rise were perhaps useless in turn, since there is no longer a present to welcome them, and because Kane died alone, recognizing the emptiness of his whole life, the sterility of all his sheets.

In *The Magnificent Ambersons*, it is no longer a suspicion induced by the singularity 'Rosebud' but a certainty which crashes headlong into the whole. The sheets of past can still be evoked and summoned: Isabelle's marriage of pride, George's child-hood, his youth, the Amberson family . . . But the images that are drawn from these are now quite useless because they can no longer be inserted into a present which would extend them into action: the town has been so transformed, the new motivity of cars has replaced that of carriages, the present has changed so profoundly that the recollections can no longer be used. This is why the film does not begin with a death, but with a commentary which precedes any image, and which finds its conclusion at the moment when the fall of the family has taken place: 'It is done, but those who wanted to be present were dead, and those who were alive had forgotten the man and what they wanted.' The recollections have lost all extension, now being useless even to give pleasure to the prophets and vengeance-seekers. The infiltration of death is so complete that there is no longer a need for a death at the beginning. All the evocations coincide with deaths, and every death coincides with the sublime death of the major, in the course of the film: 'He knew that he had to prepare himself for entering an unknown region where he wasn't even sure of being recognized as an Amberson.' The recollections fall into the void because the present has hidden itself and goes elsewhere, withdrawing any possible insertion from them. Yet it is doubtful that Welles simply wishes to show the vanity of the past. If there is a nihilism in Welles, it is not here. Death as fixed point has a different meaning. What he is showing – already in *Citizen Kane* – is this: as soon as we reach the sheets of past it is as if we were carried away by the undulations of a great wave, time gets out of joint, and we enter into temporality as a state of *permanent crisis*.[22]

A third step is taken with *The Lady from Shanghai*. Previously the sheets of past went beyond the recollection-images in all direc-tions; but their evocation made them produce images of this kind even if these images were floating and had no other application but death. The new situation is very different: the sheets or regions of past are always there, and can still be distinguished, yet they can no longer be evoked and are now accompanied by no recollection-image. But then how are they distinguished, since no recollection-image is responsible for them or draws its trademark from them? It is as if the past surfaces in itself but in the shape of personalities which are independent, alienated, off-balance, in some sense embryonic, strangely active fossils, radioactive, inexplicable in the present where they surface, and all the more harmful and autonomous. Not recollections but hallucinations. Madness, the split personality, now shows the past. The story of *The Lady from Shanghai* is that of an initially naïve hero caught in the past of others, captured, snapped up (there is a similarity here with Minnelli's subjects, without going so far as to talk of influence, which would not please Welles). We have three characters in turmoil, like three sheets of past who come and submerge the hero, without his being able to evoke anything of these sheets or even decide between them. There is Grisby, the man who appears like a spring-loaded devil; and on this sheet the hero finds himself hunted for murder, when what had been suggested to him was apparently a fake murder. There is the lawyer Bannister, with his cane, his paralysis and his outrageous limp, who wants to get him sentenced when he suggested to him a cast-iron defence. There is the woman, the lunatic queen of the Chinese quarter, by whom he is totally obsessed, whilst she makes use of his love, from the depth of an indecipherable Oriental past. The hero becomes all the more crazy because he can recognize nothing of these pasts which are realized in alienated personalities, and perhaps projections of his own past which have become independent.[23] And still the Others exist, have a reality and run the game in *The Lady from Shanghai*. A fourth step will be taken in *Mr Arkadin*: how to make *one's own* past incapable of being recalled? The hero will have to feign amnesia in order to send off an investigator who must locate the immature personalities emanating from the regions of this past, haunting different places which are now only stages in the exploration of time. These witnesses will be murdered one by one by Arkadin as he follows the trails of the investigation. He makes out that he is recouping all the splits in himself into a grandiose, paranoid unity which would know nothing but a present without memory, true amnesia at last. Welles's nihilism finds a way of being expressed which is inherited from Nietzsche: suppress your recollections, or suppress yourselves ... The fact that everything begins and ends with the disappearance of Arkadin, as in *Citizen Kane*, does not stop the inexorable progress from one film to the next: Welles is no longer content to show the pointlessness of an evocation of the past, in a permanent state of crisis of time; he shows the impossibility of any evocation, the becoming-impossible of evocation in a still more fundamental state of time. The regions of past will keep their secret, and the call to recollection remains empty. The investigator will not even tell what he knows, but, under the pressure of time, will only beg the girl to say that he has told her it.

The Trial links up with *Mr Arkadin*. In which sheet of past is the hero to look for the offence that he is guilty of? He can no longer recall anything about it, but the whole of it is hallucinatory. Characters fixed to the spot and a veiled statue. There is the region of women, there is the region of books, that of childhood and of little girls, that of art and that of religion. The present is no more than an empty door from where the past can no longer be recalled, since it has already left while it was being waited for. Each region of the past will be explored in these long shots of which Welles has the secret: for instance, the long race in a trellised walk whilst the hero is pursued by a crowd of shouting little girls (*The Lady from Shanghai* already showed a comparable race by the pseudo-murderer in a trellised space). But the regions of past no longer release recollection-images; they set free hallucinatory presences: women, books, little girls, homosexuality, paintings. Except, in all this, it is as if certain sheets have subsided, and others risen in such a way that here and there there are juxtapositions of one particular age with a different one, as in archaeology. *Nothing is decidable any more*: the coexisting sheets now juxtapose their segments. The most serious book is also a pornographic book; the most threatening adults are also children that you smack; women are at the disposition of justice, but justice is perhaps managed by little girls; and is the lawyer's secretary, with her webbed fingers, a woman, a little girl, a skimmed-through file? It is as if by breaking up and becoming unbalanced the regions of past have entered into the element of a superior justice which stirs them up; from a past in general where existences pay each other the price of their injustice (according to a pre-Socratic formulation). Welles's success in relation to Kafka is that he was able to show how spatially distant and chronologically separate regions were in touch with each other, at the bottom of a limitless time which made them contiguous: this is what depth of field is used for, the areas which are the furthest apart are in direct contact in the background.[24] But what is this background common to all the sheets, from which they emerge and into which they go back on breaking up? What is this superior justice, which all the regions are merely secondary to?

The sheets of past exist, they are strata from where we draw our recollection-images. But either they are in any case unusable, because death is a permanent present, the most contracted region; or they can no longer be recalled because they are breaking up and becoming twisted, scattered in a non-stratified substance. And perhaps the two cases come together; perhaps we find the universal substance only at the contracted point of death. But there is no confusion in this; these are two different states of time, time as perpetual crisis and, at a deeper level, time as primary matter, immense and terrifying, like universal becoming. There is a passage in Herman Melville which seems specially intended for Welles: we go from bandage to bandage, from stratum to stratum at the heart of the pyramid, at the cost of terrible effort, and all that to discover that there is no one in the funeral chamber – unless it is here that 'the substance without stratification' begins.[25] This is definitely not a transcendent element; but it is an immanent justice, the earth, and its non-chronological order in so far as each of us is directly from it and not from parents: autochthony. It is in the earth that we die and atone for our birth. In Welles, the usual way of dying is flat on your stomach, the body already in the earth, dragging yourself, crawling. All the coexistent strata are in touch and adjacent to each other in a muddy vital medium. The earth as primordial time of the autochthonous. And this is what the cohort of Welles's great characters see: the hero of *Touch of Evil* who dies in the wet, blackish earth; the one in *Trial* who dies in the hole in the ground, and, earlier, Major Amberson in great pain, speaking with difficulty: ' – and us, we came out of the earth ... So in any case we ought to be in the earth ... ' The earth was able to sink beneath the waters in order to sustain its primitive monsters, as in the aquarium scene and the story of the sharks in *The Lady from Shanghai*. And Macbeth, especially *Macbeth*. It is here that Bazin was able to see the element of Welles's characters: 'This creosoted cardboard set, these barbarian Scotsmen, wearing animal-skins and brandishing a kind of lance-cross made of gnarled wood, these strange places tinkling with water and crowned by mists which prevent any hint of a sky that would probably not have any stars in it, literally constitute a universe of prehistory, not that of our ancestors the Gauls or the but a prehistory of consciousness at the birth of time and sin, when sky and earth, water and fire, good and evil are not yet clearly separated.'[26]

3

Resnais is perhaps closest to Welles, his most independent and creative disciple, who transforms the whole problem. For, in Welles, a fixed point persists, even if it is in contact with the earth (low-angle shot). It is a present offered to our view, someone's death, sometimes given from the start, sometimes prefigured. It is also a sound-present, the story-teller's voice, the voice-off, which constitutes a radiophonic centre whose role is essential in Welles.[27] And it is in relation to this fixed point that all the strata or sheets of past coexist and confront each other. Now the first novelty in Resnais is the disappearance of the centre or fixed point. Death does not fix an actual present, so numerous are the dead who haunt the sheets of past ('9 million dead haunt this landscape', '200,000 dead in 9 seconds . . . '). The voice-off is no longer central, either because it enters into relationships of dissonance with the visual image or because it is divided or multiplied (the different voices which say 'I was born . . . ' in *My American Uncle*). As a general rule, the present begins to float, struck with uncertainty, dispersed in the characters' comings and goings or already absorbed by the past.[28] Even in the machine for going back in time (*Je t'aime je t'aime*) the present defined by the four minutes of decompression required does not have the time to become fixed, to be counted, but will send the guinea-pig back to levels that are always different. In *Muriel*, the new Boulogne has no centre, any more than the flat with the provisional furniture: none of the people has a present, except perhaps the last who finds only emptiness. In short, the confrontation between sheets of past take place directly, each capable of being present in relation to the next: for the woman, Hiroshima will be the present of Nevers, but for the man, Nevers will be the present of Hiroshima. Resnais had begun with a collective memory, that of the Nazi concentration camps, that of Guernica, that of the Bibliothèque Nationale. But he discovers the paradox of a memory for two people, or a memory for several: the different levels of past no longer relate to a single character, a single family, or a single group, but to quite different characters as to unconnected places which make up a world-memory. He attains a generalized relativity, and takes to its conclusion what was only a direction in Welles: constructing *undecidable alternatives* between sheets of past. In this way we can also understand his antagonism to Robbe-Grillet, and the productive ambiguity of the two authors' collaboration: an architecture of the memory such that it explains or develops the coexistent levels of past rather than an art of peaks which implies simultaneous presents. In both cases there is a disappearance of the centre or fixed point, but in opposite ways.[29]

Let us try to make some data sheets which would indicate an order of progress in certain of Resnais' films, rather than a dialectic and oppositions. *Je t'aime je t'aime*: despite the apparatus of science fiction, this is the simplest figure of time, because here memory concerns only one character. It is true that the memory-machine does not consist in recollecting but in reliving a precise moment of the past. However, what is possible for the animal, the mouse, is impossible for the man. For the man the past moment is like a shining point which belongs to a sheet and cannot be detached from it. An ambiguous moment can take part in two sheets, love for Catrine and the decline of this love.[30] So that the hero will only be able to relive it by crossing these sheets again, and by, from that moment, crossing many others (before he knew Catrine, after Catrine's death . . .) All kinds of regions are thus stirred up in the memory of a man jumping from one to the other, and seem to emerge one after another from an original swamp, universal lapping embodied by the eternal nature of Catrine ('You are still, you are a swamp, of night, of mud . . . You smell of low tide . . . '). *Last Year in Marienbad* is a more complex figure, because here the memory is for two characters. But it is a memory which is still shared, since it refers to the same givens, affirmed by one of them and refused or denied by the other. What happens is that the character X revolves in a circuit of past which includes A as shining point, as 'aspect', whilst A is in regions which do not include X or do so only in a nebulous way. Will A allow herself to be attracted into X's sheet, or will the latter be shattered and unhinged by A's resistances which are rolled up in her own sheets? *Hiroshima mon amour* complicates matters still more. There are two characters, but each has his or her own memory which is foreign to the other. There is no longer anything at all in common. It is like two incommensurable regions of past, Hiroshima and Nevers. And while the Japanese refuses the woman entry into his own region ('I've seen everything . . . everything . . . You've seen nothing in Hiroshima, nothing . . . '), the woman draws the Japanese into hers, willingly and with his consent, up to a certain point. Is this not a way for each of them to forget his or her own memory, and make a memory for two, as if memory was now becoming world, detaching itself from their persons? *Muriel*: there are two memories again, each marked by a war, Boulogne and Algeria. But this time each one includes several sheets or regions of past which refer to the different characters: three levels concerning the letter from Boulogne (the man who has written the letter, the man who has or has not sent it and the woman who has not received it); two levels concerning the Algerian war (the young soldier and the hotel-owner). This is a memory world, for several people, and at several levels, who contradict, accuse and grab each other. *La guerre est finie* does not, it seems to us, signal a mutation, a return to the present, but a deepening of the same problem. For the hero's present is itself no more than an 'age', a certain age of Spain which is never given as present. There is the age of the civil war, in which the committee in exile remains fixed. There is the new age of the young radical terrorists. And the present of the hero, an 'official' [*permanent*] of the organization, is itself only an age of Spain, a level which is distinct from that of the civil war no less than from the young generation who have not experienced it. What appeared as past, present and future is just as much three ages of Spain, so that something new is produced, whether in the deciding between them or at the edge of undecidability. The idea of age tends to become distinct, to take on an autonomous political, historical, or archaeological range. *My American Uncle* will continue this exploration of ages: three characters each of whom has several levels and several ages. There are constants: each age, each sheet, will be defined by a territory, lines of flight and blockages of these lines; these are the topological and cartological limits proposed by Laborit. But the distribution varies from one age to another and from one character to another. The ages become ages of the world, in their variations, because they concern animals as such (man and mouse rediscover a common fate, contrary to what happened in *Je t'aime je t'aime*), but also because they concern a superhuman cosmos, the island and its treasure. It is in this sense that Bergson spoke of durations which are inferior and superior to man, all coexisting. *Life is a Bed of Roses* finally develops the idea of three ages in its own right; three ages of the world, three ages of the château, three coexisting ages related to the human, but each possessing and absorbing its own characters rather than all relating to given people: the age of the Ancient, and utopia; the age of the Modern, and the conference, the techno-democratic organization; the age of Childhood, and legend. Throughout Resnais' work we plunge into a memory which overflows the conditions of psychology, memory for two, memory for several, memory-world, memory-ages of the world.

But the question as a whole remains: what are the sheets of past in the cinema of Resnais, whether levels of a single memory, regions of several memories, creation of a memory-world, or demonstration of the ages of the world? We must distinguish several aspects here. In the first place, each sheet of past is a continuum. If Resnais' tracking shots are famous it is because they define, or rather construct, continuums, circuits of variable speed, following the shelving in the Bibliothèque Nationale, becoming immersed in the paintings of some period of Van Gogh. But it seems to be a characteristic of each continuum, within one type, to be pliable. This is what mathematicians call 'the Boulanger transformation': a square may be pulled into a rectangle whose two halves will form a new square, with the result that the total surface is redistributed with each transformation. If we take the smallest imaginable region of this surface, two infinitely close points will end up being separated, each allocated to one half, at the end of a certain number of transformations.[31] Each transformation has an 'internal age', and we may think of a coexistence of sheets or continuums of different ages. This coexistence or these transformations form a topology. For instance, the different sections correspond to each of the characters in *My American Uncle*, or the various periods of *Van Gogh*: so many strata. In *Last Year in Marienbad*, we are in a situation for two characters, A and X, such that X settles on a sheet where he is very close to A, whilst A is on a sheet of a different age where she is on the contrary distant and separated from X. These are not simply accentuated geometric figures; it is the third character, M, who is witness here of the transformation of a single continuum. The question of knowing if two continuums of a different type, each having a 'middle age', can in turn be assimilated to the transformation of a single one surfaces with *Hiroshima mon amour*, in such a way that one is a modification of the other in all its regions: Hiroshima – Nevers (or from one character to the other in *My*

American Uncle). It is in this way that the notion of age, ages of the world and ages of memory, is profoundly justified in Resnais' cinema: events do not just succeed each other or simply follow a chronological course; they are constantly being rearranged according to whether they belong to a particular sheet of past, a particular continuum of age, all of which coexist. Did X know A or not? Did Ridder kill Catrine, or was it an accident, in *Je 'taime je t'aime*? Was the letter in *Muriel* sent and not received, and who wrote it? These are undecidable alternatives between sheets of past, because their transformations are strictly probabilistic from the point of view of the coexistence of ages. Everything depends on which sheet you are located on. And this is always the difference that we find between Resnais and Robbe-Grillet: what one gets through discontinuity of peaks of present (leaps), the other obtains by transformation of continuous sheets of past. There is a statistical probabilism in Resnais which is completely different from the indeterminism of the 'quantum' type in Robbe-Grillet.

Yet Resnais has subdued the discontinuous as much as Robbe-Grillet has subdued continuity. This is the second aspect which we see in Resnais, deriving from the first. What happens is that the transformations or new distributions of a continuum consistently and inevitably end in a fragmentation: a region, no matter how small, will be fragmented, at the same time as its closest points will each move into a half; every region of a continuum 'may begin by changing shape in a continuous way but will end up being cut in two, and its parts will in turn be fragmented' (Stengers). *Muriel*, and especially *Je t'aime je t'aime*, exhibit this inevitable fragmentation of sheets of past to the highest degree. But before them *Van Gogh* created a coexistence of periods the last of which, the one in Provence, speeds up the tracking shots across the canvases, and also multiplies the cutting shots and extends the dissolves into black, in a 'hacked montage' [*montage haché*] which ends in deep blackness.[32] In short, the continuums or strata continually fragment at the same time as they become rearranged, from one age to another. In *Je t'aime je t'aime*, a perpetual stirring will make what was faraway close and what was close faraway. The continuum continually fragments, to give a different continuum, itself in course of fragmentation. The fragmentations are inseparable from the topology, that is, from the transformation of a continuum. We see here a technical stress which is essential in the cinema. Just as with Welles, as we shall see, short montage is not opposed to wide shots or tracking shots: montage is in strict correlation with these, and marks the age of their transformation. As Godard remarked, Resnais sometimes does a tracking shot with two fixed shots, but he also produces a fragmentation by tracking, for instance from the Japanese river to the banks of the Loire.[33] It is perhaps in *Providence* that cut and continuum attain the highest unity: the one brings together states of body (organic rattlings), states of world (storm and thunder), states of history (bursts of machine-gun fire, bombs exploding), whilst the other carries out the redistributions and transformations of these states. As in mathematics, cuts no longer indicate continuity solutions but variable distributions between the points of a continuum.

In the third place, Resnais has never disguised his liking, in his preparatory works, for a complete biography of the characters, a detailed cartography of the places they go to and their itineraries, an establishment of diagrams in a true sense: even *Last Year . . .* is caught up in this requirement of his. For biographies already allow him to delimit the different 'ages' of each character. But, in addition, a map corresponds to each age, that is, to a continuum or a sheet of past. And the diagram is the set of transformations of the continuum, the piling-up of strata or the superimposing of coexistent sheets. The maps and diagrams survive, then, as integral parts of the film. The maps appear, first, as descriptions of objects, places and landscapes: series of objects are used as witnesses from *Van Gogh*, to *Muriel* and to *My American Uncle*.[34] But these objects are above all functional, and function in Resnais is not the simple use of the object but the mental function or level of thought which corresponds to it: 'Resnais conceives of cinema not as an instrument for representing reality but as the best way of approaching the way the mind functions.'[35] *Van Gogh* already set out to deal with painted things as real objects whose functions would be the artist's 'internal world'. And what makes *Night and Fog* so overpowering is that Resnais succeeds in showing, by means of things and victims, not only the functioning of the camp but also the mental functions, which are cold, diabolical, almost impossible to understand, which preside over its organization. In the Bibliothèque Nationale the books, trolleys, shelving, stairs, lifts and corridors constitute the elements and levels of a gigantic memory where men themselves are only mental functions, or 'neuronic messengers'.[36] As a result of this functionalism, cartography is essentially mental, cerebral, and Resnais has always said that what interested him was the brain, the brain as world, as memory, as 'memory of the world'. It is in the most concrete way that Resnais attains a cinema, creates a cinema which has only one single character, Thought. Each map is in this sense a mental continuum, that is, a sheet of past which makes a distribution of functions correspond to a distribution of objects. The carto-graphical method and coexistence of maps in Resnais may be distinguished from the photographic method in Robbe-Grillet, and his simultaneity of snapshots, even when the two methods result in a common product. In Resnais, the diagram will be a superimposing of maps which define a set of transformations from sheet to sheet, with redistributions of functions and fragmentations of objects: the superimposed ages of Auschwitz. *My American Uncle* will be a grand attempt at diagrammatic mental cartography, where maps are superimposed and transformed, in a single character and from one character to the next.

But, in the fourth place, it is the accent on memory which seems to create a problem. It is obvious that, if memory is reduced to the recollection-image and flashback, Resnais makes no special provision for it and has little to do with it. It is not difficult to show that dreams and nightmares, fantasies, hypotheses and antici-pations, all forms of the imaginary, are more important than flashbacks.[37] It is true that there are some well-known ones in *Hiroshima mon amour*, but in *Last Year in Marienbad* we can no longer tell what is flashback and what is not; and in *Muriel* there are none, likewise with *Je t'aime je t'aime* ('There are absolutely no flashbacks or anything of the sort,' says Resnais). *Night and Fog* could even be thought of as the sum of all the ways of escaping from the flashback, and the false piety of the recollection-image. But in this way we are not going beyond an observation that holds good for all the great film-makers of time: the flashback is just a useful convention which, when it is employed, must always be justified from elsewhere. In Resnais' case, however, this in-adequacy of the flashback does not stop his work as a whole being based on the coexistence of sheets of past, the present no longer even intervening as centre of evocation. The machine of *Je t'aime je t'aime* stirs up and fragments sheets of past in which the character is totally caught up and relives. *Night and Fog* sets out to invent a memory which is all the more alive for no longer passing through recollection-image. How can we explain such an appar-ently paradoxical situation?

We must go back to the Bergsonian distinction between the

'pure recollection', which is always virtual, and 'the recollection-image', which makes it actual only in relation to a present. In a crucial passage, Bergson says that pure recollection should definitely not be confused with the recollection-image which derives from it; it remains a 'magnetizer' behind the hallucinations which it prompts.[38] On each occasion, pure recollection is in a sheet or continuum which is preserved in time. Each sheet of past has its distribution, its fragmentation, its shining points, its nebulae, in short an age. When I take up position on such a sheet, two things can happen: either I discover there the point I was looking for, which will thus be actualized in a recollection-image, but it is clear that the latter does not possess in itself the mark of the past which it only inherits; or I do not discover the point, because it is on a different sheet which is inaccessible to me, belonging to a different age. *Last Year in Marienbad* is precisely a story of magnetism, hypnotism, in which we might say that X has recollection-images and that A does not, or only very vague ones, because they are not on the same sheet.[39] But a third case can arise: we constitute a continuum with fragments of different ages; we make use of transformations which take place between two sheets to constitute a sheet *of* transformation. For instance, in a dream, there is no longer one recollection-image which embodies one particular point of a given sheet; there are a number of images which are embodied within each other, each referring to a different point of the sheet. Perhaps, when we read a book, watch a show, or look at a painting, and especially when we are ourselves the author, an analogous process can be triggered: we constitute a sheet of transformation which invents a kind of transverse continuity or communication between several sheets, and weaves a network of non-localizable relations between them. In this way we extract non-chronological time. We draw out a sheet which, across all the rest, catches and extends the trajectory of points, the evolution of regions. This is evidently a task which runs the risk of failure: sometimes we only produce an incoherent dust made out of juxtaposed borrowings; sometimes we only form generalities which retain mere resemblances. All this is the territory of false recollections with which we trick ourselves or try to trick others (*Muriel*). But it is possible for the work of art to succeed in inventing these paradoxical hypnotic and hallucinatory sheets whose property is to be at once a past and always to come. It is a third possibility which was suggested for Marienbad: M would be the dramatist-storyteller of whom X and

A would be simply the characters, or better the two sheets from which he will draw out a transverse one. It is above all in *Providence*, one of Resnais' finest films, that we witness these redistributions, fragmentations and transformations which go continually from one sheet to another, so creating a new one which takes them all away, goes back to the animal and extends to the edges of the world. There are many difficulties and failures in this work of the drunken old story-teller: for instance, three terraces borrowed from three ages, and the footballer, which sheet has he come from, and should he keep it? Benayoun goes to the heart of the matter when he says: 'The absence of the childhood-adolescence-adult age succession in Resnais . . . perhaps pushes him to reconstitute a synthesis of the life-cycle on the creative plane, starting with birth and perhaps foetal age, up to death and its preceding experiences, even if he combines them all on occasion in the same character.'[40] The work of art crosses coexistent ages, unless it is prevented from doing so, fixed on an exhausted sheet, in a mortified fragmentation (*Les statues meurent aussi*). Success appears when the artist, like Van Gogh, reaches that excess which transforms the ages of memory or the world: a 'magnetic' operation, and this operation explains the 'montage' rather than the other way round.

No author is less bound up in the past. It is a cinema which, in an endeavour to sketch the present, prevents the past from being debased into recollection. Each sheet of past, each age calls up all the mental functions simultaneously: recollection, but equally forgetting, false recollection, imagination, planning, judgement . . . What is loaded with all these functions, each time, is feeling. *Life is a Bed of Roses* begins with 'love, love'. It is feeling which stretches out on a sheet and is modified according to its fragmentation. Resnais has often declared that it is not characters that interest him but the feelings that they could extract from them like their shadows, depending on which regions of past they are placed in. Characters are of the present, but feelings plunge into the past. Feelings become characters, as in the painted shadows in the sunless park (*Last Year in Marienbad*). This is where music becomes specially important. Resnais may therefore some-times think that he is going beyond psychology, sometimes that he is remaining within it, depending on whether we are talking about a psychology of characters or a psychology of pure feelings. And feeling is that which is in continual exchange, circulating from one sheet to another according to what transformations occur. But when transformations themselves form a sheet which crosses all the others it is as if feelings set free the consciousness or thought with which they were loaded: a becoming conscious according to which shadows are the living realities of a mental theatre and feelings the true figures in a 'cerebral game' which is very concrete. It is hypnosis which reveals thought to itself. In a single movement, Resnais goes beyond characters towards feelings, and beyond feelings towards the thought of which they are the characters. This is why Resnais is always saying that he is interested only in what happens in the brain, in cerebral mechanisms – monstrous, chaotic, or creative mechanisms.[41] If feelings are ages of the world, thought is the non-chronological time which corresponds to them. If feelings are sheets of past, thought, the brain, is the set of non-localizable relations between all these sheets, the continuity which rolls them up and unrolls them like so many lobes, preventing them from halting and becoming fixed in a death-position. According to the novelist Belyi, 'we are the unrolling of a cinematographic film subject to the minute action of occult forces: should the film stop, we will be fixed for ever in an artificial pose of terror'.[42] In cinema, Resnais says, something ought to happen 'around the image, behind the image and even inside the image'. This is what happens when the image becomes time-image. The world has become memory, brain, superimposition of ages or lobes, but the brain itself has become consciousness, continuation of ages, creation or growth of ever new lobes, re-creation of matter as with styrene. The screen itself is the cerebral membrane where immediate and direct confrontations take place between the past and the future, the inside and the outside, at a distance impossible to determine, independent of any fixed point (which is perhaps what creates the strangeness of *Stavisky*). The image no longer has space and movement as its primary characteristics but topology and time.

6 The powers of the false

1

Two regimes of the image can be contrasted point by point; an organic regime and a crystalline regime, or more generally a kinetic regime and a chronic regime. The first point concerns descriptions. A description which assumes the independence of its object will be called 'organic'. It is not a matter of knowing if the object is really independent, it is not a matter of knowing if these are exteriors or scenery. What counts is that, whether they are scenery or exteriors, the setting described is presented as independent of the description which the camera gives of it, and stands for a supposedly pre-existing reality. In contrast, what we will call a crystalline description stands for its object, replaces it, both creates and erases it – as Robbe-Grillet puts it – and constantly gives way to other descriptions which contradict, displace, or modify the preceding ones. It is now the description itself which constitutes the sole decomposed and multiplied object. We see it in a whole variety of areas, the flat views and flat tints of colour in the musical comedy, the 'anti-perspective frontal transparencies' of Syberberg. Sometimes we go from one regime to the other, as in *An Actor's Revenge*(Ichikawa) where a yellow fog blurs and passes across a painted canvas. But the difference is not between scenery and exteriors. Neo-realism and the new wave constantly filmed on location, in order to extract from it those pure descriptions which develop a creative and destructive function. In fact, organic descriptions which presuppose the independence of a setting serve to define sensory-motor situations, while crystalline descriptions, which constitute their own object, refer to purely optical and sound situations detached from their motor extension: this is a cinema of the seer and no longer of the agent [*de voyant, non plus d'actant*].

The second point is a consequence of the first, and concerns the relation between the real and the imaginary. In an organic description, the real that is assumed is recognizable by its continuity – even if it is interrupted – by the continuity shots which establish it and by the laws which determine successions, simultaneities and permanences: it is a regime of localizable relations, actual linkages, legal, causal and logical connections. It is clear that this system includes the unreal, the recollection, the dream and the imaginary but as contrast. Thus the imaginary will appear in the forms of caprice and discontinuity, each image being in a state of disconnection with another into which it is transformed. This will be a second pole of existence, which will be defined by pure appearance to consciousness, and no longer by legal connections. Images of this type will be actualized in consciousness, in accordance with the needs of the present actual or the crises of the real. A film may be entirely made up of dream-images; these will retain their capacity for perpetual disconnection and change which contrasts them with real-images. The organic system will, therefore, consist of these two modes of existence as two poles in opposition to each other: linkages of actuals from the point of view of the real, and actualizations in consciousness from the point of view of the imaginary. The crystalline regime is completely different: the actual is cut off from its motor linkages, or the real from its legal connections, and the virtual, for its part, detaches itself from its actualizations, starts to be valid for itself. The two modes of existence are now combined in a circuit where the real and the imaginary, the actual and the virtual, chase after each other, exchange their roles and become indiscernible.[1] It is here that we may speak the most precisely of crystal-image: the coalescence of an actual image and *its* virtual image, the indiscernibility of two distinct images. Passages from one regime to the other, from the organic to the crystalline, can take place imperceptibly or there can be constant overlapping (Mankiewicz, for instance). There are none the less two regimes which differ in nature.

The third point no longer concerns description, but narration. Organic narration consists of the development of sensory-motor schemata as a result of which the characters react to situations or act in such a way as to disclose the situation. This is a truthful narration in the sense that it claims to be true, even in fiction. Such a regime is complex because it can produce interventions from breaks (ellipses), insertions of recollections and dreams, and above all because it implies a certain usage of speech as a development factor. However, we are not yet considering the specific nature of this factor. We simply note that the sensory-motor schema is concretely located in a 'hodological space' (Kurt Lewin), which is defined by a field of forces, oppositions and tensions between these forces, resolutions of these tensions according to the distribution of goals, obstacles, means, detours. The corresponding abstract form is Euclidean space, because this is the setting in which tensions are resolved according to a principle of economy, according to the so-called laws of extremum, of minimum and maximum: for example, the simplest route, the most appropriate detour, the most effective speech, the minimum means for a maximum effect. This economy of narration, then, appears both in the concrete shape of the action-image and hodological space and in the abstract figure of the movement-image and Euclidean space. Movements and actions may present many obvious anomalies, breaks, insertions, superimpositions and decompositions; they none the less obey laws which are based on the distribution of *centres of forces* in space. We can say in general that time is the object of an indirect representation in so far as it is a consequence of action, is dependent on movement and is inferred from space. Hence, no matter how disordered it is, it remains in principle a chronological time.

Crystalline narration is quite different, since it implies a collapse of sensory-motor schemata. Sensory-motor situations have given way to pure optical and sound situations to which characters, who have become seers, cannot or will not react, so great is their need to 'see' properly what there is in the situation. This is the Dostoevskian condition as taken up by Kurosawa: in the most pressing situations, *The Idiot* feels the need to see the terms of a problem which is more profound than the situation, and even more pressing (the same is true for most of Kurosawa's films). But, in Ozu, in neo-realism and in the new wave, vision is no longer even a presupposition added to action, a preliminary which presents itself as a condition; it occupies all the room and takes the place of action. Thus movement can tend to zero, the character, or the shot itself, remain immobile: rediscovery of the fixed shot. But this is not what is important, because movement may also be exaggerated, be incessant, become a world movement, a Brownian movement, a trampling, a to-and-fro, a multiplicity of movements on different scales. What is important is that the anomalies of movement become the essential point instead of being accidental or contingent. This is the era of false continuity shots as inaugurated by Dreyer.[2] In other words crystalline narration will fracture the complementarity of a lived hodological space and a represented Euclidean space. Having lost its sensory-motor connections, concrete space ceases to be organized according to tensions and resolutions of tension, according to goals, obstacles, means, or even detours. It can be said, from a perspective unconnected with cinema, but which is fully confirmed by it: 'Before hodological space, there is that overlapping of perspectives which does not allow the grasping of a given object because there are no dimensions in relation to which the unique set would be ordered. The *fluctuatio animi* which precedes resolute action is not hesitation between several objects or between several directions, but a mobile covering-up of sets which are incompatible, almost alike and yet disparate.'[3] It is here that a crystalline narration will extend crystalline descriptions, their repetitions and variations, through a crisis of action. But, at the same time as concrete space ceases to be hodological, abstract space ceases to be Euclidean, losing in turn the legal connections and laws of extremum which governed it. Of course, we realize the dangers of citing scientific propositions outside their own sphere. It is the danger of arbitrary metaphor or of forced application. But perhaps these dangers are averted if we restrict ourselves to taking from scientific operators a particular conceptualizable character which itself refers to non-scientific areas, and converges with science without applying it or making it a metaphor. It is in this sense that we can talk about Riemanian spaces in Bresson, in neo-realism, in the new wave and in the New York school, of quantum spaces in Robbe-Grillet, of probabilistic and topological spaces in Resnais, of crystallized spaces in Herzog and Tarkovsky. We say, for example, that there is Riemanian space when the connecting of parts is not predetermined but can take place in many ways: it is a space which is disconnected, purely optical, sound or even tactile (in the style of Bresson). There are also empty and amorphous spaces which lose their Euclidean co-ordinates, in the style of Ozu or Antonioni. There are crystallized spaces, when the landscapes become hallucinatory in a setting which now retains only crystalline seeds and crystallizable materials.

Now what characterizes these spaces is that their nature cannot be explained in a simply spatial way. They imply non-localizable relations. These are direct presentations of time. We no longer have an indirect image of time which derives from movement, but a direct time-image from which movement derives. We no longer have a chronological time which can be overturned by movements which are contingently abnormal; we have a chronic non-chronological time which produces movements necessarily 'abnormal', essentially 'false'. It can also be said that montage tends to disappear in favour of the sequence shot, with or without depth. But this is not true in principle, and montage remains in most cases the essential cinematographic act. It simply changes its sense: instead of composing movement-images in such a way that an indirect image of time emerges from them, it decomposes the relations in a direct time-image in such a way that all the possible movements emerge from it. It is not recollections or dreams which determine these chronic relations. Recollection- or dream-images are on the way to actualization in sensory-motor schemata, and presuppose their broadening or weakening, but not their breaking in favour of something else. If time appears directly, it is in *de-actualized peaks of present*; it is in *virtual sheets of past*. The indirect image of time is constructed in the organic regime in accordance with sensory-motor situations, but the two direct time-images appear in the crystalline system in consequence of pure optical and sound situations.

A fourth point, more complex or more general, follows on from this. If we take the history of thought, we see that time has always put the notion of truth into crisis. Not that truth varies depending on the epoch. It is not the simple empirical content, it is the form or rather the pure force of time which puts truth into crisis. Since antiquity this crisis has burst out in the paradox of 'contingent futures'. If it is *true* that a naval battle *may* take place tomorrow, how are we to avoid one of the true following consequences: either the impossible proceeds from the possible (since, if the battle takes place, it is no longer possible that it may not take place), or the past is not necessarily true (since the battle could not have taken place).[4] It is easy to regard this paradox as a sophism. It none the less shows the difficulty of conceiving a direct relation between truth and the form of time, and obliges us to keep the true away from the existent, in the eternal or in what imitates the eternal. We have to wait for Leibniz to get the most ingenious, but also the strangest and most convoluted, solution to this paradox. Leibniz says that the naval battle may or may not take place, but that this is not in the same world: it takes place in one world and does not take place in a different world, and these two worlds are possible, are not 'compossible' with each other.[5] He is thus obliged to forge the wonderful notion of incompossibility (very different from contradiction) in order to resolve the paradox while saving truth: according to him, it is not the impossible, but only the incompossible that proceeds from the possible; and the past may be true without being necessarily true.

But the crisis of truth thus enjoys a pause rather than a solution. For nothing prevents us from affirming that incompossibles belong to the same world, that incompossible worlds belong to the same universe: 'Fang, for example, has a secret; a stranger calls at his door . . . Fang can kill the intruder, the intruder can kill Fang, they can both escape, they can both die, and so forth . . . you arrive at this house, but in one of the possible pasts you are my enemy, in another, my friend . . .'[6] This is Borges's reply to Leibniz: the straight line as force of time, as labyrinth of time, is also the line which forks and keeps on forking, passing through *incompossible presents*, returning to *not-necessarily true pasts*.

A new status of narration follows from this: narration ceases to be truthful, that is, to claim to be true, and becomes fundamentally falsifying. This is not at all a case of 'each has its own truth', a variability of content. It is a power of the false which replaces and supersedes the form of the true, because it poses the simultaneity of incompossible presents, or the coexistence of not-necessarily true pasts. Crystalline description was already reaching the indiscernibility of the real and the imaginary, but the falsifying narration which corresponds to it goes a step further and poses inexplicable differences to the present and alternatives which are undecidable between true and false to the past. The truthful man dies, every model of truth collapses, in favour of the new narration. We have not mentioned the author who is essential in this regard: it is Nietzsche, who, under the name of 'will to power', substitutes the power of the false for the form of the true, and resolves the crisis of truth, wanting to settle it once and for all, but, in opposition to Leibniz, in favour of the false and its artistic, creative power . . .

From the novel to the cinema, Robbe-Grillet's work testifies to the power of the false as principle of production of images. This is not a simple principle of reflection or becoming aware: 'Beware! this is cinema'. It is a source of inspiration. The images must be produced in such a way that the past is not necessarily true, or that the impossible comes from the possible. When Robbe-Grillet appeals to the detail which falsifies in the image (for instance, *The Man Who Lies* should not have the same suit and tie several years later), we see that the power of the false is also the most general principle that determines all the relationships in the direct time-image. In one world, two characters know each other, in another world they don't know each other, in another one the first knows the second, in another, finally, the second knows the first. Or two characters betray each other, only the first betrays the second, neither betrays, the first and second are the same person who betrays himself under two different names: contrary to what Leibniz believed, all these worlds belong to the same universe and constitute modifications of the same story. Narration is no longer a truthful narration which is linked to real (sensory-motor) descriptions. Description becomes its own object and narration becomes temporal *and* falsifying at exactly the same time. The formation of the crystal, the force of time and the power of the false are strictly complementary, and constantly imply each other as the new co-ordinates of the image. There is no value-judgement here, because this new regime – no less than the old one – throws up its ready-made formulas, its set procedures, its laboured and empty applications, its failures, its conventional and 'second-hand' examples offered to us as masterpieces. What is interesting is the new status of the image, this new type of narration-description in so far as it initially inspires very different great authors.[7] All this could be summed up by saying that the forger becomes *the* character of the cinema: not the criminal, the cowboy, the psycho-social man, the historical hero, the holder of power, etc., as in the action-image, but the forger pure and simple, to the detriment of all action. The forger could previously exist in a determinate form, liar or traitor, but he now assumes an unlimited figure which permeates the whole film. He is simultaneously the man of pure descriptions and the maker of the crystal-image, the indiscernibility of the real and the imaginary; he passes into the crystal, and makes the direct time-image visible; he provokes undecidable alternatives and inexplicable differences between the true and the false, and thereby imposes a power of the false as adequate to time, in contrast to any form of the true which would control time. *The Man Who Lies* is one of Robbe-Grillet's finest films: this is not a localized liar, but an unlocalizable and chronic forger in paradoxical spaces. We would also say that *Stavisky* is not just one film among others in Resnais' work: even if it is not the most important, it contains the secret of the others, a bit like Henry James's 'The Figure in the Carpet'. We might also select from Godard a film which is even more minor yet crucial, because it presents in a systematic and concise way what will be the constant inspiration for all his work, a power of the false which Godard was able to impose as a new style and which moves from pure descriptions to falsifying narration from the point of view of a direct time-image: we mean *Le grand escroc*, a free interpretation of an episode in Herman Melville's great novel.[8] *The Man Who Lies* and *Stavisky* would also be like *Le grand escroc*; they would together form the simplified, overblown, provocative, badly received, 'badly viewed and reviewed' manifesto of the new cinema.

Truthful narration is developed organically, according to legal connections in space and chronological relations in time. Of course, the elsewhere may be close to the here, and the former to the present; but this variability of places and moments does not call the relations and connections into question. They rather determine its terms or elements, so that narration implies an inquiry or testimonies which connect it to the true. The investigator and witnesses may even take on an autonomous and explicit shape, as in literally 'judicial' films. But, whether explicitly or not, narration always refers to a *system of judgement*: even when acquittal takes place due to the benefit of the doubt, or when the guilty is so only because of fate. Falsifying narration, by contrast, frees itself from this system; it shatters the system of judgement because the power of the false (not error or doubt) affects the investigator and the witness as much as the person presumed guilty. 'In *Stavisky* the testimonies come from the very living of the character who refutes them. Then, within these testimonies, other witnesses appear, who are already talking about a dead man.'[9] The point is that the elements themselves are constantly changing with the relations of time into which they enter, and the terms with their connections. Narration is constantly being completely modified, in each of its episodes, not according to subjective variations, but as a consequence of disconnected places and de-chronologized moments. There is a fundamental reason for this new situation: contrary to the form of the true which is unifying and tends to the identification of a character (his discovery or simply his coherence), the power of the false cannot be separated from an irreducible multiplicity. 'I is another' ['*Je est un autre*'] has replaced Ego = Ego.

The power of the false exists only from the perspective of a series of powers, always referring to each other and passing into one another. So that investigators, witnesses and innocent or guilty heroes will participate in the same power of the false the degrees of which they will embody, at each stage of the narration. Even 'the truthful man ends up realizing that he has never stopped lying' as Nietzsche said. The forger will thus be inseparable from a chain of forgers into whom he metamorphoses.

There is no unique forger, and, if the forger reveals something, it is the existence behind him of another forger, if only the state as in the financial operations in *Stavisky* or in *Le grand escroc*. The truthful man will form part of the chain, at one end like the artist, at the other end, the nth power of the false. And the only content of narration will be the presentation of these forgers, their sliding from one to the other, their metamorphoses into each other. In literature and philosophy, the two greatest texts to have developed such chains of forgers or such series of powers are the last book of *Zarathustra*, in Nietzsche, and Melville's novel, *The Confidence Man*. The former presents the 'multiple cry' of the higher man who passes through the divine, the two kings, the man with the leeches, the sorcerer, the last pope, the ugliest man, the voluntary beggar and the shadow: they are all forgers. The latter presents a series of forgers which includes a dumb albino, a legless negro, a man in mourning, a man in grey, a man in a cap, a man with an account book, a herbal doctor, up to the cosmopolitan with the colourful clothes, the great hypnotist, the 'metaphysical scoundrel', each metamorphosing into the other, all confronting 'truthful men' who are no less false than they are.[10] Godard outlines a similar series whose characters will be the representatives of *cinéma-vérité*, the policeman, the confidence man himself and finally the author, the portrait of the artist in a fez. *Last Year in Marienbad* only connected the hypnotized woman (the truthful woman?) to the hypnotist provided that it revealed, behind, yet another hypnotist. Or the series in *Muriel*, all forgers in some respect. Robbe-Grillet's series develop in the style of *Trans-Europe Express*: Elias, the man of the false, connects with Eva, the double agent, from the perspective of the gangster Frank who presupposes an organization, itself connecting with Jean and Marc, the author and his critic, who pass over into Commissioner Lorentz . . . Such a construction seems common to some very different films and very independent authors. We might mention Hugo Santiago's film *The Others*, in which Borges and Casares collaborated: after the death of his son, the bookseller metamorphoses into a series of forgers, the magician, the man with the wand, the man in the mirror, and the son himself, who constitute the whole narration, whilst the camera jumps from point to point to carry out pure descriptions (the empty observatory). Everywhere it is the metamorphoses of the false which replace the form of the true.

This is the essential point: how the new regime of the image (the direct time-image) works with pure crystalline optical and sound descriptions, and falsifying, purely chronic narrations. Description stops presupposing a reality and narration stops referring to a form of the true at one and the same time: hence Agnès Varda's *Documenteur*, where the documentary describes situations which are now only optical and of sound (walls, the city), for a story which now invokes only the abolition of the true, following the disconnected gestures of the heroine. Undoubtedly each great author has his own way of conceiving description, narration and their relationships.[11] The visual and the spoken also enter into new relations each time. For, as we shall see, a third element now intervenes, which is the story, distinct from description and narration. But, to remain with these two instances, we must propose that they form the framework which, after the new wave, is indispensable. The neo-realist resolution still retained a reference to a form of the true, although it profoundly renewed it, and certain authors were freed from it in their development (Fellini, and even Visconti). But the new wave deliberately broke with the form of the true to replace it by the powers of life, cinematographic powers considered to be more profound. If we look for the inheritance of the new wave or the influence of Godard in certain recent films, we immediately see characteristics which are sufficient to define its most obvious aspect. Bergala and Limosin's *Faux-fuyants* tells the story of a man in a car who accidentally runs over another man and makes off, then makes enquiries and enters into closer and closer relation with the daughter of his victim without us knowing what he wants. But the narration does not develop organically, it is rather as if the offence of making off was sliding along a chain, metamorphosing each time, *following* the characters like so many forgers each of whom comes up with an excuse [*opère un faux-fuyant*] for his own purposes (we can count eight in all), until the offence is reversed, and the original witness in turn becomes the offender whom a final offence of flight will leave to die in the snow, whilst the circuit is completed by a telephone call which reports this death to the first character. Now, such a falsifying narration appears to be intercut with strange scenes whose sole function is pure description; the man telephones the girl, who is baby-sitting, simply for her to describe the flat where she is; then he asks the girl to come and watch him, for no reason, when there is strictly nothing to see, when he is preparing to go into the cinema with a girlfriend; and the girl will repay him this 'politeness', asking him to be there when she in turn is simply out walking with a girlfriend. Doillon's *La pirate* proceeds quite differently, but on the same basis: the film presents us with a passion between three characters who want to be 'judged', but who simply fall under the purely descriptive gaze of a little girl, and into the plot of a detective who wonders which story he will be able to draw from it. Passion becomes the essential element of this cinema because, as against action, it ties falsifying narration to pure descriptions.

If there is a unity to the new German cinema – Wenders, Fassbinder, Schmid, Schroeter, or Schlöndorff – it is also here, as a result of the war, in the constantly variable link between these elements: spaces reduced to their own descriptions (city-deserts or places which are constantly being destroyed), direct present-ations of an oppressive, useless and unsummonable time which haunt the characters; and, from one pole to the other, the powers of the false which weave a narration, in so far as they take effect in 'false movements'. The German passion has become fear, but fear is also man's final reason, his nobility announcing something new, the creation which comes from fear as a noble passion. If we were looking for an example not to sum up all the others, but among others, it would be precisely Schlöndorff's *Circle of Deceit* in a devastated and divided Beirut, a man from a different past, caught in a chain of forgers, blankly watching the movement of a windscreen wiper.

Semiology of a linguistic inspiration, semiocritique, has addressed the problem of falsifying narrations as part of rich and complex studies of the 'dysnarrative'.[12] But, since it identified the cinematographic image with an utterance, and every sequence with a narration in general, the differences between narrations could come only from language processes which constituted an intellectual structure underlying the images. What constituted this structure was the syntagm and the paradigm, which were both complementary, but under conditions which meant that the second remained weak and undetermined while the first alone was decisive in traditional narration (Christian Metz). Hence, it only needs the paradigm to become crucial to the structural order, or the structure to become 'serial', for narration to lose the accumulative, homogeneous and identifiable character that it owed to the primacy of the syntagm. 'Grand syntagmatics' is overtaken, the Great Lady is dead, subverted, and the minor elements eat away at her or make her multiply. New syntagms may arise (for example, the 'projective syntagms' of Chateau and

Jost), but they show the change in predominance. The cinema is always narrative, and more and more narrative, but it is dysnarrative in so far as narration is affected by repetitions, permutations and transformations which are explicable in detail by the new structure. However, a pure semiotics is unable to follow in the tracks of this semiology, because there is no narration (nor description) which is as 'given' of images. The diversity of narrations cannot be explained by the avatars of the signifier, by the states of a linguistic structure which is assumed to underlie images in general. It relates only to perceptible forms of images and to corresponding sensory signs which presuppose no narration but from which derives one narration rather than another. Perceptible types cannot be replaced by the processes of language. It is in this sense that falsifying narration depends directly on the time-image, on opsigns and chronosigns, whilst traditional narration relates to forms of the movement-image and sensory-motor signs.

2

Orson Welles is the first: he isolates a direct time-image and makes the image go over to the power of the false. These two aspects are undoubtedly closely linked, but recent writers have attached increasing importance to the second, which culminates in *It's All True*. There is a Nietzscheanism in Welles, as if Welles were retracing the main points of Nietzsche's critique of truth: the 'true world' does not exist, and, if it did, would be inaccessible, impossible to describe, and, if it could be described, would be useless, superfluous. The true world implies a 'truthful man', a man who wants the truth, but such a man has strange motives, as if he were hiding another man in him, a revenge: Othello wants the truth, but out of jealousy, or, worse, out of revenge for being black, and Vargas, the epitome of the truthful man, for a long time seems indifferent to the fate of his wife, engrossed in the archives in amassing proofs against his enemy. The truthful man in the end wants nothing other than to judge life; he holds up a superior value, the good, in the name of which he will be able to judge, he is craving to judge, he sees in life an evil, a fault which is to be atoned for: the moral origin of the notion of truth. In the Nietzschean fashion, Welles has constantly battled against the system of judgement: there is no value superior to life, life is not to be judged or justified, it is innocent, it has 'the innocence of becoming', beyond good and evil . . .[13]

This problem of judgement is no less familiar to the cinema than to the theatre, and has undergone a complex evolution. Since expressionism, it is the struggle between good and evil, as between light and darkness, that constitutes the metaphysics of the true (find truth in light and atonement). But Lang's position is already unique because he creates a human rather than Faustian dimension of evil, whether in the shape of a hypnotic genius (Mabuse), or of irresistible impulse (*M*). This time the question of truth, that is, of tribunal and judgement, will reveal its full ambiguity: *M* can be tried by a court of thieves which is hardly motivated by truth. And the evolution accelerates when Lang moves to America and finds there a genre of literally judicial films whose assumptions he will renew. It is not simply a matter of pointing out the difficulty of reaching the true, taking into account the shortcomings of the investigation and of those who judge (this will again be the case in Lumet's *Twelve Angry Men*). In Lang, and also in Preminger, it is the very possibility of judging which is called into question. For Lang, it is as if there is no truth any more, but only appearances. The American Lang becomes the greatest film-maker of appearances, of false images (hence the evolution of the Mabuses). Everything is appearance, and yet this novel state transforms rather than suppresses the system of judgement. In fact appearance is what betrays itself; the great moments in Lang are those where a character betrays himself. Appearances betray themselves, not because they would give way to a more profound truth, but simply because they reveal themselves as non-true; the character makes a blunder, he knows the visitor's first name (*Beyond a Reasonable Doubt*) or he knows German (*Hangmen Die Too*). In these conditions, it remains possible to make new appearances arise, in the light of which the first ones will be judicable and judged. The resistance fighters, for instance, will bring out false witnesses who will get the traitor who knew German condemned by the Gestapo. The system of judgement thus undergoes a great transformation, because it moves within the conditions which determine the relations on which appearances depend: Lang invents a Protagoras-style relativism where judgement expresses the 'best' point of view, that is, the relation under which appearances have a chance of being turned around to the benefit of an individual or of a humanity of higher value (judgement as 'revenge', or displacement of appearances). Ultimately, we can understand the encounter betweenLang and Brecht and the misunderstandings of this encounter. For, in Lang as in Brecht, judgement can no longer be directly exercised in the image, but passes to the side of the viewer, to which the conditions of possibility of judging the image itself are given. What in Brecht rested on a reality of contradictions, in Lang, in contrast, rests on a relativity of appearances.[14] In both of them, the system of judgement, if it undergoes a crisis, is none the less saved and transformed. Things are very different in Welles (even though he made a 'Langian', but disowned, film: *The Stranger*, where the character betrays himself). In Welles, the system of judgement becomes definitively impossible, even and especially for the viewer. The ransacking of the judge's office in *The Lady from Shanghai*, and especially the infinite sham of judgement in *The Trial*, will be evidence of this new impossibility. Welles constantly constructs characters who are unjudicable and who have not to be judged, who evade any possible judgement. If the ideal of truth crumbles, the relations of appearance will no longer be sufficient to maintain the possibility of judgement. In Nietzsche's phrase, 'with the real world we have also abolished the apparent world'.[15*]

What remains? There remain bodies, which are forces, nothing but forces. But force no longer refers to a centre, any more than it confronts a setting or obstacles. It only confronts other forces, it refers to other forces, that it affects or that affect it. Power (what Nietzsche calls 'will to power' and Welles, 'character') is this power to affect and be affected, this relation between one force and others. This power is always fulfilled, and this relation is necessarily carried out, even if in a variable manner according to the forces which are present.[16] We already sense that short, cut-up and piecemeal montage, and the long sequence shot serve the same purpose. The one presents bodies in a successive way, each of which exercises its force or experiences that of another: 'each shot shows a blow, a counter-blow, a blow received, a blow struck'.[17] The other presents in a simultaneous way a relation of forces in its variability, in its instability, its proliferation of centres and multiplication of vectors (the scene of the questioning in *Touch of Evil*).[18] In both cases, there is the shock of forces, in the image or of the images between themselves. Sometimes a short montage reproduces a sequence shot, through cutting, as in the battle in *Chimes at Midnight*, or a sequence shot produces a short

montage, through constant reframing, as in *Touch of Evil*. We
have seen how Resnais rediscovered this complementarity, by
other means.

Is this to say that, in life, everything is a matter of forces? Yes, if
it is understood that the relation of forces is not quantitative, but
necessarily implies certain 'qualities'. There are forces which are
now able to respond to others only in a single, uniform and
invariable way: the scorpion in *Mr Arkadin* knows only how to
string, and stings the frog that carries him over the water, even if
it means death by drowning. Variability thus survives in the
relation of forces, since the scorpion's sting turns against itself,
when it is directed in this case at the frog. None the less, the
scorpion is the type of a force which no longer knows how to
metamorphose itself according to the variations of what it can
affect and what it can be affected by. Bannister is a big scorpion
who knows only how to sting. Arkadin knows only how to kill, and
Quinlan how to fix the evidence. This is a type of exhausted force,
even when it has remained quantitatively very large, and it can
only destroy and kill, before destroying itself, and perhaps in
order to kill itself. It is here that it rediscovers a centre, but one
which coincides with death. No matter how large it is, it is
exhausted because it no longer knows how to transform itself. It is
thus descending, decadent and degenerate: it represents impotence in bodies, that is, that precise point where the 'will to
power' is nothing but a will-to-dominate, a being for death, which
thirsts for its own death, as long as it can pass through that of
others. Welles multiples the list of these all-powerful impotents:
Bannister and his artificial limbs, Quinlan and his cane; Arkadin
and his helplessness when he no longer has an aeroplane; Iago,
the impotent *par excellence*.[19] These are men of revenge: not in the
same way, however, as the truthful man who claimed to judge life
in the name of higher values. They, on the contrary, take
themselves to be *higher men*, these are higher men who claim to
judge life by their own standards, by their own authority. But is
this not the same spirit of revenge in two forms: Vargas, the
truthful man who invokes the laws for judging, but also his
double, Quinlan, who gives himself the right to judge without
law; Othello, the man of duty and virtue, but also his double,
Iago, who takes revenge by nature and perversion? It is what
Nietzsche called the stages of nihilism, the spirit of revenge in
various shapes. Behind the truthful man, who judges life from
the perspective of supposedly higher values, there is the sick man,

'the man sick with himself', who judges life from the perspective of his sickness, his degeneration and his exhaustion. And this is perhaps better than the truthful man, because a life of sickness is still life, it contrasts life with death, rather than contrasting it with 'higher values' . . . Nietzsche said: behind the truthful man, who judges life, there is the sick man, sick with life itself. And Welles adds: behind the frog, the epitome of the truthful animal, there is the scorpion, the animal sick with itself. The first is an idiot and the second is a bastard.[20] They are, however, complementary as two figures of nihilism, two figures of the will to power.

Does this not amount to restoring a system of judgement? Welles constantly says of Quinlan, Arkadin, etc., that he 'detests them morally' (even if he does not detest them 'humanly', according to the amount of *Life* they have kept).[21] But it is not a matter of judging life in the name of a higher authority which would be the good, the true; it is a matter, on the contrary, of evaluating every being, every action and passion, even every value, in relation to the life which they involve. Affect as immanent evaluation, instead of judgement as transcendent value: 'I love or I hate' instead of 'I judge'. Nietzsche, who had already substituted affect for judgement, warned his readers: beyond good and evil does not in the least mean *beyond the good and the bad*. This bad is exhausted and degenerating life, all the more terrible, and apt to multiply itself. But the good is outpouring, ascending life, the kind which knows how to transform itself, to metamorphose itself according to the forces it encounters, and which forms a constantly larger force with them, always increasing the power to live, always opening new 'possibilities'. Of course there is no more truth in one life than in the other; there is only becoming, and becoming is the power of the false of life, the will to power. But there is good and bad, that is, noble and base. According to physicists, noble energy is the kind which is capable of transforming itself, while the base kind can no longer do so. There is will to power on both sides, but the latter is nothing more than will-to-dominate in the exhausted becoming of life, while the former is artistic will or 'virtue which gives', the creation of new possibilities, in the outpouring becoming. The so-called higher men are base or bad. But the good has only one name; it is 'generosity', and this is the trait by which Welles defines his favourite character, Falstaff; it is also the trait which we suppose is dominant in Don Quixote's eternal project. If becoming is the power of the false, then the good, the generous, the noble is what raises the false to the nth power or the will to power to the level of artistic becoming. Falstaff and Don Quixote may appear to be braggarts or to be pitiful, history having passed them by; they are experts in metamorphoses of life; they oppose becoming to history. Incommensurable to any judgement, they have the innocence of becoming.[22] And it is clear that becoming is always innocent, even in crime, even in the exhausted life in so far as it is still a becoming. But only the good allows itself to be exhausted by life rather than exhausting it, always putting itself at the service of what is reborn from life, what metamorphoses and creates. Out of becoming it makes a Being, so protean, instead of despatching it into non-being, from the height of a uniform and fixed being. There are two states of life which are in opposition at the heart of immanent becoming, and not one instance which would claim to be superior to becoming, whether in order to judge life, or to appropriate it, and in any event to exhaust it. What Welles sees in Falstaff and Don Quixote is the 'goodness' of life in itself, a strange goodness which carries the living being to creation. It is in this sense that we can talk about an authentic or a spontaneous Nietzscheanism in Welles.

Nevertheless, in becoming, the earth has lost all centre, not only in itself, but in that it no longer has a centre around which to turn. Bodies no longer have centres except that of their death when they are exhausted and return to the earth to dissolve there. Force no longer has a centre precisely because it is inseparable from its relation to other forces: so, as Didier Goldschmidt said, short shots constantly topple to right and left and the sequence shot likewise throws up a jumble of vanishing centres (the opening of *Touch of Evil*). Weights have lost the centres of equilibrium around which they were distributed; masses have lost the centres of gravity around which they were ordered, forces have lost the dynamic centres around which they organize space; movements themselves have lost the centres of revolution around which they develop. There is here, in Welles, a mutation which is as much cinematographic as metaphysical. For what contrasts with the ideal of truth is not movement: movement remains perfectly consistent with the true while it presents invariants, point of gravity of the moving body, privileged points through which it passes and point of fixity in relation to which it moves. This is why the movement-image, in its very essence, is answerable to the effect of truth which it invokes while movement preserves its centres. And this is what we have been trying to say from the beginning of this study: a cinematographic mutation occurs when aberrations of movement take on their independence; that is, when the moving bodies and movements lose their invariants. There then occurs a reversal where movement ceases to demand the true and where time ceases to be subordinate to movement: both at once. *Movement which is fundamentally decentred becomes false movement, and time which is fundamentally liberated becomes power of the false which is now brought into effect in false movement* (Arkadin always already there). Welles seems to be the first to have opened this breach, where neo-realism and the new wave were to be introduced with completely different methods. Welles, through his conception of bodies, forces and movement, constructs a world which has lost all motor centre or 'configuration'; the earth.

Nevertheless we have seen that Welles's cinema kept some essential centres (and it is on this very point that Resnais parts company from Welles). But what we have to evaluate here is the radical change to which Welles subjected the very notion of centre. The question of depth of field already took up in a new way a transformation of painting in the seventeenth century. It is possible that Welles's cinema has been able to re-create, for the use of our modern world, a transformation of thought which originally took place in that distant century. If we follow an important analysis by Michel Serres, the seventeenth century was not the 'classical' age of the ideal of the true, but the baroque age *par excellence* which was inseparable from what is called classical and where truth passed through a definitive crisis. It was no longer a question of knowing where the centre was, the sun or the earth, because the primary question became 'Is there a centre or not at all?' All the centres, of gravity, equilibrium, force, revolution, in short, of configuration, were collapsing. It was at that point that a restoration of centres undoubtedly occurred, but at the price of a profound change, of a great evolution of the sciences and the arts. On the one hand, the centre became *purely optical*; the point became point of view. This 'perspectivism' was *not* defined by variation of external points of view on a supposedly invariable object (the ideal of the true would be preserved). Here, on the contrary, the point of view was constant, but always internal to the different objects which were henceforth presented as the metamorphosis of one and the same thing in the process of becoming. This was *projective geometry*, which lodged the eye at the apex of the cone and gave us 'projections' as variable as the sectional planes, circle, ellipse, hyperbola, point and straight lines, the object itself, at the limit, being only the connection of its own projections, the collection or series of its own metamorphoses. Perspectives and projections – these are neither truth nor appearance.

However, this new perspective does not yet give us the means of establishing a true progression in the figures so described, or of spacing out the volumes on the flat sections. Thus we must, on the other hand, link it to the *theory of shadows*, which is, as it were, the inverse of the projective: the luminous source now occupies the apex of the cone, the body projected is the opaque and the projections are produced by reliefs or bands of shadow.[23] These are the two aspects which form an 'architecture of vision'. We see them particularly in Welles's art; and they give us the final reason for the complementarity between short montage and the sequence shot. Short montage presents flat and flattened images which are so many perspectives and projections, in the strong sense, and which express the metamorphoses of an immanent thing or being. Hence the appearance of a succession of 'numbers' which often marks Welles's films; for example, the different witnesses to the past in *Mr Arkadin* could be considered as a series of projections of Arkadin himself, who is simultaneously what is projected on to each plane and the commanding point of view according to which we pass from one projection to the next; similarly in *The Trial* all the characters, policemen, colleagues, student, concierge, lawyer, little girls, painter and priest, constitute the projective series of a single instance which does not exist outside its metamorphoses. But, from the other aspect, the sequence shot with depth of field powerfully emphasizes volumes and reliefs, the bands of shadow from which bodies emerge and into which they return, oppositions and combinations of light and dark, violent stripes which affect bodies when they are in a see-through space (*The Lady from Shanghai, The Trial*; a whole neo-expressionism which has rid itself both of its moral assumptions and the ideal of the true).[24] One might say that Welles subjected the notion of centre to a double transformation which established the new cinema: the centre ceased to be sensory-motor and, on the one hand, became optical, determining a new regime of description; on the other hand, at the same time, it became luminous, determining a new progression of narration. The descriptive or projective, and the narrative or gloomy . . .

By raising the false to power, life freed itself of appearances as well as truth: neither true nor false, an undecidable alternative, but power of the false, decisive will. It is Welles who, beginning with *The Lady from Shanghai*, imposes one single character, the forger. But the forger exists only in a series of forgers who are his metamorphoses, because the power itself exists only in the form of a series of powers which are its exponents. There is always a character destined to betray the other (Welles stresses that the prince *must* betray Falstaff, Menzies must betray Quinlan), because the other is already a traitor, and betrayal is the link between forgers throughout the series. Since Welles has a strong personality, we forget that his constant theme, precisely as a result of this personality, is to be a person no longer, in the manner of Virginia Woolf's Mrs Dalloway.[25] A becoming, an irreducible multiplicity, characters or forms are now valid only as transformations of each other. And this is the diabolical trio of *The Lady from Shanghai*, the strange relay-characters of Mr Arkadin, the chain which unites those in *Touch of Evil*, the unlimited transformation for those of *The Trial*, the journey of the false which constantly passes through the king, his son and Falstaff, all three imposters and usurpers in some way, culminating in the scene where the roles are exchanged. It is finally the great series in *It's All True*, which is the manifesto for all of Welles's work, and his reflection on cinema. F for Falstaff, but above all *F for fake*. Welles certainly has a conscious affinity with Herman Melville, even more important than his less conscious affinity with Nietzsche. It is in *It's All True* that Welles constructs a series of forgers as extensive and perfect as that in Melville's *The Confidence Man*, Welles scrupulously playing the role of the cosmopolitan hypnotist. This great series of Welles, the story that is continually being modified, may be summed up as follows: 1. 'presentation of Oja Kadar, whom all men turn to look at in the street'; 2. 'presentation of Welles as conjuror'; 3. presentation of the journalist, author of a book about a forger of paintings, but also of false memoirs of Hughes, the millionaire forger with a multiplicity of doubles, concerning whom we do not know if he has himself harmed the journalist; 4. conversation or exchange between the journalist and the forger of paintings; 5. intervention of Welles who assures us that, for an hour, the viewer will neither see nor hear anything else false; 6. Welles recounts his life, and reflects on man in front of Chartres Cathedral; 7. Oja Kadar's affair with Picasso at the end of which Welles arrives to say that the hour has passed and the affair was invented in every respect.[26]

Nevertheless, everything is not equivalent to everything else, and all the forgers are not all so to the same degree or with the same power. The truthful man forms part of them, like the frog, Vargas, or Othello, and Welles in front of Chartres Cathedral: for he invokes a true world, but the true world itself implies the truthful man. In itself, it is an *inaccessible and useless* world. Like the cathedral, its only quality is to have been made by men. Thus it is not hidden by appearances; it is it, on the contrary, which hides appearances and provides them with an alibi. Behind the truthful man there is the forger, the scorpion, and the one constantly refers back to the other. The expert in truth gives approval to Van Megeeren's false Vermeers precisely because the forger has created them by reference to the expert's own criteria. In short, the forger cannot be reduced to a simple copier, nor to a liar, because what is false is not simply a copy, but already the model. Should we not say, then, that the artist, even Vermeer, even Picasso, is a forger, since he makes a model with appearances, even if the next artist gives the model back to appearances in order to make a new model? Where does the 'bad' relation of Elmer the forger of Picasso end and the 'good' relation of Picasso and Velázquez begin? From the truthful man to the artist, the chain of forgers is long. This is obviously why it is so difficult to define 'the' forger, because we do not take into account his multiplicity, his ubiquity, and because we are content to refer to a historical and ultimately chronological time. But everything is changed in the perspective of time as becoming. What we can criticize in the forgers, as well as in the truthful man, is their exaggerated taste for *form*: they have neither the sense nor the power of metamorphosis; they reveal an impoverishment of the vital force [*élan vital*], of an already exhausted life. The difference between the forger, the expert and Vermeer is that the first two barely know how to change. Only the creative artist takes the power of the false to a degree which is realized, not in form, but in transformation. There is no longer either truth or appearance. There is no longer either invariable form or variable point of view on to a form. There is a point of view which belongs so much to the thing that the thing is constantly being transformed in a becoming identical to point of view. Metamorphosis of the true. What the artist is, is *creator of truth*, because truth is not to be achieved, formed, or reproduced; it has to be created. There is no other truth than the creation of the New: creativity, emergence, what Melville called 'shape' in contrast to 'form'. Art is the continual production of *shapes*, reliefs and projections. The truthful man and the forger form part of the same chain, but, in the end, it is not they who are projected, elevated, or excavated; it is the artist, creator of the true, in the very place where the false attains its final power: goodness, generosity. Nietzsche drew up a list of the characters of the 'will to power': the truthful man, then all the forgers who presuppose him and that he presupposes, the long, exhausted cohort of 'superior men', but, still behind, the new man, Zarathustra, the artist or outpouring life.[27] There is only a slim chance, so great is the capacity of nihilism to overcome it, for exhausted life to get control of the New from its birth, and for completed forms to ossify metamorphosis and to reconstitute models and copies. The power of the false is delicate, allowing itself to be recaptured by frogs and scorpions. But it is the only chance for art or life, the Nietzschean, Melvillian, Bergsonian, Wellesian chance . . . Kamler's *Chronopolis* shows that the elements of time require an extraordinary encounter with man in order to produce something new.

3

There would be still a third instance beyond description and narration: the story [*récit*]. If we attempt a provisional definition, as we have done for the other instances, still without taking into account the special importance of the talkie factor, we believe that the story in general concerns the subject-object relationship and the development of this relationship (whilst narration concerned the development of the sensory-motor schema). The model of truth thus finds its full expression, not in the sensory-motor connection, but in the 'adequation' of the subject and the object. We must, however, specify what the subject and the object are in the conditions of the cinema. According to convention, what the camera 'sees' is called objective, and what the character sees is called subjective. Such a convention has a place only in the cinema, not in the theatre. Now it is essential that the camera sees the character himself: it is one and the same character who sometimes sees and sometimes is seen. But it is also the same camera which gives us the character seen and what the character sees. We may, then, consider the story as the development of two kinds of images, objective and subjective, their complex relation which can go as far as antagonism, but which ought to find resolution in an identity of the type Ego = Ego; identity of the character seen and who sees, but equally well identity of the camera/film-maker who sees the character and is what the character sees. This identity passes through many trials which specifically represent the false (confusion between two characters seen, for example, in Hitchcock, or confusion in what the character sees, for example, in Ford), but ends up affirming itself for itself by constituting the True, even if the character has to die because of it. We might say that the film begins with the distinction between the two kinds of images, and ends with their identification, their identity recognized. The variations are infinite, because both the distinction and the synthetic identity can be established in all kinds of ways. The basic conditions of cinema are none the less here, from the point of view of the *veracity* of every possible story.[28]

The distinction between the objective and the subjective, but also their identification, are brought into question in another kind of story. Here again, the American Lang was the great forerunner of a critique of veracity in the story.[29] And the critique was taken up and extended by Welles, starting with *Citizen Kane*, where the distinction between the two kinds of images tends to vanish in what the witnesses have seen, without its being possible to agree on an identity for the character ('no trespassing'), nor even an identity for the film-maker, about which Welles always had doubts, which he was to push to the limit in *It's All True*. Pasolini, for his part, drew out the consequences of this new situation in what he called 'cinema of poetry', in contrast to the so-called cinema of prose. In the cinema of poetry, the distinction between what the character saw subjectively and what the camera saw objectively vanished, not in favour of one or the other, but because the camera assumed a subjective presence, acquired an internal vision, which entered into a relation of *simulation* ('mimesis') with the character's way of seeing. It is here, according to our earlier discussion, that Pasolini discovered how to go beyond the two elements of the traditional story, the objective, indirect story from the camera's point of view and the subjective, direct story from the character's point of view, to achieve the very special form of a 'free indirect discourse', of a 'free, indirect subjective'. A contamination of the two kinds of image was established, so that bizarre visions of the camera (alternation of different lenses, zoom, extraordinary angles, abnormal movements, halts . . .) expressed the singular visions of the character, and the latter were expressed in the former, but by bringing the whole to the power of the false. The story no longer refers to an ideal of the true which constitutes its veracity, but becomes a 'pseudo-story', a poem, a story which simulates or rather a simulation of the story.[30] Objective and subjective images lose their distinction, but also their identification, in favour of a new circuit where they are wholly replaced, or contaminate each other, or are decomposed and recomposed. Pasolini brings his analysis to bear on Antonioni, Bertolucci and Godard, but the origin of this transformation of the story is perhaps in Lang and Welles (the study of *The Immortal Story* would be important here).

We would like to consider an aspect of this new type of story, as it appears in a quite different area. If we go to the forms which for a long time challenged fiction, we see that the cinema of reality sometimes claimed objectively to show us real settings, situations and characters, and sometimes claimed subjectively to show the ways of seeing of these characters themselves, the way in which they themselves saw their situation, their setting, their problems. In short, there was the documentary or ethnographic pole, and the investigation or reportage pole. These two poles inspired masterpieces and in any case intermingled (Flaherty on one hand, and on the other Grierson and Leacock). But, in challenging fiction, if this cinema discovered new paths, it also preserved and sublimated an ideal of truth *which was dependent on cinematographic fiction itself*: there was what the camera sees, what the character sees, the possible antagonism and necessary resolution of the two. And the character himself retained or acquired a kind of identity in so far as he was seen or saw. And the camera/film-maker also had his identity, as ethnologist or reporter. It was very important to challenge the established fictions in favour of a reality that cinema could capture or discover. But fiction was being abandoned in favour of the real, whilst retaining a model of truth which presupposed fiction and was a consequence of it. What Nietzsche had shown, that the ideal of the true was the most profound fiction, at the heart of the real, had not yet been discovered by the cinema. The veracity of the story continued to be grounded in fiction. When the ideal or model of the true was applied to the real, it began to change many things, since the camera was being directed to a pre-existing real, but, in another sense, nothing had changed in the conditions of the story: the objective and the subjective were displaced, not transformed; identities were defined in a different way, but remained defined; the story remained truthful, really-truthful instead of fictionally-truthful. But the veracity of the story had not stopped being a fiction.

The break is not between fiction and reality, but in the new mode of story which affects both of them. A change occurred around the 1960s, in quite independent places, in the direct cinema of Cassavetes and Shirley Clarke, in the 'cinema of the lived' of Pierre Perrault, in the '*cinéma-vérité*' of Jean Rouch. Thus, when Perrault criticizes all fiction, it is in the sense that it forms a model of pre-established truth, which necessarily expresses the dominant ideas or the point of view of the colonizer, even when it is forged by the film's author. Fiction is inseparable from a 'reverence' which presents it as true, in religion, in society, in cinema, in the systems of images. Never has Nietzsche's dictum, 'suppress your reverences', been so well understood as by Perrault. When Perrault is addressing his real characters of Quebec, it is not simply to eliminate fiction but to free it from the model of truth which penetrates it, and on the contrary to rediscover the pure and simple *story-telling function* which is opposed to this model. What is opposed to fiction is not the real; it is not the truth which is always that of the masters or colonizers; it is the story-telling function of the poor, in so far as it gives the false the power which makes it into a memory, a legend, a monster. Hence the white dolphin of *Pour la suite du monde*, the caribou of *Le pays de la terre sans arbres* and above all the luminous beast, the Dionysus of *La bête lumineuse*. What cinema must grasp is not the identity of a character, whether real *or* fictional, through his objective and subjective aspects. It is the becoming of the real character when he himself starts to 'make fiction', when he enters into 'the flagrant offence of making up legends' and so contributes to the invention of his people. The character is inseparable from a before and an after, but he reunites these in the passage from one state to the other. He himself becomes another, when he begins to tell stories without ever being fictional. And the film-maker for his part becomes another when there are 'interposed', in this way, real characters, who wholly replace his own fictions by their own story-telling. Both communicate in the invention of a people. I interposed on behalf of Alexis (*Le règne du jour*), and the whole of Quebec, in order to get to know who I was, 'in such a way that to speak to myself I just have to let them speak'.[31] This is the simulation of a story, the legend and its metamorphosis, free indirect discourse of Quebec, a discourse with a thousand heads 'little by little'. Thus the cinema can call itself *cinéma-vérité*, all the more because it will have destroyed every model of the true so as to become creator and producer of truth: this will not be a cinema of truth but the truth of cinema.

This is the sense intended by Jean Rouch when he spoke of '*cinéma-vérité*'. Just like Perrault, with reporting investigations, Rouch had begun with ethnographic films. The evolution of the two authors would be difficult to explain if we restricted ourselves to pointing out the impossibility of achieving a raw real; everybody has always known that the camera has an active effect on situations, and that characters react to the presence of the camera, and it hardly troubled Flaherty or Leacock, who already saw only false problems in it. In Rouch and Perrault, the novelty has other sources. It begins to be clearly expressed in Rouch in *Les maîtres fous*, when the characters in the ritual, possessed, drunk, foaming and in trances, are first shown in their daily reality where they are waiters, navvies and labourers, as they become again after the ceremony. What they were before . . . Conversely, in *Moi un Noir*, there are real characters who are shown through the roles of their story-telling, Dorothy Lamour the little prostitute, Lemmy Caution the unemployed man from Treichville, even if they themselves then comment on and correct the function that they have released.[32] In *Jaguar*, the three characters, especially the 'gallant', share out roles which they are made to confront like so many legendary powers, by the realities of their journey – the encounter with the fetishists, the organization of work, the making of gold ingots which they lock away and which are useless, the flying visit to the central market, finally the invention of their little business under a title which replaces a ready-made formula with a figure capable of making legends: 'little by little the bird makes his . . . bonnet'. And they will return to their country, like ancestors, full of exploits and lies where the least incident becomes power. There is always passage from one state to another at the heart of the character, as when the hunter baptizes a lion the American, or when the travellers in *Cocorico Monsieur Poulet* encounter the female devil. To restrict ourselves to these masterpieces, we notice in the first place that the character has ceased to be real or fictional, in so far as he has ceased to be seen objectively or to see subjectively: it is a character who goes over crossings and frontiers because he invents as a real character, and becomes all the more real because he has been better at inventing. *Dionysos* is a great synthesis by Rouch: the image of industrial society which brings together a Hungarian mechanic, an Ivory Coast riveter, a West Indian metalworker, a Turkish carpenter, a German woman mechanic, plunges into a before that is Dionysian haunted by the three maenads, the white, the black and the yellow, but this before is also an after, like the post-industrial horizon where one worker has become a flautist, another a tambourine player, cellist, soprano, forming the Dionysian cortège which reaches the forest of Meudon. The 'ciné-trance' and its music are a temporalization of the image which never stays in the present, continually crossing the limit in both directions, all driven by a teacher who turns out to be a forger, nothing but a forger, the power of the false of Dionysus himself. If the real-fictional alternative is so completely surpassed it is because the camera instead of marking out a fictional or real present, constantly reattaches the character to the before and after which constitute a direct time-image. The character must first of all be real if he is to affirm fiction as a power and not as a model: he has to start to tell stories in order to affirm himself all the more as real and not fictional. The character is continually becoming another, and is no longer separable from this becoming which merges with a people.

But what we are saying about the character is also valid in the second place, and in particular, for the film-maker himself. He too becomes another, in so far as he takes real characters as intercessors and replaces his fictions by their own story-telling, but, conversely, gives these story-tellings the shape of legends, carrying out their 'making into legend'. Rouch makes his own free indirect discourse at the same time as his characters make that of Africa. Perrault makes his own free indirect discourse at the sametime as his characters make that of Quebec. There is undoubtedly a big difference in situation between Perrault and Rouch, a difference which is not simply personal but cinemato-graphic and formal. For Perrault, the concern is to belong to his dominated people, and to rediscover a lost and repressed collective identity. For Rouch, it is a matter of getting out of his dominant civilization and reaching the premises of another identity. Hence the possibility of misunderstandings between the two authors. Nevertheless each one as a film-maker sets off with the same slender material, camera on the shoulder and synchronized tape-recorder; they must become others, with their characters, at the same time as their characters must become others themselves. The famous formula, 'what is suitable for the documentary is that one knows who one is and whom one is filming', ceases to be valid. The Ego = Ego form of identity (or its degenerate form, them = them) ceases to be valid for the characters and for the film-maker, in the real as well as in the fiction. What allows itself to be glimpsed instead, by profound degrees, is Rimbaud's 'I is another' [*Je est un entre*]: Godard said this in relation to Rouch; not only for the characters themselves, but for the film-maker who 'white just like Rimbaud, himself declares that *I is another*', that is, *me a black*.[33] When Rimbaud exclaims, 'I am of inferior race for all eternity . . . I am a beast, a negro . . .', it is in the course of passing through a whole series of forgers, 'Merchant you are a negro, magistrate you are a negro, general you are a negro, mangy old emperor you are a negro . . .', up to that highest power of the false which means that a black must himself become black, through his white roles, whilst the white here finds a chance of becoming black too ('I can be saved . . .'). And, for his part, Perrault has no less a need to become another so as to join his own people. This is no longer *Birth of a Nation*, but constitution or reconstitution of a people, where the film-maker and his characters become others together and the one through the other, a collectivity which gradually wins from place to place, from person to person, from intercessor to intercessor. I am a caribou, an original . . . 'I is another' is the formation of a story which simulates, of a simulation of a story or of a story of simulation which deposes the form of the truthful story. Poetry is what Pasolini held up against prose, but which can be found in the place that he did not look for it, in the domain of a cinema presented as direct.[34]

In Shirley Clarke or Cassavetes, an analogous phenomenon occurs, once again with many differences. It is as if the three great themes were turning and forming their combinations; the character is continually passing the frontier between the real and the fictional (the power of the false, the story-telling function), the film-maker has to reach what the character was 'before' and will be 'after'; he has to bring together the before and the after in the incessant passage from one state to the other (the direct time-image); the becoming of the film-maker and of his character already belongs to a people, to a community, to a minority whose expression they practise and set free (free, indirect discourse).

With Shirley Clarke's *The Connexion*, the levels of organization mingle, because the roles of drug-addicts refer to pre-existing characters who themselves refer *alternatively* to their role. And in *A Portrait of Jason* it is the passage which must be grasped in all its possible 'distances', in relation to the character and to his roles, but always internal distances, as if the white camera had slid into the great black forger; the 'I is another' of Shirley Clarke consists in this: that the film that she wanted to make about herself became the one she made about Jason. What has to be filmed is the frontier, on condition that this is equally crossed by the film-maker in one direction and by the real character in the opposite direction: time is necessary here; a certain time is necessary which constitutes an integral part of the film.[35] This is what Cassavetes was already saying in *Shadows* and then *Faces*; what constitutes part of the film is interesting oneself in the people more than in the film, in the 'human problems' more than in the 'problems of *mise-en-scène*', so that the people do not pass over to the side of the camera without the camera having passed over to the side of the people. In *Shadows* it is the two white Negroes who constitute the frontier, and its perpetual crossing in a double reality which is no longer distinguishable from the film. The frontier can be grasped only in flight, when we no longer know where it passes, between the white and the black, but also between the film and the non-film; it is characteristic of film to be always outside its marks, breaking with 'the right distance', always overflowing 'the reserved zone' where we would have liked to hold it in space and time.[36]

We will see how Godard draws a generalized method of the image from this; where something ends, where something else begins, what a frontier is and how to see it, but through crossing and displacing it endlessly. In *Masculin féminin*, the fictional interview with the characters and the real interview with the actors mix together so that they seem to be speaking to each other, and to speak for themselves, by speaking to the film-maker.[37] The method can be developed only where the camera is constantly reaching a before or an after in the characters which constitute the real, at the very point where story-telling is set in motion. 'To know what they were before being placed in the *picture*, and after . . .'[38] *France tour détour deux enfants* already makes use of this as a principle; 'Him before, and the story after, or him after and the story before.' Godard, who has often acknowledged his debt to Rouch, increasingly emphasizes this point: the image has to include the before and the after; it thus has to bring together in this way the conditions of a new, direct time-image, instead of being in the present 'as in bad films'. It is under these conditions of the time-image that the same transformation involves the cinema of fiction and the cinema of reality and blurs their differences; in the same movement, descriptions become pure, purely optical and sound, narrations falsifying and stories, simulations. The whole cinema becomes a free, indirect discourse, operating in reality. The forger and his power, the film-maker and his character, or the reverse, since they only exist through this community which allows them to say 'we, creators of truth'. This is a third time-image, distinct from those we saw in the previous chapter. The two earlier ones essentially concerned the *order of time*, that is, the coexistence of relations or the simultaneity of the elements internal to time. The third concerns the *series of time*, which brings together the before and the after in a becoming, instead of separating them; its paradox is to introduce an enduring interval in the moment itself.[39] The three time-images all break with indirect representation, but also shatter the empirical continuation of time, the chronological succession, the separation of the before and the after. They are thus connected with each other and interpenetrate (Welles, Resnais, Godard, Robbe-Grillet), but allow the distinction of their signs to subsist in a particular work.

7 Thought and cinema

1

Those who first made and thought about cinema began from a simple idea: cinema as industrial art achieves self-movement, automatic movement, it makes movement the immediate given of the image. This kind of movement no longer depends on a moving body or an object which realizes it, nor on a spirit which reconstitutes it. It is the image which itself moves in itself. In this sense, therefore, it is neither figurative nor abstract. It could be said that this was already the case with all artistic images; and Eisenstein constantly analyses the paintings of Da Vinci and El Greco as if they were cinematographic images (as Elie Faure does with Tintoretto). But pictorial images are nevertheless immobile in themselves so that it is the mind which has to 'make' movement. And choreographic or dramatic images remain attached to a moving body. It is only when movement becomes automatic that the artistic essence of the image is realized: *producing a shock to thought, communicating vibrations to the cortex, touching the nervous and cerebral system directly.* Because the cinematographic image itself 'makes' movement, because it makes what the other arts are restricted to demanding (or to saying), it brings together what is essential in the other arts; it inherits it, it is as it were the directions for use of the other images, it converts into potential what was only possibility. *Automatic movement* gives rise to a *spiritual automaton* in us, which reacts in turn on movement.[1] The spiritual automaton no longer designates – as it does in classical philosophy – the logical or abstract possibility of formally deducing thoughts from each other, but the circuit into which they enter with the movement-image, the shared power of what forces thinking and what thinks under the shock; a *nooshock*.[2]* Heidegger said: 'Man can think in the sense that he possesses the possibility to do so. This possibility alone, however, is no guarantee to us that we are capable of thinking.'[3] It is this capacity, this power, and not the simple logical possibility, that cinema claims to give us in communicating the shock. It is as if cinema were telling us: with me, with the movement-image, you can't escape the shock which arouses the thinker in you. A subjective and collective automaton for an automatic movement: the art of the 'masses'.

Everyone knows that, if an art necessarily imposed the shock or vibration, the world would have changed long ago, and men would have been thinking for a long time. So this pretension of the cinema, at least among the greatest pioneers, raises a smile today. They believed that cinema was capable of imposing the shock, and imposing it on the masses, the people (Vertov, Eisenstein, Gance, Elie Faure . . .). However, they foresaw that cinema would encounter and was already encountering all the ambiguities of the other arts; that it would be overlaid with experimental abstractions, 'formalist antics' and commercial configurations of sex and blood. The shock would be confused, in bad cinema, with the figurative violence of the represented instead of achieving that other violence of a movement-image developing its vibrations in a moving sequence which embeds itself within us. Worse still, the spiritual automaton was in danger of becoming the dummy of every kind of propaganda: the art of the masses was already showing a disquieting face.[4] Thus the power or capacity of cinema was in turn revealed to be only a pure and simple logical possibility. At least the possible took on a new form here, even if the people were not yet a match for it, and even if thought was still to come. Something was in play, in a *sublime* conception of cinema. In fact, what constitutes the sublime is that the imagination suffers a shock which pushes it to the limit and forces thought to think the whole as intellectual totality which goes beyond the imagination. The sublime, as we have seen, may be mathematical, as in Gance, or dynamic, as in Murnau and Lang, or dialectical, as in Eisenstein. We will take the example of Eisenstein because the dialectical method allows him to decompose the nooshock into particularly well-determined moments (but the whole of the analysis is valid for classical cinema, the cinema of the movement-image, in general).

According to Eisenstein, the first moment goes from the image to thought, from the percept to the concept. The movement-image (cell) is essentially multiple and divisible in accordance with the objects between which it is established, which are its integral parts. There is shock of images between themselves according to their dominant characteristic, or shock in the image itself depending on its components, and, again, shock of images depending on all their components; the shock is the very form of communication of movement in images. And Eisenstein criticizes

Pudovkin for having retained only the simplest case of shock. *Opposition* defines the general formula, or the violence of the image. We saw earlier Eisenstein's concrete analyses of *Battleship Potemkin* and *The General Line*, and the abstract schema which is revealed: the shock has an effect on the spirit, it forces it to think, and to think the Whole. The Whole can only be thought, because it is the indirect representation of time which follows from movement. It does not follow like a logical effect, analytically, but synthetically as the dynamic effect of images 'on the whole cortex'. Thus it relies on montage, although it follows from the image: it is not a sum, but a 'product', a unity of a higher order. The whole is the organic totality which presents itself by opposing and overcoming its own parts, and which is constructed like the great Spiral in accordance with the laws of dialectic. The whole is the concept. This is why cinema is dubbed 'intellectual cinema', and montage 'thought-montage'. Montage is in thought 'the intellectual process' itself, or that which, under the shock, thinks the shock. Whether it is visual or of sound, the image already has harmonics which accompany the perceived dominant image, and enter in their own ways into suprasensory relations (for example, the saturation of heat in the procession in *The General Line*): this is the shock wave or the nervous vibration, which means that we can no longer say 'I see, I hear', but I FEEL, 'totally physiological sensation'. And it is the set of harmonics acting on the cortex which gives rise to thought, the cinematographic I THINK: the whole as subject. If Eisenstein is a dialectician, it is because he conceives of the violence of the shock in the form of opposition and the thought of the whole in the form of opposition overcome, or of the transformation of opposites: 'From the shock of two factors a concept is born'.[5] This is the cinema of the *punch* – 'Soviet cinema must break heads.' But in this way he dialecticizes the most general given of the movement-image; he thinks that any other conception weakens the shock and leaves thought optional. The cinematographic image must have a shock effect on thought, and force thought to think itself as much as thinking the whole. This is the very definition of the sublime.

But there is a second moment which goes from the concept to the affect, or which returns from thought to the image. It is a matter of giving 'emotional fullness' or 'passion' back to the intellectual process. Not only is the second moment inseparable from the first, but we cannot say which is first. Which is first, montage or movement-image? The whole is produced by the parts but also the opposite: there is a dialectical circle or spiral, 'monism' (which Eisenstein contrasts with Griffith-style dualism). The whole as dynamic effect is also the presupposition of its cause, the spiral. This is why Eisenstein continually reminds us that 'intellectual cinema' has as correlate 'sensory thought' or 'emotional intelligence', and is worthless without it. The organic has as correlate the pathetic. The highest form of consciousness in the work of art has as correlate the deepest form of the subconscious, following a 'double process' or two coexisting moments. In this second moment, we no longer go from the movement-image to the clear thinking of the whole that it expresses; we go from a thinking of the whole which is presupposed and obscure to the agitated, mixed-up images which express it. The whole is no longer the logos which unifies the parts, but the drunkenness, the pathos which bathes them and spreads out in them. From this point of view images constitute a malleable mass, a descriptive material loaded with visual and sound features of expression, synchronized or not, zig-zags of forms, elements of action, gestures and profiles, syntactic sequences. This is a primitive language or thought, or rather an *internal monologue*, a drunken monologue, working through figures, metonymies, synecdoches, metaphors, inversions, attractions . . . From the outset, Eisenstein thought that the internal monologue found its extension and importance in cinema rather than literature, but he still restricted it to the 'course of thought of a man'. It is in the 1935 speech that he discovers it to be appropriate for the spiritual automaton, that is, to the whole film. Internal monologue goes beyond dream, which is much too individual, and constitutes the segments or links of a truly collective thought. He develops a pathos-filled power of imagination which reaches the limits of the universe, an 'orgy of sensory representations', a visual music which is like mass, fountains of cream, fountains of luminous water, spurting fires, zig-zags forming numbers, as in the famous sequence in *The General Line*. Earlier, we went from the shock-image to the formal and conscious concept, but now from the unconscious concept to the material-image, the figure-image which embodies it and produces shock in turn. The figure gives the image an affective charge which will intensify the sensory shock. The two moments are mixed up, interlaced, as in the ascent in *The General Line* where zig-zags of numbers repeat the conscious concept.[6]

Here again it will be noted that Eisenstein dialecticizes a very general aspect of the movement-image and montage. The view that the cinematographic image proceeds through figures, and reconstitutes a kind of primitive thought, is to be found in many authors, notably Epstein. Even when the European cinema restricts itself to dream, fantasy, or day-dreaming, its ambition is to bring the *unconscious mechanisms of thought* to consciousness.[7] It is true that cinema's capacity for metaphor has been called into question. Jakobson noted that cinema is typically metonymic, because it essentially proceeds by juxtaposition and contiguity: it does not have metaphor's specific power of giving a 'subject' the verb or action of another subject; it has to juxtapose the two subjects, and so make the metaphor subject to a metonymy.[8] Cinema cannot say with the poet: 'hands flutter'; it must first show hands being moved about quickly and then leaves fluttering. But this restriction is only partially true. It is true if we compare the cinematographic image to an utterance. It is false if we take the cinematographic image for what it is; movement-image which, as well as dividing movement by connecting it to the objects between which it is established (metonymy which separates images), can *dissolve* movement by connecting it with the whole that it expresses (metaphor which connects images). It thus appears to us correct to say that Griffith's montage is metonymic but Eisenstein's metaphoric.[9] If we talk about fusion, we are not just thinking of superimposition as a technique, but of an affective fusion which is explained, in Eisenstein's terms, because two distinct images can have the same harmonics and so constitute metaphor. Metaphor is defined precisely by the harmonics of the image. We find the example of a metaphor which is authentic to the cinema in Eisenstein's *Strike*: the boss's big spy is first shown the wrong way round, head downwards, his massive legs rising like two tubes which end in a puddle at the top of the screen; then we see the two factory chimneys which seem embedded in a cloud. This is a metaphor with double inversion, since the spy is shown first, and shown upside-down. The puddle and the cloud, the legs and the chimneys have the same harmonics: it is a metaphor through montage. But cinema also achieves metaphors in the image and without montage. In this respect, it is in an American film that we find the finest metaphor in the history of cinema: Keaton's *The Navigator*, where the hero in the life-jacket, strangled, dying, drowning in his life-jacket, is going to be awkwardly saved by the girl. She takes him between her legs to make sure of a grip and finally manages to open the jacket by cutting it, whereupon a flood of water escapes from it. Never has an image rendered so well the violent metaphor of giving birth, by caesarian section and explosion of the amniotic sac.

Eisenstein had a similar idea when he distinguished the different cases of affective composition: the one where nature reflects the hero's state, two images having the same harmonics (for example, a sad nature for a sad hero); the other, more difficult, where a single image captures the harmonics of a different image which is not shown (for example, adultery as 'crime', the lovers having the gestures of a murder victim and a mad assassin).[10] Metaphor is sometimes extrinsic, sometimes intrinsic. But, in both cases, the composition does not simply express the way in which the character experiences himself, but also expresses the way in which the author and the viewer judge him, it integrates thought into the image: what Eisenstein called 'the new sphere of filmic rhetoric, the possibility of bearing an abstract social judgement'. A circuit which includes simultaneously the author, the film and the viewer is elaborated. The complete circuit thus includes the sensory shock which raises us from the images to conscious thought, then the thinking in figures which takes us back to the images and gives us an affective shock again. Making the two coexist, joining the highest degree of consciousness to the deepest level of the unconscious: this is the dialectical automaton. The whole is constantly *open* (the spiral), but so that it can internalize the sequence of images, as well as becoming externalized in this sequence. The whole forms a knowledge, in the Hegelian fashion, which brings together the image and the concept as two movements each of which goes towards the other.

There is still a third moment, equally present in the two previous ones. Not from image to concept, or from concept to image, but the identity of concept and image. The concept is in itself in the image, and the image is for itself in the concept. This is no longer organic and pathetic but dramatic, pragmatic, praxis, or action-thought. This action-thought indicates *the relation between man and the world*, between man and nature, the sensory-motor unity, but by raising it to a supreme power ('monism'). Cinema seems to have a real vocation in this respect. As Bazin said, the cinematographic image contrasts with the theatrical image in that it goes from the outside to the inside, from the setting to the character, from nature to man (even if it begins from human action, it does so as if from an outside, and even if it starts from a human face, it does so as if from a nature or a landscape).[11] It is thus all the more suitable for showing the reaction of man on nature, or the externalization of man. In the sublime there is a sensory-motor unity of nature and man, which means that nature must be named *the non-indifferent*. This is already what effective or metaphoric composition expresses, for example, in *Battleship Potemkin* where three elements, water, earth and air, harmonically reveal an external nature in mourning around the human victim, whilst man's reaction will externalize itself in the development of the fourth element, the fire, which brings a new quality to nature in revolutionary conflagration.[12] But it is also man who passes to a new quality, in becoming the collective subject of his own reaction, whilst nature becomes the objective human relation. Action-thought simultaneously posits the unity of nature and man, of the individual and the mass: cinema as art of the masses. It is for this reason that Eisenstein justifies the primacy of montage: cinema does not have the individual as its subject, nor a plot or history as its object; its object is nature, and its subject the masses, the individuation of mass and not that of a person. What theatre and especially opera had unsuccessfully attempted, cinema achieves (*Battleship Potemkin, October*): to reach the Dividual, that is, to individuate a mass as such, instead of leaving it in a qualitative homogeneity or reducing it to a quantitive divisibility.[13]

It is all the more interesting to note how Eisenstein replies to the criticisms addressed to him by the Stalinists. He is criticized for not capturing the truly dramatic element of action-thought, for presenting the sensory-motor connection in an external and very general way: without showing how it is formed in the character. The criticism is simultaneously ideological, technical and political: Eisenstein goes no further than an idealist conception of nature, which replaces 'history', a dominating conception of montage, which crushes the image or shot, an abstract conception of the masses, which obscures the conscious personal hero. Eisenstein understands extremely well what is at stake here and surrenders to a self-criticism in which prudence and irony play an equal part. This is the great speech of 1935. Yes, he bungled the role of the hero, that is of the party and its leaders, because he remained too external to events, the simple observer or fellow-traveller. But it was the first period of Soviet cinema, before 'the Bolshevization of the masses' which gives rise to personal and conscious heroes. Nor was everything bad in this first period, which makes the following one possible. And the following one would have to keep montage, even if it integrated it better into the image and even into the playing of the actors. Eisenstein was going to concern himself with properly dramatic heroes, *Ivan the Terrible, Alexander Nevsky*, while preserving the earlier achievements, the non-indifference of nature and the individuation of the masses. At the most he could note that the second period had, to date, produced only mediocre works, and that it was in danger, if they were not careful, of losing the specificity of the Soviet cinema. They must avoid the Soviet cinema's coming close to the American, which had specialized in personal heroes and dramatic actions . . .

It is indeed true that the three relationships between cinema and thought are encountered together everywhere in the cinema of the movement-image: *the relationship with a whole which can only be thought in a higher awareness, the relationship with a thought which can only be shaped in the subconscious unfolding of images, the sensory-motor relationship between world and man, nature and thought.* Critical thought, hypnotic thought, action-thought. What Eisenstein criticizes in others, and primarily in Griffith, is having badly understood the whole, because they were content with a diversity of images without reaching the constituent oppositions, having composed figures badly, because they do not achieve true metaphors or harmonics; to have reduced action to a melodrama, because they were content to have a personal hero caught in a psychological rather than a social situation.[14] In short, they lacked dialectical practice and theory. It is still true that American cinema, in its own way, displayed the three fundamental relationships. The action-image could go from the situation to the action, or conversely, from the action to the situation; it was inseparable from acts of comprehension through which the hero evaluated what was given in the problem or situation, or from acts of inference by which he guessed what was not given (thus, as we have seen, the lightning reasoning-images of Lubitsch). And these acts of thought in the image extended in a double direction, relation of the images with a thought whole and with figures of thought. Let us return to an extreme example: if Hitchcock's cinema appeared to us the very culmination of the movement-image, it is because it goes beyond the action-image towards the 'mental relations' which frame it and constitute its linkage, but at the same time returns to the image in accordance with 'natural relations' which make up a framework. From the image to the relation, and from the relation to the image: all the functions of thought are included in this circuit. In accordance with the English genius, this is definitely not a dialectic, it is a logic of relations (which particularly explains the fact that 'suspense' replaces 'shock').[15] There are, therefore, many ways in which cinema can carry its relationships with thought into effect. But these three relationships seem to be well defined at the level of the movement-image.

2

How strangely the great declarations, of Eisenstein, of Gance, ring today; we put them to one side like declarations worthy of a museum, all the hopes put into cinema, art of the masses and new thought. We can always say that cinema has drowned in the nullity of its productions. What becomes of Hitchcock's suspense, Eisenstein's shock and Gance's sublimity when they are taken up by mediocre authors? When the violence is no longer that of the image and its vibrations but that of the represented, we move into a blood-red arbitrariness. When grandeur is no longer that of the composition, but a pure and simple inflation of the represented, there is no cerebral stimulation or birth of thought. It is rather a generalized shortcoming in author and viewers. Nevertheless a current mediocrity has never prevented great painting; but it is not the same in the conditions of an industrial art, where the proportion of disgraceful works calls the most basic goals and capacities directly into question. Cinema is dying, then, from its quantitative   mediocrity. But there is a still more important reason: the mass-art, the treatment of masses, which should not have been separable from an accession of the masses to the status of true subject, has degenerated into state propaganda and manipulation, into a kind of fascism which brought together Hitler and Hollywood, Hollywood and Hitler. The spiritual automaton became fascist man. As Serge Daney says, what has brought the whole cinema of the movement-image into question are 'the great political *mises-en-scène*, state propaganda turned *tableaux vivants*, the first handlings of masses of humans', and their backdrop, the camps.[16] This was the death-knell for the ambitions of 'the old cinema': not, or not only, the mediocrity and vulgarity of current production but rather Leni Riefenstahl, who was not mediocre.

And the situation is still worse if we accept Virilio's thesis: there has been no diversion or alienation in an art of the masses initially founded by the movement-image; on the contrary the movement-image was from the beginning linked to the organization of war, state propaganda, ordinary fascism, historically and essentially.[17] These two joint reasons, mediocrity of products and fascism of production, can explain a great many things. For a brief moment, Artaud 'believes' in cinema, and makes a number of declarations which seen to coincide with those of Eisenstein or Gance; new art, new thought. But he very quickly renounces it. 'The imbecile world of images caught as if by glue in millions of retinas will never perfect the image that has been made of it. The poetry which can emerge from it all is only a possible poetry, the poetry of what might be, and it is not from cinema that we should expect . . .'[18]

Perhaps there is a third reason, oddly capable of restoring hope in a possibility of thinking in cinema through cinema. We must study the case of Artaud more closely, because it may well be of crucial importance. For, during the brief period that he believed, Artaud seems at first sight to take up the great themes of the movement-image in its relations with thought. He says specifically that cinema must avoid two pitfalls, abstract experimental cinema, which was developing at the time, and commercial figurative cinema, which Hollywood was imposing. He says that cinema is a matter of neuro-physiological vibrations, and that the image must produce a shock, a nerve-wave which gives rise to thought, 'for thought is a matron who has not always existed'. Thought has no other reason to function than its own birth, always the repetition of its own birth, secret and profound. He says that the image thus has as object the functioning of thought, and that the functioning of thought is also the real subject which brings us back to the images. He adds that the dream as it appears in the European cinema inspired by surrealism, is an interesting approximation, but inadequate in relation to this goal: the dream is too easy a solution to the 'problem' of thought. Artaud believes more in an appropriateness between cinema and *automatic writing*, as long as we understand that automatic writing is not at all an absence of composition, but a higher control which brings together critical and conscious thought and the unconscious in thought: the spiritual automaton (which is very different from the dream, which brings together a censure or repression with an unconscious made up of impulses). He adds that his point of view is much ahead of its time and is in danger of being misunderstood, even by the surrealists, to which his relations with Germaine Dulac testify, as she goes back and forth from an abstract cinema to a dream-cinema.[19]

At first sight, there is nothing to bring these declarations of Artaud into conflict with those of Eisenstein: from the image to thought there is shock or vibration, which must give rise to thought in thought; from thought to the image, there is the figure which must be realized in a kind of internal monologue (rather than in a dream), capable of giving us the shock again. And yet there is something quite different in Artaud: a recognition of powerlessness, which does not yet have a bearing *on* cinema, but on the contrary defines the real object-subject of cinema. What cinema advances is not the power of thought but its 'impower',[20]* and thought has never had any other problem. It is precisely this which is much more important than the dream: this difficulty of being, this powerlessness at the heart of thought. What the enemies of cinema criticized it for (like Georges Duhamel, 'I can no longer think what I want, the moving images are substituted for my own thoughts'), is just what Artaud makes into the dark glory and profundity of cinema. In fact, the problem for him is not of a simple inhibition that the cinema would bring to us from the outside, but of this central inhibition, of this internal collapse and fossilization, of this 'theft of thoughts' of which thought is a constant agent and victim. Artaud would stop believing in the cinema when he considered that cinema was sidetracking and could produce only the abstract or the figurative or the dream. But he believes in the cinema as long as he considers that cinema is essentially suited to reveal this powerlessness to think at the heart of thought. If we consider Artaud's actual scripts, the vampire in *32*, the madman in *La révolte du boucher*, and especially the suicide case in *Dix-huit secondes*, the hero 'has become incapable of achieving his thoughts', 'he is reduced to only seeing a parade of images within him, an excess of contradictory images', his 'spirit has been stolen'. The spiritual or mental automaton is no longer defined by the logical possibility of a thought which would formally deduce his ideas from each other.[21] But no more through the physical power of a thought that would be placed in a circuit with the automatic image. The spiritual automaton has become the Mummy, this dismantled, paralysed, petrified, frozen instance which testifies to 'the impossibility of thinking that is thought'.[22] It could be said that expressionism had already made us familiar with all this, theft of thoughts, splitting in two of personality, hypnotic petrification, hallucination, raging schizophrenia. But, here again, we are in danger of misconstruing Artaud's originality: it is no longer thought which confronts repression, the unconscious, dream, sexuality or death, as in expressionism (and also in surrealism), it is all these determinations which confront thought as higher 'problem', or which enter into relation with the undeterminable, the unreferable.[23] The navel, or the Mummy, is no longer the irreducible core of the dream which thought comes up against, on the contrary, it is the core of thought, 'the reverse side of thoughts', which itself is what dreams come up against and rebound, break. Whilst expressionism makes wakefulness pass through a nocturnal treatment, Artaud *makes dream pass through a diurnal treatment*. Artaud's vigilambulist, in *Dix-huit secondes* or *La coquille et le clergyman* is the opposite of the expressionist somnambulist.

In spite of a superficial similarity of words, there is, therefore, an absolute opposition between Artaud's project and a conception such as Eisenstein's. It is indeed a matter, as Artaud puts it, 'of bringing cinema together with the innermost reality of the brain', but this innermost reality is not the Whole, but on the contrary a fissure, a crack.[24] As long as he believes in cinema, he credits it, not with the power of making us think the whole, but on the contrary with a 'dissociative force' which would introduce a 'figure of nothingness', a 'hole in appearances'. As long as he believes in cinema, he credits it, not with the power of returning to images, and linking them according to the demands of an internal monologue and the rhythm of metaphors, but of 'un-linking' them, according to multiple voices, internal dialogues, always a voice in another voice. In short, it is the totality of cinema-thought relations that Artaud overturns: on the one hand there is no longer a whole thinkable through montage, on the other hand there is no longer an internal monologue utterable through image. It might be said that Artaud turns round Eisenstein's argument: if it is true that thought depends on a shock which gives birth to it (the nerve, the brain matter), it can only think one thing, *the fact that we are not yet thinking*, the powerlessness to think the whole and to think oneself, thought which is always fossilized, dislocated, collapsed. A being of thought which is always to come is what Heidegger discovered in a universal form, but it is what Artaud lived as the most singular problem, his own problem.[25] Between Heidegger and Artaud,

Maurice Blanchot was able to give the fundamental question of what makes us think, what forces us to think, back to Artaud: what forces us to think is 'the inpower [*impouvoir*] of thought', the figure of nothingness, the inexistence of a whole which could be thought. What Blanchot diagnoses everywhere in literature is particularly clear in cinema: on the one hand the presence of an unthinkable in thought, which would be both its source and barrier; on the other hand the presence to infinity of another thinker in the thinker, who shatters every monologue of a thinking self.

But the question is: in what respect does all this essentially concern the cinema? It is perhaps the question for literature, or philosophy, or even psychiatry. But in what respect is it the question for the cinema; that is, a question that touches on its specificity, on its difference from other disciplines? The cinema does not in fact deal with this question in the same way, although it is encountered elsewhere with other means of expression. By what means does cinema approach this question of thought, its fundamental powerlessness and the consequences of this? It is true that bad cinema (and sometimes good) limits itself to a dream state induced in the viewer, or – as has been the subject of frequent analysis – to an imaginary participation. But the essence of cinema – which is not the majority of films – has thought as its higher purpose, nothing but thought and its functioning. In this regard, the strength of Jean-Louis Schefer's book is in having replied to the question: in what respect and how is cinema concerned with a thought whose essential character is not yet to be? He says that the cinematographic image, as soon as it takes on its aberration of movement, carries out a *suspension of the world* or affects the visible with a *disturbance*, which, far from making thought visible, as Eisenstein wanted, are on the contrary directed to what does not let itself be thought in thought, and equally to what does not let itself be seen in vision. This is perhaps not 'crime', as he believes, but simply the power of the false. He says that thought, in cinema, is brought face to face with its own impossibility, and yet draws from this a higher power of birth. He adds that the condition of cinema has only one equivalent, not imaginary participation but the rain when you leave the auditorium; not dream, but the blackness and insomnia. Schefer is close to Artaud. His conception of cinema now finds a complete match in the work of Garrel: the dancing grains which are not made to be seen, the luminous dust which is not a prefiguration of bodies, the flakes of snow and blankets of soot.[26] Provided that we can show persuasively that such works, far from being boring or abstract, represent the most entertaining, lively and disquieting things that can be done in cinema. As well as the great scene with the mill and the white flour piling up, at the end of Dreyer's *Vampyr*, Schefer proposes the example of the beginning of Kurosawa's *Cobweb Castle* (Macbeth): the grey, the steam and the mist constitute 'a whole this side of the image', which is not a blurred veil put in front of things, but 'a thought, without body and without image'. This was also the case with Welles's *Macbeth*, where the indiscernibility of earth and water, sky and land, good and evil constituted a 'prehistory of consciousness' (Bazin) which produced the thought of its own impossibility. Was this not already the mists of Odessa, despite Eisenstein's intentions? According to Schefer, it is the suspension of the world, rather than movement, which gives the visible to thought, not as its object, but as an act which is constantly arising and being revealed in thought: 'not that it is here a matter of thought become visible, the visible is affected and irremediably infected by the initial incoherence of thought, this inchoate quality'. This is the description of *the ordinary man in cinema*: the spiritual automaton, 'mechanical man', 'experimental dummy', Cartesian diver in us, unknown body which we have only at the back of our heads whose age is neither ours nor that of our childhood, but a little time in the pure state.

If this experience of thought essentially (but not exclusively) concerns modern cinema, it is first as a result of the change which affects the image: the image has ceased to be sensory-motor. If Artaud is a forerunner, from a specifically cinematographic perspective, it is because he points to 'real psychic situations between which trapped thought looks for a subtle way out', *'purely visual situations* whose drama would flow from a knock made for the eyes, drawn out, if we may put it this way, in the very substance of the gaze'.[27] Now this sensory-motor break finds its condition at a higher level and itself comes back to a break in the link between man and the world. The sensory-motor break makes man a seer who finds himself struck by something intolerable in the world, and confronted by something unthinkable in thought. Between the two, thought undergoes a strange fossilization, which is as it were its powerlessness to function, to be, its dispossession of itself and the world. For it is not in the name of a better or truer world that thought captures the intolerable in this world, but, on the contrary, it is because this world is intolerable that it can no longer think a world or think itself. The intolerable is no longer a serious injustice, but the permanent state of a daily banality. Man *is not himself* a world other than the one in which he experiences the intolerable and feels himself trapped. The spiritual automaton is in the psychic situation of the seer, who sees better and further than he can react, that is, think. Which, then, is the subtle way out? To believe, not in a different world, but in a link between man and the world, in love or life, to believe in this as in the impossible, the unthinkable, which none the less cannot but be thought: 'something possible, otherwise I will suffocate'. It is this belief that makes the unthought the specific power of thought, through the absurd, by virtue of the absurd. Artaud never understood powerlessness to think as a simple inferiority which would strike us in relation to thought. It is part of thought, so that we should make our way of thinking from it, without claiming to be restoring an all-powerful thought. We should rather make use of this powerlessness to believe in life, and to discover the identity of thought and life: 'I think of life, all the systems that I shall be able to build will never match my cries of a man engaged in remaking his life . . . ' Was there in Artaud an affinity with Dreyer? Was Dreyer an Artaud to whom reason would have been 'restored', once again by virtue of the absurd? Drouzy has noted Dreyer's great psychic crisis, his schizophrenic journey.[28] But, even more to the point, Véronique Tacquin has been able to show how the mummy (the spiritual automaton) haunts his last films. This was already true of *Vampyr*, where the mummy appeared as the diabolic force of the world, the Vampire itself, but also as the uncertain hero, who does not know what to think and dreams his own fossilization. In *Ordet*, the mummy has become thought itself, the young, dead, cataleptic woman: it is the madman of the family who restores her to life and love, precisely because he has ceased to be mad, that is, to believe *himself* to be another world, and because he now knows what believing means . . . *Gertrud* finally develops all the implications and the new relation between cinema and thought: the 'psychic' situation which replaces all sensory-motor situations; the perpetual break of the link with the world, the perpetual hole in appearances, embodied in false continuity; the grasping of the intolerable even in the everyday and insignificant (the long scene in tracking shot that Gertrud will not be able to bear, the schoolboys coming rhythmically along, like robots, to thank the poet for having taught them love and freedom); the encounter with the unthinkable which cannot even be spoken, but sung, to the point of Gertrud's passing-out; the fossilization, the 'mummifying' of the heroine, who becomes conscious of belief as thought of the unthinkable ('Have I been young? No but I have loved. Have I been beautiful? No but I have loved. Have I been in life? No but I have loved.'). In all these respects, *Gertrud* inaugurates a new cinema, whose sequel will be Rossellini's *Europe 51*. Rossellini expresses his position in relation to this: the less human the world is, the more it is the artist's duty to believe and produce belief in a relation between man and the world, because the world is made by men.[29] The heroine of *Europe 51*, a mummy radiating tenderness.

It is clear from the outset that cinema had a special relationship with belief. There is a Catholic quality to cinema (there are many explicitly Catholic authors, even in America, and those who are not have complex relationships with Catholicism). Is there not in Catholicism a grand *mise-en-scène*, but also, in the cinema, a cult which takes over the circuit of the cathedrals, as Elie Faure said?[30] Cinema seems wholly within Nietzsche's formula: 'How we are still pious.' Or better, from the outset, Christianity and revolution, the Christian faith and revolutionary faith, were the two poles which attracted the art of the masses. For the cinematographic image, in contrast to the theatre, showed us the link between the man and the world. Hence it developed either in the direction of a transformation of the world by man, or in the discovery of an internal and higher world that man himself was . . . It cannot be said today that these two poles of cinema have become weakened: a certain Catholic quality has continued to inspire a great number of authors, and revolutionary passion has passed into third world cinema. What has changed is, however, the crucial point, and there is as much difference between the Catholicism of Rossellini or Bresson, and that of Ford, as between the revolutionary qualities of Rocha or Güney, and those of Eisenstein.

The modern fact is that we no longer believe in this world. We do not even believe in the events which happen to us, love, death, as if they only half concerned us. It is not we who make cinema; it is the world which looks to us like a bad film. Godard said, about *Bande à part*: 'These are people who are real and it's the world that is a breakaway group. It is the world that is making cinema for itself. It is the world that is out of synch; they are right, they are true, they represent life. They live a simple story; it is the world around them which is living a bad script.'[31] The link between man and the world is broken. Henceforth, this link must become an object of belief: it is the impossible which can only be restored within a faith. Belief is no longer addressed to a different or transformed world. Man is in the world as if in a pure optical and sound situation. The reaction of which man has been dispossessed can be replaced only by belief. Only belief in the world can reconnect man to what he sees and hears. The cinema must film, not the world, but belief in this world, our only link. The nature of the cinematographic illusion has often been considered. Restoring our belief in the world – this is the power of modern cinema (when it stops being bad). Whether we are Christians or atheists, in our universal schizophrenia, *we need reasons to believe in this world.* It is a whole transformation of belief. It was already a great turning-point in philosophy, from Pascal to Nietzsche: to replace the model of knowledge with belief.[32] But belief replaces knowledge only when it becomes belief in this world, as it is. With Dreyer, then Rossellini, cinema takes the same turn. In his last works, Rossellini loses interest in art, which he reproaches for being infantile and sorrowful, for revelling in a loss of world: he wants to replace it with a morality which would restore a belief capable of perpetuating life. Rossellini undoubtedly still retains the ideal of knowledge, he will never abandon this Socratic ideal, but he does need to establish it in a belief in simple faith in man and the world. What made *Joan of Arc at the Stake* a misunderstood work? The fact that Joan of Arc needs to be in the sky to believe in the tatters of this world.[33] It is from the height of eternity that she can believe in this world. There is a return of Christian belief in Rossellini, which is the highest paradox. Belief, even in the case of holy characters, Mary, Joseph and the Child, is quite prepared to go over to the side of the atheist. In Godard, the ideal of knowledge, the Socratic ideal which is still present in Rossellini, collapses: the 'good' discourse, of the militant, the revolutionary, the feminist, the philosopher, the film-maker, etc., gets no better treatment than the bad.[34] Because the point is to discover and restore belief in the world, before or beyond words. Is it enough to go to live in the sky, be it the sky of art and painting, to find reasons to believe (*Passion*)? Or shouldn't we invent a 'medium level' between earth and sky (*First Name Carmen*)?[35] What is certain is that believing is no longer believing in another world, or in a transformed world. It is only, it is simply believing in the body. It is giving discourse to the body, and, for this purpose, reaching the body before discourses, before words, before things are named: the 'first name', and even before the first name.[36] Artaud said the same thing, believe in the *flesh*: 'I am a man who has lost his life and is searching by all means possible to make it regain its place.' Godard foreshadows *Hail Mary*: what did Joseph and Mary say to each other, what did they say to each other *before*? Give words back to the body, to the flesh. In this respect, the influence between Godard and Garrel is exchanged or reversed. The only object of Garrel's work has been making use of Mary, Joseph and the Child to believe in the body. When Garrel is compared to Artaud, or Rimbaud, there is something true that goes beyond a simple generality. Our belief can have no object but 'the flesh', we need very special reasons to make us believe in the body ('the Angels do not know, for all true knowledge is obscure . . . '). We must believe in the body, but as in the germ of life, the seed which splits open the paving-stones, which has been preserved and lives on in the holy shroud or the mummy's bandages, and which bears witness to life, in this world as it is. We need an ethic or a faith, which makes fools laugh; it is not a need to believe in something else, but a need to believe in this world, of which fools are a part.

3

This is the first aspect of the new cinema: the break in the sensory-motor link (action-image), and more profoundly in the link between man and the world (great organic composition). The second aspect is the abandoning of figures, metonymy as much as metaphor, and at a deeper level the dislocation of the internal monologue as descriptive material of the cinema. For example, in regard to depth of field as introduced by Renoir and Welles, it has been noted that this opened up a new direction for the cinema, no longer metaphorically or even metonymically 'figurative', but more demanding, more constraining, in some sense *theorematic*. This is what Astruc says: depth of field has the physical effect of a snow-plough; it makes characters enter and leave beneath the camera, or at the back of the scene, and not now back and forth; but it also has a mental effect of a theorem, it makes the unrolling of the film a theorem rather than an association of images, it makes thought immanent to the image.[37] Astruc himself learnt Welles's lesson: the camera-pen gives up metaphor and metonymy of montage, it writes with camera-movements, high-angle shots, low-angle shots, back-shots, it carries out a construction (*The Crimson Curtain*). There is now no room for metaphor, there is not even any metonymy, because the necessity which belongs to relations of thought in the image has replaced the contiguity of relations of images (shot-reverse shot). The author who became most committed to this theorematic direction, even independently of depth of field, was Pasolini: undoubtedly in all his work but in particular in *Theorem* and *Salo*, which present themselves as geometrical demonstrations in action (the Sadean inspiration in *Salo* comes from the fact that, already in Sade, unbearable corporeal figures are strictly subordinated to the progress of a demonstration). *Theorem* and *Salo* aspire to have the paths of its own *necessity* follow on from thought, and to carry the image to the point where it becomes deductive and automatic, to substitute the formal linkages of thought for sensory-motor representative or figurative linkages. Is it possible that cinema achieves a truly mathematical rigour in this way, a rigour which no longer simply concerns the image (as in the old cinema which already subjected this to metrical and harmonic relations), but the thought of the image, the thought in the image? Cinema of cruelty, of which Artaud said that it 'does not tell a story but develops a sequence of spiritual states which are deduced from one another as thought is deduced from thought'.[38]

Nevertheless, is this not the direction expressly rejected by Artaud, the conception that he challenged of the spiritual automaton as linking thoughts over which it would have formal power, in a model of knowledge? We should perhaps understand something else, in Pasolini's work as well as in Artaud's projects. In fact, there are two mathematical instances which constantly refer to each other, one enveloping the second, the second sliding into the first, but both very different in spite of their union: these are the theorem and the problem. A problem lives in the theorem, and gives it life, even when removing its power. The problematic is distinguished from the theorematic (or constructivism from the axiomatic) in that the theorem develops internal relationships from principle to consequences, while the problem introduces an event from the outside – removal, addition, cutting – which constitutes its own conditions and determines the 'case' or cases: hence the ellipse, hyperbola, parabola, straight lines and the point are cases of projection of the circle on its secant planes, in relation to the apex of a cone. This outside of the problem is not reducible to the exteriority of the physical world any more than to the psychological interiority of a thinking ego. Astruc's *The Crimson Curtain* already introduces an unfathomable problem rather than a theorem: what is the young girl's case? What has happened for the silent young girl to sacrifice herself, and not even explain the love-sickness which is killing her? There is a decision on which everything depends, deeper than all the explanations that can be given for it. (Likewise the woman-traitor in Godard: there is something in her decision which goes beyond the simple desire to show herself that she is not in love). As Kierkegaard says, 'the profound movements of the soul disarm psychology', precisely because they do not come from within. An author's strength is measured by the way he is able to impose this problematic, uncertain and yet non-arbitrary point: grace or chance. It is in this sense that Pasolini's deduction in *Theorem* must be understood: a problematic rather than a theorematic deduction. The envoy from outside is the instance on the basis of which each member of the family experiences a decisive event or affect, constituting one case of the problem, or the section of a hyper-spatial figure. Each case, each section will be considered as a mummy, the paralysed girl, the mother fixed in her erotic quest, the blindfolded son urinating on his painter's canvas, the maid a victim of a mystical levitation, the animalized, naturalized father. What gives them life is being the projections of an outside which makes them pass into each other, like conical projections or metamorphoses. In *Salo*, on the contrary, there is no longer a problem because there is no outside: Pasolini presents, not even fascism *in vivo*, but fascism at bay, shut away in the little town, reduced to a pure interiority, coinciding with the conditions of closure in which Sade's demonstrations took place. *Salo* is a pure, dead theorem, a theorem of death, as Pasolini wanted, while *Theorem* is a living problem. Hence Pasolini's insistence, in *Theorem*, on invoking a problem towards which everything converges, as towards the always extrinsic point of thought, the uncertain point, the leitmotif of the film: 'I am haunted by a question to which I cannot reply.' Far from restoring knowledge, or the internal certainty that it lacks, to thought, the problematic deduction puts the unthought into thought, because it takes away all its interiority tò excavate an outside in it, an irreducible reverse-side, which consumes its substance.[39] Thought finds itself taken over by the exteriority of a 'belief', outside any interiority of a mode of knowledge. Was this Pasolini's way of still being

Catholic? Was it on the contrary his way of being a radical atheist?
Has he not, like Nietzsche, torn belief from every faith in order to
give it back to rigorous thought?

If the problem is defined by a point of the outside we can better
understand the two values that the sequence shot can take on –
depth (Welles, Mizoguchi) or planitude (Dreyer and often
Kurosawa). Thus the apex of the cone: when it is occupied by the
eye, we find ourselves in front of flat projections or clear outlines
to which light is subordinate; but when it is occupied by the light
source itself, we are in the presence of volumes, reliefs, chiaroscu-
ros, concavities and convexities which subordinate the viewpoint
in a high-angle or low-angle shot. It is in this sense that Welles's
expanses of shadow contrast with Dreyer's frontal perspectives
(even if the Dreyer of *Gertrud* or the Rohmer of *Perceval le Gallois*
succeed in giving a curvature to flattened space). But what both
share is the position of an outside as instance which creates the
problem: the depth of the image has become the pure viewpoint
in Dreyer. In both cases, 'focusing' has jumped out of the image.
What has been broken is the sensory-motor space which had its
own focuses and drew paths and obstacles between them.[40] A
problem is not an obstacle. When Kurosawa takes up Dostoevsky's method, he shows us characters constantly seeking the
givens of a 'problem' which is even deeper than the situation in
which they find themselves caught: in this way he goes beyond the
limits of knowledge, but also the conditions of action. He reaches
a purely optical world, where the thing to be is a seer, a perfect
'Idiot'. Welles's depth is of the same type, and is not situated in
relation to obstacles or concealed things, but in relation to a light
which makes us see beings and objects according to their opacity.
Just as clairvoyance replaces sight, 'lux' replaces 'lumen'. In a text
which is relevant not only to Dreyer's flat image but Welles's
depth, Daney writes: 'The question about this scenography is no
longer: what is there to see behind? But rather: can I hold my
gaze on what I am seeing anyway? And which is unfolding in a
single shot?'[41] What I am seeing anyway is the formula of the
unendurable. It expresses a new relation between thought and
seeing, or between thought and the light source, which constantly
sets the thought outside itself, outside knowledge, outside action.

It is characteristic of the problem that it is inseparable from a
choice. In mathematics, cutting a straight line into two equal parts
is a problem, because it may be cut into unequal parts; setting an
equilateral triangle in a circle is a problem, whilst setting a right

angle in a semicircle is a theorem, every angle in the semicircle being a right angle. Now when the problem concerns existential determinations and not mathematical matters, we see clearly that choice is increasingly identified with living thought, and with an unfathomable decision. Choice no longer concerns a particular term, but the mode of existence of the one who chooses. This was already the sense of Pascal's wager: the problem was not that of choosing between the existence or non-existence of God, but between the mode of existence of the one who believes in God, and the mode of existence of the one who does not. Again a greater number of modes of existence were in play: there was the person who saw the existence of God like a theorem (the devout person), there was the one who did not know how to or was unable to choose (the uncertain, the sceptic . . .). In short, choice covered as great an area as thought, because it went from non-choice to choice, and was itself formed between choosing and not choosing. Kierkegaard drew all the consequences of this: choice being posed between choice and non-choice (and all their variants) sends us back to an absolute relation with the outside, beyond the inward psychological consciousness, but equally beyond the relative external world, and finds that it alone is capable of restoring the world and the ego to us. We have seen how a cinema of Christian inspiration was not content to apply these conceptions but revealed them as the highest theme of the film, in Dreyer, Bresson, or Rohmer: the identity of thought with choice as determination of the indeterminable. *Gertrud* herself passes through all the states, between her father who said that we do not make choices in life and her boyfriend who is writing a book about choice. The formidable man of good or the devout person (he for whom there is no question of choosing), the uncertain or indifferent (he who does not know how to, or is unable to choose), the terrible man of evil (he who chooses a first time, but can then no longer choose, can no longer repeat his own choice), finally the man of choice or belief (he who chooses choice or reiterates it): this is a cinema of modes of existence, of confrontation of these modes, and of their relation to an outside on which both the world and the ego depend. This point of the outside, is it grace, or chance? For his part, Rohmer takes up the Kierkegaardian stages 'on the path of life': the aesthetic stage in *La Collectionneuse*, the ethical stage in *Beau marriage*, for example, and the religious stage in *My Night at Maud's*, or especially in *Perceval le Gallois*.[42] Dreyer had himself run through the different stages of the devout person's over-certainty, the mystic's mad certainty and the aesthete's uncertainty, as far as the simple belief of the one who chooses to choose (and restores the world and life). Bresson rediscovered Pascal's emphases, to show the man of good, the man of evil, the uncertain, but also the man of grace or awareness of choice (the relation with outside, 'the wind blows where it will'). And in all three cases, it is not simply a question of a film-content: it is cinema-form, according to these authors, which is capable of revealing to us this higher determination of thought, choice, this point deeper than any link with the world. Thus Dreyer only secures the reign of the flat image cut off from the world; Bresson the reign of the disconnected and fragmented image, and Rohmer that of a crystalline or miniaturized image, in order to reach the fourth or fifth dimension, the Spirit, he who blows where he will. In Dreyer, in Bresson and in Rohmer, in three different ways, this is a cinema of the spirit which does not fail to be more concrete, more fascinating and more amusing than any other (cf. Dreyer's comic aspect).

It is cinema's automatic character which gives it this capacity – in contrast to the theatre. The automatic image demands a new conception of the role or of the actor but also of thought itself. Only he who is chosen chooses well or effectively: this could be one of Rohmer's proverbs, but equally a subtitle of Bresson's or an epigraph of Dreyer's. What constitutes the whole is the relation between automatism, the unthought and thought. Dreyer's mummy was cut off from an over-rigid, over-burdensome, or over-superficial external world: she was none the less permeated by feelings, by an over-fullness of feeling, which she neither could nor should outwardly express, but which would be revealed in consequence of the deeper outside.[43] In Rohmer, the mummy gives way to a marionette, at the same time as feelings give way to an obsessive 'idea', which will inspire it from the outside: even if it means abandoning it to return it to the void. With Bresson, a third state appears, where the automaton is pure, as bereft of ideas as of feelings, reduced to the automatism of segmented daily gestures, but endowed with autonomy: this is what Bresson calls the 'model' peculiar to cinema, the authentic Vigilambulist, in contrast to the theatre actor. And it is precisely the automaton, petrified in this way, that thought seizes from the outside, as the unthinkable in thought.[44] This question is very different from that of distancing; it is the question of properly cinematographic automatism, and its consequences. It is the material automatism of images which produces from the outside a thought which it imposes, as the unthinkable in our intellectual automatism.

The automaton is cut off from the outside world, but there is a more profound outside which will animate it. The first consequence is a new status of the Whole in modern cinema. Nevertheless, there does not seem to be a great difference between what we are saying now, *the whole is the outside*, and what we were saying about classical cinema, *the whole was the open*. But the open merged with the indirect representation of time: everywhere where there was movement, there was a changing whole open somewhere, in time. This was why the cinematographic image essentially had an out-of-field which referred on the one hand to an external world which was actualizable in other images, on the other hand to a changing whole which was expressed in the set of associated images. Even false continuity could be introduced, and prefigure the modern cinema; but it seemed to constitute a mere anomaly of movement or an association-disorder, which showed the indirect action of the whole on the parts of the set. We have examined these aspects. The whole was thus being continually made, in cinema, by internalizing the images and externalizing itself in the images, following a double attraction. This was the process of an always open totalization, which defined montage or the power of thought. When we say 'the whole is the outside', the point is quite different. In the first place, the question is no longer that of the association or attraction of images. What counts is on the contrary the *interstice* between images, between two images: a spacing which means that each image is plucked from the void and falls back into it.[45] Godard's strength is not just in using this mode of construction in all his work (constructivism) but in making it a method which cinema must ponder at the same time as it uses it. *Ici et ailleurs* marks a first peak in this reflection, which is afterwards transferred to television in *Six fois deux*. It can, in fact, always be objected that there is only an interstice between associated images. From this point of view, images like those which bring together Golda Meir and Hitler in *Ici et ailleurs* would be intolerable. But this is perhaps proof that we are not yet ready for a true 'reading' of the visual image. For, in Godard's method, it is not a question of association. Given one image, another image has to be chosen which will induce an interstice *between* the two. This is not an operation of association, but of differentiation, as mathematicians say, or of disappearance, as physicists say: given one potential, another one has to be chosen, not any whatever, but in such a way that a difference of potential is established between the two, which will be productive of a third or of something new. *Ici et ailleurs* chooses the French couple who enter into disparity with the group of fedayeen. In other words, the interstice is primary in relation to association, or irreducible difference allows resemblances to be graded. The fissure has become primary, and as such grows larger. It is not a matter of following a chain of images, even across voids, but of getting out of the chain or the association. Film ceases to be 'images in a chain ... an uninterrupted chain of images each one the slave of the next', and whose slave we are (*Ici et ailleurs*). It is the method of BETWEEN, 'between two images', which does away with all cinema of the One. It is the method of AND, 'this and then that', which does away with all the cinema of Being = is. Between two actions, between two affections, between two perceptions, between two visual images, between two sound images, between the sound and the visual: make the indiscernible, that is the frontier, visible (*Six fois deux*). The whole undergoes a mutation, because it has ceased to be the One-Being, in order to become the constitutive 'and' of things, the constitutive between-two of images. The whole thus merges with that Blanchot calls the force of 'dispersal of the Outside', or 'the vertigo of spacing': that void which is no longer a motor-part of the image, and which the image would cross in order to continue, but is the radical calling into question of the image (just as there is a silence which is no longer the motor-part or the breathing-space of discourse but its radical calling into question).[46] False continuity, then, takes on a new meaning, at the same time as it becomes the law.

Just as the image is itself cut off from the outside world, the out-of-field in turn undergoes a transformation. When cinema became talkie, the out-of-field seems to have initially found a confirmation of its two aspects: first, noises and voices could have a source external to the visual image; secondly, a voice or a piece of music could show the changing whole, behind or beyond the visual image. Hence the notion of 'voice-off' as sound expression of the out-of-field. But if we ask in what conditions cinema draws out the consequences of the talkie, and so becomes truly talking, everything is inverted: this is when the sound itself becomes the object of a specific framing which *imposes an interstice* with the visual framing. The notion of voice-off tends to disappear in favour of a difference between what is seen and what is heard, and this difference is constitutive of the image. There is no more out-of-field. The outside of the image is replaced by the interstice between the two frames in the image (here again Bresson was a pioneer).[47] Godard draws all the consequences from this when he declares that mixing ousts montage, it being understood that mixing does not just consist of a distribution of the different sound elements, but the allocation of their differential relations with the visual elements. Interstices thus proliferate everywhere, in the visual image, in the sound image, between the sound image and the visual image. That is not to say that the discontinuous prevails over the continuous. On the contrary, the cuts or breaks in cinema have always formed the power of the continuous. But cinema and mathematics are the same here: sometimes the cut, so-called *rational*, forms part of one of the two sets which it separates (end of one or beginning of the other). This is the case with 'classical' cinema. Sometimes, as in modern cinema, the cut has become the interstice, *it is irrational and does not form part of either set, one of which has no more an end than the other has a beginning*: false continuity is such an irrational cut.[48] Thus, in Godard, the interaction of two images engenders or traces a frontier which belongs to neither one nor the other.

Epstein had already demonstrated that the continuous and the discontinuous were never opposed to each other in the cinema. What are opposed, or at least distinguished, are rather two ways of reconciling them, according to the transformation of the Whole. It is here that montage comes into its own. As long as the whole is the indirect representation of time, the continuous is reconciled with the discontinuous in the form of rational points and according to commensurable relations (Eisenstein explicitly found their mathematical theory in the golden section). But, when the whole becomes the power of the outside which passes into the interstice, then it is the direct presentation of time, or the continuity which is reconciled with the sequence of irrational points, according to non-chronological time relationships. It is in this sense that, already in Welles, then in Resnais, and also in Godard, montage takes on a new sense, determining relations in the direct time-image, and reconciling the cut-up with the sequence shot. We have seen that the power of thought gave way, then, to an unthought in thought, to an irrational proper to thought, a point of outside beyond the outside world, but capable of restoring our belief in the world. The question is no longer: does cinema give us the illusion of the world? But: how does cinema restore our belief in the world? This irrational point is the *unsummonable* of Welles, the *inexplicable* of Robbe-Grillet, the *undecidable* of Resnais, the *impossible* of Marguerite Duras, or again what might be called the *incommensurable* of Godard (between two things).

There is another consequence, correlative to the change of status of the whole. What is correlatively produced is a dislocation of the internal monologue. According to Eisenstein's musical conception, the internal monologue constituted a descriptive material loaded with features of visual and sound expression which were associated or linked together with each other: each image had a dominant tonality, but also harmonics which defined its possibilities of harmony and metaphor (there was metaphor when two images had the same harmonics). There was thus a whole of the film which encompassed the author, the world and the characters, whatever the differences or contrasts. The author's way of seeing, that of the characters, and the way in which the world was seen formed a signifying unity, working through figures which were themselves significant. A first blow to this conception was struck when the internal monologue lost its personal or collective unity, and shattered into anonymous debris: stereotypes, clichés, ready-made visions and formulas took away the outside world and the interiority of characters in the same decomposition. The *Married Woman* merged with the pages of the weekly that she was flicking through, and with a catalogue of 'spare parts'. The internal monologue exploded under the weight of the same poverty on the inside and the outside: this was the transformation that Dos Passos had introduced into the novel, by already invoking cinematographic methods, and which Godard was to bring to completion in *A Married Woman*. But this was only the negative or critical aspect of a more profound and more important positive transformation. From this other perspective, the internal monologue gives way to sequences of images, each sequence being independent, and each image in the sequence standing for itself in relation to the preceding and following ones: a different descriptive material. There are no longer any perfect and 'resolved' harmonies, but only dissonant tunings or irrational cuts, because there are no more harmonics of the image, but only 'unlinked' tones forming the series. What disappears is all metaphor or figure. The formula in *Weekend*, 'it's not blood, it's red', signifies that blood has ceased to be a harmonic of red, and that this red is the unique tone of blood. One must speak and show literally, or else not show and speak at all. If, according to ready-made formulas, the revolutionaries are at our doors, besieging us like cannibals, they must be shown in the scrub of Seine-et-Oise, eating human flesh. If bankers are killers, schoolchildren prisoners, photographers pimps, if the workers are being screwed by their bosses, this has to be shown, not 'metaphorized', and series have to be constructed in consequence. If it is said that a weekly does not 'stand up' in its advertising pages, this has to be shown, literally, by tearing them out so as to let us see that the weekly no longer stands upright: this is no longer a metaphor but a demonstration (*Six fois deux*).

With Godard, the 'unlinked' image (this was Artaud's term) becomes serial and atonal, in a precise sense.[49] The problem of the relation between images is no longer of knowing if it works or it does not work [*si ça va ou si ça va pas*], according to the requirements of the harmonics or of the resolved tunings, but of knowing *How it's going* [*Comment ça va*]. Like this or like that, 'how it's going' [*comment ça va*] is the constitution of series, of their irrational cuts, of their dissonant tunings, of their unlinked terms. Each series refers to a way of seeing or speaking, for its own purposes, a way which may be that of current opinion operating through slogans, but equally that of a class, a sort, a typical character operating through thesis, hypothesis, paradox or even pretended cleverness, abrupt change of subject. Each series will be the way in which the author expresses himself indirectly in a sequence of images attributable to another, or, conversely, the way in which something or someone is expressed indirectly in the vision of the author considered as other. In any case, there is no longer the unity of the author, the characters and the world such as was guaranteed by the internal monologue. There is formation of 'free indirect discourse', of a *free indirect vision*, which goes from one to the other, so that either the author expresses himself through the intercession of an autonomous, independent character other than the author or any role fixed by the author, or the character acts and speaks himself as if his own gestures and his own words were already reported by a third party. The first case is that of the cinema incorrectly called 'direct', of Rouch and Perrault; the second, that of an atonal cinema, in Bresson, in Rohmer.[50] In short, Pasolini had a profound insight about modern cinema when he characterized it by a sliding of ground, breaking the uniformity of the internal monologue to replace it by the diversity, the deformity, the otherness of a free indirect discourse.[51]

Godard has used every method of free indirect vision. Not that he has limited himself to borrowing and renewing; on the contrary, he created the original method which allowed him to make a new synthesis, and in so doing to identify himself with modern cinema. If we are looking for the most general formula for the series in Godard, we should call every sequence of images *in so far as it is reflected in a genre* a series. An entire film may correspond to a dominant genre, as *Une femme est une femme* does to musical comedy, or *Made in USA* does to the strip cartoon. But even in this case the film moves through sub-genres, and the general rule is that there are several genres, hence several series. The passage from one genre to the next day may be through straight discontinuity, or equally in an imperceptible and continuous manner with 'intercalary genres', or again through recurrence or feedback,[52*] with electronic procedures (new possibilities are opening everywhere for montage). This reflective status of genre has important consequences: instead of genre subsuming images which naturally belong to it, it constitutes the limit of images which do not belong to it but àre reflected in it.[53] Amengual rightly pointed this out for *Une femme est une femme*: whilst dance, in a classical musical comedy, informs all the images, even preparatory or intercalary ones, it arises here, in contrast, as a 'moment' in the behaviour of the heroes, as the limit towards which a sequence of images is moving, a limit which will be realized only by forming another sequence moving towards another limit.[54] This is the case of dance not only in *Une femme . . .*, but in the café scene in *Bande à part*, or that of the pinewood in *Pierrot le fou*, a passage from the wander-genre to the ballad-genre.[55*] These are three great moments in Godard's work. Losing its capacities for subsuming or constituting in favour of a free power of reflection, genre may be said to be all the purer for marking the direction of pre-existing images, more than the character of the present images (Amengual shows that the scenery of *Une femme . . .*, the great square pillar in the middle of the bedroom and the patch of white wall between two doors, contributes all the more to dance in that it 'demolishes what is danced', in a kind of pure and empty reflection which gives the virtual a specific reality: the virtualities of the heroine).

Godard's reflexive genres, in this sense, are genuine *categories* through which the film passes. And the table of montage is conceived as a table of categories. There is something Aristotelian in Godard. Godard's films are syllogisms, which simultaneously integrate degrees of probability and paradoxes of logic. It is not a matter of a cataloguing procedure or one of 'collage', as Aragon suggested, but of a method of constitution of series, each marked by a category (the types of series can be very varied). It is as if Godard were taking the reverse route to the one we followed earlier, and was finding 'theorems' at the edge of 'problems'. The mathematician Bouligand distinguished, as two inseparable instances, on the one hand problems and on the other theorems or the overall synthesis: while problems impose conditions of series on unknown elements, overall synthesis fixes categories from where these elements are extracted (points, straight lines, curves, planes, spheres, etc.)[56] Godard is constantly creating categories: hence the very special role of discourse in many of his films where, as Daney noted, one genre of discourse always leads to a discourse of a different genre. Godard goes from problems to categories, even if the categories end up presenting him with a problem again. For instance, the structure of *Slow Motion*: the four great categories, 'the Imaginary', 'Fear', 'Business', 'Music', lead to a new problem, 'What is passion?', 'Passion is not this . . . ', which is to be the object of the next film.

According to Godard, categories are not fixed once and for all. They are redistributed, reshaped and reinvented for each film. A montage of categories, which is new each time, corresponds to a cutting of categories. The categories must, each time, surprise us, and yet not be arbitrary, must be well founded, and must have strong, indirect relations between themselves: they must not be derived from each other, so that their relation is of the 'And . . . ' type, this 'and' must achieve necessity. It is often the case that the written word indicates the category, while the visual images constitute the series: hence the very special primacy of the word over the image and the presentation of the screen as blackboard. And, in the written phrase, the conjunction 'and' can assume an isolated and magnified value (*Ici et ailleurs*). This re-creation of the interstice does not necessarily mark a discontinuity between the series of images: we can pass without break from one series to another, at the same time as the relation of one category to the next becomes unlocalizable, as we pass from the wandering [*balade*] to the ballad [*ballade*] in *Pierrot le fou*, or from daily life to the theatre in *Une femme est une femme*, or from the housework scene to the epic in *Le mépris*. Or again, the written word can be the object of an electronic processing introducing mutation, recurrence and retroaction (as already on the notebook in *Pierrot le fou, la . . . rt* is changed into *la mort*.[57] Categories, then, are never final answers but categories of problems which introduce reflection into the image itself. They are problematic or propositional functions. Henceforth, the question for each of Godard's films is: what performs the function of categories or of reflexive genres? In the simplest case, it can be aesthetic genres, the epic, theatre, the novel, dance, cinema itself. It is characteristic of cinema to reflect itself, and reflect the other genres, without the visual images referring to a pre-established dance, novel, theatre, or film, but themselves setting out to 'do' cinema, to do dance, to do novel, to do theatre, throughout a series, for an episode.[58] The categories of genres can also be psychic faculties (imagination, memory, forgetting . . .). But sometimes the category or genre assumes much more unusual aspects, for example in the well-known interventions of reflexive types, that is, original individuals who exhibit for what it is, in its singularity, the limit towards which a given series of visual images was moving and would move in the future: these are thinkers, like Jean-Pierre Melville in *Breathless*, Brice Parain in *Vivre sa vie*, Jeanson in *La Chinoise*; they are burlesque like Devos or the queen of the Lebanon in *Pierrot le fou*; they are examples like the extras in *Two or Three Things I Know About Her* (my name is this, I do this, I like that . . .). They are all interceders who function as a category, by giving it a complete individuation: the most moving example is perhaps the intervention of Brice Parain who exhibits and individuates the category of language, as the limit towards which the heroine was moving, with all her energy, through the series of images (the problem of Nana).

In short, the categories can be words, things, acts, people. *Les carabiniers* is not another film *about* war, to glorify or attack it. It films the categories of war, which is something quite different. Now, as Godard says, these can be specific things, armies of sea, earth and air, or 'specific ideas', occupation, countryside, resistance, or 'specific feelings', violence, rout, absence of passion, derision, disorder, surprise, void, or 'specific phenomena', noise, silence.[59] It will be noted that colours themselves can fulfil the function of categories. Not only do they affect things and people, and even written words; but they form categories in themselves: red is one in *Weekend*. If Godard is a great colourist, it is because he uses colours as great, individuated genres in which the image is reflected. This is Godard's consistent method in the films in colour (unless there is rather reflection in music, or in both at once). The *Letter to Freddy Buache* releases the chromatic procedure in the pure state: there is the high and the low, the blue, celestial Lausanne, and the green, terrestrial and aquatic Lausanne. Two curves or peripheries, and, between the two, there is grey, the centre, the straight lines. The colours have become almost mathematical categories in which the town reflects its images and makes a problem out of them. Three series, three states of matter, the problem of Lausanne. All the technical aspects of the film, its high-angle shots, low-angle shots, halts on the image, are at the service of this reflection. He will be criticized for not having fulfilled the brief of a film 'about' Lausanne: this is because he has inverted the relation between Lausanne and the colours; he has made Lausanne pass into the colours as on a table of categories which was, however, applicable only to Lausanne. This is definitely constructivism: he has reconstructed Lausanne with colours, the discourse of Lausanne, its indirect vision.

Cinema ceases to be narrative, but it is with Godard that it becomes the most 'novelesque'. As *Pierrot le fou* puts it, 'Next chapter. Despair. Next chapter. Freedom. Bitterness.' Bakhtine defined the novel, in contrast to the epic or tragedy, as no longer having the collective or distributive unity through which the characters still spoke one and the same language. On the contrary, the novel necessarily borrows sometimes the everyday anonymous language, sometimes the language of a class, a group, a profession, sometimes the particular language of a character. To the extent that the characters, classes and genres form the free indirect discourse of the author, as much as the author forms their free indirect vision (what they see, what they know or do not know). Or rather the characters express themselves freely in the author's discourse-vision, and the author, indirectly, in that of the characters. In short, it is reflection in genres, anonymous or personified, which constitutes the novel, its 'plurilingualism', its speech and its vision.[60] Godard gives cinema the particular powers of the novel. He provides himself with the reflexive types as so many interceders through whom I is always another. It is a broken line, a zig-zag line, which brings together the author, his characters and the world, and which passes between them. Thus modern cinema develops new relations with thought from three points of view: the obliteration of a whole or of a totalization of images, in favour of an outside which is inserted between them;

the erasure of the internal monologue as whole of the film, in favour of a free indirect discourse and vision; the erasure of the unity of man and the world, in favour of a break which now leaves us with only a belief in this world.

8 Cinema, body and brain, thought

1

'Give me a body then': this is the formula of philosophical reversal. The body is no longer the obstacle that separates thought from itself, that which it has to overcome to reach thinking. It is on the contrary that which it plunges into or must plunge into, in order to reach the unthought, that is life. Not that the body thinks, but, obstinate and stubborn, it forces us to think, and forces us to think what is concealed from thought, life. Life will no longer be made to appear before the categories of thought; thought will be thrown into the categories of life. The categories of life are precisely the attitudes of the body, its postures. 'We do not even know what a body can do':in its sleep, in its drunkenness, in its efforts and resistances. To think is to learn what a non-thinking body is capable of, its capacity, its postures. It is through the body (and no longer through the intermediary of the body) that cinema forms its alliance with the spirit, with thought. 'Give me a body then' is first to mount the camera on an everyday body. The body is never in the present, it contains the before and the after, tiredness and waiting. Tiredness and waiting, even despair are the attitudes of the body. No one has gone further than Antonioni in this direction. His method: the interior *through* behavior, no longer experience, but 'what remains of past experiences', 'what comes afterwards, when everything has been said', such a method necessarily proceeds via the attitudes or postures of the body.[1] This is a time-image, the series of time. The daily attitude is what puts the before and after into the body, time into the body, the body as a revealer of the deadline. The attitude of the body relates thought to time as to that outside which is infinitely further than the outside world. Perhaps tiredness is the first and last attitude, because it simultaneously contains the before and the after: what Blanchot says is also what Antonioni shows, *not* the drama of communication, but the immense tiredness of the body, the tiredness there is beneath *The Outcry*, and which suggests to thought 'something to incommunicate', the 'unthought', life.

But there is another pole to the body, another cinema-body-thought link. 'To give' a body, to mount a camera on the body, takes on a different sense: it is no longer a matter of following and trailing the everyday body, but of making it pass through a ceremony, of introducing it into a glass cage or a crystal, of imposing a carnival or a masquerade on it which makes it into a grotesque body, but also brings out of it a gracious and glorious body, until at last the disappearance of the visible body is achieved.Carmelo Bene is one of the greatest constructors of crystal-images: the palace in *Notre-Dame des Turcs* floats in the image, or rather it is the whole image which moves or throbs, reflections take on a violent colour, the colours themselves crystallize in *Don Juan*, in the dance of the veils in *Capricci* where the material comes between the dancer and the camera. Eyes haunt the crystal, like the eye in the monstrance, but what we are first allowed to see are the skeletons in *Notre-Dame*, the old men in *Capricci*, the old, decrepit saint in *Salomé*, who exhaust themselves with useless gestures endlessly taken up again, with constantly inhibited and recommenced attitudes, up to the impossible posture (the Christ in *Salomé* who can't manage to crucify himself alone: how could the last hand nail itself?). The ceremony in Bene begins with parody, which affects the sounds as much as the gestures, for gestures are also vocal, and apraxia and aphasia are the two sides of the same posture. But what emerges from the grotesque, what is torn from it, is the gracious body of woman as superior mechanic, whether she dances among the old men, or goes through the stylized attitudes of a secret wish, or becomes fixed in an attitude of ecstasy. Is this not done in order finally to free the third body, that of the 'protagonist', or master of ceremonies, who passes through all the other bodies? It is already his eye which was sliding into the crystal, it is he who communicates with the crystalline setting, as in *Notre-Dame* where the history of the palace becomes an autobiography of the protagonist. It is he who takes up inhibited or incomplete gestures, as in *Notre-Dame* where he is continually missing his own death, a totally bandaged mummy who can no longer give himself an injection, the impossible posture. It is he who must desecrate the gracious body, or use it in some respect, in order finally to acquire the power to disappear, like the poet in *Capricci* who looks for the best position to die in. To disappear is already Salomé's obscure desire, when she went away, back turned, towards the moon. But, when the protagonist takes up everything in this way, it is because he has reached that point of non-desire which now defines the pathetic, the Schopenhaurian point, Hamlet's point in *Un Hamlet de moins*, the point where the visible body disappears. What is freed in non-desire is music and speech, their intertwining in a body which is now only sound, a body of new opera. Even aphasia then becomes the noble and musical language. It is no longer the characters who have a voice, it is the voices, or rather the vocal modes of the protagonist (whisper, breathing, shout, eructation . . .) which become the sole, true characters in the ceremony in what has become a musical setting: as in the prodigious monologues of Herod Antipas in *Salomé*, which rise from his leprosy-covered body, and which carry out the sound powers of the cinema.[2] In this undertaking, Carmelo Bene must be the director closest to Artaud. He has the same experience: he 'believes' in cinema, he believes that cinema can bring about a more profound theatricalization than theatre itself, but he only believes this for a short time. He soon thinks that theatre is more capable of renewing itself, and freeing sound powers, than a still limited, over-visual cinema, even if this means that the theatricalization has to include electronic rather than cinematographic aids. None the less he believed in it for a while, the time of a work too soon interrupted, voluntarily interrupted: the capacity that cinema would have to *give* a body, that is, to make it, to bring about its birth and disappearance in a ceremony, in a liturgy. It is perhaps here that we shall be able to grasp a stake in the theatre-cinema relationship.

These two poles, the everyday body and the ceremonial body, are discovered or rediscovered in experimental cinema. The latter is not necessarily more advanced; it can even come afterwards. The difference between experimental cinema and the other cinema is that the former experiments, whilst the other discovers, by virtue of a *different* necessity from that of the filmic process. In experimental cinema, sometimes the process mounts the camera on the everyday body; these are Warhol's famous essays, six and half hours on the man asleep in a fixed shot, three-quarters of an hour on the man eating a mushroom (*Sleep, Eat*).[3] Sometimes, on the contrary, this cinema of the body mounts a ceremony, takes on an initiatory and liturgical aspect, and attempts to summon all the metallic and liquid powers of a sacred body, to the point of honour or revulsion, as in the essays of the Vienna school, Brus, Müehl and Nitsch.[4] But can we talk in terms of opposite poles except in extreme cases which are not necessarily the most successful? In the best instances, the everyday body might rather be said to lend itself to a ceremony which, perhaps, will never arrive, to prepare itself for a ceremony which, perhaps, will consist of waiting: as in the long preparation of the couple in *Mechanics of Love* by Maas and Moore, or that of the prostitute in *Flesh* by Morrissey and Warhol. By making marginals the characters of its cinema, the underground provided itself with the methods of an everydayness which continually leaked from the preparations for a stereotype ceremony, drugs, prostitution, transvestism. Attitudes and postures pass into this slow, everyday theatricalization of the body, as in *Flesh*, one of the finest of these films, with its fatigues and expectations, but also with the moment of relaxation, the game of three fundamental bodies, man woman, and child.

What is important is less the difference between poles than the passage from one to another, the imperceptible passage of attitudes or postures to 'gest'. It is Brecht who created the notion of gest, making it the essence of theatre, irreducible to the plot or the 'subject': for him,the gest should be social, although he recognizes that there are other kinds of gest.[5] What we call gest in general is the link or knot of attitudes between themselves, their co-ordination with each other, in so far as they do not depend on a previous story, a pre-existing plot or an action-image. On the contrary, the gest is the development of attitudes themselves, and, as such, carries out a direct theatricalization of bodies, often very discreet, because it takes place independently of any role. The greatness of Cassavetes's work is to have undone the story, plot, or action,but also space, in order to get to attitudes as to categories which put time into the body, as well as thought into life. When Cassavetes says that characters must not come from a story or plot, but that the story should be secreted by the characters, he sums up the requirement of the cinema of bodies: the character is reduced to his own bodily attitudes, and what ought to result is the gest, that is, a 'spectacle', a theatricalization or dramatization which is valid for all plots. *Faces* is constructed on the attitudes of the bodies presented as faces going as far as the grimace, expressing waiting, fatigue, vertigo and depression. And on the basis of the attitudes of blacks, and the attitudes of whites, *Shadows* revealed the social gest which forms around the attitude of the white Negro, put in a position where it is impossible to choose, lonely, on the verge of evanescence. Comolli speaks of a cinema of *revelation*, where the only constraint is that of bodies, and the only logic that of linkages of attitudes: characters 'are constituted gesture by gesture and word by word, as the film proceeds; they construct themselves, the shooting acting on them like a revel-ation, each advancement of the film allowing them a new development in their behaviour, their own duration very pre-cisely coinciding with that of the film'.[6] And, in the succeeding films, the spectacle can pass through a script: the point of this is less to tell a story than to develop and transform bodily attitudes, as in *A Woman under the Influence*: or in *Gloria*, where the abandoned child sticks to the body of the woman who first tries to push it away. In *Love Streams*, there is the brother and sister: the first can only experience his existence in an amassing of female bodies; the other in an amassing of luggage, or of animals which she offers to the brother. How can one exist, personally, if one cannot do so all alone? How can something be made to pass through these packets of body, which are at once both obstacle and means? Every time, space is made up of these excrescences of body, girls, luggage, animals, in search of a 'current' which would pass from one body to the next. But the lonely sister will leave on a dream, and the brother will remain under a hallucination: a hopeless story. As a general rule, Cassavetes keeps only the parts of space connected to bodies; he composes space with disconnec-ted bits solely linked by a gest. This is association of images being replaced by formal linkage of attitudes.

The new wave, in France, has taken this cinema of attitudes and postures (whose model actor would be Jean-Pierre Léaud) a long way. The scenery is often made according to the attitudes of the body that it demands and the degrees of freedom that it allows them, like the flat in *Le mépris* or the bedroom in *Vivre sa vie*, in Godard. Embracing, striking, intertwining and bumping bodies animate major scenes as in *First Name Carmen* again, where the two lovers attempt to grab each other in doors or windows.[7] Not only do bodies bang into each other, but the camera bangs against the bodies. in *Passion* each body not only has its space, but also its light. The body is sound as well as visible. all the components of the image come together on the body. Daney's formula when he defines *Ici et ailleurs* – restore images to the bodies on which they have been taken – applies to the whole of Godard's cinema and to the new wave. *Ici et ailleurs* does it politically, but the other films have at least a politics of the image, to restore the image to the attitudes and postures of the body. A characteristic image is that of a body leant against a wall, which lets itself go and falls to a

sitting position on the ground in a sliding of postures. Throughout his work, Rivette elaborates a formula where cinema, theatre
and theatricality specific to cinema confront each other: *L'amour
par terre* is its most perfect expression, that becomes dull as soon as
it is presented in a theoretical way, whilst it sets in motion the most
supple combinations. The characters are rehearsing a play; but
the rehearsal precisely implies that they have not yet achieved the
theatrical attitudes which correspond to the roles and to the plot
of the play which goes beyond them; on the contrary, they resort
to para-theatrical attitudes which they assume in relation to the
play, in relation to their role, and each in relation to the others,
and these second attitudes are all the purer and more independent for being free from all pre-existing plot, which exists only in
the play. These attitudes will thus secrete a gest which is neither
real nor imaginary, neither everyday nor ceremonial, but on the
boundary between the two, and which will point from this
position to the functioning of a truly visionary or hallucinatory
sense (the magic sweet in *Celine and Julie Go Boating*, the
magician's projections in *L'amour par terre*). It is as if the characters
spring to life again on the walls of the theatre, and discover pure
attitudes as independent of the theatrical role as they are of a real
action, although echoing both of them. One of the finest
instances, in Rivette, is *L'amour fou*, when the couple enclosed in a
room take up and pass through all the postures, a refuge-posture,
an aggressive posture, an amorous posture . . . It is a marvellous
demonstration of postures. In this sense, Rivette invents a
theatricality of cinema totally distinct from the theatricality of the
theatre (even when cinema uses it as a reference).

Godard's solution is different, and seems at first sight simpler:
it is, as we have seen, that characters begin to play for themselves,
to dance and to mimic for themselves, in a theatricalization which
directly extends their everyday attitudes. The character makes a
theatre for himself. In *Pierrot le fou* we continually move from the
attitude of the body to the theatrical gest which joins the attitudes
together and produces further ones, up to the final suicide which
absorbs all the others. In Godard, the attitudes of body are the
categories of the spirit itself, and the gest is the thread which goes
from one category to another. *Les carabiniers* is the Gesture of
war. The gest is necessarily social and political, following Brecht's
requirements, but it is necessarily something different as well (for
Rivette as much as Godard). It is bio-vital, metaphysical and
aesthetic.[8] For Godard, in *Passion*, the postures of the boss, the

female owner, and the female worker, refer to a pictorial or para-pictorial gest. And in *First Name Carmen*, the attitudes of body continually refer to a musical gest which co-ordinates them independently of the plot; which takes them up and subjects to them to a higher linkage, but also frees all their potentialities; the rehearsals of the quartet are not limited to developing and directing the sound qualities of the image, but also the visual qualities, in the sense that the curve of the violinist's arm modifies the movement of the bodies which are embracing. The fact is that, in Godard, sounds and colours are attitudes of the body, that is, categories: they thus find their thread in the aesthetic composition which passes through them, no less than in the social and political organization which underpins them. *First Name Carmen*, from the outset, makes sounds depend on a body which collides with things, and collides with itself, bangs itself on the head. Godard's cinema goes from the attitudes of the body, visual and sound, to the pluri-dimensional, pictorial and musical gest, which constitutes their ceremony, liturgy and aesthetic organization. This was already true of *Slow Motion*, where music constituted the virtual directional thread going from one attitude to another, 'What is that music?', before it is revealed for itself, at the end of the film. The attitude of the body is like a time-image, the one which puts the before and the after in the body, the series of time; but the gest is already a different time-image, the order or organization of time, the simultaneity of its peaks, the coexistence of its sheets. In the passage from one to the other, Godard thus achieves a great complexity. All the more because he may follow the reverse procedure, and begin from a continuous gest initially given, in order to break it up into attitudes or categories: as in the halts on the image in *Slow Motion* (Where does the caress end and the slap begin? Where does the embrace end and the struggle begin?).[9] There is not only the gest 'between' two attitudes; there is also the sound and the visual in the attitudes and in the gest and 'between' the attitudes and the gest itself, and inversely: as, again, in the visual and sound breaking down of the pornographic postures.

The post-new wave will continually work and invent in these directions: the attitudes and postures of the body, the valorizing of what happens on the ground or in bed, the speed and violence of co-ordination, the ceremony or theatre of cinema which is revealed (Chéreau's *La chair de l'orchidée* and especially his *L'homme blessé* are already very powerful in this respect). Certainly

the cinema of bodies does not proceed without risk: a glorification
of marginal characters who make their daily life into an insipid
ceremony; a cult of gratuitous violence in the linkage of postures;
a cultivation of catatonic, hysterical or simply refuge-attitudes –
Godard makes a kind of parody of these at the beginning of *First
Name Carmen*. And we end up being tired of all these bodies who
slide along the wall and then find themselves squatting on the
ground. But since the new wave, every time there was a fine and
powerful film, there was a new exploration of the body in it.
Starting with *Jeanne Dielman*, Chantal Akerman wants to show
'gestures in their fullness'. Enclosed in the bedroom, the heroine
of *Je Tu Il Elle* links involutive refuge- and infantile postures in a
mode which is that of waiting, counting the days: a ceremony of
anorexia. Chantal Akerman's novelty lies in showing in this way
bodily attitudes as the sign of states of body particular to the
female character, whilst the men speak for society, the environment, the part which is their due, the piece of history which they
bring with them (*Anna's Rendezvous*). But the chain of states of
female body is *not* closed: descending from the mother or going
back to the mother, it serves as a revelation to men, who now talk
about themselves, and on a deeper level to the environment,
which now makes itself seen or heard only through the window of
a room, or a train, a whole art of sound. In the same place or in
space, a woman's body achieves a strange nomadism which makes
it cross ages, situations and places (this was Virginia Woolf's secret
in literature). The states of the body secrete the slow ceremony
which joins together the corresponding attitudes, and develop a
female gest which overcomes the history of men and the crisis of
the world. It is this gest which reacts on the body giving it a
hieratism like an austere theatricalization, or rather a 'stylization'.
Whether it is possible to avoid the excess of stylization which
tends, in the end, to enclose film and character is the problem that
Chantal Akerman herself poses.[10] The gest may become more
burlesque, without concealing anything, and pass on to the film a
lightness, an irresistible gaiety: already in *Toute une nuit*, but
especially in the episode in *Paris vu par . . . 20 ans après*, whose title
itself stimulates the whole of Akerman's work, 'I am hungry, I am
cold', the states of body have become burlesque, sources of a
ballad.

Female authors, female directors, do not owe their importance
to a militant feminism. What is more important is the way they
have produced innovations in this cinema of bodies, as if women

had to conquer the source of their own attitudes and the temporality which corresponds to them as individual or common gest (*Cleo from 5 to 7*, *One Sings, the Other Doesn't* by Agnès Varda, *Mon coeur est rouge* by Michèle Rosier). With *Mur murs* and *Documenteur*, Varda constructs a diptych whose second part presents the day-to-day attitudes and gestures of a woman lost in Los Angeles, while the first part shows, in the eyes of another woman walking in the same city, the historical and political gest of a minority community, murals by Chicanoes in exasperated shapes and colours.

The cinema of the body or of attitudes also took new directions. From *Le cochon* and *La rosière de Pessac*, Eustache filmed cyclical festivals integrating collective attitudes and constituting a social gest. There was undoubtedly a whole context, an organization of power, of political aims, a whole history surrounding these ceremonies, in these ceremonies. But, following the lesson of *cinéma-vérité*, this history would not be told: it would be revealed, and all the more so for being less shown; the only thing to be shown would be the way the attitudes of the body are co-ordinated in the ceremony, so as to reveal what did not allow itself to be shown.[11] Eustache's cinema was henceforth to develop in several directions. The attitude of the body was no less vocal than gestural, one of the principal aims of cinema being, as Philippon puts it, *to film speech*. Attitudes and postures would engender their gest through a power of the false, from which bodies sometimes hid themselves, and to which they sometimes gave themselves fully, but always being confronted in this way with the pure act of cinema. If the attitude had been made to be seen and heard, it necessarily referred to a voyeur and a listener who were equally postures of the body and also attitudes, to the extent that the gest was made up of the attitude and its voyeur, and vice versa, likewise for speech. In the end, the diptych became the fundamental form of cinema, in very varied shapes but each time having the effect of putting time into bodies. Eustache was to make a second *Rosière de Pessac* years later, to confront and co-ordinate them on the basis of the second: 'It is the idea of time which interests me.' *Mes petites amoureuses* was organized as a diptych of which the first panel showed the attitudes of childish bodies, in the countryside, but the second, the 'false' adolescent attitudes of which the child , in the city, was now only the voyeur or hearer, until he returns to the countryside, having grown up with his new knowledge. *Une sale histoire* constituted the two degrees where on both sides, attitude and speech, hearer and voyeur were joined together. All these aspects already made *The Mother and the Whore* a masterpiece of the cinema of bodies, of their gestural and vocal attitudes.

If modern cinema has been constructed on the ruins of the sensory-motor schema or of the action-image, it finds in the 'posture-voyeurism' couple a new element which functions all the better because the postures are innocent. The richness of such a cinema cannot be exhausted by one author, Akerman or Eustache. It is an abundance, in which only different styles can be recognized, and which founds the unity of a category ('the post-new wave') by passing through very different authors. *Faux-fuyants*, by Bergala and Limosin can be mentioned, as showing a strange ceremony, which consists, for an adult (the man with the camera?), of inspiring and co-ordinating only attitudes of the body in young people of whom he makes himself the voyeur, constituting a gest which links all the unexpected offences of flight, and replaces narration, from one crime to the next.[12] With *La drôlesse*, Jacques Doillon made an important film of postures, a mentally handicapped man took a wild little girl and subjected her to the innocent attitudes imposed by the décor of a barn, lying down, sitting down, eating, sleeping, under the surveillance of a fake viewing appparatus ineptly stuck together (it would be the police's business not to believe this, and to invent a non-existent story, that is, an action film with abduction and rape). And in most of his films, from *Doigts dans la tête*, which takes up a theme related to *The Mother and the Whore*, to *La pirate*, which pushes attitudes of body to a frenzy under the gaze of a stern watching little girl, Doillon uses a very supple diptych form, which is able to show the postural poles between which the body oscillates. Each time, the stylization of attitudes forms a theatricalization of cinema which is very different from theatre. But it is Philippe Garrel who goes furthest in this direction, because he provides himself with a genuine liturgy of bodies, because he restores them to a secret ceremony whose only characters are now Mary, Joseph and the Child, or their equivalents (*Le lit de la vierge, Marie pour mémoire, Le révélateur, L'enfant secret*). This is hardly a pious cinema, even though it is a cinema of revelation. If the ceremony is secret, it is precisely because Garrel takes the three characters 'before' the legend, before they have made a legend or constituted a holy story: the question posed by Godard, 'What did Joseph and Mary say to each other before having the baby?', not only heralds a project of Godard's but sums up Garrel's experiences. The theatrical hieratism of characters, noticeable in his first films, is increasingly focused on a physics of fundamental bodies. What Garrel expresses in cinema, is the problem of the three bodies: the man, the woman and the child. The holy story as gesture. The fine opening of *Le révélateur* lets us guess that there is a child perched in the dark on top of the wardrobe, then shows the door opening on to the over-exposed silhouette of the father, and finally reveals, in front of him, the mother on her knees. Each will embrace one of the other two, in three combinations, in a big bed which resembles a cloud on the floor. Sometimes, the constantly invoked child is missing (*Marie pour mémoire*) or is a different one from the one we see (*L'enfant secret*): this is the sign that the problem of the three bodies remains cinematographically as well as physically insoluble. The child is in himself the problematic point. It is around him that the gest is composed, as in the episode in *Paris vu par . . . 20 ans après* ('Rue Fontaine'): the first attitude is that of the man in the middle of telling the story of a woman who said 'I want a child' and who disappeared; the second, that of the same man sitting in a woman's house and waiting; the third, they become lovers, attitudes and postures; the fourth, they have split up, he wants to see her again, but she tells him that she had a child who died; the fifth, he learns that she has been found dead herself, and he kills himself, his body toppling slowly over in a long image to become one with snow, as in a posture which has no end. The child thus appears as the undecidable point in terms of which the attitudes of a man and a woman are distributed. In Garrel as well, the diptych form is thus imposed, around an empty turning-point, unattainable limit, or irrational cut. It distributes not only attitudes, but the white and black, the cold and hot, as the conditions on which attitudes depend or the elements of which the bodies are made. There are the two coloured rooms, on each side of the bed, the cold one and the warm one, in *La concentration*. There are the two big landscapes in the *Lit de la vierge*, the white Arab village and the dark Brittany castle, the mystery of Christ and the quest for the Grail. There are the two quite distinct parts of *Liberté la nuit*, the black image of the couple where the man betrays the woman (the deserted woman who knits crying in the dark, empty theatre), the white image of the couple where the woman betrays the man (the two characters embracing in a field where the washing is drying, a sheet caught by the wind coming to cover them and cover the screen). There are the alternations of hot and cold, the heat of the fire or a light in the night, but also the cold of the white drug caught in a mirror (as in *L'enfant secret* where we see the café window, the man with his back turned, and, in the window, the image of the woman also from the back crossing the street and going to meet the dealer). In Garrel, over-exposed and under-exposed, white and black, cold and hot, became the components of the body and the elements of its postures.[13] They are the catagories which 'give' a body.

'The absence of image', the black screen or the white screen, have a decisive importance in contemporary cinema. For, as Noël Burch has shown, they no longer have a simple function of punctuation, as if they marked a change, but enter into a dialectical relation between the image and its absence, and assume a properly structural value (as in Brakhage's *Reflections on Black* in experimental cinema).[14] This new value of the black or white screen seems to us to correspond to the characteristics analysed earlier: on the one hand, what is important is no longer the association of images, the way in which they associate, but the interstice between two images; on the other hand, the cut in a sequence of images is not now a rational cut which marks the end of one *or* the beginning of another, but a so-called irrational cut which belongs neither to one nor the other, and sets out to be valid for itself. Garrel was able to give an extraordinary intensity to these irrational cuts, so that the series of anterior images has no end, while the series of subsequent images likewise has no beginning, the two series converging towards the white or black screen as their common limit. Moreover, used in this way, the screen becomes the medium for variations: the black screen and the under-exposed image, the intense blackness which lets us guess at dark volumes in process of being constituted, or the black marked by a fixed or moving luminous point, and all the combinations of black and fire; the white screen and the over-exposed image, the milky image, or the snowy image whose dancing seeds are to take shape . . . And, in *L'enfant secret*, it is often the flash which gives rise to the images and gathers together the powers of black and white. Throughout Garrel's films, the black or white screen no longer has only a structural value, but has a genetic one: with its variations and tonalities, it acquires the power of a constitution of bodies (primordial bodies from this point, Man, Woman and Child), the power of the genesis of postures.[15] This may be the first case of a cinema of constitution, one which is truly constitutive: constituting bodies, and in this way restoring our belief in the world, restoring our reason ... It is doubtful if cinema is sufficient for this; but, if the world has become a bad cinema, in which we no longer believe, surely a true cinema can contribute to giving us back reasons to believe in the world and in vanished bodies? The price to be paid, in cinema as elsewhere, was always a confrontation with madness.[16]

In what sense is Garrel one of the greatest modern authors, whose work, alas, may well develop its effects only in the long term, endowing the cinema with powers that are as yet not well known? We have to go back to a very old problem, which already brought theatre and cinema into opposition. Those who deeply loved the theatre objected that cinema always lacked something, *presence*, the presence of bodies which remained the prerogative of theatre: cinema only showed us waves and dancing corpuscles with which it simulated bodies. When André Bazin takes up the problem, he looks for a sense in which there is a different mode of presence, a cinematographic one, which rivals that of theatre and may even outdo it with different methods.[17] But, if cinema does not give us the presence of the body and cannot give us it, this is perhaps also because it sets itself a different objective; it spreads an 'experimental night' or a white space over us; it works with 'dancing seeds' and a 'luminous dust'; it affects the visible with a fundamental disturbance, and the world with a suspension, which contradicts all natural perception. What it produces in this way is the genesis of an 'unknown body' which we have in the back of our heads, like the unthought in thought, the birth of the visible which is still hidden from view. These responses which change the problem are those of Jean-Louis Schefer in *L'homme ordinaire du cinéma*. They consist in saying that the object of cinema is not to reconstitute a presence of bodies, in perception and action, but to carry out a primordial genesis of bodies in terms of a white, or a black or a grey (or even in terms of colours), in terms of a 'beginning of visible which is not yet a figure, which is not yet an action'. Is this what Bresson's project, *Genèse*, is? In any case, we believe that what Schefer seeks rare examples of in the history of cinema, in Dreyer and Kurosawa, is what Garrel draws on, not for a systematic recapitulation, but as a revitalizing inspiration which means that cinema thus coincides with its own essence, at least with one of its essences: a proceeding, a process of constitution of bodies from the neutral image, white or black, snowy or flashed. The problem is *not* that of a presence of bodies, but that of a belief which is capable of restoring the world and the body to us on the basis of what signifies their absence. The camera must invent the movements or positions which correspond to the genesis of bodies, and which are the formal linkages of their primordial postures. Garrel's special role in the cinema of bodies can be found in a geometry which in turn goes to make up the world, with points, circles and semicircles. A little like in Cézanne, the dawn of the world is linked to the point, the plane, volume and section, not as abstract figures but as genesis and birth. In *Le révélateur*, the woman is often a fixed point, immobile and contradictory, whilst the child turns, around the woman, around the bed, around the trees, and the man does semicircles which maintain his relationship with the woman and the child. In *Les enfants désaccordés*, the camera which is initially a fixed point on to the dance, begins to turn around two dancers, approaching and moving away according to their rhythm, and the changing light; at the beginning of *La cicatrice intérieure* the circular tracking shot allows the character to make a complete turn, the camera remaining fixed on him as if it were moving laterally to find still the same speaker; and, in *Marie pour mémoire*, while Mary is imprisoned in the clinic, Joseph turns as he watches the camera, which changes position as if it were in a succession of different cars on a traffic interchange. On each occasion there is a construction of space as this is attached to bodies. And what is valid for the three fundamental bodies is also valid for the other trinity, that of the characters, the film-maker and the camera: placing them 'in the best possible posture, in the sense that we say of a configuration of stars that it is in an astrologically favourable position'.[18]

What is special to Doillon is the situation of the body caught between two sets, caught simultaneously in two exclusive sets. Truffaut had opened the way (*Jules and Jim*, *The Two English Girls*), and Eustache in *The Mother and the Whore* was able to construct the particular space of the non-choice. But Doillon renews and explores this ambiguous space. The character-body, the apprentice baker of *Doigts dans la tête*, the husband of *La femme qui pleure*, the young woman in *La pirate*, oscillate between two women, or between a woman and a man, but above all between two groupings, two modes of life, two sets demanding different attitudes. One of the two sets can always be said to prevail: the temporary girl sends the baker back to his constant fiancée; the happy woman sends the man back to the crying woman, as soon as she realizes that she is herself only an excuse or pretext. And, in *La pirate*, if the predominance does not seem fixed in advance, it is, according to Doillon's own pronouncements, the tendering of a higher bid which should decide the heroine's life, or her reserve price. But there is something else. It is not that the character finds himself indecisive. It appears rather that two sets are really distinct, but that the character, or rather the body in the character, has no way of choosing between the two. He is in an impossible posture. The character in Doillon is in the situation of not being able to make out the distinct: he is not psychologically indecisive, he would be even the opposite. But the predominance is useless to him, because he inhabits his body like a zone of indiscernibility. Who is the mother, who is the whore? Even if it is decided for him, this changes nothing. His body will always retain the imprint of an undecidability which was just the passing of life. It may be here that the cinema of the body fundamentally contrasted with the cinema of action. The action-image presupposes a space in which ends, obstacles, means, subordinations, the principle and the secondary, predominances and loathings are distributed: a whole space which can be called 'hodological'. But the body is initially caught in a quite different space, where disparate sets overlap and rival each other, without being able to organize themselves according to sensory-motor schemata. They fit over each other, in an overlapping of perspectives which means that there is no way to distinguish them even though they are distinct and also incompatible. This is space before action, always haunted by a child, or by a clown, or by both at once. It is a pre-hodological space, like a *fluctuatio animi* which does not point to an indecision of the spirit, but to an undecidability of the body. The obstacle does not, as in the action-image, allow itself to be determined in relation to goals and means which would unify the set, but is dispersed in 'a plurality of ways of being present in the world', of belonging to sets, all incompatible and yet coexistent.[19] Doillon's strength is to have made this pre-hodological space, this space of overlappings, the special object of a cinema of bodies. He leads his characters there; he creates this space where regression becomes discovery (*La fille prodigue*). Not only does he thereby undo the action-image of classical cinema, he reveals a non-choice of the body as the unthought, the other side or reversal of the spiritual choice. As in the dialogue exchanged in Godard's *Slow Motion*: 'You choose . . . No I'm not choosing . . . You choose . . . I'm not choosing . . .'

2

'Give me a brain' would be the other figure of modern cinema.
This is an intellectual cinema, as distinct from the physical
cinema. Experimental cinema is shared between these two areas:
the physics of the body, everyday or ceremonial; the formal or
informal 'eidetics' of the spirit (to use Bertetto's formulation). But
experimental cinema develops the distinction according to two
processes, one concretive, the other abstractive. The abstract and
the concrete, however, are not the right criteria, in a cinema
which creates rather than experiments. We saw that Eisenstein
already laid claim to an intellectual or cerebral cinema, which he
considered to be more concrete than the physics of bodies in
Pudovkin, or physical formalism in Vertov. There is no less of the
concrete and abstract on the one side than on the other: there is as
much feeling or intensity. passion, in a cinema of the brain as in a
cinema of the body. Godard initiates a cinema of the body,
Resnais, a cinema of the brain, but one is not more abstract or
more concrete than the other. Body or brain is what cinema
demands be given to it, what it gives to itself, what it invents itself,
to construct its work according to two directions, each one of
which is simultaneously abstract and concrete. The distinction is
thus not between the concrete and the abstract (except in
experimental cases and, even there, it is fairly consistently
confused). The intellectual cinema of the brain and the physical
cinema of the body will find the source of their distinction
elsewhere, a very variable source, whether with authors who are
attracted by one of the two poles, or with those who compose with
both of them.

Antonioni would be the perfect example of a double composition. The unity of his work has often been sought in the
established themes of solitude and incommunicability, as characteristics of the poverty of the modern world. Nevertheless,
according to him, we walk at two very different paces, one for the
body, one for the brain. In a fine passage, he explains that our
knowledge does not hesitate to renew itself, to confront great
mutations, whilst our morality and feelings remain prisoners of
unadapted values of myths that no one believes any more, and
find only poor excuses – cynical, erotic, or neurotic – for freeing
themselves. Antonioni does not criticize the modern world, in
whose possibilities he profoundly 'believes': he criticizes the
coexistence in the world of a modern brain and a tired, worn-out,

neurotic body. So that his work, in a fundamental sense passes through a dualism which corresponds to the two aspects of the time-image: a cinema of the body, which puts all the weight of the past into the body, all the tiredness of the world and modern neurosis; but also a cinema of the brain, which reveals the creativity of the world, its colours aroused by a new space-time, its powers multiplied by artificial brains.[20] If Antonioni is a great colourist, it is because he has always believed in the colours of the world, in the possibility of creating them, and of renewing all our cerebral knowledge. He is not an author who moans about the impossibility of communicating in the world. It is just that the world is painted in splendid colours, while the bodies which people it are still insipid and colourless. The world awaits its inhabitants, who are still lost in neurosis. But this is one more reason to pay attention to the body, to scrutinize its tiredness and neurosis, to take tints from it. The unity of Antonioni's work is the confrontation of the body-character with his weariness and his past, and of the brain-colour with all its future potentialities, but the two making up one and the same world, ours, its hopes and its despair.

Antonioni's formula is valid for him only, it is he who invents it. Bodies are not destined for wearing out, any more than the brain is destined for novelty. But what is important is the possibility of a cinema of the brain which brings together all the powers, as much as the cinema of the body equally brought them together as well: there are, then, two different styles, where the difference itself is constantly varying, cinema of the body in Godard and cinema of the brain in Resnais, cinema of the body in Cassavetes and cinema of the brain in Kubrick. There is as much thought in the body as there is shock and violence in the brain. There is an equal amount of feeling in both of them. The brain gives orders to the body which is just an outgrowth of it, but the body also gives orders to the brain which is just a part of it: in both cases, these will not be the same bodily attitudes nor the same cerebral gest. Hence the specificity of a cinema of the brain, in relation to that of the cinema of bodies. If we look at Kubrick's work, we see the degree to which it is the brain which is *mis en scène*. Attitudes of body achieve a maximum level of violence, but they depend on the brain. For, in Kubrick, the world itself is a brain, there is identity of brain and world, as in the great circular and luminous table in *Doctor Strangelove*, the giant computer in *2001 A Space Odyssey*, the Overlook hotel in *The Shining*. The black stone of *2001* presides over both cosmic states and cerebral stages: it is the soul of the three bodies, earth, sun and moon, but also the seed of the three brains, animal, human, machine. Kubrick is renewing the theme of the initiatory journey because every journey in the world is an exploration of the brain. The world-brain is *A Clockwork Orange*, or again, a spherical game of chess where the general can calculate his chances of promotion on the basis of the relation between soldiers killed and positions captured (*Paths of Glory*). But if the calculation fails, if the computer breaks down, it is because the brain is no more reasonable a system than the world is a rational one. The identity of world and brain, the automaton, does not form a whole, but rather a limit, a membrane which puts an outside and an inside in contact, makes them present to each other, confronts them or makes them clash. The inside is psychology, the past, involution, a whole psychology of depths which excavate the brain. The outside is the cosmology of galaxies, the future, evolution, a whole supernatural which makes the world explode. The two forces are forces of death which embrace, are ultimately exchanged and become ultimately indiscernible. The insane violence of Alex in *Clockwork Orange* is the force of the outside before passing into the service of an insane internal order. In *Space Odyssey*, the robot breaks down from the inside, before being lobotomized by the astronaut who penetrates it from the outside. And, in *The Shining*, how can we decide what comes from the inside and what comes from the outside, the extra-sensory perceptions or hallucinatory projections?[21] The world-brain is strictly inseparable from the forces of death which pierce the membrane in both directions. Unless a reconciliation is carried out in another dimension, a regeneration of the membrane which would pacify the outside and the inside, and re-create a world-brain as a whole in the harmony of the spheres. At the end of *Space Odyssey*, it is in consequence of a fourth dimension that the sphere of the foetus and the sphere of the earth have a chance of entering into a new, incommensurable, unknown relation, which would convert death into a new life.

In France, at the same time as the new wave launched a cinema of bodies which mobilized the whole of thought, Resnais was creating a cinema of the brain which empowered bodies. We saw how states of the world and the brain found their common expression in the bio-psychic stages of *My American Uncle* (the three brains), or in the historical epochs in *Life is a bed of roses* (the three epochs). Landscapes are mental states, just as mental states are cartographies, both crystallized in each other, geometrized, mineralized (the torrent in *L'amour à mort*). The identity of brain and world is the noosphere of *Je t'aime je t'aime*, it can be the diabolic organization of the extermination camps, but also the cosmo-spiritual structure of the Bibliothèque Nationale.[22] In Resnais this identity already appears less in a whole than at the level of a polarized membrane which is constantly making relative outsides and insides communicate or exchange, putting them in contact with each other, extending them, and referring them to each other. This is not a whole, but rather like two zones which communicate all the more, or are all the more in contact, because they cease to be symmetrical and synchronous, like the halves of the brain in *Stavisky*.[23] In *Providence*, the bombshell is in the state of body of the old, alcoholic novelist, who rattles in every direction, but also in the state of the cosmos in thunder and lightning, and in the social state in machine-gun and rifle bursts. This membrane which makes the outside and the inside present to each other is called memory. If memory is the explicit theme of Resnais' work, there is no reason to look for a latent content which would be more subtle; it is better to evaluate the transformation that the notion of memory is made to undergo in Resnais (a transformation as important as that carried out by Proust or Bergson). For memory is clearly no longer the faculty of having recollections: it is the membrane which, in the most varied ways (continuity, but also discontinuity, envelopment, etc.), makes sheets of past and layers of reality correspond, the first emanating from an inside which is always already there, the second arriving from an outside always to come, the two gnawing at the present which is now only their encounter. These themes have been analysed earlier; and, if the cinema of bodies referred in particular to one aspect of the direct time-image – series of time according to the before and the after, the cinema of the brain develops the other aspect – the order of time according to the coexistence of its own relations.

But, if memory makes relative insides and outsides communicate like interiors and exteriors, an absolute outside and inside must confront each other and be co-present. Réné Prédal has shown the extent to which Auschwitz and Hiroshima remained the horizon of all Resnais' work, how close the hero in Resnais is to the 'Lazarean hero' which Cayrol made the soul of the new novel, in a fundamental relation with the extermination camps.[24] The character in Resnais' cinema is Lazarean precisely because he returns from death, from the land of the dead; he has passed through death and is born from death, whose sensory-motor disturbances he retains. Even if he was not personally in Auschwitz, even if he was not personally in Hiroshima . . . He passed through a clinical death, he was born from an apparent death, he returns from the dead, Auschwitz or Hiroshima, Guernica or the Algerian war. The hero of *Je t'aime je t'aime* has not simply commited suicide; he speaks of Catrine, the woman he loves, as a marsh, a low tide, night, mud, which means that the dead are always victims of drowning. This is what a character in *Stavisky* says. It should be understood that, beyond all the sheets of memory, there is this lapping which stirs them, this death from the inside which forms an absolute, and from which he who has been able to escape it is reborn. And he who escapes, he who has been able to be reborn, moves inexorably towards a death from the outside, which comes to him as the other side of the absolute. *Je t'aime je t'aime* will make the two deaths coincide, the death from the inside from which he returns, the death from the outside which comes to him. *L'amour à mort*, which seems to us to be one of the most ambitious films in the history of cinema, moves from the clinical death from which the hero comes back to life, to the definitive death into which he goes down, 'a shallow stream' separating the two (it is clear that the Doctor had not been mistaken the first time, it was not an illusion, there had been apparent or clinical death, brain-death). Between one death and the other, the absolute inside and the absolute outside enter into contact, an inside deeper than all the sheets of past, an outside more distant than all the layers of external reality. Between the two, in the in-between, it is as if zombies peopled the brain-world for a moment: Resnais 'insists on preserving the ghostly character of the beings he shows, and on maintaining them in a society of spectres destined to be included for a moment in our mental universe; these shivering heroes . . . like to wear warm, out-of-date clothes'.[25] Resnais' characters do not just return from Auschwitz or Hiroshima, they are philosophers, thinkers, beings of thought in another way too. For philosophers are beings who have passed through a death, who are born from it, and go towards another death, perhaps the same one. In a very happy story, Pauline Harvey says that she understands nothing about philosophy, but is very fond of philosophers because they give her a double impression: they themselves believe that they are dead, that they have passed through death; and they also believe that, although dead, they continue to live, but in a shivering way, with tiredness and prudence.[26] According to Pauline Harvey, this would be a double mistake, which amuses her. Acording to us, it is a double truth, although this is cause for amusement as well: the philosopher is someone who believes he has returned from the dead, rightly or wrongly, and who returns to the dead in full consciousness. The philosopher has returned from the dead and goes back there. This has been the living formulation of philosophy since Plato. When we say that Resnais' characters are philosophers, we are certainly not saying that these characters talk about philosophy, or that Resnais 'applies' philosophical ideas to a cinema, but that he invents a cinema of philosophy, a cinema of thought, which is totally new in the history of cinema and totally alive in the history of philosophy, creating, with his unique collaborators, a rare marriage between philosophy and cinema. The great post-war philosophers and writers demonstrated that thought has something to do with Aushchwitz, with Hiroshima, but this was also demonstrated by the great cinema authors from Welles to Resnais – this time in the most serious way.

This is the opposite of a cult of death. Between the two sides of the absolute, between the two deaths – death from the inside or past, death from the outside or future – the internal sheets of memory and the external layers of reality will be mixed up, extended, short-circuited and form a whole moving life, which is at once that of the cosmos and of the brain, which sends out flashes from one pole to the other. Hence zombies sing a song, but it is that of life. Resnais' *Van Gogh* is a masterpiece because it shows that, between the apparent death from inside, the attack of madness, and the definitive death from outside as suicide, the sheets of internal life and the layers of external world plunge, extend and intersect with increasing speed up to the final black screen.[27] But, between the two, what flashes of lightning there will have been; these were life itself. From one pole to the other a creation will be constructed, which is true creation only because it will be carried out between the two deaths, the apparent and the real, all the more intense because it illuminates this interstice. The sheets of past come down and the layers of reality go up, in mutual embraces which are flashes of life: what Resnais calls 'feeling' or 'love', as mental function.

Resnais has always said that what interested him was the cerebral mechanism, mental functioning, the process of thought, and that here was the true element of cinema. A cinema which is cerebral or intellectual, but not abstract, because it is clear to what extent feeling, affect, or passion are the principal characters of the brain-world. The question is rather that of knowing what difference there is between the 'classical' intellectual cinema, for example, Eisenstein's, and the modern, for example, Resnais'. For Eisenstein already identified cinema with the process of thought as this necessarily develops in the brain, as it necessarily envelops feeling or passion. Intellectual cinema was already the cerebral whole which brought together pathos and the organic. Resnais' pronouncements may be close to those of Eisenstein: the cerebral process as object and motor of cinema.[28] Nevertheless, something has changed,which undoubtedly has something to do with scientific knowledge of the brain, but still more with our personal relationship with the brain. So that intellectual cinema has changed, not because it has become more concrete (it was so from the outset), but because there has been a simultaneous change in our conception of the brain and our relationship with the brain. The 'classical' conception developed along two axes; on the one hand integration and differentiation, on the other association, through contiguity or similarity. The first axis is the law of the concept: it constitutes movement as continually integrating itself into a whole whose change it expresses, and as continually differentiating itself in accordance with the objects between which it is established. This integration-differentiation thus defines movement as movement of the concept. The second axis is the law of the image: similarity and contiguity determine the way in which we pass from one image to another. The two axes cut across each other, according to a principle of attraction, in order to achieve the identity of image and concept: indeed, the concept as whole does not become differentiated without externalizing itself in a sequence of associated images, and the images do not associate without being internalized in a concept as the whole which integrates them. Hence the ideal of knowledge as harmonious totality, which sustains this classical representation. Even the fundamentally open character of the whole does not compromise this model, on the contrary, because the out-of-field shows an associability which extends and goes beyond the given images, but also expresses the changing whole which integrates the extendable sequences of images (the two aspects of the out-of-field). We have seen how Eisenstein, like a cinematographic Hegel, presented the grand synthesis of this conception: the open spiral, with its commensurabilities and attractions. Eisenstein himself did not hide the cerebral model which drove the whole synthesis, and which made cinema the cerebral art *par excellence*, the internal monologue of the brain-world; 'The form of montage is a restoration of the laws of the process of thought, which in turn restores moving reality in process of unrolling.' For the brain was both the vertical organization of intergration-differentiation, and the horizontal organization of association. Our relationship with the brain has followed these axes for a long time. Of course, Bergson (who was, with Schopenhauer, one of the rare philosophers to propose a new conception of the brain) introduced a profound element of transformation: the brain was now only an interval [*écart*], a void, nothing but a void, between a stimulation and a response. But, whatever the importance of the discovery, this interval [*écart*] remained subject to an integrating whole which was embodied in it, and to associations which traversed it.[29] In yet another area, it could be said that linguistics maintained the classic cerebral model, both from the point of view of metaphor and metonymy (similarity-contiguity) and from the point of view of the syntagm and paradigm (integration-differentiation).[30]

Scientific knowledge of the brain has evolved, and carried out a general rearrangement. The situation is so complicated that we should not speak of a break, but rather of new orientations which only produce an effect of a break with the classical image at the limit. But perhaps our own relationship with the brain changed at the same time, and, on its own account, independently of science, and consummated the break with the old relationship. On the one hand, the organic process of integration and differentiation increasingly pointed to relative levels of interiority and exteriority and, through them, to an absolute outside and inside, in contact topologically: this was the discovery of a topological cerebral space, which passed through relative mediums [*milieux*] to achieve the co-presence of an inside deeper than any internal medium, and an outside more distant than any external medium.[31] On the other hand, the process of association increasingly came up against cuts in the continuous network of the brain; everywhere there were micro-fissures which were not simply voids to be crossed, but random mechanisms introducing themselves at each moment between the sending and receiving of an association message: this was the discovery of a probabilistic or semi-fortuitous cerebral space, 'an uncertain system'.[32] It is perhaps through these two aspects that the brain can be defined as an acentred system.[33] It is obviously not through the influence of science that our relationship with the brain changed: perhaps it was the opposite, our relationship with the brain having changed first, obscurely guiding science. Pyschology has a good deal to say about a lived relationship with the brain, of a lived body, but it has less to say about a lived brain. Our lived relationship with the brain becomes increasingly fragile, less and less 'Euclidean' and goes through little cerebral deaths. The brain becomes our problem or our illness, our passion, rather than our mastery, our solution or decision. We are not copying Artaud, but Artaud lived and said something about the brain that concerns all of us: that 'its antennae turned towards the invisible', that it has a capacity to 'resume a resurrection from death'.

We no longer believe in a whole as interiority of thought – even an open one; we believe in a force from the outside which hollows itself out, grabs us and attracts the inside. We no longer believe in an association of images – even crossing voids; we believe in breaks which take on an absolute value and subordinate all association. This is not abstracting, these two aspects define the new 'intellectual' cinema and examples can be found in particular in Téchiné, and Benoit Jacquot. Both are able to take the sensory-motor collapse on which modern cinema is constituted as read. But they distinguish themselves from the cinema of bodies because for them (as for Resnais) it is the brain which initially orders attitudes. The brain cuts or puts to flight all internal associations, it summons an outside beyond any external world. In Téchiné, associated images slide and flee on windows, following currents up which the character must go back to move towards an outside which calls them, but which he will perhaps not be able to meet up with (the boat in *Barocco*, and then *L'hôtel des Ameiriques*).[34] In Jacquot, by contrast, it is a function of literalness of the image (flattened, redundancies and tautologies) which will shatter associations, to replace them with an infinity of interpretation whose only limit is an absolute outside (*L'assassin musicien*, *Les enfants du placard*).[35] In both cases, this is a cinema inspired by neo-psychoanalytical themes: give me a slip [*lapsus*], an act that is lacking and I will reconstruct the brain. The new cerebral images are defined by a topological structure of the outside and the inside, and a fortuitous character at each stage of the linkages or mediations.

The great corresponding novel is Andrei Bely's *Petersburg*. This masterpiece evolves in a noosphere, where a corridor is hollowed out inside the brain, in order to communicate with a cosmic void.

It no longer works by totalization, but by application of the inside on the outside, of the two sides of a membrane (the bomb of the inside and of the outside, in the belly and in the house). It no longer works through linkage of images, but through continual relinked parcellings (the fiendish appearances of the red domino). This is the constructivist novel as 'cerebral game'.[36] Resnais seems to us close to Bely because he makes cinema the cerebral game *par excellence*: hence the organic-cosmic bomb of *Providence* and the fragmentations through transformation of sheets in *Je t'aime je t'aime*. The hero is sent back to a minute of his past, but this is perpetually relinked in variable sequences, through succeeding drafts. Or again the ghostly city, as world and brain, Boulogne as much as Petersburg. This is a space which is both topological and probabilistic. In this respect, we can return to the great difference between classical cinema and modern cinema. The so-called classical cinema works above all through linkage of images, and subordinates cuts to this linkage. On the mathematical analogy, the cuts which divide up two series of images are rational, in the sense that they constitute either the final image of the first series, or the first image of the second. This is the case of the 'dissolve' in its various forms. But even when there is a pure optical cut, and likewise when there is false continuity, the optical cut and the false continuity function as simple lacunae, that is, as voids which are still motor, which the linked images must cross. In short, rational cuts always determine commensurable relations between series of images, and thereby constitute the whole rhythmic system and harmony of classical cinema, at the same time as they integrate associated images in an always open totality. Time here is, therefore, essentially the object of an indirect representation, according to the commensurable relations and rational cuts which organize the sequence or linkage of movement-images. This grandiose conception finds its apogee in the theory and practice of Eisenstein.[37] Now, modern cinema can communicate with the old, and the distinction between the two can be very relative. However, it will be defined ideally by a reversal where the image is unlinked and the cut begins to have an importance in itself. The cut, or interstice, between two series of images no longer forms part of either of the two series: it is the equivalent of an irrational cut, which determines the non-commensurable relations between images. It is thus no longer a lacuna that the associated images would be assumed to cross; the images are certainly not abandoned to chance, but there are only relinkages subject to the cut, instead of cuts subject to the linkage. As in *Je t'aime je t'aime*, there is return to the same image, but caught up in a new series. Ultimately, there are no longer any rational cuts, but only irrational ones. There is thus no longer association through metaphor or metonymy, but relinkage on the literal image; there is no longer linkage of associated images, but only relinkages of independent images. Instead of one image after the other, there is one image *plus* another, and each shot is deframed in relation to the framing of the following shot.[38] We saw this detail in the case of Godard's intersticial method, and, more generally, it is the relinked parcelling that is found in Bresson, in Resnais, and in Jacquot and Téchiné. It is a whole new system of rhythm, and a serial or atonal cinema, a new conception of montage. The cut may now be extended and appear in its own right, as the black screen, the white screen and their derivatives and combinations: hence the great blue image of night, where little feathers or corpuscules flutter at various speeds and in various arrangements, which keeps reappearing in Resnais' *L'amour à mort*. In the first place, the cinematographic image becomes a direct presentation of time, according to non-commensurable relations and irrational cuts. In the second place, this time-image puts thought into contact with an unthought, the unsummonable, the inexplicable, the undecidable, the incommensurable. The outside or the obverse of the images has replaced the whole, at the same time as the interstice or the cut has replaced association.

Even abstract or 'eidetic' cinema shows a similar evolution. According to a rough periodization, the first epoch is that of geometrical figures, taken at the intersection of two axes, a vertical axis which concerns the integration and differentiation of their intelligible elements and a horizontal axis which concerns their linkages and transformations in a movement-material. A powerful organic life therefore sustains the figure, from one axis to the other, and sometimes gives it a linear 'tension' similar to Kandinsky (Eggeling's *Diagonal Symphony*), sometimes a punctual expansion closer to Paul Klee (Richter's *Rhytmus 23*). In a second period, line and point are freed from the figure, at the same time as life is freed from the axes of organic representation: power has passed into a non-organic life, which sometimes traces a continuous arabesque directly on to the film from which it will draw images by point-cuts, and sometimes generates the image by making the point flicker on and off on the void of a dark film.

This is the camera-less cinema of McLaren, which implies a new relationship with sound, whether in *Begone Dull Care* or *Workshop Experiment in Animated Sound*, or *Blinkity Blank*. But although these elements already had an important role, a third epoch appears when the black or white screen stands for the outside of all the images, when the flickerings multiply the interstices like irrational cuts (Tony Conrad's *The Flicker*), when proceeding by loops effects relinkages (George Landow's *The Film that Rises to the Surface of Clarified Butter*). The film does not record the filmic process in this way without projecting a cerebral process. A flickering brain, which relinks or creates loops – this is cinema. Lettrism had already gone a long way in this direction, and, after the geometric epoch and the 'engraving' epoch, proclaimed a cinema of expansion without camera, and also without screen or film stock. Everything can be used as a screen, the body of a protagonist or even the bodies of the spectators; everything can replace the film stock, in a virtual film which now only goes on in the head, behind the pupils, with sound sources taken as required from the auditorium. A disturbed brain-death or a new brain which would be at once the screen, the film stock and the camera, each time membrane of the outside and the inside?[39]

In short, the three cerebral components are the point-cut, relinkage and the black or white screen. If the cut no longer forms part of either of the two series of images which it determines, there are only relinkages on either side. And, if it grows larger, if it absorbs all the images, then it becomes the screen, as contact independent of distance, co-presence or application of black and white, of negative and positive, of place and obverse, of full and empty, of past and future, of brain and cosmos, of the inside and the outside. It is these three aspects, topological, of probabilistic and irrational. which constitute the new image of thought. Each is easily inferred from the others, and forms with the others a circulation: the noosphere.

3

Resnais and the Straubs are probably the greatest political film-makers in the West, in modern cinema. But, oddly, this is not through the presence of the people. On the contrary, it is because they know how to show how the people are what is missing, what is not there. Thus Resnais, in *La guerre est finie*, in relation to a Spain that will not be seen: do the people in the old central committee stand with the young terrorists or the tired militant? And the German people in the Straubs' *Unreconciled*: has there ever been a German people, in a country which has bungled its revolutions, and was constituted under Bismarck and Hitler, to be separated again? This is the first big difference between classical and modern cinema. For in classical cinema, the people are there, even though they are oppressed, tricked, subject, even though blind or unconscious. Soviet cinema is an example: the people are already there in Eisenstein, who shows them performing a qualitative leap in *The General Line (Old and New)*, or who, in *Ivan the Terrible*, makes them the advanced edge held in check by the tsar; and, in Pudovkin, it is on each occasion the progression of a certain awareness which means that the people already has a virtual existence in process of being actualized; and in Vertov and Dovzhenko, in two different ways, there is a unanimity which calls the different peoples into the same melting-pot from which the future emerges. But unanimity is also the political character of American cinema before and during the war: this time, it is not the twists and turns of class struggle and the confrontation of ideologies, but the economic crises, the fight against moral prejudice, profiteers and demagogues, which mark the awareness of a people, at the lowest point of their misfortune as well as at the peak of their hope (the unanimism of King Vidor, Capra, or Ford, for the problem runs through the Western as much as through the social drama, both testifying to the existence of a people, in hardships as well as in ways of recovering and rediscovering itself).[40] In American and in Soviet cinema, the people are already there, real before being actual, ideal without being abstract. Hence the idea that the cinema, as art of the masses, could be the supreme revolutionary or democratic art, which makes the masses a true subject. But a great many factors were to compromise this belief: the rise of Hitler, which gave cinema as its object not the masses become subject but the masses subjected; Stalinism, which replaced the unanimism of peoples with the tyrannical unity of a party; the break-up of the American people, who could no longer believe themselves to be either the melting-pot of peoples past or the seed of a people to come (it was the neo-Western that first demonstrated this break-up). In short, if there were a modern political cinema, it would be on this basis: the people no longer exist, or not yet . . . *the people are missing.*

No doubt this truth also applied to the West, but very few authors discovered it, because it was hidden by the mechanisms of power and the systems of majority. On the other hand, it was absolutely clear in the third world, where oppressed and exploited nations remained in a state of perpetual minorities, in a collective identity crisis. Third world and minorities gave rise to authors who would be in a position, in relation to their nation and their personal situation in that nation, to say: the people are what is missing. Kafka and Klee had been the first to state this explicitly. The first said that minor literatures, 'in the small nations', ought to supplement a 'national consciousness which is often inert and always in process of disintegration', and fulfil collective tasks in the absence of a people; the second said that painting, to bring together all the parts of its 'great work', needed a 'final force', the people who were still missing.[41] This was all the more true for cinema as mass-art. Sometimes the third world film-maker finds himself before an illiterate public, swamped by American, Egyptian or Indian serials, and karate films, and he has to go through all this, it is this material that he has to work on, to extract from it the elements of a people who are still missing (Lino Brocka). Sometimes the minority film-maker finds himself in the impasse described by Kafka: the impossibility of not 'writing', the impossibility of writing in the dominant language, the impossibility of writing differently (Pierre Perrrault encounters this situation in *Un pays sans bon sens*, the impossibility of not speaking, the impossibility of speaking other than in English, the impossibility of speaking English, the impossibility of settling in France in order to speak French . . .), and it is through this state of crisis that he has to pass, it is this that has to be resolved. This acknowledgement of a people who are missing is not a renunciation of political cinema, but on the contrary the new basis on which it is founded, in the third world and for minorities. Art, and especially cinematographic art, must take part in this task: not that of addressing a people, which is presupposed already there, but of contributing to the invention of a people. The moment the master, or the colonizer, proclaims 'There have never been people here', the missing people are a becoming, they invent themselves, in shanty towns and camps, or in ghettos, in new conditions of struggle to which a neccessarily political art must contribute.

There is a second big difference between classical and modern political cinema, which concerns the relationship between the political and the private. Kafka suggested that 'major' literatures always maintained a border between the political and the private, however mobile, whilst, in minor literature, the private affair was immediately political and 'entailed a verdict of life or death'. And it is true that, in the large nations, the family, the couple, the individual himself go about their own business, even though this business necessarily expresses social contradictions and problems, or directly suffers their effects. The private element can thus become the place of a becoming conscious, in so far as it goes back to root causes, or reveals the 'object' that it expresses. In this sense, classical cinema constantly maintained this boundary which marked the correlation of the political and the private, and which allowed, through the intermediary of an awareness, passage from one social force to another, from one political position to another: Pudovkin's *Mother* discovers the son's real object in fighting, and takes it over; in Ford's *The Grapes of Wrath*, it is the mother who sees clearly up to a certain point, and who is relieved by the son when conditions change. This is no longer the case in modern political cinema, where no boundary survives to provide a minimum distance or evolution: the private affair merges with the social – or political – immediate. In Güney's *Yol*, the family clans form a network of alliances, a fabric of relationships so close-knit that one character must marry the wife of his dead brother, and another go far away to look for his guilty wife, across a desert of snow, to have her punished in the proper place; and, in *The Flock* as in *Yol*, the most progressive hero is condemned to death in advance. It could be said that this is a matter of archaic pastoral families. But, in fact, what is important is that there is no longer a 'general line', that is, of evolution from the Old to the New, or of revolution which produces a leap from one to the other. There is rather, as in South American cinema, a juxtaposition or compenetration of the old and the new which 'makes up an absurdity', which assumes 'the form of aberration'.[42] What replaces the correlation of the political and the private is the coexistence, to the point of absurdity, of very different social stages. It is in this way that, in Glauber Rocha's work, the myths of the people, prophetism and banditism, are the archaic obverse of capitalist violence, as if the people were turning and increasing against themselves the violence that they suffer from somewhere else out of a need for idolization (*Black God and White Devil*). Gaining awareness is disallowed either because it takes place in the air, as with the intellectual, or because it is compressed into a hollow, as with Antonio das Mortes, capable only of grasping the juxtaposition of two violences and the continuation of one by the other.

What, then, is left? The greatest 'agitprop' cinema that has ever been made: the agitprop is no longer a result of a becoming conscious, but consists of *putting everthing into a trance*, the people and its masters, and the camera itself, pushing everything into a state of aberration, in order to communicate violences as well as to make private business pass into the political, and political affairs into the private (*Earth Entranced*). Hence the very specific aspect assumed by the critique of myth in Rocha: it is not a matter of analysing myth in order to discover its archaic meaning or structure, but of connecting archaic myth to the state of the drives in an absolutely contemporary society, hunger, thirst , sexuality, power, death, worship. In Asia, in Brocka's work, we can also find the immediacy of the raw drive and social violence underneath the myth, for the former is no more 'natural' than the latter is 'cultural'.[43] A lived actual which at the same time indicates the impossibility of living can be extracted from myth in other ways, but continues to constitute the new object of political cinema: putting into a trance, putting into a crisis. In Pierre Perrault, it is a matter of a state of crisis and not of trance. It is a matter of stubborn quests rather than of violent drives. However, the aberrant quest for French ancestors (*Le règne du jour, Un pays sans bon sens, C'était un Québécois en Bretagne*) testifies in its own way, beneath the myth of origins, to the absence of boundary between the private and the political, but also to the impossibility of living in these conditions, for the colonized person who comes up against an impasse in every direction.[44] It is as if modern political cinema were no longer constituted on the basis of a possibility of evolution and revolution, like the classical cinema, but on impossibilities, in the style of Kafka: *the intolerable*. Western authors cannot save themselves from this impasse, unless they settle for a cardboard people and paper revolutionaries: it is a condition which makes Comolli a true political film-maker when he takes as his object a double impossibility, that of forming a group *and* that of not forming a group, 'the impossibility of escaping from the group and the impossibility of being satisfied with it' (*L'ombre rouge*).[45]

If the people are missing, if there is no longer consciousness, evolution or revolution, it is the scheme of reversal which itself becomes impossible. There will no longer be conquest of power by a proletariat, or by a united or unified people. The best third world film-makers could believe in this for a time: Rocha's Guevarism, Chahine's Nasserism, black American cinema's black-powerism. But this was the perspective from which these authors were still taking part in the classical conception, so slow, imperceptible and difficult to site clearly. The death-knell for becoming conscious was precisely the consciousness that there were no people, but always several peoples, an infinity of peoples, who remained to be united, or should not be united, in order for the problem to change. It is in this way that third world cinema is a cinema of minorities, because the people exist only in the condition of minority, which is why they are missing. It is in minorities that private business is immediately political. Acknowledging the failure of fusions or unifications which did not re-create a tyrannical unity, and did not turn back against the people, modern political cinema has been created on this fragmentation, this break-up. This is its third difference. After the 1970s, black American cinema makes a return to the ghettos, returns to this side of a consciousness, and, instead of replacing a · negative image of the black with a positive one, multiplies types and 'characters', and each time creates or re-creates only a small part of the image which no longer corresponds to a linkage of actions, but to shattered states of emotions or drives, expressible in pure images and sounds: the specificity of black cinema is now defined by a new form, 'the struggle that must bear on the medium itself' (Charles Burnett, Robert Gardner, Haile Gerima, Charles Lane).[46] In another style,this is the compositional mode of Chahine in Arab cinema: *Why Alexandria?* reveals a plurality of intertwined lines, primed from the beginning, one of these lines being the principal one (the story of the boy), the others having to be pushed until they cut across the principal one; and *Memory* leaves no place for the principal line, and pursues the multiple threads which end in the author's heart attack, conceived as internal trial and verdict, in a kind of *Why Me?*, but where the arteries of the inside are in immediate contact with the lines of the outside. In Chahine's work, the question 'why' takes on a properly cinematographic value, just as much as the question 'how' in Godard. 'Why?' is the question of the inside, the question of the I: for, if the people are missing, if they are breaking up into minorities, it is I who am first of all a people, the people of my atoms as Carmelo Bene said, the people of my arteries as Chahine said (for his part, Gerima says that, if there is a plurality of black 'movements', each film-maker is a movement in himself). 'But why?' is also the question from the outside, the question of the world, the question of the people who, missing, invent themselves, who have a chance to invent themselves by asking the I the question that it asked them: Alexandria-I, I-Alexandria. Many third world films invoke memory, implicitly or even in their title, Perrault's *Pour la suite du monde*, Chahine's *Memory*, Khleifi's *Fertile Memory*. This is not a psychological memory as faculty for summoning recollections, or even a collective memory as that of an existing people. It is, as we have seen, the strange faculty which puts into immediate contact the outside and the inside, the people's business and private business, the people who are missing and the I who is absent, a membrane, a double becoming. Kafka spoke of this power taken on by memory in small nations: 'The memory of a small nation is no shorter than that of a large one, hence it works on the existing material at a deeper level.' It gains in depth and distance what it lacks in extent. It is no longer psychological nor collective, because each person 'in a little country' inherits only the portion due to him, and has no goal other than this portion, even if he neither recognizes nor maintains it. Communication of the world and the I in a fragmented world and in a fragmented I which are constantly being exchanged. It is as if the whole memory of the world is set down on each oppressed people, and the whole memory of the I comes into play in an organic crisis. The arteries of the people to which I belong, or the people of my arteries . . .

But is this I not the I of the third world intellectual, whose portrait Rocha and Chahine among others have often sketched, and who has to break with the condition of the colonized, but can do so only by going over to the colonizer's side, even if only aesthetically, through artistic influences? Kafka pointed to another path, a narrow path between the two dangers: precisely because 'great talents' or superior individualities are rare in minor literatures, the author is not in a condition to produce individual utterances which would be like invented stories; but also, because the people are missing, the author is in a situation of producing utterances which are already collective, which are like the seeds of the people to come, and whose political impact is immediate and inescapable. The author can be marginalized or separate from his more or less illiterate community as much as you like; this condition puts him all the more in a position to express potential forces and, in his very solitude, to be a true collective agent, a collective leaven, a catalyst. What Kafka suggests for literature is even more valid for cinema, in as much as it brings collective conditions together through itself. And this is in fact the last characteristic of a modern political cinema. The cinema author finds himself before a people which, from the point of view of culture, is doubly colonized: colonized by stories that have come from elsewhere, but also by their own myths become impersonal entities at the service of the colonizer. The author must not, then, make himself into the ethnologist of his people, nor himself invent a fiction which would be one more private story: for every personal fiction, like every impersonal myth, is on the side of the 'masters'. It is in this way that we see Rocha destroying myths from the inside, and Perrault repudiating every fiction that an author could create. There remains the possibility of the author providing himself with 'intercessors', that is, of taking real and not fictional characters, but putting these very characters in the condition of 'making up fiction', of 'making legends', of 'story-telling'. The author takes a step towards his characters, but the characters take a step towards the author: double becoming. Story-telling is not an impersonal myth, but neither is it a personal fiction: it is a word in act, a speech-act through which the character continually crosses the boundary which would separate his private business from politics, and which *itself produces collective utterances*.

Daney observed that African cinema (but this applies to the whole third world) is not, as the West would like, a cinema which dances, but a cinema which talks, a cinema of the speech-act. It is in this way that it avoids fiction and ethnology. In *Ceddo*, Ousmane Sembene extracts the story-telling which is the basis of living speech, which ensures its freedom and circulation, which gives it the value of collective utterance, thus contrasting it with the myths of the Islamic colonist.[47] Was this not already Rocha's way of operating on the myths of Brazil? His internal critique would first isolate a lived present beneath the myth, which could be intolerable, the unbelievable, the impossibility of living now in 'this' society (*Black God and White Devil*) (*Earth Entranced*); then he had to seize from the unliving a speech-act which could not be forced into silence, an act of story-telling which would not be a return to myth but a production of collective utterances capable of raising misery to a strange positivity, the invention of a people (*Antonio das Mortes, The Lion Has Seven Heads, Severed Heads*).[48] The trance, the putting into trances, are a transition, a passage, or a becoming; it is the trance which makes the speech-act possible, through the ideology of the colonizer, the myths of the colonized and the discourse of the intellectual. The author puts the parties in trances in order to contribute to the invention of his people who, alone, can constitute the whole [*ensemble*]. The parties are again not exactly real in Rocha, but reconstructed (and in Sembene they are reconstituted in a story which goes back to the seventeenth century). It is Perrault, at the other end of America, who addresses real characters, his 'intercessors', in order to prevent any fiction, but also to carry out the critique of myth. Operating by putting into crisis, Perrault will isolate the story-telling speech-act, sometimes as the generator of action (the reinvention of porpoise-fishing in *Pour la suite du monde*), sometimes taking itself as object (the search for ancestors in *Le règne du jour*), sometimes bringing about a creative simulation (the elk-hunt in *La bête lumineuse*), but always in such a way that story-telling is itself memory, and memory is invention of a people. Everything perhaps culminates in *Le pays de la terre sans arbres*, which brings all the ways together, or, by contrast, in *Un pays sans bon sens*, which minimizes them (for, here, the real character has the most solitude, and does not even belong to Quebec, but to a tiny French minority in an English country, and leaps from Winnipeg to Paris the better to invent his belonging to Quebec, and to produce a collective utterance for it).[49] Not the myth of a past people, but the story-telling of the people to come. The speech-act must create itself as a foreign language in a dominant language, precisely in order to express an impossibility of living under domination. It is the real character who leaves his private condition, at the same time as the author his abstract condition, to form, between the two, between several, the utterances of Quebec, about Quebec, about America, about Britanny and Paris (free indirect discourse). In Jean Rouch, in Africa, the trance of the *Maîtres fous* is extended in a double becoming, through which the real characters become another by story-telling, but the author, too, himself becomes another, by providing himself with real characters. It may be objected that Jean Rouch can only with difficulty be considered a third world author, but no one has done so much to put the West to flight, to flee himself, to break with a cinema of ethnology and say *Moi un Noir*, at a time when blacks play roles in American series or those of hip Parisians. The speech-act has several heads, and, little by little, plants the elements of a people to come as the free indirect discourse of Africa about itself, about

America or about Paris. As a general rule, third world cinema has this aim: through trance or crisis, to constitute an assemblage which brings real parties together, in order to make them produce collective utterances as the prefiguration of the people who are missing (and, as Klee says, 'we can do no more').

9 The components of the image

1

The break between the talkie and the silent picture, and the resistances which it produced, have often been emphasized. But it has been shown with as much justification how the silent film called for the talkie, already implied it: the silent film was not silent, but only 'noiseless', as Mitry says, or only 'deaf', as Michel Chion says. What the talkie seemed to lose was the universal language, and the omnipotence of montage; what it seemed to gain according to Mitry, was a continuity in the passage from one place to another, from one moment to another. But another difference perhaps appears if we compare the components of the silent image with those of the talking image. The silent image is composed from the seen image, and the intertitle which is read (second function of the eye). The intertitle includes, among other elements, speech-acts. Being scriptual, those passed into the indirect style (the intertitle, 'I'm going to kill you', is read in the form 'He says he's going to kill him'), took on an abstract universality and expressed in some sense a law. Whilst the seen image kept and developed something natural, took on the natural aspect of things and beings. Analysing Murnau's *Tabu* (1931), Louis Audibert observes that it is not only a film kept silent at the time of the talkie, but a way of justifying the permanence of the silent film: for, by virtue of its most profound theme, the visual image points to an innocent physical nature, to an immediate life which has no need of language, whilst the intertitle or piece of writing shows the law, the forbidden, the transmitted order, which come to shatter this innocence, as in Rousseau.[1]

It will be objected that this division is closely linked to the exotic subject of *Tabu*. But this is not clear. Silent cinema constantly showed civilization, the city, the flat, everyday objects, objects of art or cult, every possible artefact. However, it passes on a kind of naturalness to them, which is as it were the secret and beauty of the silent image.[2] Even the great film sets as such have their own naturalness. Even faces take on the appearance of natural phenomena, to adopt Bazin's observation on *The Passion of Joan of Arc*. The visual image shows the structure of a society, its situation, its places and functions, the attitudes and roles, the actions and reactions of the individuals, in short the form and the contents. And, no doubt, it grips speech-acts so tightly that it can make us see the lamentations of the poor or the cry of the rebels. It shows the condition of a speech-act, its immediate consequences and even its phonation. But what it reaches in this way is the nature of a society, the social physics of actions and reactions, even the physics of speech. Eisenstein said that, in Griffith, the poor and the rich were so by nature. But Eisenstein himself preserves the identity of society or of history with nature, with the important reservation that identity is now dialectical, and passes through the transformation of the natural being of man, and of the human being of nature: non-indifferent nature (hence, we have seen, a different conception of montage).[3] In short, in the silent cinema in general, the visual image is, as it were, naturalized, as far as it presents us with the natural being of man in history or society, whilst the other element, the other plane which is as distinct from history as from nature, passes into a discourse that is necessarily 'written', that is read, and put into an indirect style.[4] Hence, silent cinema must intertwine the seen image and the read image to the highest possible degree, whether by forming real blocs with the intertitle, in the style of Vertov or Eisenstein, or by making particularly important scriptual elements pass into the visual (as in the written orders and messages in *Tabu*, or, in Keaton's *Our Hospitality*, the vengeful father who sees the framed motto 'Love thy neighbour as thyself' over his daughter's head . . .), or at any rate, by developing graphic research on the written text (for example, the repetition of the word 'Brothers' whose letters grow larger in *Battleship Potemkin*).

What happens with the talking cinema? The speech-act is no longer connected with the second function of the eye, it is no longer read but heard. It becomes direct, and recovers the distinctive features of 'discourse' which were altered in the silent or written film (the distinctive feature of discourse, according to Benveniste, is the I-You relation between persons). It will be noticed that cinema does not become audio-visual as a result of this. In contrast to the intertitle, which was an image other than the visual image, the talkie, the sound film are heard, but as *a new dimension of the visual image, a new component*. It is even for this reason that they are image.[5] This is a situation which is completely different from that in theatre. It is likely, from this point, that the talkie modifies the visual image: in so far as it is heard, it *makes visible* in itself something that did not freely appear in the silent film. It is as if the visual image is de-naturalized. In effect, it takes on an area that might even be called *human interactions*, which are distinct from both previous structures and consequent actions or reactions. Of course, interactions are closely bound up with structures, actions and reactions. But the latter are conditions or consequences of the speech-act, whilst the former are the correlate of the act, and only show themselves in it, through it, as the reciprocities of perspective in the I-You relationship, the interferences corresponding to communication. A sociology of communication is constituted on this basis: interactions caught at the point where they do not derive from pre-existing social structures and are not the same as psychic actions and reactions, but are the correlate of speech-acts or silence, stripping the social of its naturalness, forming systems which are far from being in equilibrium or invent their own equilibrium (socialization-desocialization) – interactions are established in the margins or at the crossroads, constituting a whole *mise-en-scène* or dramaturgy of daily life (uneasinesses, deceptions and conflicts in interaction), opening up a field of special perception, of specific visibility, and provoking a 'hypertrophy of the eye'.[6] Interactions *make themselves seen* in speech-acts. Interactions do not simply concern the partners in a speech-act precisely because they are not explained through individuals, any more than they derive from a structure: rather it is the speech-act which, through its continuous circulation, propagation and autonomous evolution, will create the interaction between individuals or groups who are far away, dispersed, indifferent to each other. As in a song which crosses places, spaces and people (one of the first examples of this was Mamoulian's *Love Me Tonight*). If it is true that the talking cinema is an interactionist sociology in action, or rather the other way round, if it is true that interactionism is a talking cinema, it will come as no surprise that rumour has been a cinematographically privileged object: Ford's *The Whole Town's Talking*, Mankiewicz's *People Will Talk*, and already Lang's *M*.

As Noël Burch summarizes it, one of the first sequences in *M* appears like this: 'A man reads out a police poster, in front of which a crowd has gathered, in a loud voice; the same text is continued in the form, first, of a radio announcement, then in that of the reading in a loud voice of a newspaper in the café which serves as frame . . . and where excited customers end up coming to blows, the victim accusing his assailant of being a stainer of reputation. This phrase, by which the scene is interrupted, goes hand in hand with "*What a Slanderer!*" shouted out by a man whose apartment the police are going through on the basis of an anonymous letter; finally, when this man, unjustly suspected, suggests that the killer could be anybody in the street, this response introduces the fourth episode in the series: somebody gets manhandled by the crowd as a result of a tragic misunderstanding.'[7] Of course there is a situation, actions and reactions; but another, irreducible dimension is mixed with these. It will be noticed, in the example of Lang as in many others, that the written (the poster, the newspaper) is there to be rendered by the voice, taken up by determinate speech-acts which make each scene go hand in hand with the next. To the extent that, in fact, it is one and the same indeterminate speech-act (rumour) which circulates and spreads, making visible the live interactions between independent characters and separate places. And the more autonomous the speech-act becomes as it goes beyond determinate characters, the more the field of visual perception that it opens up is presented as problematic, positioned on a problematic point at the limit of tangled lines of interaction: as in the killer 'leaning with his back against the wall' whom we can barely see (or the doubles in Ford's film and the forkings in that of Mankiewicz). Structure and situation continue to condition interactions, as they did actions and reactions, but they are regulative and no longer constitute conditions. 'Interaction remains structured by such conditions, but *stays problematic in the course of action.*'[8]

We can see from all this the extent to which talking cinema had nothing in common with the theatre and that the two could only be confused at the level of bad films. The question: What innovations did talking cinema bring to the silent film?, then loses its ambiguity and may be dealt with briefly. Take a theme like that of police-gangster collaboration: in Eisenstein's *Strike*, this collaboration which puts the barrel workers at the service of the management is caught in a play of actions and reactions which matches the natural dependence of the gangster and derives from the structure of a capitalist society; in *M* the collaboration passes through a speech-act which becomes independent of the two parties concerned, because a phrase begun by the commissioner will be continued, extended, or transformed by the leader of the gang, in two different places, and will make visible a problematic interaction of parties which are themselves independent, as a function of 'circumstances' (sociology of situations, of circumstances). Or take another theme like that of degradation: in Murnau's *The Last Laugh* the degradation of the head porter is able to pass through a ceremonial and a phonatory (even though silent) scene in the manager's office; it can include visual rhymes, between the revolving-doors at the beginning, the dream of the doors, and the doors to the lavatories where the man ends up; the film's splendour consists of a physics of social degradation, where an individual goes down through the places and functions in a structure in the big hotel, which has a 'natural' or constitutive role. In Sternberg's *The Blue Angel*, in contrast, the teacher's cock-a-doodle-doo is a sound drama, a speech-act, which is this time emitted only by a single individual but none the less takes on an autonomy, and makes visible the interaction of two independent places, the school which the teacher leaves for the cabaret in a first cock-a-doodle-doo, shy and becoming intoxicated with himself, then the cabaret which the teacher leaves to return to die in the school, after another cock-a-doodle-doo which marks the climax of the degradation and abjectness that he has suffered. There is something here that the silent film could not achieve, even and especially with alternate montage.[9] If Sternberg's film is a great work of talking cinema, it is because the two separate places, the school and the club, respectively pass through the ordeal of silence and sound, and enter all the more into interaction because the cock-a-doodle-doo goes from the first to the second, then from the second to the first, in two different times, in consequence of interactions internal to the teacher himself.

The silent cinema carried out a division of the visible image and the readable speech. But when speech makes itself heard, it is as if it makes something new visible, and the visible image, denaturalized, begins to become readable in turn, *as* something visible or visual. The latter, from this point, acquires problematic values or a certain equivocal quality which it did not have in the silent cinema. What the speech-act makes visible, interaction, may always be badly deciphered, read, seen: hence a whole rise in the lie, in deception, which takes place in the visual image. Jean Douchet defined Mankiewicz by 'the cinematographic power of language'.[10] And certainly no author has made such use of the speech-act, which nevertheless owes nothing to the theatre. For the speech-act in Mankiewicz makes visible interactions, but ones which remain at the time imperceptible to many participants, or badly seen, and which allow themselves to be deciphered only by privileged characters gifted with hypertrophy of the eye. So that these interactions (forkings) which come from speech will return to speech: second speech or voice-off, which can only make visible afterwards what initially escaped the view, because it was too strong, too incredible, or too awful.[11] It is forking which becomes the visual correlate of a double speech-act in Mankiewicz, once as voice-off, once as voice in action.

It was inevitable that the talkie took what appeared to be the most superficial social forms as its privileged object: encounters with the other, other sex, other class, other region, other nation, other civilization. The less of a pre-existing social structure there is, the better is revealed, not a silent natural life, but pure forms of sociability necessarily passing through *conversation*. And conversation is undoubtedly inseparable from structures, places and functions, from interests and motives, from actions and reactions which are external to it. But it also possesses the power of artificially subordinating all these determinations, of making them a stake, or rather of making them the variables of an interaction which corresponds to it. Interests, feeling or love no longer determine conversation, they themselves depend on the division of stimulation in conversation, the latter determining relations of force and structurations which are particular to it. This is why there is always something mad, schizophrenic, in a conversation taken for itself (with bar conversations, lovers' conversations, money conversations, or small talk as its essence). Psychiatrists have studied the conversation of schizophrenics, with its mannerisms, its interactional bringing closer and putting at a distance, but all conversation is schizophrenic, conservation is a model of schizophrenia, not the other way round. Berthet rightly says: 'Seeing conversation as the whole of what comes to be said, what polycephalic, and almost half-mad, subject is to be imagined to utter it?'[12] It would be wrong to consider conversation in terms of partners who are already joined or linked. Even in this case, the specificity of conversation lies in its redistributing the stakes, and its initiation of interactions between supposedly dispersed and independent people who pass through the scene by chance: so that conversation is a contracted rumour, and rumour an expanded conversation, both of which reveal the autonomy of communication or circulation. This time, it is not conversation which provides the model of interaction; it is interaction between separated people, or within one and the same person, which is the model of conversation. What might be called sociability, or 'small talk',[13*] in a very general sense, is never identical with society: it is a matter of the interactions which coincide with speech-acts, and not actions and reactions which pass through them according to a prior structure. This essence of small talk in conversation, as distinct from society, is what Proust discovered, but also the sociologist Simmel. It is strange to note how powerless theatre and even the novel were to grasp conversation for itself, except in authors contemporary with cinema (Proust, James), or even directly influenced by it (Wilson in the theatre, or Dos Passos and Nathalie Sarraute in the novel).[14] In fact, the talking cinema was in absolutely no danger of being confused with filmed theatre or novel, except at its lowest level. What cinema invented was the sound conversation which, until then, had escaped the theatre and novel alike, and the visual or readable interactions which corresponded to conversation. Perhaps the lowest level was always in danger of drawing cinema into a dead-end: filmed dialogue. So that it would take neo-realism and especially the new wave to rediscover conversation and interaction: this was a great reactivation, in a positive, parodic, or critical mode, in Truffaut, Godard and Chabrol. But conversation and interaction were none the less, from the beginning of the talkie, cinema's triumph, as it made them a special genre, the properly cinematographic 'comedy', the American comedy *par excellence* (but also the French comedy, with more ambiguity, in Pagnol and Guitry).

Conversation will produce the interactions which tighten or loosen the bonds between individuals, which oblige them to be winners or losers, to modify or even reverse their perspective independently of its contents or objects.[15] For example, is the old lady going to finance the enterprise, is the young girl going to seduce the man? It is the stimulation of the play of interactions which decides economic or amorous contents, not the other way round. The cinematographic talkie, whose potential is realized from the outset by the American comedy, is defined by the way that speech-acts fill space, in increasingly numerous and delicate conditions which on each occasion constitute the 'right form', bringing together talking speed and the space shown. Everybody talks at once, or the speech of one person fills the space so well that it reduces the other to vain attempts, stammerings, efforts to interrupt. The ordinary madness in the American family, and the constant intrusion of the stranger or the abnormal – like a disequilibrium in systems which are themselves far from equilibrium – will produce the classics of comedy (Capra's *Arsenic and Old Lace*). An actress like Katharine Hepburn reveals her mastery in the sociability stakes through the speed of her retorts, the way that she disorients her partner and ties him in a knot, the indifference to contents, the variety or reversal of perspectives through which she passes. Cukor, McCarey and Hawks make *conversation*, the craziness of conversation, the essence of American comedy, and Hawks was able to give it an unprecedented speed. Lubitsch conquers a whole area of *subconversation* (somewhat as Nathalie Sarraute defines it). Capra achieves *discourse* as element of comedy, precisely because he shows an interaction with the public within discourse itself. In *Ruggles of Red Gap*, McCarey already contrasted English reserve and conciseness with free American discourse founded on Lincoln's declaration. And it is understandable that discourse as cinematographic object could make Capra go from comedy to the series 'Why we fight', in so far as the very form of sociability, despite its relations of forces and the cruelty essential to its stakes, appears in democracy, defined as 'artificial world' where individuals have abandoned the objective aspects of their situation and the personal aspects of their activity in order to produce a pure interaction between themselves. American comedy mobilizes nations (confrontation of America with England, France, the USSR . . .), but also regions (the man from Texas), classes and also those outside classes (the drifter, the tramp, the adventurer, all characters dear to interactionist sociology), so as to make visible interactions, discontents in interaction, reversals in interaction. And, if objective social contents are blurred in favour of forms of sociability, subjects survive, in the accents and intonations of country or class, as subjects of speech-acts, or as variables of the speech-act caught in its intersubjective whole. Perhaps in a different cinematographic genre, in certain adventure films, subjects themselves disappear. In this case the rapid voices become atonal and accentless, horizontal, looking for the shortest route, voices which are already blank in the same sense as blank weapons, replicas each of which could just as well be uttered by someone else, to the point where conversation reveals its madness all the more because it now merges with the autonomous whole of what 'comes to be said', and where interaction is revealed in a purer form because it has become oddly neutral: as in the Bogart-Lauren Bacall couple in certain Hawks films, like *To Have and Have Not* or *The Big Sleep*.[16]

The heard speech-act, as component of the visual image, makes something visible in that image. It is perhaps in this sense that Comolli's hypothesis is to be understood: the abandonment of depth of field, and the taking on of a certain flatness of the image, would have had as one of their principal causes the talkie, which constituted a fourth dimension of the visual image, supplementing the third.[17] But, as such, the speech-act is not restricted to making visible; it sometimes itself sees (Michel Chion has analysed the special case of these 'seeing voices', which have 'an eye in the voice', like that of Lang's *The Testament of Dr Mabuse*, or that of the computer in Kubrick's *2001*, to which could be added Mankiewicz's voices).[18] And, more generally, the heard speech-act is itself in a sense seen. It is not just its source which may (or may not) be seen. In being heard, it is itself seen, as itself tracing a path in the visual image. It is true that silent cinema could already show the space covered by an unheard speech-act and supplement it: the passing on of a slogan [*mot d'ordre*] in Eisenstein, the seductress's whistle which makes the man jump in Murnau's *Sunrise*, the call of the look-out which goes through progressive close-ups in Murnau's *Tabu*, the siren and noises of machines, through beams of light in Lang's *Metropolis*. These are great moments of silent film. But it was the space covered which allowed the silent speech-act to be reconstituted in this way. Whilst it is now the heard voice which spreads in visual space, or fills it, trying to reach its addressee across obstacles and diversions. It hollows out space. Bogart's voice at the microphone is like a guided missile which strives to reach the woman in the crowd who must get the urgent warning (*The Enforcer* by Walsh and Windust), the mother's song has to go up the stairs and through the rooms before its refrain finally reaches the imprisoned child (Hitchcock's *The Man Who Knew Too Much*). Whale's *The Invisible Man* was a masterpiece of the talking cinema because speech became all the more visible in it. What Philippon says about Alaouie's *Beyrouth la rencontre* applies to all talking cinema worthy of the name, in its fundamental difference from theatre: 'Speech is truly seen forcing a difficult path through the ruins . . . [The author] has filmed speech as something visible, as a material in movement.'[19] The reversal which tends to be produced in the talkie, in relation to the silent cinema, thus appears: instead of a seen image *and* a read speech, the speech-act becomes visible at the same time as it makes itself heard, but also the visual image becomes legible as such, as visual image in which the speech-act is inserted as a component.

2

We are sometimes reminded that there is not just one soundtrack, but at least three groups, words, noises, music. Perhaps an even greater number of sound components should be distinguished: noises (which isolate an object and are isolated from each other), sounds (which indicate relationships and are themselves in mutual relation), phonations (which cut into these relations, which can be shouts, but also genuine 'jargons', as in the talking burlesque of Chaplin or Jerry Lewis), words, music. It is clear that these different elements can enter into a rivalry, fight each other, supplement each other, overlap, transform each other: this was the object of thorough research from the outset of talking cinema by René Clair; it was one of the most important aspects of Tati's work, where intrinsic relations of sounds are systematically deformed, but also where elementary noises become characters (the ping-pong ball, the car in *Mr Hulot's Holiday*), and where, conversely, characters enter into conversation through noises (the pfff conversation in *Playtime*).[20] All this would be a sign, following a fundamental thesis of Fano, that there is already a single sound continuum, whose elements are separate only in terms of an ultimate referent or signified, but not of a 'signifier'.[21] The voice is not separable from noises, from the sounds which on occasion make it inaudible: this is indeed the second important difference between cinematographic and theatrical speech-acts. Fano cites the example of Mizoguchi's *A Story from Chikmatsu*, 'where Japanese phenomena, sound effects and punctuations by percussion weave a continuum whose mesh is so fine that it seems impossible to find its weft'. All of Mizoguchi's sound work goes in this direction. With Godard, not only can music hide the voice, as at the beginning of *Week-end*, but *First Name Carmen* uses musical movements, speech-acts, sounds of doors, sounds of the sea or the Métro, cries of seagulls, pluckings of strings, revolver-shots, slidings of bows and machine-gun bursts, the 'attack' of music and the 'attack' in the bank, the correspondences between these elements, and especially their displacements, their cuts, in such a way as to form the power of one and the same sound continuum. Rather than invoking the signifier and the signified, we might say that the sound components are separate only in the abstraction of their pure hearing. But, in so far as they are a specific dimension, a fourth dimension of the visual image (which does not mean that they merge with a referent or a signified), then they all form together one single component, a continuum. And so far as they rival, overlap, cross and cut into each other, they trace a path full of obstacles in visual space, and they do not make themselves heard without also being seen, for themselves, independently of their sources, at the same time as they make the image readable, a little like a musical score.

If the continuum (or the sound component) does not have separable elements, it is none the less differentiated at each moment into two diverging directions which express its relation to the visual image. This double relation passes through the out-of-field, even though the latter is fully part of the cinematographic visual image. It is true that it is not sound that invents the out-of-field, but it is sound which dwells in it, and which fills the visual not-seen with a specific presence. From the outset, the problem of sound was: how could sound and speech be used so that they were not simply an unnecessary addition to what was seen? This problem was not a denial that sound and talking were a component of the visual image; on the contrary: it was because it was a specific component that sound did not have to be unnecessary in relation to what was seen in the visual. The famous Soviet manifesto already proposed that sound referred to a source out-of-field, and would therefore be a visual counterpoint, and not the double of a seen point: the noise of boots is all the more interesting when they are not seen.[22] We may recall René Clair's great successes in this area, like *Under the Roofs of Paris*, where the young man and the young girl pursue their conversation, lying in the dark, all the lights out. Bresson maintains this principle of non-redundancy, non-coincidence, very firmly: 'When a sound can suppress an image, suppress the image or neutralize it.'[23] This is the third difference from theatre. In short, sound in all its forms comes to fill the out-of-field of the visual image, and realizes itself all the more in this sense as component of that image: at the level of the voice, it is what is called voice-off, whose source is not seen.

In Volume 1 we considered the two aspects of the out-of-field, the to-the-side and the elsewhere, the relative and the absolute.

Sometimes the out-of-field is linked to a visual space, by right, which naturally extends the space seen in the image: in this case the sound-off prefigures what it comes from, something that will soon be seen, or which could be seen in a subsequent image. For instance, the noise of a lorry that is not yet visible, or the sounds of a conversation only one of whose participants is visible. This first relation is that of a given set with a larger set which extends or encompasses it, but which is of the same nature. Sometimes, in contrast, the out-of-field shows a power of a different kind, exceeding any space or set: it is connected in this case to the Whole which is expressed in sets, to the change which is expressed in movement, to the duration which is expressed in space, to the living concept which is expressed in the image, to the spirit which is expressed in matter. In this second case, the sound or voice-off consists rather of music, and of very particular speech-acts which are reflexive and not now interactive ones (the voice which evokes, comments, knows, endowed with an omnipotence or a strong power over the sequence of images). These two relations of the out-of-field, the actualizable relation with other sets, the virtual relation with the whole, are inversely proportional; but both of them are alike strictly inseparable from the visual image, and already appear in the silent film (for instance, Dreyer's *The Passion of Joan of Arc*). When cinema acquires sound, when sound fills the out-of-field, it therefore does so in consequence of these two aspects, of their complementarity and inverse proportionality, even if it is destined to produce new effects. Pascal Bonitzer and then Michel Chion have called the unity of voice-off into question, by showing how it was necessarily divided according to the two relations.[24] In effect it seems as if the sound continuum was constantly differentiated in two directions, one of which carries noises and interactive speech-acts, the other reflexive speech-acts and music. Godard once said that two soundtracks are needed because we have two hands, and cinema is a manual and tactile art. And it is true that sound has a special relation with touch, hitting on things, on bodies, as at the beginning of *First Name Carmen*. But even for a person with no arms, the sound continuum would continue to be differentiated in accordance with the two relations of the visual image, its actualizable relation with other possible images, realized or not, and its virtual relation with a totality of images which is unrealizable.

The differentiation of the aspects in the sound continuum is not a separation, but a communication, a circulation which constantly reconstitutes the continuum. Take, for example, *The Testament of Dr Mabuse* according to Michel Chion's exemplary analysis: the terrible voice seems to be always to the side, in accordance with the first aspect of the out-of-field, but, as soon as there is a move to the side, it is already elsewhere, omnipotent, in accordance with the second aspect, until it is localized, identified in the image seen (voice-in). None of these aspects, however, negates or reduces the others, and each survives in the others: there is no last word. This is also true of music: in Antonioni's *Eclipse*, the music that first surrounds the lovers in the park is discovered to come from a pianist whom we do not see, but who is to the side; the sound-off thus changes its status, passes from one out-of-field to the other, then goes back in the opposite direction, when it continues to make itself heard far from the park, following the lovers in the street.[25] But, because the out-of-field belongs to the visual image, the circuit passes equally through the sounds-in situated in the seen image (hence all the instances where the music's source is seen, as in the dances beloved of the French school). This is a network of sound communication and permutation, bearing noises, sounds, reflexive or interactive speech-acts and music, which enter the visual image, from outside and from inside, and make it all the more 'legible'. The prime example of such a cinematographic network is Mankiewicz, and especially *People Will Talk* where all the speech-acts intercommunicate but also both the visual image to which these speech-acts refer, and the music which harmonizes and goes beyond them, carrying away the image itself. Hence, we are moving towards a problem which does not now concern only the intercommunication of sound elements on the basis of the visual image, but the intercommunication of the latter: in all its forms of belonging, with something that goes beyond it, without being able to do without it, without ever being able to do without it. The circuit is not only that of sound elements, including musical elements, in relation to the visual image, but the relation of the visual image itself with the musical element *par excellence* which slips everywhere, in, off, noises, sounds, speeches.

Movement in space expresses a whole which changes, rather as the migration of birds expresses a seasonal variation. Everywhere that a movement is established between things and persons, a variation or a change is established in time, that is, in an open whole which includes them and into which they plunge. We saw this earlier: the movement-image is necessarily the expression of a whole; it forms in this sense an indirect representation of time. This is the very reason that the movement-image has two out-of-fields: the one relative, according to which movement concerning the set of an image is pursued or can be pursued in a larger set of the same nature; the other absolute, according to which movement, whatever the set which it is taken as part of, refers to a changing whole which it expresses. According to the first dimension, the visual image links up with other images. According to the other dimension the linked images are internalized in the whole, and the whole is externalized in the images, itself changing at the same time as the images move and link up. Of course, the movement-image does not only have extensive movements (space), but also intensive movements (light) and affective movements (the soul). Time as open and changing totality none the less goes beyond all the movements, even the personal changes of the soul or affective movements, even though it cannot do without them. It is thus caught in an indirect representation, because it cannot do without movement-images which express it, and yet goes beyond all relative movements forcing us to think an absolute of the movement of bodies, an infinity of the movement of light, a backgroundless [*sans fond*] of the movement of souls: the sublime. From the movement-image to the living concept, and vice versa . . . Now all this already applied to silent cinema. If we ask now what cinema music contributes, the elements of a reply appear. Silent cinema certainly included a music, improvised or programmed. But this music found itself subject to a certain obligation to *correspond* to the visual image, or to serve descriptive, illustrative and narrative ends, acting as a form of intertitle. When cinema develops sound and talking, music is in a sense emancipated, and can take flight.[26] But what does this flight and this emancipation consist of? Eisenstein gave a first response, in his analyses of Prokofiev's music for *Alexander Nevsky*: the image and the music had themselves to form a whole, revealing an element common to the visual and the sound, which would be movement or even vibration. There would be a certain way of *reading* the visual image, corresponding to the hearing of the music. But this thesis does not conceal its intention of assimilating the mixing, or 'audio-visual montage', to silent montage of which it would just be a special case; it fully preserves the idea of correspondence, and replaces external or illustrative correspondence by an internal correspondence; it believes that the whole should be formed by the visual and sound which go beyond themselves in a higher unity.[27] But, since the silent visual image already expressed a whole, how can we ensure that the sound and visual whole is not the same, or, if it is the same, does not give rise to two redundant expressions? For Eisenstein, it is a matter of forming a whole with two expressions whose common measure would be discovered (always commensurability). Whilst the achievement of sound consisted rather in expressing the whole in two incommensurable, non-corresponding ways.

It is in fact in this direction that the problem of cinema music finds a Nietzschean solution, rather than Eisenstein's Hegelian one. According to Nietzsche, or at least according to the still Schopenhaurian Nietzsche of *The Birth of Tragedy*, the visual image comes from Apollo, who causes it to move according to a measure, and makes it represent the whole indirectly, mediately, through the intermediary of lyric poetry or drama. But the whole is also capable of a direct presentation, of an 'immediate image' incommensurable with the first, and this time musical, dionysian: closer to an inexhaustible Will [*Vouloir sans fond*] than to a movement.[28] In tragedy, the musical immediate image is like the core of fire which is surrounded by apollonian visual images, and cannot do without their procession. In the case of cinema, which is first of all a visual art, it will be music which will be thought to add the immediate image to mediate images which represented the whole indirectly. But the essential point has not changed, namely the difference in nature between indirect representation and direct presentation. According to musicians like Pierre Jansen, or, to a lesser degree, Philippe Arthuys, cinema music must be abstract and autonomous, a true 'foreign body' in the visual image, rather like a speck of dust in the eye, and must accompany 'something that is in the film without being shown or suggested in it'.[29] There is certainly a relation, but it is not an external correspondence *nor even an internal one* which would lead us back to an imitation; it is a reaction between the musical foreign body and the completely different visual images, or rather an interaction independent of any common structure. Internal correspondence is no more valid than external, and a barcarole finds just as good a correlate in the movement of light and water as in the embrace of a Venetian couple. Hans Eisler demonstrated this, criticizing Eisenstein: there is no movement common to the visual and to sound, and music does not act as movement, but as 'stimulant to movement without being its double' (that is, as will).[30] For movement-images, visual images in movement, express a whole that changes, but they express it indirectly, so that change as property of the whole does not regularly coincide with any relative movement of persons or things, not even with the affective movement internal to a character or a group: it is expressed directly in music, but as contrast or even in conflict, in disparity with the movement of the visual images. Pudovkin gave an instructive example: the failure of a proletarian demon-stration should not be accompanied by melancholic or even violent music, but constitutes only the drama in interaction with the music, with the change of the whole as rising will of the proletariat. Eisler gives many examples of this 'pathetic distance' between music and images: an incisive fast music for a passive or depressing image, the tenderness or serenity of a barcarole as spirit of place in relation to violent events which are happening, a hymn to solidarity for images of oppression . . . In short, sound cinema adds *a direct, but musical and only musical, non-corresponding presentation* to the indirect representation of time as changing whole. This is the living concept, which goes beyond the visual image, without being able to do without it.

It will be noticed that direct presentation, as Nietzsche said, is not identical to what it presents, to the changing whole or time. It may therefore have a very discontinuous, or rarefied, presence. Moreover, other sound elements may assume a function anal-ogous to that of music: hence the voice-off in its absolute dimension as omnipotent and omniscient voice (Welles's mo-dulation of the voice in *The Magnificent Ambersons*). Or again the voice-in: if Greta Garbo's voice stood out in the talkie, it is because, at a certain point in each of her films, it was capable not only of expressing the internal, personal change of the heroine as affective movement, but of bringing together to form a whole the past, the present and the future, crude intonations, amorous cooings, cold decisions in the present, reminders from memory, bursts of imagination (from her first talking film, *Anna Christie*).[31] Delphine Seyrig perhaps achieves a similar effect in Resnais' *Muriel*, gathering together in her voice the changing whole, from one war to the other, from one Boulogne to the other. As a general rule, music itself becomes 'in'[32*] as soon as its source is seen in the visual image, but without losing its power. These permutations are better explained if an apparent contradiction between the two conceptions that we have discussed, of Fano's 'sound continuum', and of Jansen's 'foreign body', is cleared up.

It is not enough that they are both opposed to the principle of correspondence. In fact, all the sound elements, including music, including silence, form a continuum as something which belongs to the visual image. Which does not prevent this continuum from being continually differentiated in accordance with the two aspects of the out-of-field which also belong to the visual image, one relative, and the other absolute. It is in so far as it presents or fills the absolute that music interacts as a foreign body. But the absolute, or the changing whole, does not merge with its direct presentation: this is why it continually reconstitutes the sound continuum, off and in, and relates it to the visual images which indirectly express it. Now this second movement does not cancel out the other, and preserves for music its autonomous, special power.[33] At the present juncture, cinema remains a fundamentally visual art in relation to which the sound continuum is differentiated in two directions, two heterogeneous streams, but is also re-formed and reconstituted. This is the powerful movement by which, already in the silent film, visual images are internalized in a changing whole, but at the same time as the changing whole is externalized in visual images. With sound, speech and music, the circuit of the movement-image achieves a different figure, different dimensions or components; however, it maintains the communication between the image and a whole which has become increasingly rich and complex. It is in this sense that the talkie perfects the silent film. Silent or talkie, we have seen, cinema constitutes an immense 'internal monologue' which constantly internalizes and externalizes itself: not a language, but a visual material which is the utterable of language (its 'signified of power' the linguist Gustave Guillaume would say), and which refers in one case to indirect utterances (intertitles), in the other case to direct enunciations (acts of speech and of music).

3

We have already relied on 'modern' authors in relation to some aspects of our discussion. But it was still not in this that they were modern. The difference between a so-called classic cinema and a so-called modern cinema does not coincide with that between the silent film and the talkie. The modern implies a new use of the talking, sound and the musical. It is as if, to a first approximation, the speech-act tended to extricate itself from its dependencies in relation to the visual image, and assumed a value for itself, an autonomy which was nevertheless non-theatrical. The silent film set the speech-act in an indirect style, because it made it read like an intertitle; the essence of the talkie, in contrast, was to make the speech-act achieve the direct style, and to make it interact with the visual image, while still being part of this image, voice-off included. But it is here that with modern cinema there arises a very special use of the voice, which might be called the free indirect style, and which goes beyond the opposition of the direct and the indirect. It is not a mixture of indirect and direct, but an original irreducible dimension, in various forms.[34] We have encountered it several times in the previous chapters, whether at the level of a cinema wrongly called direct, or at the level of a cinema of composition which it would be wrong to call indirect. To limit ourselves to this second case, free indirect speech may be presented as a passage from the indirect to the direct, or the other way round, although this is not a mixture. Thus Rohmer has often said, when explaining his practice, that the 'Contes moraux' were *mises-en-scène* of texts first written in an indirect style, then changing to the condition of dialogues: the voice-off is obliterated, even the narrator enters into a direct relation with another (for instance the woman writer in *Claire's Knee*), but in such conditions that the direct style keeps the marks of an indirect origin and does not allow itself to be fixed with the first person. Outside of the series of 'Contes' and that of the 'Proverbes', the two great films, *The Marquise of O* and *Perceval le Gallois*, successfully give cinema the power of the free indirect, as it appears in Kleist's writings, or in the medieval romance, where the characters can speak of themselves in the third person ('She is crying', sings Blanchefleur).[35] It is as if Rohmer has taken the opposite path to Bresson, who had already used Dostoevsky twice and the medieval romance once. For, in Bresson, it is not indirect discourse which is treated as direct, it was the opposite; it was the direct, the dialogue, which was treated as if it were reported by someone else: hence the famous Bressonian voice, the voice of the 'model' in opposition to the voice of the theatre actor, where the character speaks as if he were listening to his own words reported by someone else, hence achieving a *literalness* of the voice, cutting it off from any direct resonance, and making it produce a free indirect speech.[36]

If it is true that modern cinema implies the collapse of the sensory-motor schema, the speech-act is no longer inserted in the linkage of actions and reactions, and does not reveal a web of interactions any more. It turns in on itself; it is no longer a dependant or something which is part of the visual image; it becomes a completely separate sound image; it takes on a cinematographic autonomy and cinema becomes truly audio-visual. It is this which produces the unity of all the new forms of speech-act, when it moves into this regime of the free-indirect: this act through which the talkie finally becomes autonomous. Thus it is no longer a question of action-reaction, nor of interaction, nor even of reflection. The speech-act has changed its status. If we go to 'direct' cinema, we fully discover this new status which gives speech the value of a free indirect one: this is story-telling. The speech-act becomes act of *story-telling*, in Rouch or in Perrault, what Perrault calls 'the flagrant offence of making up legends' [*légender*], and which takes on the political dimension of the constitution of a people (it is through this alone that a cinema presented as direct or lived may be defined). And, in a cinema of composition as in Bresson or Rohmer, a similar result would be achieved at other levels and with other means. According to Rohmer, it is the analysis of morals in a society in crisis which allows speech to be revealed as 'realizing fabrication', creative of the event.[37] With Bresson, conversely, it is the event that speech must get back to from the inside in order to draw from it the spiritual part of which we are the eternal contemporary: that which produces memory or legend, Peguy's 'internal'. Free indirect, the speech-act becomes political act of story-telling, moral act of tale, supra-historical act of legend.[38] On occasion, Rohmer, like Robbe-Grillet, simply begins with an act of lying, which the cinema, in contrast to the theatre, is capable of; but it is clear in both authors that the normal concept of the lie is left strikingly behind.

The break in the sensory-motor link does not only affect the speech-act turning in on itself and hollowing itself out, and in which the voice now refers only to itself and to other voices. It also affects the visual image, which now reveals the any-space-whatevers, empty or disconnected spaces characteristic of modern cinema. It is as if, speech having withdrawn from the image to become founding act, the image, for its part, raised the foundations of space, the 'strata', those silent powers of before or after speech, before or after man. The visual image becomes *archaeological, stratigraphic, tectonic*. Not that we are taken back to prehistory (there is an archaeology of the present), but to the deserted layers of our time which bury our own phantoms; to the lacunary layers which we juxtaposed according to variable orientations and connections. These are the deserts in German cities. These are the deserts of Pasolini, which make prehistory the abstract poetic element, the 'essence' co-present with our history, the archaean base which reveals an interminable history beneath our own. Or the deserts of Antonioni, which ultimately retain only abstract routes, and conceal the multiple fragments of a primordial couple. These are Bresson's fragmentations which link up or relink fragments of space each of which is closed on its own account. In Rohmer, it is the female body which suffers fragmentations, undoubtedly as fetishes, but also as pieces of a vase or an iridescent piece of pottery that has come out of the sea: the 'Contes' are an archaeological collection of our time. And the sea or, above all, space in *Perceval* are affected by a curve which imposes itself with almost abstract trajectories. Perrault, in *Un royaume vous attend*, shows the slow tractors which from dawn take away the prefabricated houses to return the landscape to emptiness: men had been brought here; today they are withdrawn. *Le pays de la terre sans arbres* is a masterpiece where geographic and archaeological images are juxtaposed, over the trail of the almost vanished moose which has become abstract. Resnais plunges the image into ages of the world and variable orders of layers, which cross characters themselves, and bring together in *L'amour à mort*, for instance, the botanist and the archaeologist returned from the dead. But they are again essentially the empty and lacunary stratigraphic landscapes of Straub, where the camera movements (when there are any, notably pan shots) trace the abstract curve of what has happened, and where the earth stands for what is buried in it: the cave in *Othon* where the resistance fighters had their weapons, the marble quarries and the Italian countryside where civil populations were massacred in *Fortini Cani*, the cornfield in *Della Nube alla Resistenza* fertilized by the blood of the sacrificial victims (or the shot of the grass and acacias), the French countryside and the Egyptian countryside in *Trop tôt trop tard*.[39] To the question: what is a Straubian shot?, one can reply, as in a manual of stratigraphy, that it is a section comprising the stippled [*pointillées*] lines of vanished *features* and the complete lines of those that are still touched. The visual image, in Straub, is the rock.

'Empty' and 'disconnected' are not the best words. An empty

space, without characters (or in which the characters themselves show the void) has a fullness in which there is nothing missing. Disconnected, unlinked fragments of space are the object of a specific relinkage over the gap: the absence of match is only the appearance of a linking-up which can take place in an infinite number of ways. In this sense, the archaeological, or stratigraphic, image is *read* at the same time as it is seen. Noël Burch put it very well when he said that, when images cease to be linked together 'naturally', when they relate to a systematic use of false continuity or a continuity shot at 180°, it is as if the shots are themselves turning, or 'turning round', and grasping them 'requires a considerable effort of memory and imagination, in other words, a *reading*'. This is the case in Straub: according to Daney, *Moses et Aaron*, are, as it were, the figures which come to be inscribed on the two sides of the white or empty image, the right side and the reverse of a single piece, 'something that is unified and then is separated in such a way that its two aspects are made visible simultaneously'; and in the ambigious landscapes themselves, there is produced a whole 'coalescence' of the perceived with the remembered, the imagined, the known.[40] Not in the sense that it used to be said: to perceive *is* to know, is to imagine, is to recall, but in the sense that reading is a function of the eye, a perception of perception, a perception which does not grasp perception without also grasping its reverse, imagination, memory, or knowledge. In short, what we call reading of the visual image is the stratigraphic condition, the reversal of the image, the corresponding act of perception which constantly converts the empty into full, right side into its reverse. To read is to relink instead of link; it is to turn, and turn round, instead of to follow on the right side: a new Analytic of the image. No doubt, from the beginning of the talkie, the visual image began to become readable as such. But this was because the talkie, as a part of something, or dependent, made something seen in this image, and was itself seen. Eisenstein created the notion of *read image*, in a relation to the musical, but here again this was because music made things visible by imposing an irreversible orientation on the eye. It is no longer the same now, in this second stage of the talkie. It is the opposite because the heard speech ceases to make seen and be seen; it is because it becomes independent of the visual image, that the visual image attains to the new readability of things on its own account, and becomes an archaeological or rather stratigraphic section which must be read: 'Rock is not touched in words', it is said in *Della Nube* . . . And, in *Fortini Cani*, Jean-Claude Bonnet analyses the 'great central fissure', the 'telluric, geological, geophysical' sequence without words, 'where the landscape is given to be read as place of inscription of struggles, empty theatre of operations'.[41] A new sense of 'readable' appears for the visual image, at the same time as the speech-act becomes for itself an autonomous sound image.

It has often been observed that modern cinema is in some sense closer to silent cinema than to the first-stage talkie: not only because it sometimes reintroduces intertitle but also because it uses, through the other approach of the silent film, injections of scriptual elements into the visual image (notebooks, letters, and, repeatedly in Straub, lapidary or petrified inscriptions 'commemorative plaques, monuments to the dead, street-names . . .').[42] Nevertheless there is no basis for bringing together modern and silent cinema rather than the first stage of the talkie. For, in silent cinema, we found ourselves faced with two kinds of images, one seen and the other read (intertitle), or before two elements of the image (scriptual injections). Whilst, now, it is the visual image in its entirety that must be read, intertitles and injections being now only the stipplings [*pointillées*] of a stratigraphic layer, or the variable connections from one layer to another, the passages from one to the other (hence, for instance, the electronic transformations of the scriptual in Godard).[43] In short, in modern cinema, the readability of the visual image, the 'duty' of reading the image, no longer relates to a specific element as in the silent, nor to an overall effect of the speech-act in the seen image, as in the first stage of the talkie. It is because the speech-act has gone elsewhere and assumed its autonomy that the visual image for its part reveals an archaeology or a stratigraphy, that is, a reading which concerns it in its entirety, and concerns it uniquely. The aesthetic of the visual image therefore takes on a new character: its pictorial or sculptural qualities depend on a geological, tectonic power as in Cézanne's mountains. This is what is developed to its highest point in Straub.[44] The visual image reveals its geological strata or foundations, whilst the act of speech and also of music becomes for its part founder, ethereal. The huge paradox of Ozu is perhaps explicable in this way: for Ozu was, already in silent film, the one who invented empty and disconnected spaces, and even still lifes, which revealed the strata of the visual image and submitted it as such to a stratigraphic reading; in this way he anticipated modern cinema to the extent that he had no need of the talkie; and when he came to the talkie, very late, but again as a forerunner, it was to treat it directly in a second stage, in a 'dissociation' of the two powers which strengthens each of them, in a 'division of labour between presentational image and representational voice'.[45] In modern cinema, the visual image acquires a new aesthetic: it becomes legible for itself, assuming a power which did not generally exist in the silent cinema, whilst the speech-act has gone elsewhere, assuming a power which did not exist in the first stage of the talkie. The ethereal speech-act creates the event, but always placed crosswise over tectonic visual layers: there are two trajectories crossing each other. It creates the event, but in a space empty of events. What defines modern cinema is a 'to-ing and fro-ing between speech and image', which has to invent their new relationship (not only Ozu and Straub, but Rohmer, Resnais and Robbe-Grillet . . .).[46]

In the simplest case, this new arrangement of the visual and talking occurs in the same, but consequently audio-visual, image. A whole pedagogy is required here, because we have to read the visual as well as hear the speech-act in a new way. This is why Serge Daney refers to a 'Godardian pedagogy', a 'Straubian pedagogy'. And the first manifestation of great pedagogy, in the simplest and already decisive instance, would be the last works of Rossellini. It is as if Rossellini was able to reinvent a primary, absolutely fundamental, school, with its lesson in things and its lesson in words, its grammar of discourse and its handling of objects. This pedagogy, which is not the same as a documentary or investigation, is particularly clear in *The Rise of Louis XIV*: Louis XIV gives the tailor a lesson in things by making him add ribbons and bows to the prototype court-costume which is to keep the nobility occupied, and elsewhere gives the lesson in a new grammar, where the king becomes the sole subject of enunciation, whilst things happen according to his designs. Rossellini's pedagogy, or rather his 'didactics', does not consist in reporting discourses and showing things, but in revealing the simple structure of speech, the speech-act, and the everyday manufacture of objects, small or large works, crafts or industry. *The Messiah* combines parables as Christ's speech-act with the manufacture of craft objects; *Agostino di Ippona* combines the act of faith with the new sculpture (similarly the objects in *Blaise Pascal*, the market in *Socrates* . . .). Two trajectories are combined. What interests Rossellini is to make 'the struggle' comprehensible as emergence of the new: not a struggle between two trajectories, but a struggle which can only be revealed through the two, thanks to their to-ing and fro-ing. Underneath discourses there has to be found the new style of speech-act which is revealed on each occasion, in a language struggle with the old, and, underneath things, the new space which is formed, in tectonic opposition to the old. The space of Louis XIV is Versailles, the laid-out space which contrasts with the packing together of Mazarin, but also the industrial space where things will be produced in series. Whether it is Socrates, Christ, Augustine, Louis XIV, Pascal, or Descartes, the speech-act is torn away from the old style, at the same time as space forms a new layer which tends to cover over the old; everywhere a struggle marking the itinerary of a world which emerges from one historical moment to enter into another, the difficult birth of a new world, under the double forceps of words and things, speech-act and stratified space. It is a conception of history which simultaneously calls up the comic and the dramatic, the extraordinary and the everyday: new types of speech-act and new structurations of space. An 'archaeological' conception almost in Michel Foucault's sense. It is a method that Godard was to inherit, and which he would make the basis of his own pedagogy, his own didacticism: the lessons in things and the lessons in words in *Six fois deux*, up to the famous sequence in *Slow Motion*, where the lesson in things bears on the postures that the client imposes on the whore, and the lesson in words on the phonemes that she has to come out with, the two being quite separate.

The new regime of the image is constructed on this pedagogical base. This new regime, as we have seen, consists of this: images and sequences are no longer linked by rational cuts; which end the first or begin the second, but are relinked on top of irrational cuts, which no longer belong to either of the two and are valid for themselves (interstices). Irrational cuts thus have a disjunctive, and no longer a conjunctive, value.[47] In the complex case that we are now considering, the question is: where do these cuts occur, and what do they consist of, since they have an autonomy? We find ourselves before a first sequence of visual images with a sound and talking component, as in the first stage of the talkie; but they are moving towards a limit which no longer belongs to them, any more than it belongs to the second sequence. Now this limit, this irrational cut, may present itself in quite diverse visual forms: whether in the steady form of a sequence of unusual, 'anomalous' images, which come and interrupt the normal linkage of the two sequences; or in the enlarged form of the black screen, or the white screen, and their derivatives. *But on each occasion, the irrational cut implies the new stage of the talkie, the new figure of sound.* This may be an act of silence, in the sense that it is the talkie and the musical which invent silence. It may be a speech-act, but in the story-telling or founding aspect which it takes on here, in contrast to its 'classical' aspects. There are numerous instances in the new wave: Truffaut's *Shoot the Piano Player*, for example, where a strange speech-act comes and interrupts the motor pursuit, all the more strange in that it retains the appearance of a simple chance conversation; however, the procedure takes on its full force with Godard, because the irrational cut towards which a normal sequence tends is the genre or category personified, which precisely requires the speech-act as founder (the intercession of Brice Parain in *Vivre sa vie*), as story-teller (the intercession of Devos in *Pierrot le fou*). It can also be an act of music, in the sense that music would find its natural place in the snowy black screen which comes and cuts the sequences of images, and will fill this gap, so as to divide the images into two constantly revised series: this is the organization of Resnais' *L'amour à mort*, where Henze's music makes itself heard only in the gaps, assuming a mobile disjunctive function between the two series, from death to life and from life to death. Things can be even more complex, when the series of images not only tends towards a musical limit, as cut or category (as in Godard's *Slow Motion*, where the question rings out: what is that music?), but when this cut, this limit, itself forms a series which is superimposed in the first (as in the vertical construction of *First Name Carmen*, where the images of the quartet develop into a series which can be superimposed on the series whose cuts it ensures). Godard is definitely one of the authors who has thought most about visual-sound relationships. But his tendency to reinvest the visual with sound, with the ultimate aim (as Daney puts it) of 'restoring' both to the body from which they have been taken, produces a system of disengagements or micro-cuts in all directions: cuts spread and no longer pass between the sound and the visual, but in the visual, in the sound, and in their multiplied connections.[48] In contrast, what happens when the irrational cut, the interstice or interval, pass between visual and sound elements which are purified, disjunctive, freed from each other?

To return to a demonstrative pedagogy, Eustache's film *Les photos d'Alix* reduces the visual to photos, the voice to a commentary, but between the commentary and the photo a gap is progressively excavated, without, however, the observer being surprised at this growing heterogeneity. In *Last Year in Marienbad*, and in all his work, Robbe-Grillet put into play a new asynchrony, where the talking and the visual were no longer held together, no longer corresponded, but belied and contradicted themselves, without it being possible to say that one rather than the other is 'right': something undecidable between the two (as Gardies observes, the visual has no special claim to authenticity, and includes as many implausibilities as speech). And the contradictions no longer allow us simply to confront the heard and the seen bit by bit, or one by one, pedagogically: their role is to induce a system of unhookings and intertwinings which in turn determine the different presents through anticipation or regression, in a direct time-image, or which organize a series of powers, capable of regression or progression under the sign of the false.[49] The visual and the talking may in each case take over the distinction between the real and the imaginary, sometimes one, sometimes the other, or the alternative of the true and the false; but a sequence of audio-visual images necessarily makes the distinct indiscernible, and the alternative undecidable. The first characteristic of this new image is that 'asynchrony' is no longer in any way what was invoked by the Soviet manifesto and Pudovkin in particular: it is no longer a matter of making heard words and sound whose source is in a relative out-of-field, and which thus relate to the visual image whose givens they simply avoid doubling. Nor is it a matter of a voice-off which realizes an absolute out-of-field or relation with the whole, a relation which itself still belongs to the visual image. Entering into rivalry or heterogeneity with the visual images, the voice-off no longer has the power which only exceeded these in so far as it defined itself in relation to their limits: it has lost the omnipotence which characterized it in the first stage of the talkie. It has ceased to see everything; it has become questionable, uncertain, ambiguous, as in Robbe-Grillet's *The Man Who Lies* or Marguerite Duras's *India Song*, because it has broken from its moorings with the visual images which delegated to it the omnipotence which they lacked. The voice-off loses its omnipotence but by gaining autonomy. This is the transformation comprehensively analysed by Michel Chion, and which led Bonitzer to propose the notion of 'voice-off-off'.[50]

The other novelty (or the development of the first), is perhaps that there is now no out-of-field whatsoever nor voice-off in any sense. In the first place, the talkie and the whole of sound have won autonomy: they have escaped from Balazs's curse (there is no sound image . . .); they have ceased to be a component of the visual image as in the first stage; they have become a whole image apart. The sound image is born, in its very break, from its break with the visual image. There are no longer even two autonomous components of a single audio-visual image, as in Rossellini, but two 'heautonomous' images, one visual and one sound, with a fault, an interstice, an irrational cut between them.[51] Marguerite Duras says of *La femme du Gange*: 'There are two films, the film of the image and the film of the voices . . . The two films are there, with total autonomy . . . Neither are (the voices) voices-off, in the conventional sense of the term: they do not facilitate the unrolling of the film: on the contrary, they hamper and disturb it. They ought not to be linked with the film of the image.'[52] For, in the second place, and simultaneously, the second of Balazs's curses is also effaced: he acknowledged the existence of sound close-ups, and dissolves, etc., but excluded any possibility of a sound framing, because, he said, sound did not have sides.[53] However, visual framing is now defined less by the choice of a pre-existing side of the visible object than by the invention of a point of view which disconnects the sides, or establishes a void between them, in such a way as to extract a pure space, an any-space-whatever, from the space given in objects. A sound framing will be defined by the invention of a pure act of speech, of music, or even of silence, which must be extracted from the audible given continuum in noises, sounds, words and pieces of music. There is thus no longer an out-of-field, any more than there are sounds-off to inhabit it, because the two forms of the out-of-field, and the corresponding sound distributions, were still part of the visual image. But now the visual image has given up its externality; it has cut itself off from the world and conquered its reverse side; it has made itself free from what depended on it. In the same way, the sound image has shaken off its own dependency; it has become autonomous, has mastered its own framing. The externality of the visual image as uniquely framed (out-of-field) has been replaced by *the interstice between two framings, the visual and the sound*, the irrational cut between two images, the visual and the sound. This is what in our view defines the second stage of the talkie (and undoubtedly this second stage would never have arisen without television; it is television which made it possible; but, because television abandoned most of its own creative possibilities, and did not even understand them, it needed cinema to give it a pedagogical lesson; it needed great cinema authors to show what it could do and what it would be able to do; if it is true that television kills cinema, cinema on the other hand is continually revitalizing television, not only because it feeds it with films, but because the great cinema authors invent the audio-visual image, which they are quite ready to 'give back' to television if it gives them the opportunity, as we can see in Rossellini's last works, in Godard's interventions, in the consistent aims of Straub, and equally in Renoir, in Antonioni . . .).

We find ourselves, then, faced with two problems. According to the first, if it is true that sound framing consists in freeing a pure act of speech or music, in the creative conditions of cinema, what does this act consist of? This is what can be called 'properly cinematographic utterance or enunciation'. But, at the same time, the question clearly goes beyond cinema. Socio-linguistics has been much concerned with speech-acts and the possibilities of classifying them. Does not the talking cinema, in its history and without setting out to do so, offer a classification which could be of benefit elsewhere and could have a philosophical importance? Cinema invited us to distinguish interactive speech-acts, mostly in the relative sound-in and sound-off; reflexive speech-acts, mostly in the absolute sound-off; and finally more mysterious speech-acts, acts of story-telling, 'flagrant offences of making up legends' [*flagrants délits de légender*], which would be pure in so far as they would be autonomous and would no longer belong to the visual image.[54] The first problem is thus that of getting to know the nature of these pure cinematographic acts. And the second problem would be this: when speech-acts are taken to be pure, that is, are no longer components or dimensions of the visual image, the status of the image changes, because the visual and the sound have become two autonomous components of a single, truly audio-visual image (Rossellini, for example). But this movement cannot be stopped: the visual and the sound will give way to two heautonomous images, an auditory image and an optical image, continually separated, dissociated, or unhooked by irrational cuts between them (Robbe-Grillet, Straub, Marguerite Duras). Nevertheless, the image, having become audio-visual, does not burst into pieces; on the contrary, it gains a new consistency which depends on a more complex link between the visual image *and* the sound image. So that we do not believe

Marguerite Duras's statement about *La femme du Gange*: the two images would be linked only by a 'material concomitance', both written on the same film stock and being seen at the same time. It is a humorous or provocative pronouncement, which moreover proclaims what it claims to deny, because it attributes to each of the two images the power of the other. Otherwise, the work of art would have no necessity of its own; there would be only a contingency and a gratuitousness, anything about anything else, as in the mass of bad arty films, or in the form that Mitry criticizes Marguerite Duras for. The heautonomy of the two images does not suppress but reinforces the audio-visual nature of the image, it strengthens the victory of the audio-visual. The second problem thus concerns the complex link between the two heterogeneous, non-corresponding disparate images: this new intertwining, a specific relinkage.

The first aspect of the work of Jean-Marie Straub and Danièle Huillet is the isolating of the pure speech-act, the properly cinematographic utterance or the sound image: this act must be torn from its written support, text, book, letters, or documents. This tearing-away does not take place in a fit of rage or passion; it presupposes a certain resistance of the text, and all the more respect for the text, but on each occasion a special effort to draw the speech-act out of it. In *Chronicle of Anna Magdalena Bach*, the supposed voice of Anna Magdalena recites the letters of Bach himself and the accounts of a son, so that she speaks as Bach wrote and spoke, thus reaching a kind of free indirect discourse. In *Fortini Cani*, the book is seen, the pages are seen, the hands that turn them, the author Fortini reading the passages which he has not himself chosen, but it is ten years later, reduced to 'listening to himself speak', overcome with tiredness, the voice passing through amazement, astonishment, or approval, non-recognition or the already heard. And certainly *Othon* shows neither text nor theatrical representation, but implies them all the more because the majority of actors have not mastered the language (Italian, English, Argentinian accents): what they tear from the representation is a cinematographic act, what they tear from the text is a rhythm or a tempo; what they tear from language is an 'aphasia'.[55] In *Della Nube alla Resistenza*, the speech-act is extracted from myths ('No, I don't want to . . .'), and it is perhaps only in the second, modern part that it manages to overcome the resistance of the text, of the pre-established language of the gods. There are always conditions of strangeness which will reveal or, as Marguerite Duras says, 'frame' the pure speech-act.[56] Moses himself is the herald of an invisible God or pure Word which overcomes the resistance of the old gods and does not even allow itself to be fixed in its own tablets. And perhaps what explains the Straubs' encounter with Kafka is that Kafka also thought that we had a speech-act only to overcome the resistance of the dominant texts, the pre-established laws and the already decided verdicts. But, if this is so, in *Moses and Aaron*, and in *Amerika, rapports de classes*, it is no longer enough to say that the speech-act must be torn from what is resisting it: it is the speech-act which is resisting, *it is the act of resistance*. The speech-act is not isolated from what is resisting it without its being made itself resistant, against what is threatening it. It is itself the violence which helps 'in the place where violence reigns': Bach's *Hinaus!* Is it not already in this way that the speech-act is act of music, in the *'sprech-gesang'* [spoken song] of Moses, but also the performance of Bach's music which is torn from its scores, still more than the voice of Anna Magdalena is torn from letters and documents? The act of speech or music is a struggle: it must be economical and sparse, infinitely patient, in order to impose itself on what resists it, but extremely violent in order to be itself a resistance, an act of resistance.[57] Irresistibly, it rises.

In *Unreconciled*, the speech-act is that of the old lady, this time schizophrenic rather than aphasic, which rises to the sound image of the final revolver-shots: 'I noticed how time went past; it seethed, it struggled, paid a million for a sweet then didn't have two ha'pennies for a bit of bread.' It is as if the speech-act is placed cross-wise over all the visual images it crosses, and which are themselves organized like so many geological sections, archaeo-logical layers, in variable order according to the breaks and gaps: Hindenburg, Hitler, Adenauer, 1910, 1914, 1942, 1945 . . . This is certainly the comparative status of the sound image and the visual image in the Straubs: people talk in an empty space, and, whilst speech rises, the space is sunk into the ground, and does not let us see it, but makes its archaeological buryings, its stratigraphic thicknesses readable; it testifies to the work that had to be done and the victims slaughtered in order to fertilize a field, the struggles that took place and the corpses thrown out. (*Della Nube . . . Fortini Cani*). History is inseparable from the earth [*terre*], struggle is underground [*sous terre*], and, if we want to grasp an event, we must not show it, we must not pass along the event, but plunge into it, go through all the geological layers that are its internal history (and not simply a more or less distant past). I do not believe in great resounding events, Nietzsche said. To grasp an event is to connect it to the silent layers of earth which make up its true continuity, or which inscribe it in the class struggle. There is something peasant in history. It is therefore now the visual image, the stratigraphic landscape, which in turn resists the speech-act and opposes it with a silent piling-up. Even letters, books and documents, that which the speech-act has torn itself from, have passed into the landscape, with the monuments, the ossuaries, the lapidary inscriptions. The word 'resistance' has a lot of meaning with the Straubs, and it is now the earth, the tree and the rock which resist the speech-act, resist Moses. Moses is the speech-act or sound image, but Aaron is the visual image; he 'makes visible', and, what he makes visible is the continuity of the land. Moses is the new nomad, the one who wants no other earth than the always wandering word of God, but Aaron wants a territory, and 'reads' it already as the aim of movement. Between the two, the desert, but equally the people, who 'are still missing' and yet already there. Aaron resists Moses, the people resist Moses. What will the people choose, the visual image or the sound image, the speech-act or the earth?[58] Moses drives Aaron into the ground, but Moses without Aaron has no connection with the people, with the earth. Moses and Aaron might be said to be the two parts of the Idea; these parts, however, will never form a whole again, but a disjunction of resistance, which should prevent speech being despotic and the earth belonging, being possessed, subjected to its final layer. It is like in Cézanne, the Straubs' mentor: on the one hand the 'stubborn geometry' of the visual image (drawing) which goes deep and makes the 'geological strata' readable, on the other hand this thick cloud, this 'aerial logic' (colour and light, Cézanne said), but equally speech-act which rises from the land towards the sun.[59] The two trajectories: 'The voice comes from the other side of the image.' One resists the other, but it is in this always re-created disjunction that the history under the ground takes on an emotional aesthetic value, and that the speech-act towards the sun assumes an intense political value. The speech-acts of the nomad (Moses), of the bastard (*Della Nube . . .*), of the exile (*Amerika . . .*), are political acts, and it is in this way that they were from the outset acts of resistance. If the Straubs give a film taken from Kafka the title *Amerika, rapports de classes*, it is because, from the outset, the hero takes on the defence of the underground man, the driver from

below, then has to confront the machinations of the class above
who separate him from his uncle (the delivery of the letter): the
speech-act, the sound image, is act of resistance as much in the
case of Bach, who over-turned the division between sacred and
profane, as in that of Moses, who transformed that of the priests
and the people. But, conversely, the visual image, the telluric
landscape, develops a whole aesthetic power which reveals the
layers of history and political struggles on which it is built. In
Toute révolution est un coup de dés, some people recite Mallarmé's
poem on the hill of the cemetery where the bodies of the
communards are buried: they share out the poem's elements
according to their typographical characters, like so many disinter-
red objects. It must be simultaneously maintained that speech
creates the event, makes it rise up, and that the silent event is
covered over by the earth. The event is always resistance, between
what the speech-act seizes and what the earth buries. It is a cycle of
sky and earth, of external light and underground fire, and even
more of the sound and the visual, which never re-forms into a
whole, but each time constitutes the disjunction of the two images,
at the same time as their new type of relation, a relation of very
precise incommensurability, not an absence of relation.

What constitutes the audio-visual image is a disjunction, a
dissociation of the visual and the sound, each heautonomous, but
at the same time an incommensurable or 'irrational' relation
which connects them to each other, without forming a whole,
without offering the least whole. It is a resistance stemming from
the collapse of the sensory-motor schema, and which separates
the visual image and the sound image, but puts them all the more
into a non-totalizable relation. Marguerite Duras would go
further and further in this direction: as centre of a trilogy, *India
Song* establishes an extraordinary metastable equilibrium between a sound image which makes us hear all the voices (in and
off, relative and absolute, attributable and non-attributable, all
competing and plotting, being unaware of and forgetting each
other, without any one having omnipotence or the last word), and
a visual image which makes us read a silent stratigraphy (characters who keep their mouths closed even when they are speaking
from the other side, so that what they say is already in the perfect
tense while place and event, the dance at the embassy, are the
dead layer that covers up an old burning stratum, the other dance
in another place).[60] In the visual image there is revealed the life
beneath the ashes or behind the mirrors, just as in the sound

image a pure but polyvocal speech-act is extracted which splits off from theatre, and tears itself from writing. The 'untimely' voices are like four sides of an entity of sound, which confronts the visual entity: the visual and the sound are perspectives in a love-story, to infinity, the same one and yet different. Before *India Song*, *La femme du Gange* had already founded the heautonomy of the sound image on the two timeless voices, and defined the end of the film when the sound and the visual 'touch' at the point at infinity whose perspectives they are, losing their respective sides.[61] And, after, *Son nom de Venise dans Calcutta désert* would under-line the heautonomy of a visual image brought to ruins, revealing a still more ancient stratum as a young girl's name underneath the married woman's name, but always tending towards an end, when she touches the common point of the two images, to infinity (it is as if the visual and the sound ended in the tactile, in 'junc-tion'). *Le camion* can restore a body to voices, at the back, but inasmuch as the visible becomes disembodied or empties itself (the cab, the journey, the appearances of the ghost-lorry): 'There are only places of a story left and of story the one which does not take place.'[62*]

Marguerite Duras's first films were marked by all the powers of the house, or of house and grounds together, fear and desire, talking and being quiet, going out and coming back, creating the event and burying it, etc. Marguerite Duras was a great film-maker of the house, such an important theme in cinema, not simply because women 'inhabit' houses, in every sense, but be-cause passions 'inhabit' women: as in *Destroy She Said*, and especi-ally *Nathalie Granger* and, later still, *Vera Baxter*. But why does she see *Vera Baxter* as a regression of her work, and equally *Nathalie Granger* as a preparation for the trilogy which was to follow? It is not the first time that an artist can think that what has been fully achieved is only a step, forwards or backwards, in relation to a deeper aim. In the case of Marguerite Duras, the house ceases to satisfy her because she can bring about only autonomy of the visual and sound components for one and the same audio-visual image (the house is still a place, a locus, in the double sense of speech and space). But going further, achieving the heautonomy of a sound image and a visual image, making the two images the perspectives of a common point situated at infinity, this new conception of the irrational cut cannot take place in the house, nor even with it. The house-grounds undoubtedly already had most of the properties of an any-space-whatever, the voids and

the disconnections. But the house had to be left, abolished, so that
the any-space-whatever could only be constructed in flight, at the
same time as the speech-act had to 'get out and away'. It is only in
flight that characters had to be brought together, to reply to each
other. The uninhabitable had to be restored, space made
uninhabitable (beach-sea instead of house-grounds), so that it
achieved a heautonomy, comparable with that of the speech-act,
which for its part had become unattributable: a story [*histoire*] that
no longer has a place (sound image) for places that no longer have
a history [*histoire*] (visual image).[63] And it would be this new design
of the irrational cut, this new way of conceiving of it, which would
constitute the audio-visual relation.

In the disjunction between the sound image become pure
speech-act, and the visual image become readable or stratigraphic, what distinguishes the work of Marguerite Duras from that
of the Straubs? A first difference would be that, for Duras, the
speech-act to be reached is total love or absolute desire. It is this
which can be silence, or song, or shout like the shout of the
vice-consul in *India Song*.[64] It is this which has control over
memory and forgetting, over suffering and hope. And it is above
all this which is creative story-telling coextensive with the whole of
the text from which it tears itself, constituting an infinite writing
deeper than writing, an unlimited reading deeper than reading.
The second difference consists of a liquid quality which increasingly marks the visual image in Marguerite Duras: it is the tropical
Indian humidity which rises from the river, but which spreads out
on the beach and in the sea as well; it is the dampness of
Normandy which already drew *Le camion* from the Beauce to the
sea; and the disused room in *Agatha* is not so much a house as a
slow phantom ship moving on to the beach, while the speech-act
unfolds (*L'homme atlantique* would come out of this as a natural
consequence). That Marguerite Duras creates seascapes in this
way has important consequences: not only because she is related
to what is most important in the French school, daylight grey, the
specific movement of the light, the alternation of solar and lunar
light, the sun setting in water, liquid perception. But also because
the visual image, in contrast to the Straubs, tends to go beyond its
stratigraphic or 'archaeological' values towards a peaceful power
of river and sea which stands for the eternal, which mixes up
strata and carries away statues. We are not restored to the earth
but to the sea. Things are erased by the tide rather than being
buried in dry earth. The beginning of *Aurélia Steiner* seems

comparable with that of *Della Nube* . . .: it is a matter of tearing the speech-act from myth, the act of story-telling from fable; but the statues give way to the tracking shot from the front of a car, then to the river-barge, then to the fixed shots of waves.[65] In short, the specific readability of the visual image becomes oceanographic rather than telluric and stratigraphic. *Agatha et les lectures illimitées* refers reading to this marine perception that is deeper than that of things, at the same time as it refers writing to this speech-act deeper than a text. Cinematographically, Marguerite Duras can be compared to a great painter who might say: if only I could manage to capture a wave, just a wave, or a bit of wet sand . . . There would be yet a third difference, undoubtedly connected with the two previous ones. In the Straubs, the class struggle is the relation which keeps circulating between the two incommensurable images, the visual and the sound, the sound image which does not tear the speech-act from the speech of the gods or bosses without the intercession of someone who could be described as a 'traitor to his own class' (Fortini's position, but it might also be said of Bach, Mallarmé and Kafka), and the visual image which does not take on its stratigraphic values without the earth being nourished by the struggles of workers and particularly peasants, all the great resistances.[66] This is why the Straubs could present their work as profoundly Marxist, even taking into account the cases of the bastard or the exile (including the very pure class-relations which drive *Amerika*). But, in her estrangement from Marxism, Marguerite Duras does not limit herself to characters who would be traitors to their own class; she calls up those outside classes, the beggar woman and the lepers, the vice-consul and the child, commercial travellers and cats, to make up a 'class of violence'. The function of this class of violence, first introduced in *Nathalie Granger*, is not to be seen in savage images; this class fulfils the function of circulating between the two kinds of image, and making them connect, the absolute act of speech-desire in the sound image, the unlimited power of river-ocean in the visual image: the beggar woman of the Ganges at the crossing-point of the river and the song.[67]

In the second stage, then, talking and sound cease to be components of the visual image: the visual and the sound become two autonomous components of an audio-visual image, or, better, two heautonomous images. In this case we can say with Blanchot: 'Talking is not seeing.' It seems here that talking ceases to see, to make visible and also to be seen. But a preliminary observation is required: talking breaks with its visual links in this way only by giving up its particular habitual or empirical exercise; by managing to turn towards a limit which is at once, as it were, the unspeakable and yet what can only be spoken ('different speech, which carries here and there, and itself differs from speaking . . .'). If the limit is the pure speech-act, this can equally take the shape of a cry, of musical or non-musical sounds, the whole of the series being made up of independent elements each of which, here and there, can in turn constitute a limit in relation to the possibilities of cutting, of reversal, of retrogression, of anticipation. The sound continuum thus ceases to be differentiated according to what the visual image belongs to or the dimensions of the out-of-field, and music no longer ensures a direct presentation of an assumed whole. This continuum now takes on the value of innovation claimed by Maurice Fano in Robbe-Grillet's films (notably in *The Man Who Lies*: it ensures the heautonomy of the sound images, and must achieve both the speech-act as limit – which does not necessarily consist of a speech in the strict sense – and the musical organization of the series, which does not necessarily consist of musical elements (similarly, with Marguerite Duras, music will be collated with the organization of the voices and with the absolute act of desire, vice-consul's shout or burnt voice in *La femme du Gange*, or, with Straub, the organization of Anna Magdalena's words with the performance of the music and Bach's shout. But it would be wrong to conclude that there is a prevalence of sound in modern cinema. The same observation is also valid for the visual image: seeing wins a heautonomy only if it is torn from its empirical exercise and is carried to a limit which is at once invisible and yet can only be seen (a kind of clairvoyance, differing from seeing, and passing through any-space-whatevers, empty or disconnected spaces).[68] It is the vision of a blind man, of Tiresias, as speech was that of an aphasic or amnesic. Henceforth, *neither of the two faculties is raised to higher exercise without reaching the limit which separates it from the other, but connects it to the other through separating it*. What speech utters is also the invisible that sight sees only through clairvoyance; and what sight sees is the unutterable uttered by speech. Marguerite Duras could invoke the 'seeing voices' and make them so often say 'I see', 'I see without seeing, yes that's it.' Philippon's general idea, filming speech as something visible, remains valid, but all the more so in that seeing and speaking in this way take on a new meaning. When the sound image and the visual image become heautonomóus, they still constitute no less of an audio-visual image, all the purer in that the new correspondence is born from the determinate forms of their non-correspondence: it is the limit of each which connects it to the other. This is not an arbitrary construction, but a very rigorous one as in *La femme du Gange*, which has them dying as they touch, but only touching over the limit which keeps them separate, 'for that reason uncrossable, yet always crossed because uncrossable'. The visual image and the sound image are in a special relationship, a free indirect relationship. We are in fact no longer in the classical regime where a whole would internalize images and be externalized in images, constituting an indirect representation of time, and being able to receive from music a direct presentation. What has now become direct is a time-image for itself, with its two dissymetric, non-totalizable sides, fatal when they touch, that of an outside more distant than any exterior, and that of an inside deeper than any interior, here where a musical speech rises and is torn away, there where the visible is covered over or buried.[69]

10   Conclusions

1

Cinema is not a universal or primitive language system [*langue*], nor a language [*langage*]. It brings to light an intelligible content which is like a presupposition, a condition, a necessary correlate through which language constructs its own 'objects' (signifying units and operations). But this correlate, though inseparable, is specific: it consists of movements and thought-processes (pre-linguistic images), and of points of view on these movements and processes (pre-signifying signs). It constitutes a whole 'psychome-chanics', the spiritual automaton, the utterable of a language system which has its own logic. The language system takes utterances of language, with signifying units and operations from it, but the utterable itself, its images and signs, are of another nature. This would be what Hjelmslev calls non-linguistically formed 'content', whilst the language system works through form and substance. Or rather, it is the first signifiable, anterior to all significance, which Gustave Guillaume made the condition of linguistics.[1] We can understand from this the ambiguity which runs through semiotics and semiology: semiology, which is of linguistic inspiration, tends to close the 'signifier' in on itself, and cut language off from the images and signs which make up its raw material.[2] Semiotics, by contrast, is the discipline which considers language only in relation to this specific content, images and signs. Of course, when language takes over the content or the utterable it makes from them properly linguistic utterances which are no longer expressed in images and signs. But even the utterances are in turn reinvested in images and signs, and provide the utterable afresh. It seemed to us that cinema, precisely through its automatic or psychomechanical qualities, was the system of pre-linguistic images and signs, and that it took utterances up again in the images and signs proper to this system (the read image of the silent cinema, the sound components of the visual image in the first stage of the talkie, the sound image itself in the second stage of the talkie). This is why the break between the silent film and the talkie has never seemed fundamental in cinema's evolution. By contrast, what has seemed fundamental to us in this system of images and signs is the distinction between two kinds of images with their corresponding signs, movement-images and time-images which were only to appear and develop later. Kinostructures and chronogeneses are the two successive chapters of a pure semiotics.

Cinema considered as psychomechanics, or spiritual automaton, is reflected in its own content, its themes, situations and characters. But the relationship is complicated, because this reflection gives way to oppositions and inversions as well as to resolutions or reconciliations. The automaton has always had two coexistent, complementary senses, even when they were in conflict. On one hand, the great spiritual automaton indicates the highest exercise of thought, the way in which thought thinks and itself thinks itself in the fantastic effort of an autonomy; it is in this sense that Jean-Louis Schefer can credit cinema with being a giant in the back of our heads, Cartesian diver, dummy or machine, mechanical man without birth who brings the world into suspense.[3] But, on the other hand, the automaton is also the psychological automaton who no longer depends on the outside because he is autonomous but because he is dispossessed of his own thought, and obeys an internal impression which develops solely in visions or rudimentary actions (from the dreamer to the somnambulist, and conversely through the intermediary of hypnosis, suggestion, hallucination, obsession, etc.).[4] Hence there is something specific to cinema which has nothing to do with theatre. If cinema is automatism become spiritual art – that is, initially movement-image – it confronts automata, not accidentally, but fundamentally. The French school never lost its taste for clockwork automata and clock-making characters, but also confronted machines with moving parts, like the American or Soviet schools. The man-machine assemblage varies from case to case, but always with the intention of posing the question of the future. And machines can take hold so fully on man that it awakens the most ancient powers, and the moving machine becomes one with the psychological automaton pure and simple, at the service of a frightening new order: this is the procession of somnambulists, the hallucinators, hypnotizers-hypnotized in expressionism, from *The Cabinet of Dr Caligari* to *Testament of Dr Mabuse* via *Metropolis* and its robot. German cinema summoned up primitive powers, but it was perhaps best placed to announce something new which was to change cinema, horribly to 'realize' it and thus to modify its basic themes.

What is interesting in Krackauer's book *From Caligari to Hitler* is that it shows how expressionist cinema reflected the rise of the Hitlerian automaton in the German soul. But it still took an external viewpoint, whilst Walter Benjamin's article set itself inside cinema in order to show how the art of automatic movement (or, as he ambiguously said, the art of reproduction) was itself to coincide with the automization of the masses, state direction, politics become 'art': Hitler as film-maker . . . And it is true that up to the end Nazism thinks of itself in competition with Hollywood. The revolutionary courtship of the movement-image and an art of the masses become subject was broken off, giving way to the masses subjected as psychological automaton, and to their leader as great spiritual automaton. This is what compels Syberberg to say that the end-product of the movement-image is Leni Riefenstahl, and if Hitler is to be put on trial by cinema, it must be inside cinema, against Hitler the film-maker, in order to 'defeat him cinematographically, turning his weapons against him'.[5] It is as if Syberberg felt the need to add a second volume to Krackauer's book, but this second volume would be a film: not now from Caligari (or from a film from Germany) to Hitler, but from Hitler to *A Film from Germany*, the change taking place inside cinema, against Hitler, but also against Hollywood, against represented violence, against pornography, against business . . . But at what price? A true psychomechanics will not be found unless it is based on *new associations*, by reconstituting the great mental automata whose place was taken by Hitler, by reviving the psychological automata that he enslaved. The movement-image, that is, the bond that cinema had introduced between movement and image from the outset, would have to be abandoned, in order to set free other powers that it kept subordinate, and which had not had the time to develop their effects: projection and back-projection.[6] There is also a more general problem: for projection and back-projection are only technical means which directly carry the time-image, which substitute the time-image for the movement-image. The film set is transformed, but in that 'space here is born from time' (*Parsifal*). Is there a new regime of images like that of automatism?

A return to the extrinsic point of view obviously becomes necessary: the technological and social evolution of automata. Clockwork automata, but also motor automata, in short, automata of movement, made way for a new computer and cybernetic race, automata of computation and thought, automata with controls and feedback. The configuration of power was also inverted, and, instead of converging on a single, mysterious leader, inspirer of dreams, commander of actions, power was diluted in an information network where 'decision-makers' managed control, processing and stock across intersections of insomniacs and seers (as in, for example, the world-conspiracy we saw in Rivette, or Godard's *Alphaville*, the listening and surveillance system in Lumet, but above all, the evolution of Lang's three Mabuses, the third Mabuse, the Mabuse of the return to Germany, after the war).[7] And, in frequently explicit forms, the new automata were to people cinema, for better and for worse (the better would be Kubrick's giant computer in *2001*), and restore to it, particularly through science fiction, the possibility of huge *mises-en-scènes* that the impasse in the movement-image had provisionally ruled out. But new automata did not invade content without a new automatism bringing about a mutation of form. The modern configuration of the automaton is the correlate of an electronic automatism. The electronic image, that is, the tele and video image, the numerical image coming into being, either had to transform cinema or to replace it, to mark its death. We do not claim to be producing an analysis of the new images, which would be beyond our aims, but only to indicate certain effects whose relation to the cinematographic image remains to be determined.[8] The new images no longer have any outside (out-of-field), any more than they are internalized in a whole; rather, they have a right side and a reverse, reversible and non-superimposable, like a power to turn back on themselves. They are the object of a perpetual reorganization, in which a new image can arise from any point whatever of the preceding image. The organization of space here loses its privileged directions, and first of all the privilege of the vertical which the position of the screen still displays, in favour of an omni-directional space which constantly varies its angles and co-ordinates, to exchange the vertical and the horizontal. And the screen itself, even if it keeps a vertical position by convention, no longer seems to refer to the human posture, like a window or a painting, but rather constitutes a table of information, an opaque surface on which are inscribed 'data', information replacing nature, and the brain-city, the third eye, replacing the eyes of nature. Finally, sound achieving an autonomy which increasingly lends it the status of image, the two images, sound and visual, enter into complex relations with neither subordination nor commensurability, and reach a common limit in so far as each reaches its own limit. In all these senses, the new spiritual automatism in turn refers to new psychological automata.

But we are all the time circling the question: cerebral creation or deficiency of the cerebellum? The new automatism is worthless in itself if it is not put to the service of a powerful, obscure, condensed will to art, aspiring to deploy itself through involuntary movements which none the less do not restrict it. An original will to art has already been defined by us in the change affecting the intelligible content of cinema itself: the substitution of the time-image for the movement-image. So that electronic images will have to be based on still another will to art, or on as yet unknown aspects of the time-image. The artist is always in the situation of saying simultaneously: I claim new methods, and I am afraid that the new methods may invalidate all will to art, or make it into a business, a pornography, a Hitlerism . . .[9] What is important is that the cinematographic image was already achieving effects which were not like those of electronics, but which had autonomous anticipatory functions in the time-image as will to art. Thus Bresson's cinema has no need of computing or cybernetic machines; yet the 'model' is a modern psychological automaton, because it is defined in relation to the speech-act, and no longer, as before, by motor action (Bresson was constantly thinking about automatism). Similarly Rohmer's puppet characters, Robbe-Grillet's hypnotized ones, and Resnais' zombies are defined in terms of speech or information, not of energy or motivity. In Resnais, there are no more flashbacks, but rather feedbacks and failed feedbacks, which, however, need no special machinery (except in the deliberately rudimentary case of *Je t'aime je t'aime*). In Ozu, it is the daring of the continuity shots at 180° that is enough to assemble an image 'end to end with its obverse', and to make 'the shot turn round'.[10] Space muddles its directions, its orientations, and loses all primacy of the vertical axis that could determine them, as in Snow's *The Central Region*, using only a single camera and a rotary machine obeying electronic sounds. And the vertical of the screen now has only a conventional meaning when it ceases to make us see a world in movement, when it tends to become an opaque surface which receives, in order to disorder, and on which characters, objects and words are inscribed as 'data'. The readability of the image makes it as independent of the vertical human position as a newspaper can be. Bazin's alternative, either the screen acts as a frame of painting or as a mask (window), was never sufficient; for there was also the frame-mirror in the style of Ophüls, the wallpaper frame in the style of Hitchcock. But, when the frame or the screen functions as instrument panel, printing or computing table, the image is constantly being cut into another image, being printed through a visible mesh, sliding over other images in an 'incessant stream of messages', and the shot itself is less like an eye than an overloaded brain endlessly absorbing information: it is the brain-information, brain-city couple which replaces that of eye-Nature.[11] Godard will move in this direction (*A Married Woman, Two or Three Things I Know about Her*), even before starting to use video methods. And, in the Straubs, and in Marguerite Duras, in Syberberg, the sound framing, the disjunction of the sound image and the visual image, use cinematographic methods, or simple video methods, instead of calling on new technologies. The reasons are not simply economic. The fact is that the new spiritual automatism and the new psychological automata depend on an aesthetic before depending on technology. It is the time-image which calls on an original regime of images and signs, before electronics spoils it or, in contrast, relaunches it. When Jean-Louis Schefer invokes the great spiritual automaton or the dummy at the back of our heads as principles of the cinema, he is right in defining it today by a brain which has a direct experience of time, anterior to all motivity of bodies (even if the apparatus invoked, the mill in Dreyer's *Vampyr*, still refers to a clockwork automaton).

The Straubs, Marguerite Duras and Syberberg have, with some justification, often been grouped together in the project of forming a whole audio-visual system, whatever the differences between these authors.[12] In Syberberg we effectively encounter the two great characteristics that we have tried to identify in the other cases. First, the disjunction of the sound and the visual appears clearly in *Le cuisinier du roi*, between the cook's flux of words and the deserted spaces, castles, shacks, sometimes an engraving. Similarly, in *Hitler* the visual space of the chancellery becomes deserted, while some children in a corner make heard the record of one of Hitler's speeches. This disjunction takes on aspects peculiar to Syberberg's style. Sometimes it is the objective dissociation of what is said and what is seen: front-projection and the frequent use of slides provide a visual space not only not seen by the actor himself, but with which he is associated without ever being a part of it, reduced to his words and a few accessories (for instance, in *Hitler* the giant furniture, the giant telephone, while the dwarf servant talks about the master's underpants). Sometimes it is the subjective dissociation of the voices and the body: the body is here replaced by a puppet, a jumping jack facing the voice of the actor or reciter; or as in *Parsifal* the playback is perfectly synchronized, but with a body which remains foreign to the voice it gives itself, a living puppet, whether a girl's body for a man's voice or two competing bodies for the same voice.[13] In other words, there is no whole: the regime of the 'tear', where the division into body and voice forms a genesis of the image as 'non-representable by a single individual', 'appearance divided in itself and in a non-psychological way'.[14] The puppet and the reciter, the body and the voice, constitute neither a whole nor an individual, but the automaton. This is the psychological automaton, in the sense of a profoundly divided essence of the psyche, even though it is not at all psychological in the sense that this division would be interpreted as a state of the non-machine individual. As in Kleist, or Japanese theatre, the soul is made from the 'mechanical movement' of the puppet, in so far as the latter appoints itself an 'internal voice'. But, if the division is thus valid in itself, it is nevertheless not valid for itself. For, in the second place, a pure speech-act as creative story-telling or legend-making must extricate itself from all the spoken information (the most striking example is *Karl May* who must become a legend through his own lies and their exposure), but also the visual data must be organized in superimposed layers, endlessly mixed up, with variable outcrops, retro-active relations, heavings, sinkings, collapses, a rendering into muddle from which the speech-act will emerge, will rise up on the other side (these are the three layers of the history of Germany which correspond to the trilogy, Ludwig, Karl May, Hitler, and in each film the superimposition of slides like so many layers the last of which is the end of the world, 'a frozen and murdered landscape'). As if it were necessary for the world to be broken and buried for the speech-act to rise up. Something similar to what we have seen in Straub and Duras happens with Syberberg: the visual and the sound do not reconstitute a whole, but enter into an 'irrational' relation according to two dissymetrical trajectories. The audio-visual image is not a whole, it is 'a *fusion* of the tear'.

But one of Syberberg's originalities is to stretch out a vast space of information, like a complex, heterogeneous, anarchic space where the trivial and the cultural, the public and the private, the historic and the anecdotal, the imaginary and the real are brought close together, and sometimes on the side of speech, discourses, commentaries, familiar or ancillary testimonies, sometimes on the side of sight, of existing or no longer existing settings, engravings, plans and projects, acts of seeing with acts of clairvoyance, all of equal importance and forming a network, in kinds of relationship which are never those of causality. The modern world is that in which information replaces nature. It is what Jean-Pierre Oudart calls the 'media-effect' in Syberberg.[15] And it is an essential aspect of Syberberg's work, because the disjunction, the division of the visual and the sound, will be specifically entrusted with experiencing this *complexity* of informational space. This goes beyond the psychological individual just as it makes a whole impossible: a non-totalizable complexity, 'non-representable by a single individual', and which finds its representation only in the automaton. Syberberg takes the image of Hitler as enemy, not Hitler the individual, who does not exist, but neither a totality which could produce him according to relations of causality. 'Hitler in us' not only indicates that we made Hitler as much as he made us, or that we all have potential fascist elements, but that Hitler exists only through pieces of information which constitute his image in ourselves.[16] It could be said that the Nazi regime, the war, the concentration camps, were not images, and that Syberberg's position is not without ambiguity. But Syberberg's powerful idea is that *no information, whatever it might be, is sufficient to defeat Hitler.*[17] All the documents could be shown, all the testimonies could be heard, but in vain: what makes information all-powerful (the newspapers, and then the radio, and then the television), is its very nullity, its radical ineffectiveness. Information plays on its ineffectiveness in order to establish its power, its very power is to be ineffective, and thereby all the more dangerous. This is why it is necessary to go beyond information in order to defeat Hitler or turn the image over. Now, going beyond information is achieved on two sides at once, towards two questions: *what is the source and what is the addressee?* These are also the two questions of the Godardian pedagogy. Informatics replies to neither question, because the source of information is not a piece of information any more than is the person informed. If there is no debasement of information, it is because information itself is a debasement. It is thus necessary to go beyond all the pieces of spoken information; to extract from them a pure speech-act, creative story-telling which is as it were the obverse side of the dominant myths, of current words and their supporters; an act capable of creating the myth instead of drawing profit or business from it.[18] It is also necessary to go beyond all the visual layers; to set up a pure informed person capable of emerging from the debris, of surviving the end of the world, hence capable of receiving into his visible body the pure act of speech. In *Parsifal* the first aspect is taken up in the huge head of Wagner, which gives the speech-act as song its creative function, the power of a myth of which Ludwig, Karl May and Hitler are only the derisory, or perverse, putting to use, the debasement. The other aspect is taken up in Parsifal, who moves through all the visual spaces, themselves emerged from the great head, and who leaves the last end of world space divided in two, when the head itself divides, and the girl Parsifal does not utter, but receives into her whole being the redemptive voice.[19] The irrational cycle of the visual and the sound is related by Syberberg to information and its overcoming. Redemption, art beyond knowledge, is also creation beyond information. Redemption arrives too late (the point shared by Syberberg and Visconti); it appears when information has already gained control of speech-acts, and when Hitler has already captured the German myth or irrational.[20] But the too-late is not only negative; it is the sign of the time-image in the place where time makes visible the stratigraphy of space and audible the story-telling of the speech-act. The life or the afterlife of cinema depends on its internal struggle with informatics. It is necessary to set up against the latter the question which goes beyond it, that of its source and that of its addressee, the head of Wagner as spiritual automaton, the Parsifal couple as psychic automata.[21]

2

We can now summarize the constitution of this time-image in modern cinema, and the new signs that it implies or initiates. There are many possible transformations, almost imperceptible passages, and also combinations between the movement-image and the time-image. It cannot be said that one is more important than the other, whether more beautiful or more profound. All that can be said is that the movement-image does not give us a time-image. Nevertheless, it does give us many things in connection with it. On one hand, the movement-image constitutes time in its empirical form, the course of time: a successive present in an extrinsic relation of before and after, so that the past is a former present, and the future a present to come. Inadequate reflection would lead us to conclude from this that the cinematographic image is necessarily in the present. But this ready-made idea, disastrous for any understanding of cinema, is less the fault of the movement-image than of an over-hasty reflection. For, on the other hand, the movement-image gives rise to an image *of* time which is distinguished from it by excess or default, over or under the present as empirical progression: in this case, time is no longer measured by movement, but is itself the number or measure of movement (metaphysical representation). This number in turn has two aspects, which we saw in the first volume: it is the minimum unity of time as interval of movement or the totality of time as maximum of movement in the universe. The subtle and the sublime. But, from either aspect, time is distinguished in this way from movement only as indirect representation. Time as progression derives from the movement-image or from successive shots. But time as unity or as totality depends on montage which still relates it back to movement or to the succession of shots. This is why the movement-image is fundamentally linked to an indirect representation of time, and does not give us a direct presentation of it, that is, does not give us a time-image. The only direct presentation, then, appears in music. But in modern cinema, by contrast, the time-image is no longer empirical, nor metaphysical; it is 'transcendental' in the sense that Kant gives this word: time is out of joint and presents itself in the pure state.[22] The time-image does not imply the absence of movement (even though it often includes its increased scarcity) but it implies the reversal of the subordination; it is no longer time which is subordinate to movement; it is movement which subordinates itself to time. It is no longer time which derives from movement, from its norm and its corrected aberrations; it is movement as *false movement*, as aberrant movement which now depends on time. The time-image has become direct, just as time has discovered new aspects, as movement has become aberrant in essence and not by accident, as montage has taken on a new sense, and as a so-called modern cinema has been constituted post-war. However close its relations with classical cinema, modern cinema asks the question: what are the new forces at work in the image, and the new signs invading the screen?

The first factor is the break of the sensory-motor link. For the movement-image, as soon as it referred itself back to its interval, constituted the action-image: the latter, in its widest sense, comprised received movement (perception, situation), imprint (affection, the interval itself), and executed movement (action properly speaking and reaction). The sensory-motor link was thus the unity of movement and its interval, the specification of the movement-image or the action-image *par excellence*. There is no reason to talk of a narrative cinema which would correspond to this first moment, for narration results from the sensory-motor schema, and not the other way round. But precisely what brings this cinema of action into question after the war is the very break-up of the sensory-motor schema: the rise of situations to which one can no longer react, of environments with which there are now only chance relations, of empty or disconnected any-space-whatevers replacing qualified extended space. It is here that situations no longer extend into action or reaction in accordance with the requirements of the movement-image. These are pure optical and sound situations, in which the character does not know how to respond, abandoned spaces in which he ceases to experience and to act so that he enters into flight, goes on a trip, comes and goes, vaguely indifferent to what happens to him, undecided as to what must be done. But he has gained in an ability to see what he has lost in action or reaction: he SEES so that the viewer's problem becomes 'What is there to see in the image?' (and not now 'What are we going to see in the next image?'). The situation no longer extends into action through the intermediary of affections. It is cut off from all its extensions, it is now important only for itself, having absorbed all its affective intensities, all its active extensions. This is no longer a sensory-motor situation, but a purely optical and sound situation, where the seer [*voyant*] has replaced the agent [*actant*]: a 'description'. We call this type of image opsigns and sonsigns, they appear after the war, through all the external reasons we can point to (the calling into question of action, the necessity of seeing and hearing, the proliferation of empty, disconnected, abandoned spaces) but also through the internal push of a cinema being reborn, re-creating its conditions, neo-realism, new wave, new American cinema. Now, if it is true that the sensory-motor situation governed the indirect representation of time as consequence of the movement-image, the purely optical and sound situation opens onto a direct time-image. The time-image is the correlate of the opsign and the sonsign. It never appeared more clearly than in the author who anticipated modern cinema, from before the war and in the conditions of the silent film, Ozu: opsigns, empty or disconnected spaces, open on to still lifes as the pure form of time. Instead of 'motor situation – indirect representation of time', we have 'opsign or sonsign – direct presentation of time'.

But what can purely optical and sound images link up with, since they no longer extend into action? We would like to reply: with recollection-images or dream-images. Yet, the former still come within the framework of the sensory-motor situation, whose interval they are content to fill, even though lengthening and distending it; they seize a former present in the past and thus respect the empirical progression of time, even though they introduce local regressions into it (the flashback as psychological memory). The latter, dream-images, rather affect the whole: they project the sensory-motor situation to infinity, sometimes by ensuring the constant metamorphosis of the situation, sometimes by replacing the action of characters with a movement of world. But we do not, in this way, leave behind an indirect represen-tation, even though we come close, in certain exceptional cases, to doors of time that already belong to modern cinema (for instance, the flashback as revelation of a time which forks and frees itself in Mankiewicz, or the movement of world as the coupling of a pure description and dance in the American musical comedy). How-ever, in these very cases, the recollection-image or the dream-image, the mnemosign or the onirosign, are gone beyond: for these images in themselves are virtual images, which are linked with the actual optical or sound image (description) but which are constantly being actualized on their own account, or the former in the latter to infinity. For the time-image to be born, on the contrary, the actual image must enter into relation with its *own* virtual image as such; from the outset pure description must divide in two, 'repeat itself, take itself up again, fork, contradict itself'. An image which is double-sided, mutual, both actual and virtual, must be constituted. We are no longer in the sitation of a relationship between the actual image and other virtual images, recollections, or dreams, which thus become actual in turn: this is still a mode of linkage. We are in the situation of an actual image *and* its own virtual image, to the extent that there is no longer any linkage of the real with the imaginary, but *indiscernibility of the two*, a perpetual exchange. This is a progress in relation to the opsign:

we saw how the crystal (the hyalosign) ensures the dividing in two of description, and brings about the exchange in the image which has become mutual, the exchange of the actual and the virtual, of the limpid and the opaque, of the seed and the surrounding.[23] By raising themselves to the indiscernibility of the real and the imaginary, the signs of the crystal go beyond all psychology of the recollection or dream, and all physics of action. What we see in the crystal is no longer the empirical progression of time as succession of presents, nor its indirect representation as interval or as whole; it is its direct presentation, its constitutive dividing in two into a present which is passing and a past which is preserved, the strict contemporaneity of the present with the past that it will be, of the past with the present that it has been. It is time itself which arises in the crystal, and which is constantly recommending its dividing in two without completing it, since the indiscernible exchange is always renewed and reproduced. The direct time-image or the transcendental form of time is what we see in the crystal; and hyalosigns, and crystalline signs, should therefore be called mirrors or seeds of time.

Thus we have the chronosigns which mark the various present-ations of the direct time-image. The first concerns the *order of time*: this order is not made up of succession, nor is it the same thing as the interval or the whole of indirect representation. It is a matter of the internal relations of time, in a topological or quantic form. Thus the first chronosign has two figures: sometimes it is the coexistence of all the sheets of past, with the topological transformation of these sheets, and the overtaking of psychologi-cal memory towards a world-memory (this sign can be called sheet, aspect, or *facies*). Sometimes it is the simultaneity of points of present, these points breaking with all external succession, and carrying out quantic jumps between the presents which are doubled by the past, the future and the present itself (this sign can be called point or accent). We are no longer in an indiscernible distinction between the real and the imaginary, which would characterize the crystal image, but in undecidable alternatives between sheets of past, or 'inexplicable' differences between points of present, which now concern the direct time-image. What is in play is no longer the real and the imaginary, but the true and the false. And just as the real and the imaginary become indiscernible in certain very specific conditions of the image, the true and the false now become undecidable or inextricable: the impossible proceeds from the possible, and the past is not necessarily true. A new logic has to be invented, just as earlier a new psychology had to be. It seemed to us that Resnais went furthest in the direction of coexisting sheets of past, and Robbe-Grillet in that of simultaneous peaks of present: hence the paradox of *Last Year in Marienbad*, which participates in the double system. But, in any event, the time-image has arisen through direct or transcendental presentation, as a new element in post-war cinema, and Welles was master of the time-image . . .

There is still another type of chronosign which on this occasion constitutes *time as series*: the before and after are no longer themselves a matter of external empirical succession, but of the intrinsic quality of that which becomes in time. Becoming can in fact be defined as that which transforms an empirical sequence into a series: a burst of series. A series is a sequence of images, which tend in themselves in the direction of a limit, which orients and inspires the first sequence (the before), and gives way to another sequence organized as series which tends in turn towards another limit (the after). The before and the after are then no longer successive determinations of the course of time, but the two sides of the power, or the passage of the power to a higher power. The direct time-image here does not appear in an order of coexistences or simultaneities, but in a becoming as potentialization, as series of powers. This second type of chronosign, the genesign, has therefore also the property of bringing into question the notion of truth; for the false ceases to be a simple appearance or even a lie, in order to achieve that power of becoming which constitutes series or degrees, which crosses limits, carries out metamorphoses, and develops along its whole path an act of legend, of story-telling. Beyond the true or the false, becoming as power of the false. Genesigns present several figures in this sense. Sometimes, as in Welles, they are characters forming series as so many degrees of a 'will to power' through which the world becomes a fable. Sometimes it is a character himself crossing a limit, and becoming another, in an act of story-telling which connects him to a people past or to come: we have seen the paradox by which this cinema was called '*cinéma-vérité*' at the moment that it brought every model of the true into question; and there is a double becoming superimposed for the author becomes another as much as his character does (as with Perrault who takes the character as 'intercessor' or with Rouch who tends to become a black, in a quite different non-symmetrical way). It is perhaps here that the question of the author and the

author's becoming, of his becoming-other, is already posed in its
most acute form in Welles. Sometimes again, in the third place,
characters dissolve of their own accord, and the author is effaced:
there are now only attitudes of bodies, corporeal postures
forming series, and a gest which connects them together as limit.
It is a cinema of bodies which has broken all the more with the
sensory-motor schema through action being replaced by attitude,
and supposedly true linkage by the gest which produces legend or
story-telling. Sometimes, finally, the series, their limits and
transformations, the degrees of power, may be a matter of any
kind of relation of the image: characters, states of one character,
positions of the author, attitudes of bodies, as well as colours,
aesthetic genres, psychological faculties, political powers, logical
or metaphysical categories. Every sequence of images forms a
series in that it moves in the direction of a category in which it is
reflected, the passage of one category to another determining a
change of power. What is said in the most simple terms about
Boulez' music will also be said about Godard's cinema: having put
everything in series, having brought about a generalized
serialism. Everything which functions as limit between two series
divided into two parts, the before and the after constituting the
two sides of the limit, will also be called a category (a character, a
gest, a word, a colour may be a category as easily as a genre, from
the moment that they fulfil the conditions of reflection). If the
organization of series generally takes place horizontally, as in *Slow
Motion* with the imaginary, fear, business, music, it is possible that
the limit or category in which a series is reflected itself forms
another series of a higher power, henceforth superimposed on
the first: as in the pictorial category in *Passion* or the musical one
in *First Name Carmen*. There is in this case a vertical construction
of series, which tends to return to coexistence or simultaneity,
and to combine the two types of chronosigns.

The so-called classical image had to be considered on two axes.
These two axes were the co-ordinates of the brain: on the one
hand, the images were linked or extended according to laws of
association, of continuity, resemblance, contrast, or opposition;
on the other hand, associated images were internalized in a whole
as concept (integration), which was in turn continually externalized in associable or extendable images (differentiation). This is
why the whole remained open and changing, at the same time as a
set of images was always taken from a larger set. This was the
double aspect of the movement-image, defining the out-of-field:

in the first place it was in touch with an exterior, in the second place it expressed a whole which changes. Movement in its extension was the immediate given, and the whole which changes, that is, time, was indirect or mediate representation. But there was a continual circulation of the two here, internalization in the whole, externalization in the image, circle or spiral which constituted for cinema, no less than for philosophy, the model of the True as totalization. This model inspired the noosigns of the classical image, and there were necessarily two kinds of noosign. In the first kind, the images were linked by rational cuts, and formed under this condition an extendable world: between two images or two sequences of images, the limit as interval is included as the end of the one *or* as the beginning of the other, as the last image of the first sequence or the first of the second. The other kind of noosign marked the integration of the sequences into a whole (self-awareness as internal representation), but also the differentiation of the whole into extended sequences (belief in the external world). And, from one to the other, the whole was constantly changing at the same time as the images were moving. Time as measure of movement thus ensured a general system of commensurability, in this double form of the interval and the whole. This was the splendour of the classical image.

The modern image initiates the reign of 'incommensurables' or irrational cuts: this is to say that the cut no longer forms part of one or the other image, of one or the other sequence that it separates and divides. It is on this condition that the succession or sequence becomes a series, in the sense that we have just analysed. The interval is set free, the interstice becomes irreducible and stands on its own. The first consequence is that the images are no longer linked by rational cuts, but are relinked on to irrational cuts. We gave Godard's series as an example, but they can be found everywhere, notably in Resnais (the moment around which everything turns and repasses in *Je t'aime je t'aime*, is a typical irrational cut). By relinkage must be understood, not a second linkage which would come and add itself on, but a mode of original and specific linkage, or rather a specific connection between de-linked images. There are no longer grounds for talking about a real or possible extension capable of constituting an external world: we have ceased to believe in it, and the image is cut off from the external world. But the internalization or integration of self-awareness in a whole has no less disappeared: the relinkage takes place through parcelling, whether it is a

matter of the construction of series in Godard, or of the
transformations of sheets in Resnais (relinked parcellings). This
is why thought, as power which has not always existed, is born
from an outside more distant than any external world, and, as
power which does not yet exist, confronts an inside, an unthinkable or unthought, deeper than any internal world. In the second
place, there is no longer any movement of internalization or
externalization, integration or differentiation, but a confrontation of an outside and an inside independent of distance, this
thought outside itself and this un-thought within thought. This is
the unsummonable in Welles, the undecidable in Resnais, the
inexplicable in the Straubs, the impossible in Marguerite Duras,
the irrational in Syberberg. The brain has lost its Euclidean
co-ordinates, and now emits other signs. The direct time-image
effectively has as noosigns the irrational cut between non-linked
(but always relinked) images, and the absolute contact between
non-totalizable, asymmetrical outside and inside. We move with
ease from one to the other, because the outside and the inside are
the two sides of the limit as irrational cut, and because the latter,
no longer forming part of any sequence, itself appears as an
autonomous outside which necessarily provides itself with an
inside.

The limit or interstice, the irrational cut, pass especially
between the visual image and the sound image. This implies
several novelties or changes. The sound must itself become image
instead of being a component of the visual image; the creation of
a sound framing is thus necessary, so that the cut passes between
the two framings, sound and visual; hence even if the out-of-field
survives in fact [*en fait*], it must lose all power by right [*de droit*]
because the visual image ceases to extend beyond its own frame,
in order to enter into a specific relation with the sound image
which is itself framed (the interstice between the two framings
replaces the out-of-field); the voice-off must also disappear,
because there is no more out-of-field to inhabit, but two heautonomous images to be confronted, that of voices and that of
views, each in itself, each for itself and in its frame. It is possible
for the two kinds of images to touch and join up, but this is clearly
not through flashback, as if a voice, more or less off, was evoking
what the visual image was going to give back to us: modern
cinema has killed flashback, like the voice-off and the out-of-field.
It has been able to conquer the sound image only by imposing a
dissociation between it and the visual image, a disjunction which

must not be surmounted: irrational cut between the two. And yet there is a relation between them, a free indirect or incommensurable relation, for incommensurability denotes a new relation and not an absence. Hence the sound image frames a mass or a continuity from which the pure speech act is to be extracted, that is, an act of myth or story-telling which creates the event, which makes the event rise up into the air, and which rises itself in a spiritual ascension. And the visual image for its part frames an any-space-whatever, an empty or disconnected space which takes on a new value, because it will bury the event under stratigraphic layers, and make it go down like an underground fire which is always covered over. The visual image will thus never show what the sound image utters. For example, in Marguerite Duras, the originary dance will never rise up again through flashback to totalize the two kinds of images. There will none the less be a relation between the two, a junction or a contact. This will be the contact independent of distance, between an outside where the speech-act rises, and an inside where the event is buried in the ground: a complementarity of the sound image, the speech-act as creative story-telling, and the visual image, stratigraphic or archaeological burying. And the irrational cut between the two, which forms the non-totalizable relation, the broken ring of their junction, the asymmetrical faces of their contact. This is a perpetual relinkage. Speech reaches its own limit which separates it from the visual; but the visual reaches its own limit which separates it from sound. So each one reaching its own limit which separates it from the other thus discovers the common limit which connects them to each other in the incommensurable relation of an irrational cut, the right side and its obverse, the outside and the inside. These new signs are lectosigns, which show the final aspect of the direct time-image, the common limit: the visual image become stratigraphic is for its part all the more readable in that the speech-act becomes an autonomous creator. Classical cinema was not short of lectosigns, but only to the extent that the speech-act was itself read in the silent film, or in the first stage of the talkie, making it possible to read the visual image, of which it was only one component. From classical to modern cinema, from the movement-image to the time-image, what changes are not only the chronosigns, but the noosigns and lectosigns, having said that it is always possible to multiply the passages from one regime to the other, just as to accentuate their irreducible differences.

3

The usefulness of theoretical books on cinema has been called into question (especially today, because the times are not right). Godard likes to recall that, when the future directors of the new wave were writing, they were not writing about cinema, they were not making a theory out of it, it was already their way of making films. However, this remark does not show a great understanding of what is called theory. For theory too is something which is made, no less than its object. For many people, philosophy is something which is not 'made', but is pre-existent, ready-made in a prefabricated sky. However, philosophical theory is itself a practice, just as much as its object. It is no more abstract than its object. It is a practice of concepts, and it must be judged in the light of the other practices with which it interferes. A theory of cinema is not 'about' cinema, but about the concepts that cinema gives rise to and which are themselves related to other concepts corresponding to other practices, the practice of concepts in general having no privilege over others, any more than one object has over others. It is at the level of the interference of many practices that things happen, beings, images, concepts, all the kinds of events. The theory of cinema does not bear on the cinema, but on the concepts of the cinema, which are no less practical, effective or existent than cinema itself. The great cinema authors are like the great painters or the great musicians: it is they who talk best about what they do. But, in talking, they become something else, they become philosophers or theoreticians – even Hawks who wanted no theories, even Godard when he pretends to distrust them. Cinema's concepts are not given in cinema. And yet they are cinema's concepts, not theories about cinema. So that there is always a time, midday-midnight, when we must no longer ask ourselves, 'What is cinema?' but 'What is philosophy?' Cinema itself is a new practice of images and signs, whose theory philosophy must produce as conceptual practice. For no technical determination, whether applied (psychoanalysis, linguistics) or reflexive, is sufficient to constitute the concepts of cinema itself.

Notes

1 Beyond the Movement-Image

1 Bazin, *What Is Cinema?*, trans. Hugh Gray, Berkeley: University of California Press, 1971, Vol. II, p. 37 (and the whole of the chapters on neo-realism). It is Amédée Ayfre who takes up and develops Bazin's thesis to give it a pronounced phenomenological expression: 'Du premier au second néo-réalisme', *Le néo-réalisme italien, Etudes cinématographiques.*

2 On these films, cf. Jean-Claude Bonnet, 'Rossellini ou le parti pris des choses', *Cinématographe*, no. 43, janvier 1979. This review devoted two special numbers to neo-realism, 42 and 43, with the very apt title 'Le regard néo-réaliste'.

3* Translators' note: Deleuze uses the word 'bal(l)ade', an untranslatable pun on the words *ballade* (ballad) and *balade* (trip or voyage).

4 James Cain's novel, *The Postman Always Rings Twice*, has given rise to four pieces of work in the cinema: Pierre Chenil (*Le dernier tournant*, 1939), Visconti (1942), Garnett (1946) and Rafelson (1981). The first is part of French poetic realism, and the latter two, of American action-image realism. Jacques Fieschi does a very interesting comparative analysis of the four films: *Cinématographe*, no. 70, septembre 1981, pp. 8–9 (the reader is also referred to his article on *Obsession*, no. 42).

5· These themes are analysed in *Visconti, Etudes cinématographiques* especially the articles by Bernard Dort and René Duloquin (cf. Duloquin, on the subject of *Rocco and his Brothers*, p. 86: 'From the monumental staircase of Milan to the indistinct countryside, the characters float in a set whose boundaries they cannot reach. They are real, and so is the set, but their relation is not and approaches that of a dream.').

6 On this 'communism' in *The Earth Trembles*, cf. Yves Guillaume, *Visconti*, Editions Universitaires, p. 17 f.

7 cf. the commentary by Noël Burch, *Praxis du cinéma*, Gallimard, pp. 112–18.

8 Barthélemy Amengual, 'Du spectacle au·spectaculaire', *Fellini I, Etudes cinématographiques.*

9 Pierre Leprohon has emphasized this notion of report in Antonioni: *Antonioni*, Seghers.

10* Translators' note: 'Instats' is a neologism coined by Deleuze.

11 Fellini has frequently claimed this sympathy for decadence (for instance, 'it is not a trial by a judge, it is a trial conducted by an accomplice', quoted by Amengual, op. cit., p. 9). In contrast, in relation to the world, and the feelings and characters which appear

in it, Antonioni retains a critical objectivity in which there has been discerned an almost Marxist inspiration: cf. the analysis by Gérard Gozlan, *Positif*, no. 35, juillet 1960. Gozlan points to Antonioni's fine text: how is it that men rid themselves with ease of their scientific and technical concepts when they turn out to be lacking or unsuitable, whilst they remain attached to 'moral' beliefs and feelings which no longer bring anything but their unhappiness, even when they invent an even more harmful immoralism? (Antonioni's words are reprinted in Leprohon, op. cit., pp. 104–6).

12 Antonioni, *Cinéma 58*, septembre 1958. And Leprohon's formulation, op. cit., p. 76: 'The story can only be read in filigree, through images which are consequences and no longer act.'

13 Robbe-Grillet, 'Temps et description', *Pour un nouveau roman*, Editions de Minuit, p. 127 (English translation: *Snapshots, or Towards a New Novel*, trans. Barbara Wright, London: Calder & Boyars, 1965). We shall have frequent recourse to the theory of description in this text of Robbe-Grillet's.

14 André Labarthe, *Cahiers du cinéma*, no. 123, septembre 1961.

15 Amengual, op. cit., p. 22.

16 Claude Ollier, *Souvenirs écran*, Cahiers du cinéma, Gallimard, p. 86. It is Ollier who analyses the breaks and injections in Antonioni's images, and the role of the imaginary gaze which gives parts of space continuity. The excellent analyses by Marie-Claire Ropars-Wuilleumier may also be referred to: she shows how Antonioni does not simply move from a disconnected space to an empty one, but, simultaneously, from a person who is suffering from the absence of another to a person who is suffering still more deeply from an absence in himself and in the world ('L'espace et le temps dans l'univers d'Antonioni', *Antonioni, Etudes cinématographiques*, pp. 22, 27–8, reprinted in *L'Ecran de la mémoire*, Seuil.

17 cf. the analyses by Michel Esteve, 'Les nuits blanches ou le jeu du réel et de l'irréel', *Visconti, Etudes cinématographiques*.

18 Sadoul, *Chroniques du cinéma français*, I, Paris: UGE, p. 370.

19 Ollier, op. cit., pp. 23–4 (on the space in *Made in USA*).

20 In Volume I we saw this special sense of light in the French pre-war school, particularly in Grémillon, but Rivette carries it to a higher level, picking up Delaunay's most elevated conceptions: 'In contrast to the cubists, Delaunay does not look for the secrets of renewal in the presentation of objects, or more precisely of light at the level of objects. He holds that light creates forms by itself, independently of its reflections on matter ... If light destroys objective forms, what it brings with it is its order and movement ... It is then that Delaunay discovers that the movements which enliven light are different depending on whether the sun or the moon is more prominent ... With the two fundamental spectacles of light in movement he associates the

image of the universe, in the form of the earthly globe presented as the locus of eternal mirages' (Pierre Francastel, *Du cubisme à l'art abstrait, Robert Delaunay*, Bibliothèque de l'Ecole pratique des hautes études, pp. 19–29)..

21 Proust, *Against Sainte-Beuve* 'Gérard de Nerval'. Proust ends his analysis by noting that a mediocre dreamer is not going to see again the places that he has caught in his dream, since it is only a dream, whilst a true dreamer goes there all the more because it is a dream.

22 Godard already said in relation to *Vivre sa vie* that 'the external side of things' must allow 'the feeling of inside' to be given: 'How do we do the inside? Well, precisely by staying prudently outside', like the painter. And Godard presents *Two or Three Things* . . . as adding a 'subjective description' to the 'objective description' to give a 'feeling of a whole' (*Jean-Luc Godard par Jean-Luc Godard*, Belfond, pp. 394–5.

23 Robbe-Grillet, op. cit., p. 66.

24 Emmanuel Carrère has clearly demonstrated this 'attempt to approach tactile sensations' (*Werner Herzog*, Edilig, p. 25): not only in *Land of Silence and Darkness*, which puts before us some deaf and blind people, but in *Kaspar Hauser* which has grand dream-visions coexisting with little tactile gestures (for instance, the pressure of the thumb and fingers when Kaspar forces himself to think).

25 Donald Richie, *Ozu*, Editions Lettre du Blanc: 'When he was about to get down to the script-writing, confident of his list of themes, he rarely wondered what the story was going to be. He asked himself instead which people were to occupy his film . . . A name was assigned to each character along with an arsenal of general characteristics appropriate to his family situation, father, daughter, aunt, but few recognizable traits. This character would grow, or rather the dialogue that gave him life would grow . . . beyond all reference to the plot or story . . . Although the opening scenes are always full of dialogue, the dialogue seems to turn on no particular subject . . . The character was thus constructed and modelled almost exclusively by virtue of the conversations he had' (pp. 15–26). And, on the 'one shot, one line' principle, cf. pp. 143–5.

26 Paul Schrader, *Transcendental Style in Film: Ozu, Bresson, Dreyer* (extracts in *Cahiers du cinéma*, no. 286, mars 1978).

27 Maurice Leblanc, *La vie extravagante de Balthazar*, Le Livre de Poche.

28 On colour in Ozu, see the remarks of Renaud Bezombes, *Cinématographe*, no. 41, novembre 1978, p. 47, and no. 52, novembre 1979, p. 58.

29 Reference should be made to Noël Burch's fine analysis of the 'pillow shot' and its functions: suspension of human presence, passage to the inanimate, but also reverse passage, pivot, emblem, contribution to the flatness of the image, pictorial composition (*Pour un observateur lointain*, Cahiers du cinéma Gallimard, pp. 175–86).

We simply wonder if there is not room to distinguish two different things in these 'pillow shots'. Similarly for what Richie calls 'still lifes', pp. 164–70.

30 Dôgen, *Shôbôgenzo*, Editions de la Différence.
31 cf. Antonioni, 'The horizon of events' (*Cahiers du cinéma*, no. 290, juillet 1978, p. 11) which insists on European dualism. And, in a later interview, he returns briefly to this theme, pointing out that the Japanese raise the problem differently (no. 342, décembre 1982).
32 Paul Rozenberg sees in this the essence of English romanticism: *Le romantisme anglais*, Larousse.
33 J. M. G. Le Clezio, 'The extra-terrestrial', in 'Fellini', *L'Arc*, no. 45, p. 28.
34 On Marxist criticism on the evolution of neo-realism and its characters, cf. *Le néo-réalisme, Etudes cinématographiques*, p. 102. And on Marxist criticism in Japan, especially against Ozu, cf. Noël Burch, op. cit., p. 283. It must be emphasized that in France the new wave, in its visionary aspect, was deeply understood by Sadoul.
35 cf. *Jean-Luc Godard par Jean-Luc Godard*, p. 392.
36 Marc Chevrie analyses Jean-Pierre Léaud's playing as 'medium' in terms close to Blanchot's (*Cahiers du cinéma*, no. 351, septembre 1983, pp. 31–3).
37 Criticism of metaphor is equally present in the new wave, with Godard, and in the new novel with Robbe-Grillet (*Pour un nouveau roman*). It is true that, more recently, Godard has taken inspiration from a metaphorical form, for instance, in the case of *Passion*: 'The knights are metaphors for the bosses' (*Le Monde*, 27 mai 1982), but, as we shall see, this form draws on a genetic and chronological analysis of the image, much more than on a synthesis or comparison of images.
38 D. H. Lawrence wrote an important piece in support of the image and against clichés in relation to Cézanne. He shows how parody is not a solution; and neither is the pure optical image, with its voids and disconnections. According to him, it is in the still lifes that Cézanne wins his battle against clichés, rather than in the portraits and landscapes ('Introduction to these paintings', *Eros et le chiens*, Bourgois, pp. 253–64). We have seen how the same remarks applied to Ozu.
39 'Lectosign' refers to the Greek *lekton* or Latin *dictum*, which indicates what is expressed in a proposition independent of the relationship of this to its object. Similarly for the image when it is captured intrinsically, independent of its relationship with a supposedly external object.
40 Text of Antonioni's quoted by Leprohon, op. cit., p. 103: 'Now that we have today eliminated the problem of the bicycle (I am using a metaphor, try to understand beyond my words), it is important to see what there is in the spirit and heart of this man whose bicycle has been stolen, how he has adapted, what has stayed with him out of all

his past experiences of the war, the post-war and everything that has
happened in our country.' (And the text on Eros sick, pp. 104–6.)

41   Noël Burch is one of the first critics to have shown that the
cinematographic image ought to be read no less than seen and
heard; and this in connection with Ozu (*Pour un observateur lointain*,
p. 175). But already in *Praxis du cinéma* Burch showed how *Story of a
Love Affair* inaugurated a new relation between story and action,
and gave the camera an 'autonomy', rather like that of a reading
pp. 112–18; and on the 'continuity grasped through discrepancy',
p. 47).

2   Recapitulation of Images and Signs

1   On all these points, reference may be made to Christian Metz, *Essais
sur la signification au cinéma*, Klincksieck (particularly Vol. I, 'Langue
ou langage?', and 'Problèmes de dénotation' which analyses the
eight syntagmatic types). Raymond Bellour's book *L'analyse du film*,
Albatros, is also essential. In an unpublished work, André Parente
makes a critical study of this semiology, underlining the hypothesis
of narrativity: *Narrativité et non-narrativité filmiques*.

2   Metz, op. cit., I, pp. 96–9, and 51: Metz takes up Edgar Morin's
theme which is that the 'cinematograph' became 'cinema' by
committing itself to a narrative direction. cf. Morin, *Le cinéma ou
l'homme imaginaire*, Editions de Minuit, ch. 3.

3   Metz had begun by underlining the weakness of paradigmatics, and
the predominance of syntagmatics in the narrative code of cinema
(*Essais*, I, pp. 73, 102). But his followers propose to show that, if the
paradigm assumes a specifically cinematographic importance (and
likewise other structural factors), there result new modes of
narration, 'dysnarrative' ones. Metz returns to the question in
Psychoanalysis and the Cinema: the imaginary signifier, trans. Celia
Britton *et al.*, London: Macmillan, 1983. For all this, nothing
changed in the hypothesis of semiology, as we shall see.

4   On this view, it must first be shown that a judgement of resemblance
or analogy is already subject to codes. However, these codes are not
specifically cinematographic but socio-cultural in general. It must
therefore be shown in addition that the analogical utterances
themselves, in each area, refer to specific codes which no longer
determine resemblance but internal structure: 'It is not only from
the outside that the visual message is partly invested by a language
system . . . but equally from the inside and in its very visuality, which
is only intelligible because its structures are partly non-visual . . . Not
everything is iconic in the icon . . .' Once one has opted for analogy
by resemblance, one moves necessarily to a 'beyond analogy': cf.
Christian Metz, *Essais*, II, pp. 157–9; and Umberto Eco, 'Sémiologie
des messages visuels', *Communications*, no. 15, 1970.

5　It is odd that, in order to distinguish the cinematographic image from a photo, Metz points, not to movement, but to narrativity (I, p. 53: 'To go from one image to two images is to go from the image to language'). Moreover semiologists explicitly appeal to a suspension of movement, in contrast, as they put it, to the 'cinephilic gaze'.

6　On this 'analogical-digital' circularity, cf. Roland Barthes, *Elements of Semiology*, trans. Annette Lavers and Colin Smith, New York: Hill & Wang, 1978, pp. 51–4 (II.4.3).

7　We shall see that the notion of the 'model' (modelling) in Bresson, elaborated as a result of the problem of the actor, but going far beyond this problem, is close to modulation. Similarly the 'type' or 'typing' in Eisenstein. These notions cannot be understood without contrasting them with the workings of the mould.

8　See the whole second part of Pasolini's book, *L'expérience hérétique*, Payot. Pasolini shows *on what conditions* real objects should be considered as constituting the image, and the image as constitutive of reality. He refuses to talk of an 'impression of reality' given by cinema: it is simply reality (p. 170), 'cinema represents reality through reality', 'I always stay within the framework of reality', without interrupting it because of a symbolic or linguistic system (p. 199). It is the study of the preliminary conditions that Pasolini's critics have not understood: it is conditions of principle [*de droit*] that constitute 'cinema', even though cinema does not actually exist outside particular films. So the object can indeed be just a referent in the image, and the image an analogical image which in turn refers to codes. But there is nothing to stop film in practice overtaking itself towards principle [*droit*], towards cinema as 'Ur-code' which, independently of any language system, makes the phoneme of the image from real objects and the moneme of reality from the image. Pasolini's whole thesis loses all sense as soon as this study of the conditions of principle [*de droit*] is ignored. If it is worth making a philosophical comparison, Pasolini might be called post-Kantian (the conditions of legitimacy are the conditions of reality itself), whilst Metz and his followers remain Kantians (bringing principle down to fact).

9　Eisenstein quickly abandons his theory of the ideogram for a notion of internal monologue, to which he thinks cinema gives an even greater extension than literature: 'Film form, new problems', *Film Form*, trans. Jay Leyda, London: Dennis Dobson, 1951, pp. 122–31. He first compares internal monologue to a primitive language system or a proto-language, as certain linguists of the Marr school had (cf. Eichenbaum's text on cinema, in 1927, *Cahiers du cinéma*, nos 220–1, juin 1970). But the internal monologue is rather closer to a visual and sound method loaded with various expressional features: the great sequence in *The General Line*, after the success of the cream-making machine, would be a classic case. Pasolini, also, moved from the idea of primitive language system to that of material constituting an internal monologue: it is not arbitrary 'to say that cinema is based on a system of signs different from a system of written-spoken language systems, that is, that cinema is another language system. But not another language system in the sense that Bantu is different from Italian' (pp. 161–2). The linguist Hjelmslev calls 'content' [*matière*] precisely this element which is not linguistically formed although it is perfectly formed from other points of view. He says 'not semiotically formed' because he identifies the semiotic function with the linguistic one. This is why Metz tends to exclude this material in his interpretation of Hjelmslev (cf. *Language and Cinema*, trans. Donna Jean Umiker-Sebeck, The Hague: Mouton, 1974, ch. 10). But its specificity as signaletic material is none the less presupposed by a language: in contrast to the majority of linguists and critics of cinema inspired by linguistics, Jakobson attaches a great deal of importance to the notion of internal monologue in Eisenstein ('Entretien sur le cinéma', in *Cinéma, théorie, lectures*, Klincksieck).

10   Peirce, *Ecrits sur le signe*, commentary by Gérard Deledalle, Seuil: we reprint Deledalle's table (p. 240):

	First	Second	Third
Representamen	Qualisign (1.1)	Synsign (1.2)	Legisign (1.3)
Object	Icon (2.1)	Index (2.2)	Symbol (2.3)
Interpretant	Rheme (3.1)	Dicisign (3.2)	Argument (3.3)

11   Peirce, *ibid*, p. 30.
12   In Peirce, there are no intermediaries, but only 'degenerate' or 'accretive' types: cf. Deledalle, *Théorie et pratique du signe*, Payot, pp. 55–64.
13   Pasolini, op. cit., pp. 211–12. We already find in Epstein, from the same point of view, a fine discussion of cinema and death: 'death makes its promises to us by cinematograph' (*Ecrits sur le cinéma*, Seghers, I, p. 199).
14   Eisenstein sometimes criticizes himself for having given too much importance to montage or co-ordination in relation to the parts co-ordinated and their 'analytic deepening': as in the text 'Montague 1938', *Film Form*. But we shall see how difficult it is, in Eisenstein's texts, to distinguish what is genuine and what is a show for Stalinist critics. In practice, from the outset, Eisenstein emphasized the need to consider the image or shot as an organic 'cell', and not as an indifferent element: in a text from 1929, 'Methods of montage', rhythmic, tonal and harmonic methods already consider the intrinsic content of each shot, according to deepening which takes increasing account of all the 'potentialities' of the image. It none the less remains true that the two points of view – that of montage and that of image or shot – enter into an

oppositional relation, even if this opposition has to be 'dialectically' resolved.

15 Epstein, *Ecrits*, Seghers, pp. 184, 199 (and on 'moving spaces', 'floating periods' and 'dangling causes', pp. 364–79). On 'impossible continuity shots', cf. Eisenstein, p. 59. Noël Burch gives an analysis of the false continuities in the priest's scene in *Ivan the Terrible*, in *Praxis du cinéma*, Gallimard, pp. 61–3.

16 Jean-Louis Schefer, *L'homme ordinaire du cinéma*, Cahiers du cinéma/ Gallimard.

17 Godard, in connection with *Passion*, *Le Monde*, 27 mai 1982.

18 cf. Claude Beylie's analysis in *Visconti, Etudes cinématographiques*.

19 René Prédal, *Alain Resnais, Etudes cinématographiques*, p. 120.

20 Proust, *A la recherche du temps perdu*, Pléiade, III, p. 924.

21 Vertov, *Articles, journaux, projets*, Paris: UGE, pp. 129–32. 'Negative' is obviously not to be understood in the sense of negation, but of indirect or derived: it is the derivative of the 'visual equation' of movement, which also allows the resolution of this primitive equation. The solution will be 'the communist deciphering of reality'.

22 cf. Narboni, Sylvie Pierre and Rivette, 'Montage', *Cahiers du cinéma*, no. 210, mars 1969.

23 Robert Lapoujade, 'Du montage au montrage', in 'Fellini', *L'Arc*.

24 Bonitzer, *Le champ aveugle*, Cahiers du cinéma/Gallimard, p. 130: 'Montage becomes the order of the day again, but in an interrogative form that Eisenstein never gave it.'

25 Tarkovsky, 'De la figure cinématographique', *Positif*, no. 249, décembre 1981: 'Time in cinema becomes the basis of bases, like sound in music, colour in painting ... Montage is far from producing a new quality ...' cf. Michel Chion's comments on this text of Tarkovsky, *Cahiers du cinéma*, no. 358, avril 1984, p. 41: 'His profound intuition about the essence of cinema, when he refuses to assimilate it to a language which combines units such as shot, images, sounds, etc.'

3 From Recollection to Dreams

1 Bergson, *Matter and Memory*, trans. Nancy Margaret Paul and W. Scott Palmer, London: Macmillan, 1911, pp. 126–9; hereafter cited as *MM*. And 'Intellectual effort', in *Mind – Energy*, trans. H. Wildon Carr, London: Macmillan, 1920, pp. 164–5; hereafter cited as *M–E*. We analysed the first chapter of *MM* in Volume I. Here we deal with the second chapter, which introduces a very different point of view. The third chapter, which is particularly concerned with time, will be discussed below.

2 Claude Ollier, himself a *nouveau roman* writer, says in relation to *Carabiniers*: Godard 'produces for each shot a very quick review of

its descriptive and suggestive virtualities before concentrating on one of them, then abandoning it, as soon as it has been indicated, precisely as he constitutes the whole work through a succession of renewed approaches, and at the very moment he finds it undoes it, gives almost the impression of losing interest in it, if not of purposely destroying it' (*Souvenirs écran*, Cahiers du cinéma/ Gallimard, p. 129).

3 The theory of descriptions becomes one of the foundations of modern logic with Russell. But Bergson, in *Matter and Memory*, not only produces a psychology of recognition, but proposes a logic of description utterly different from Russell's. Robbe-Grillet's conception, very strong logically, often extends Bergson's, and is related to it. cf. 'Time and description', Snapshots, or *Towards a New Novel* ('a double movement of creation and erasure . . .').

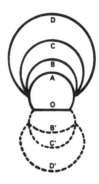

4 This is Bergson's first great schema, *MM*, pp. 127–8. The difficulty evident in this schema arises from 'the narrowest' circuit which is not presented in a form A A', but A O, because it 'contains only the object O itself with the consecutive image which returns to cover it' (memory immediately consecutive to perception). We shall see below the reason why there is such a minimum circuit which necessarily plays the role of internal limit.

5 *MM*, pp. 69–77.

6 cf. the analysis of *Jour se lève* by André Bazin, *Le cinéma français de la libération à la nouvelle vague*, Cahiers du cinéma/Editions de L'Etoile, pp. 53–75.

7* Translators' note: in *Labyrinths*, Harmondsworth: Penguin, 1970, pp. 44–54.

8 On this notion of forking, cf. Prigogine and Stengers, *Order out of Chaos: man's new dialogue with nature*, London: Heinemann, 1984, pp. 189–90.

9* Translators' note: in English in the original.

10 Philippe Carcassonne has produced an excellent analysis of the

flashback in Mankiewicz, as shattering linearity and rebutting causality: 'The flashback would suggest a complementarity of times which would go beyond the temporal dimension; the past is not simply the before of the present, it is also its missing piece, the unconscious, and very often the ellipse.' Carcassonne makes the comparison with Chabrol: 'Far from dispersing the enigma, the return back often serves to underline it, even to make it more impenetrable, by indicating the lacunary chain of enigmas which preceded it' ('Coupez!', *Cinématographe*, no. 51, octobre 1979).

11 Jean Narboni has indicated other points of comparison between the two authors: 'Mankiewicz à la troisième person', *Cahiers du cinéma*, no. 153, mars 1964.

12 This is the sense in which Janet understood it when he defined memory as story behaviour: I remember, I constitute a memory for myself to be able to tell a story. But Nietzsche had already defined memory as promise behaviour: I constitute a memory for myself in order to be capable of promising, of keeping a promise.

13 *MM*, pp. 162–3 and pp. 173–4.

14 Epstein, in all his written work, emphasized the subjective and dreamlike states which according to him characterized European cinema, especially French: *Ecrits*, II, p. 64 ff. Soviet cinema took on dream states (Eisenstein, Dovzhenko . . .), but also pathological states of the amnesic type, with reconstitution of tatters of memories: Ermler, *The Man Who Lost his Memory*. Expressionism's encounter with psychoanalysis was made directly about 1927, in the film by Pabst on which Abraham and Sachs collaborated, despite Freud's reservations: *Secrets of a Soul*, which dealt with the obsessional states of a man who dreams of killing his wife with a knife.

15 *MM*, p. 129. In chapters II and III of *Matter and Memory* and III, IV and V of *Mind – Energy*, Bergson shows his constant interest in the phenomena of memory, dream and amnesia, but also of *déjà-vu*, of 'panoramic vision' (the vision of the dying, 'the drowned and hung'). He points to something analogous to cinematographic speeding-up: *M–E*, pp. 105–6.

16 Mitry, *Le cinéma expérimental*, Seghers, p. 96.

17 Maurice Drouzy (*Luis Buñuel architecte du rêve*, Lherminier, pp. 40–3), analysing the contrast between the two films, remarks that *Un chien andalou* proceeds in particular through static shots, and includes only a few high-angle shots, dissolves and tracking shots forwards or backwards, one single low-angle shot, one wide shot, and one slow-motion shot; which is why Buñuel himself regarded it as a reaction against the avant-garde films of the time (not only *Ent'racte*, but Germaine Dulac's *La coquille et le clergyman*, whose rich store of techniques was one of the reasons that Artaud, inventor of the idea and screen writer, turned against this film). However, the restrained concept itself implies technical virtuosities of a different kind: thus, on the problems thrown up for Keaton in the dream in *Sherlock Junior* (the back-projection process not yet

being in existence), cf. David Robinson, *Buster Keaton*, Image et son, pp. 53–4.

18 Michel Devillers, 'Rêves informulés', *Cinématographe*, no. 35, février 1978. The author cites in particular Louis Malle: 'The great night in the *Lovers* rests on a dreamlike state where the implication is linked to a depersonalization.'

19 This notion ('the fact of being inhaled by the world') has its origin in the psychiatric work of Binswanger.

20 Sartre, *L'Imaginaire*, Gallimard, pp. 324–5.

21 Amengual, *Fellini II, Etudes cinématographiques*, p. 90.

22 On verticality and kaleidoscopic vision in Busby Berkeley, cf. Mitry, *Histoire du cinéma*, Delarge, IV, pp. 185–8, and V, pp. 582–3.

23 Alain Masson, *La comédie musicale*, Stock, pp. 49–50. (And, on what Masson calls 'degree zero' or 'entering dance', cf. pp. 112–14, 122, 220).

24 cf. Alain Masson's excellent analysis of Donen, ibid., pp. 99–103.

25 Tristan Renaud, 'Minnelli', *Dossiers du cinéma*: 'The film set is not integrated into the *mise-en-scène* so as to become one of its constitutive parts, it is its motor', to the extent that the dynamic of Minnelli's films, more important than the story, 'could be reduced to a journey through a certain number of film sets which would give a very precise measurement of the character's evolution'.

26 Jacques Fieschi has analysed this 'dark area' of dream in Minnelli: in *Yolande*, the cruel washerwomen attempt to capture the man with sheets; and, in *The Pirate*, the man is not simply absorbed into the girl's dream; she goes into a violent trance under the influence of the magician's ball (*Cinématographe*, no. 34, janvier 1978, pp. 16–18).

27 cf. Robert Benayoun, *Bonjour Monsieur Lewis*, Losefeld.

28* Translators' note: in English in the original.

29 The three films mentioned are by Tashlin. But the collaboration of the two men makes attribution difficult, and the active autonomy of the object remains a constant in Lewis's films. Gérard Recasens (*Jerry Lewis*, Seghers) sees grounds for Lewis's comic quality in what he calls 'the personification of the object', which he distinguishes from the tools and machines of earlier burlesque: this distinction appeals to electronics, but also to a new range of movements and gestures.

30 Gérard Rabinovitch has analysed this mutation of gestures and movements, new sports, dances and gymnastics which correspond to the electronic age (Le Monde, 27 juillet 1980, p. 13). All kinds of movements can be found in Jerry Lewis which anticipate the recent dances of the 'break' or 'smurf' type.

31 On the subject of dreaming in Lewis, cf. the two long analyses by André Labarthe (*Cahiers du cinéma*, no. 132, juin 1962) and by Jean-Louis Comolli (no. 197, février 1968). Comolli talks about a 'ubiquity of waves [which] spread out'.

32 cf. Jean-Louis Schefer 'La vitrine', and Serge Daney, 'Eloge de Tati',

Cahiers du cinéma, no. 303, septembre 1979. From Mr Hulot's
Holiday, Bazin had shown how situations opened on to a time-image
('M. Hulot et le temps', (Qu'est-ce que le cinéma?, Editions du Cerf).
33* Translators' note: a game in which the player who is 'it' must try to
gain possession of one of the four corners, rather like 'musical
chairs'.
34 Claude Ollier noted these crossings or cross-checkings of characters, and these 'slippages' of action from Lola (which Demy had
conceived as a sung comedy) onwards: Souvenirs écran, p. 42.
Similarly, in A Room in Town, Jacques Fieschi points out the scenes
that make the characters intersect with each other in the colonel's
flat, as if in a 'charmed circle' which goes beyond narration; and
Dominique Rinieri emphasizes the pictorial autonomy of the film
set, and the 'unhooking of action' in the music (cf. Cinématographe,
no. 82, octobre 1982).

4 The Crystals of Time

1 Bergson, MM, pp. 166–7, M–E, pp. 135–6: we saw in the last
chapter how the Bergsonian schema of circuits appeared to have an
anomaly when we considered 'the narrowest' circle, the one that was
'the nearest to immediate perception': MM, p. 127.
2 Jean Ricardou has developed the theory of descriptions in this
double direction of 'capture' and 'freeing': sometimes characters
and events which are apparently real become fixed in a 'representation', sometimes the opposite: Le nouveau roman, Seuil, pp. 112–
21. These procedures are common in Robbe-Grillet's films.
3 cf. what Hjelmslev says of 'content' and 'expression': 'It is impossible
to maintain that it is legitimate to call one of these dimensions
expression and the other content, and not the reverse; their
definition is a matter of solidarity involving them both, and neither
of them can be defined more specifically. Taken separately, they can
only be defined by opposition and in a relative way, as functives of a
single function which contrast with one another.' (Prolégomènes à une
théorie du langage, Editions de Minuit, p. 85).
4 Bachelard, La terre et les rêveries de la volonté, Corti, p. 290 (about the
crystal).
5 On 'camera movement through 360° with several mirrors', cf.
Ciment, Le livre de Losey, Stock, pp. 261–2, 274.
6 Serge Daney observed that, in eastern European cinema, scientific
power undergoes a significant expansion, because it is the only kind
that can be shown and subjected to criticism (political power being
out of reach): hence the coexistence of everyday life and a scientific
discourse 'off'. cf. La rampe, Cahiers du cinéma/Gallimard, p. 99 (on
the subject of Zanussi and Makavejev).
7 Peter Cowie, 'La chute d'un corps', Cinématographe, no. 87, mars

1983, p. 6. This article contains an excellent analysis of the whole of Zanussi's work.

8 cf. Jean-Marie Sabatier's analysis of Browning, *Les classiques du cinéma fantastique*, Balland, pp. 83–5: 'The whole of Browning's work rests on the spectacle-reality dialectic . . . This readiness of the actor to be transformed from real man to dreamed man, with the growth of power which that implies, is not really a consequence of the theme of the double as it occurs in the German Romantics or in the Jekyll and Hyde myth. Rather than a double, it is a matter of a reflection, a reflection that exists only because of someone else's gaze, while, beneath the mask, the face lives in shadow.'

9 On the ship, vision, the visible and the invisible, the transparent and the opaque in Melville's work, cf. Régis Durand, *Melville*, Age d'homme, and Philippe Jaworski, 'Le désert et l'empire', thesis, University of Paris VII.

10 On the resemblance between Herzog's landscapes and the crystalline and visionary painting of Friedrich, cf. Alain Masson, 'La toile et l'écran', *Positif*, no. 159.

11* Translators' note: the word 'lavé' has the sense of 'washed out' or 'watery' and of the 'wash' used by an artist.

12 Serge Daney, *Libération*, 27 janvier 1982: 'The Americans have taken the study of continuous movement a very long way . . . a movement which empties the image of its weight and its material . . . In Europe, even in the USSR, there are those who allow themselves the luxury of questioning movement in its other side: slowed down and discontinuous. Paradjanov, Tarkovsky (but already Eisenstein, Dovzhenko or Barnet) watch matter accumulate and become blocked, a geology of elements, filth and treasures being created in slow motion. They create the cinema of the Soviet Bloc, that motionless empire. Whether the empire likes it or not.'

13 Daniel Rocher has made a detailed analysis of the white and the black, the limpid and the opaque, and their distribution and exchange in *Last Year in Marienbad*: cf. *Alain Resnais et Alain Robbe-Grillet, Etudes cinématographiques*. And Robert Benayoun, stressing the tiling, the white frosts and the black jewels: Marienbad 'is a sort of fortune-teller's crystal-ball' (*Alain Resnais arpenteur de l'imaginaire*, Stock, p. 97).

14 Raymond Bellour and Alain Virmaux compared Fellini's 8½ with Gide's novel in a general way: *Fellini I, Etudes cinématographiques*.

15 Frédéric Vitoux underlines the crystalline aspect of the images of the sailor led into the house: 'A very bright yellow light falls on the sailor giving him a luminous outline, whilst the room as a whole and Mr Clay himself remain in the cold penumbra of blue-grey lights' (*Positif*, no. 167, mars 1975, p. 57).

16 The review *Cinématographe* devoted two special issues to 'money in cinema', nos 26 and 27, avril and mai 1977. Analysing the films where money plays an important role, we encounter, as it were naturally, the theme of the film reflected in the film. A forerunner is

the article by Mireille Latil, 'Bresson et l'argent', which analyses the
role and importance of money in the work of Bresson well before
the production of the film of the same name.

17 Marcel l'Herbier, 'Le cinématographe et l'espace, chronique finan-
    cière', reprinted in Noël Burch, *Marcel l'Herbier*, Seghers, pp. 97–
    104.

18 *M–E*, p. 130: 'How would recollection only arise after everything is
    over?' It will be noted that Bergson does not talk about crystal: the
    only images he points to are optical, acoustic, or magnetic.

19 *M–E*, pp. 135–8.

20 *M–E*, p. 135.

21 All these themes are dealt with in *MM*, ch. III.

22 Hence Bergson's second great schema, the famous cone of *MM*,
    p. 211.

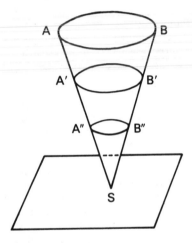

The point S is clearly the actual present; but this is not strictly
speaking a point, since it already includes the past of this present,
the virtual image which doubles the actual image. As for the AB,
A'B' . . . sections of the cone, they are not psychological circuits to
which recollections-images would correspond; they are purely
virtual circuits, each of which contains all our past as this is
preserved in itself (pure recollection). Bergson is quite unequivocal
in this respect. Psychological circuits of recollection-images or
dream-images are produced only when we 'leap' from S to one of
these sections, to actualize some virtuality of it which must then
move down into a new present S'.

23 *M–E*, p. 130. This is the third schema, which Bergson does not feel
    the need to draw:

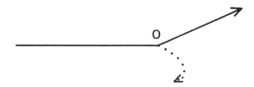

24 Jean Ricardou, p. 73. Similarly, referring to Browning's work, Sabatier said: it is a reflection, not a double.
25 Félix Guattari produced this idea of 'crystal of time': *L'inconscient machinique*, Ed. Recherches.
26 Michel Devillers, 'Ophüls ou la traversée du décor', *Cinématographe*, no. 33, décembre 1977. In the same issue, Louis Audibert ('Max Ophüls et la mise en scène') analyses a double tension in the crystal-image in Ophüls: on the one hand the transparent side and the opaque side (hiding-places, bars, fetters, spy-holes) of the crystal itself; on the other hand, the immobility, and the movement of what is seen in the crystal. Each character is followed on his course to a point of immobility which usually coincides with a stationary figure or film set, a brief moment of uncertainty . . . Movement, in fantastic ellipses, tears time from the wretched dimension of space.' As in the succession of waltzes in *Madame de* . . . .
27 Bazin pointed to this substitution of the scene by the shot, brought about by depth of field: *Jean Renoir*, Champ libre, pp. 80–4 (and *What Is Cinema?*, Vol. I, pp. 91–3). But, for him, depth of field has a reality-function, even and especially when it underlines the ambiguity of the verb. On the other hand, we think that there are many different functions of depth depending on authors and films alike. Michaël Romm saw in it a theatrical function (*L'art du cinéma de Pierre Lherminier*, Seghers, pp. 227–9). And it is often so in Renoir, even if the function changes or evolves into the flow of the sequence shot.
28 On Renoir's 'apparent casualness', cf. Bazin, pp. 69–71. The fact is that often in Renoir the actor plays the role of a character in the process of himself playing a role: thus Boudu tries successive roles in the bookshop, and, in *La règle du jeu*, the gamekeeper tries the role of manservant, as the marquis tries all aspects of the role of marquis. Rohmer will talk in this regard of a kind of exaggeration in Renoir, and points to the selective function which becomes evident in it: 'This exaggeration has its respites, as if the actor, tired of pretending, got his wind back, not by becoming himself (the actor) again, but by identifying with the character. With the result that credibility is strengthened: the character, playing his character, becomes the character again, when he is not playing, whilst the actor, playing the character, only becomes the actor again' (*Le goût de la beauté*, Cahiers du cinéma/Editions de l'Etoile, p. 208.
29 cf. Truffaut, in Bazin, pp. 260–2. It is in *The Golden Coach* that Renoir's question, 'Where does theatre end and life begin?', occurs.

30 This is true not only of Fellini. Ollier gave a complete breakdown of the types of image in *Last Year in Marienbad*: recollection-images, desire, pseudo-recollection, fantasy, hypothesis, calculation ('Ce soir à Marienbad', *La Nouvelle Revue française*, octobre et novembre 1961).

31 Barthélemy Amengual devoted two articles to the idea of spectacle and its evolution in Fellini: *Fellini I and II*. He shows how, in the earlier films, it is still a matter of leaving and finding an exit, but, from *Cabiria*, one returns; and later there is no question of getting out at all: I, pp. 15–16. Amengual analyses the halo-like and compartmentalized form of the giant Luna Park or 'universal exhibition' that Fellini constructs from one film to the next: II, pp. 89–93. He rightly contrasts him with Renoir, but in terms that are hard on Renoir (I, p. 26). We, however, do not see in what respect the theme of 'theatre-life' is less profound in Renoir than in Fellini's conception of the spectacle, as long as we place these reflections in their respective cinematographic context: outside this context, both alike are worthless.

32 cf. Mireille Latil-Le Dantec's analysis of *Clowns*, in *Fellini II*.

33 cf. Henry Miller's pages for an opera project with Varèse: *The Air-Conditioned Nightmare*, Heinemann: London, 1962, pp. 152–8.

34 Guattari specifically develops his analysis of the 'crystal of time' in relation to the ritornello or 'little phrase' in Proust's words: Guattari, op. cit., pp. 239 ff.' Reference may also be made to Clément Rosset's text on the ritornello, notably on Ravel's *Boléro*: 'Archives', *La Nouvelle Revue française*, no. 373, février 1984. And, on the gallop as musical schema identified through very different cultures, cf. François-Bernard Mâche, *Musique, mythe, nature*, Klincksieck, p. 26.

35* Translators' note: 'Augustes', strictly a type of circus clown, heavily made up and brightly costumed, who perform 'linking pieces'.

36 Philippe de Lara, *Cinématographe*, no. 30, septembre 1977, p. 20: 'If *Terra Trema* was a character-film, the most important character would be time: its rhythms, its cutting constitute the film's material; it is time which, in the argument, is the principal reason for the fishermen's failure.'

37 It is possible to make a list of themes linking Visconti and Proust: the crystalline world of aristocrats; its internal decomposition; history seen crosswise (the Dreyfus affair, the 1914 war); the too-late of lost time, which also gives the unity of art or rediscovered time; classes defined as families of spirit rather than social groups . . . Bruno Villien has made a very interesting comparative analysis of the projects of Visconti and of Losey (scenario by Harold Pinter): *Cinématographe*, no. 42, décembre 1978, pp. 25–9. However, we cannot go along with this analysis because it credits Losey–Pinter with an awareness of time which would be lacking in Visconti, who would give an almost naturalistic version of Proust. The opposite would rather be the case: Visconti is in a profound sense a

film-maker of time, while the 'naturalism' specific to Losey leads him to subordinate time to originary worlds and their drives (we have tried to show this earlier). It is a point of view which is also present in Proust.

38 Baroncelli, *Le Monde*, 18 juin 1963.

5   *Peaks of Present and Sheets of Past*

1* Translators' note: the *ratio cognoscendi* of a thing is its being in the mode of being known; the *ratio essendi* of a thing is its essence or 'formal reason'.

2 This is the development of the themes of ch. III of *Matter and Mem ry* that we saw earlier (the second schema of time, the cone): pp. 210–25.

3 This fine piece by Groethuysen ('De quelques aspects du temps', *Recherches philosophiques*, V, 1935–6) has echoes of Péguy and Bergson. In *Clio*, p. 230, Péguy made a distinction between history and memory: 'History is essentially longitudinal, memory essentially vertical. History essentially consists of passing along the event. Being inside the event, memory essentially and above all consists of not leaving it, staying in it and going back through it from within.' Bergson had proposed a schema, what might be called his fourth schema of time, to distinguish between the spatial vision which passes along the event, and the temporal vision which goes deep inside the event: *MM*, p. 184.

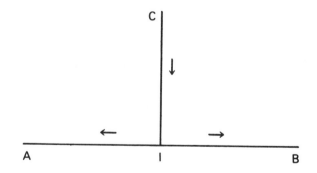

4 Kafka, *Un champion de jeune*, IV.

5 Daniel Rocher has compared *Marienbad* and Mallarmé's dice throw, 'number starry progeny', 'total addition in formation': *Alain Resnais et Alain Robbe-Grillet, Etudes cinématographiques*.

6 cf. Jean-Claude Bonnet, 'L'innocence du rêve', *Cinématographe*, no. 92, septembre 1983, p. 16.

7 'The sadistic characters in my novels are always of a special sort in

that they attempt to immobilize something which is moving'; in
Trans-Europe Express, the young woman never stops moving in every
direction: 'Him, he is there, he is watching me, and I think that you
can feel arising in him the desire to stop that.' It is thus a
transformation from a motor-situation to a purely optical situation.
The passage is quoted by André Gardies, *Alain Robbe-Grillet*,
Seghers, p. 74.

8　Mireille Latil-Le Dantec, 'Notes sur la fiction et l'imaginaire chez
Resnais et Robbe-Grillet', *Alain Resnais and Alain Robbe-Grillet*,
p. 126. On a chronology of Marienbad, cf. *Cahiers du cinéma*, nos 123
and 125.

9　Many commentators see this necessity of going beyond the level of
the real and the imaginary: beginning with the adherents of a
language-based semiology who find in Robbe-Grillet a key example
(cf. Chateau and Jost, *Nouveau cinéma nouvelle sémiologie*, Editions de
Minuit, and Gardies, *Le cinéma de Robbe-Grillet*, Albatros). But, for
them, the third level is that of the 'signifier', whilst our enquiry
concerns the time-image and its a-signifying power.

10　This is the difference suggested by Robbe-Grillet between Proust
and Faulkner (Snapshots, or *Towards a New Novel*). And, in the
chapter 'Time and description', he says that the new novel and
modern cinema are very little concerned with time; he criticizes
Resnais for being too interested in memory and forgetting.

11　cf. *MM*, p. 223.

12　Petr Kral, 'Le film comme labyrinthe', *Positif*, no. 256, juin 1982:
'We cross the court and the years that slipped away at the same
time.'

13　On the opposition between these two ideas of depth, in the sixteenth
and seventeenth centuries, cf. Wölfflin, *Principles in the History of Art*,
London: Bell, 1932, ch. II. Wölfflin analyses the 'baroque' spaces of
the seventeenth century on the basis of Tintoretto's diagonals, the
anomalies of dimension in Vermeer, the gaps in Rubens, etc.

14　Claudel said that depth, for instance, in Rembrandt, was an
'invitation to recall' ('sensation has aroused recollection, and
recollection in turn reaches and successively destroys the superimposed layers of memory', *L'oeil écoute*, Oeuvres en prose, Pléiade,
p. 195). Bergson and Merleau-Ponty showed how 'distance' (*MM*,
ch. 1), and 'depth' (*Phenomenology of Perception*) were temporal
dimensions.

15　cf. Wölfflin, op. cit., p. 97 and p. 185.

16　The Bazin–Mitry discussion is relevant to both problems. But it
seems that Mitry is much closer to Bazin than he thinks. In the first
place, is there something new in Welles's depth of field or is it the
return to an old procedure which was an inseparable part of earlier
cinema, as Mitry reminds us? Yet it is Mitry himself who shows how,
in *Intolerance*, there is only juxtaposition of parallel shots and not
interaction as in Renoir and Welles (with the great angular shots):
he thus confirms Bazin's view of this social point. cf. *Esthétique et*

psychologie du cinéma, Ed. Universitaires, II, p. 40. In the second place, is the function of this new depth a freer reality-function, or is it just as restrictive as any other depth, as Mitry believes? In any case, Bazin willingly recognized the theatrical character of depth of field, in Wyler as much as in Renoir. He analyses one of Wyler's shots, in *The Snake*, where the fixed camera records the totality of a scene in depth, as in the theatre. But, in fact, the cinematographic element means that the character situated in the sitting-room may leave the frame twice, first to the right in the foreground, then to the left in the background, before falling down the stairs: the out-of-frame has a quite different function from the wings of a theatre ('William Wyler ou le janséniste de la mise en scène', *Revue du cinéma*, nos 10 and 11, février and mars 1948). Cinema here produces an 'excess of theatricality', which will in the end strengthen the feeling of reality. What can be said, then, is that Bazin, while acknowledging the plurality of functions enjoyed by depth of field, upheld the primacy of the reality-function.

17   *MM*, p. 125: the two forms of memory are 'sheets of recollections' and the 'contraction' of the present.

18   Bazin has often analysed this kitchen scene, but without making it dependent on the function of remembering which takes place (or tries to take place) in it. Yet the same thing often happens in Wyler, depth being linked to the recollections of two characters: as in a sequence shot in *The Best Years of Our Life* analysed by Bazin in his article on Wyler, but also a shot in *L'insoumise* analysed by Mitry, where two characters meet again and confront each other in a kind of memory challenge (the heroine has put on her red dress again. . .). In this last example, depth of field produces a maximum contraction which would be impossible by shot-reverse shot: the camera is in a low-angle position behind one of the characters, and simultaneously catches the clenched hand of one and the trembling face of the other (Mitry).

19   Jean Collet, 'La soif du mal, ou Orson Welles et la soif d'une transcendance', *Orson Welles, Etudes cinématographiques*, p. 115 (there is one point where we have to disagree with this text, as we will see below, namely the appeal to transcendance).

20   *MM*, p. 133: according to Bergson these are the two principal forms of illness of memory.

21   In contrast to arbitrary comparisons, Amengual is right to make a point-by-point comparison between Rosebud (or the glass ball) and Proust's madeleine: there is no search for lost time in Welles. cf. *Etudes cinématographiques*, pp. 64–5.

22   'The very foundations of existence are tragic. Man is not living, as people are fond of saying, in a transient crisis. The whole thing has always been a crisis.' (Quoted by Michel Estève. 'Notes sur les fonctions de la mort dans l'univers de Welles', *Etudes cinématographiques*, p. 41.)

23   The hero is an ordinary man, but 'conscious of his madness'.

Confronted with these pasts that he does not know of or recognize, he says: 'I thought I was in the grip of delirium, then reason returned, and it was then that I thought I was mad.' Gérard Legrand shows that two levels may be envisaged: Welles the actor, who plays the character of O'Hara, hollowly, as a hallucinated sleepwalker; and Welles the author, who projects himself into the three hallucinating characters (*Positif*, no. 256, juin 1982).

24 It is the topography of *The Trial* (and also of *The Castle*) which calls on a depth of field: places that are very far apart or even opposed, in the foreground, are next to each other in the background. To the extent that space, as Michel Ciment puts it, is constantly disappearing: 'The viewer, as the film develops, loses all sense of space, and the painter's house, the courthouse and the church are from then on in contact with each other.' (*Les conquérants d'un nouveau monde*, Gallimard, p. 219.)

25 Herman Melville, *Pierre, or the ambiguities*, American Library: New York, 1964.

26 Bazin, *Orson Welles*, Ed. du Cerf, p. 90. Michel Chion finds the same motif earlier in the opening of *Citizen Kane*: 'To a cavernous, archaic music, disparate landscapes succeed each other in an atmosphere of primitive chaos, of total disorder where the elements of earth and water are not yet separate. The only traces of life are monkeys, a reference to a pre-human past . . .' (*La voix au cinéma*, Cahiers du cinéma Editions de l'Etoile, p. 78.)

27 Michel Chion, recalling the influence that radio continually exercised on Welles, talks about a 'central immobility of the voice', even when it is the voice of characters in movement. And, correlatively, moving bodies themselves tend to a massive inertia which will embody the fixed point of the voice. cf. 'Notes sur la voix chez Orson Welles', *Orson Welles*, *Cahiers du cinéma*, p. 93.

28 In *Hiroshima mon amour*, the present is the place of a forgetting which is already concerned with itself, and the character of the Japanese man is as it were blurred. In *Last Year in Marienbad*, Marie-Claire Ropars sums up the whole as follows: 'At the point where the account, imaginary or not, of a first meeting in Marienbad has become totally bound up with the second meeting, which it has modified, at this moment the present story of this second meeting in turn tips over into the past, and the narrator's voice begins again to recall it in the imperfect, as if a third meeting were now being prepared, overshadowing the one that has just taken place, rather as if this whole story never ceased being a past one . . .' (*L'écran de la mémoire*, Seuil, p. 115) .

29 Bernard Pingaud, in particular, underlined this disappearance of the fixed point in Resnais (in contrast to Welles), which was already in *Hiroshima mon amour*: cf. *Premier Plan*, no. 18, octobre 1961.

30 It is a matter of the precise moment when the machine is considered to be taking the hero back, the minute when he came out of the water on to the beach, which is taken up and modified throughout

the film. Gaston Bounoure comments: 'Claude has swum, swims and will swim around this minute in which his whole life is enclosed. Unassailable and inaccessible, it flashes like a diamond in the labyrinth of time.' (*Alain Resnais*, Seghers, p. 86.)

31 An analysis of the Boulanger transformations, and the notion of age which goes with them, may be found in Prigogine and Stengers, *Order out of Chaos*, pp. 267–80. The authors draw some original conclusions which link up with Bergson. There is a close relation between Prigogine's transformations and the sections of the Bergsonian cone. Our concern with all this is with its simplest and least scientific aspects. The intention, basically, is to show that Resnais does not apply scientific data to cinema but creates, in his particular cinematographic way, something that has its counterpart in mathematics and physics (and also in biology, explicitly invoked in *My American Uncle*). We might talk about an implicit relation between Resnais and Prigogine and likewise between Godard and René Thom.

32 cf. René Prédal, *Alain Resnais, Etudes cinématographiques*, p. 23.

33 One of the finest books on Resnais is that of Gaston Bounoure, because of its power and density. He is the first to suggest relations between the short and long features in which they throw light on each other. He understands memory in Resnais as a memory-world in which infinity goes beyond recollection, and mobilizes all the faculties (e.g., p. 72). And he analyses in particular the relation between the continuous shot and hacked montage as two things in correlation: cf. his commentary on *Muriel*, on what he calls 'seasons' (what we call 'ages'), and on the shared identity of cutting-continuum and cut-sliding (pp. 62–5). On fragmentation in *Muriel*, reference may also be made to Didier Goldschmidt, 'Boulogne mon amour', *Cinématographe*, no. 88, avril 1983.

34 Marie-Claire Ropars-Wuilleumier, p. 69: 'It is no accident (in *Muriel*) that everything begins in alternating close-ups of everyday objects, a door-knob, a kettle, and ends in an empty flat where static roses seem suddenly artificial.' And Robert Benayoun: 'At the opening of *My American Uncle*, Resnais makes a catalogue of model objects pass before us juxtaposed with landscapes or portraits without establishing any hierarchy between them' (*Alain Resnais arpenteur de l'imaginaire*, Stock, p. 185). The reader is also referred to René Prédal's chapter, 'Des objets plus parlants que les êtres'.

35 Youssef Ishaghpour, *D'une image à l'autre*, Médiations, p. 182.

36 Buonoure, op. cit., p. 67.

37 Robert Benayoun, for instance, challenges from the outset any interpretation of Resnais by memory, or even by time (pp. 163, 177). But he hardly justifies his view, and it seems that for him memory and time are reducible to flashback. For his part, Resnais is less simple, and more Bergsonian: 'I have always protested against the word memory, but not against the word imaginary or the word

consciousness . . . If cinema is not a method of juggling specifically with time, in any event the method which is the best adapted to it . . . This is not the consequence of a deliberate act of will. I think that the theme of memory is present each time that a piece is written or a painting painted . . . Personally, I prefer the words consciousness and imaginary rather than memory, but consciousness is obviously part of memory' (pp. 212–13).

38   *M–E*, pp. 131–2. And *MM*, pp. 170–1.
39   cf. Robbe-Grillet, *L'année dernière à Marienbad*, Editions de Minuit, p. 13: 'The whole film is the story of a persuasion.' And Resnais talks of hypnosis, *Cahiers du cinéma*, no. 123, septembre 1961.
40   Benayoun, op. cit., p. 205.
41   In his interviews, Resnais often returns to these two themes: feelings beyond characters, and the gaining of awareness or the critical thought which results. This is a method of *critical hypnosis* closer to what Dali called the critical-paranoiac method than to Brecht's methods. René Prédal has brought this aspect out well: 'If Brecht, in the theatre, achieved this result by distantiation, Resnais, by contrast, arouses a true fascination. This sort of hypnosis, of purely aesthetic origin, de-dramatizes the anecdote, prevents identification with the characters and directs the public's attention to the lonely feelings which drive the hero' (op. cit., p. 163).
42   *Je t'aime je t'aime* fits this formulation very well. There is a real affinity, it seems to us, between Resnais' work and Andrei Bely's great novel *Petersburg* which is based on what Bely calls 'the biology of shadows' and 'the cerebral game'. With Bely the city and the brain are in topological contact; 'all that passed before his eyes, paintings, piano, mirrors, mother-of-pearl, the inlay of the tables, was all just stimulation of the cerebral membrane, unless it was deficiency of the cerebellum'; and a continuum is continuously produced between visceral organic states, political states of society and meteorological states of the world. In this regard *Providence* is particularly close to Bely's novel. There is a method of critical hypnosis in both authors. cf. Bely, *Petersburg*, translated by Robert A. Maguire and John E. Malmstad, Harmondsworth: Penguin, 1983.

6   *The Powers of the False*

1   At the beginning of chapter III of *MM*, Bergson shows initially how common sense is opposed to two poles of existence, the connections which determine a continuity and discontinuous appearances to consciousness. But, from a more profound perspective, these are two elements which refuse separation and mix together to various degrees: pp. 189–91.
2   Sylvette Baudrot says, in relation to *Last Year in Marienbad*, the film 'is entirely composed of false continuities . . . there are only

continuities of feelings'. Similarly in *Muriel, or in La guerre est finie*; if the character moved from right to left in one shot, in the following shot he had to move from left to right, or come straight forward, so that there is a shock, a contrast. (*Alain Resnais, L'Arc*, no. 31, p. 50).

3   Gilbert Simondon, *L'individu et sa genèse physico-biologique*, PUF, p. 233.

4   cf. P. M. Schuhl, *Le dominateur et les possibles*, PUF (on the role of this paradox in Greek philosophy). Jules Vuillemin has taken up the whole question in *Nécessité ou contingence*, Editions de Minuit.

5   cf. Leibniz, *Theodicy*, sections 414–16; in this astonishing text, which we consider a source of all modern literature, Leibniz presents 'contingent futures' as so many compartments making up a pyramid of crystal. In one compartment Sextus does not go to Rome and cultivates his garden in Corinth; in another he becomes king in Thrace; but in another, he goes to Rome and takes power . . . It will be noticed that this text is presented in a very complex and inextricable narration, even though it presumes to save the Truth; it is first a dialogue between Valla and Antony, in which is inserted another dialogue between Sextus and the oracle of Apollo, then this is succeeded by a third dialogue, Sextus and Jupiter, which gives way to the Theodorus and Pallas discussion at the end of which Theodorus wakes up.

6   Borges, 'The garden with forking paths', in *Labyrinths*, trans. Donald A. Yates, Harmondsworth: Penguin, 1970.

7   cf. Alain Bergala, 'Le vrai, le faux, le factice', *Cahiers du cinéma*, no. 351, septembre 1983. He criticizes the ready-made formulations which follow from this new system of the image (and obviously every system of images has its imitations which appear very quickly). Bergala suggests a criterion: the film set must not remain lifeless, pretending to stand for itself, but must link up with a falsifying narration, which for its part is not arbitrary but has a justification. In relation to Welles, he entitled a block of images, 'The powers of the false' (*Orson Welles, Cahiers du cinéma*, p. 69). The reader is referred to an important article by Pascal Bonitzer, 'L'art du faux: métamorphoses' (*Raoul Ruiz, Cahiers du cinéma*).

8   Melville's novel, *The Confidence man*, has been translated by Henri Thomas with the title *Le grand escroc*, Editions de Minuit (the expression occurs in Melville). Godard's short film (1964) was part of a series making up *Les plus belles escroqueries du monde*. The breakdown of the cutting has been published in *L'Avant-scène du cinéma*, no. 46.

9   Ishaghpour, *D'une image à l'autre*, p. 206.

10 As Régis Durand says, summarizing one of Melville's narrative procedures, 'someone repeats a story that he has got from another character, who, by way of justification, invokes the testimony of other characters who are no more than the first one variously disguised'. The man with the cap comes to cast doubt on the supposed disasters whose story he has heard; now these calamities

are those which would have befallen a man who is none other than himself in another disguise, and whose story has been passed on by another individual who is also a version of himself. (*Melville, signes et métaphores*, Age d'homme, pp. 129–30.)

11   For instance, in Robbe-Grillet, it is the erotic scenes which play the role of descriptions, tending to immobility (tying up, chaining the woman), whilst the narration passes through every means of transport as sources of false movement.

12   It is on this point that the followers of Christian Metz have introduced important semiological changes concerning 'modern cinema'; on dysnarrative in Robbe-Grillet (who created the word), cf. Chateau and Jost, *Nouveau cinéma nouvelle sémiologie*, and Gardies, *Le cinéma de Robbe-Grillet*. The reader is also referred, in relation to Resnais, to the book on *Muriel*, Galilée (M. Marie, M.-C. Ropars and C. Baiblé).

13   In most interviews with Welles, the critique of the notion of truth comes back to the impossibility of judging man and life. cf. Jean Gili, 'Orson Welles ou le refus de juger', *Orson Welles, Etudes cinématographiques*.

14   The collaboration between Lang and Brecht occurred in *Hangmen Also Die*, but was very ambiguous. For instance, at the beginning of the film, the question of knowing if the resistance fighters can legitimately compromise their compatriots is raised, because the Nazis detain and kill innocent hostages; the young girl begs the resistance fighter to give himself up in order to save her father who has been taken hostage. But a little afterwards, and still to save her father, she does not hesitate in accepting the sacrifice of a woman shopkeeper who refuses to denounce her herself. There is a properly Brechtian process in this, where the viewer is made aware of a problem or a contradiction, and led to resolve them in his own way (distancing). What Lang is responsible for is a quite different process: the way in which someone betrays himself, but in such a way that the appearance will be contrasted with other appearances in a different connection (not only the informer who inadvertently 'gives himself away', but also the resistance fighter who has put traces of red on his lips, this time too perfectly, to give the impression of a love-scene). The two processes may intermingle and converge towards a similar effect, but they are very distant from each other.

15* Translators' note: *Twilight of the Idols*, trans. R. J. Hollingdale, Harmondsworth: Penguin, 1968, p. 41.

16   On body-forces, cf. Petr Kral, 'Le film comme labyrinthe', *Positif*, no. 256, juin 1982, and Jean Narboni, 'Un cinéma en plongée', *Orson Welles, Cahiers du cinéma* (Narboni compares 'character' according to Welles and the Nietzschean will to power).

17   Interview with Welles, *Cahiers du cinéma*, p. 42: about the battle in *Falstaff*. Similarly the cut-up montage of the characters in *The Lady from Shanghai* is suggestive for Didier Goldschmidt: the shots do not

link up, 'they rush at each other, the series of cross-cuttings in extreme close-up, especially of O'Hara and Grisby, tip the weight of the image from left to right; movements are brusquely interrupted; everything contributes to the freeing of an *energy* which conditions an almost exclusively plastic perception of the film' (*Cinématographe*, no. 75, février 1982, p. 64).

18 cf. Robin Wood's detailed analyses of *Touch of Evil* (*Positif*, no. 167, mars 1975): Vargas and Quinlan, 'each of the two men dominates the frame in turn, or both occupy the image in an ephemeral and precarious equilibrium'.

19 On the 'impotence' of Welles's characters, as 'price to pay for exercising the power of voice and script', cf. Michel Chion, *Orson Welles, Cahiers du cinéma*, p. 93. Similarly, Lago's assumed sexual impotence is not a motive or explanation but refers at a deeper level to a certain state or quality of life (Marienstras, 'Orson Welles interprète et continuateur de Shakespeare', *Positif*, no. 167).

20 cf. the interview, in Bazin, *Orson Welles*, Ed. du Cerf, p. 178. The frog is the truthful animal because it believes in pacts and contracts. But, in practice, there are only fluctuating 'partners' ('You talk as if there was a kind of contract between us, but there isn't, we are partners here', *Touch of Evil*). It is true that Welles begins by saying that it is better to make judgements in the name of higher values rather than 'on one's own authority' (p. 154). But, a little further on, he says that each is as dreadful as the other (p. 160).

21 This is the problem which dominates the Bazin interview. Welles is happy to acknowledge the 'ambiguity' of his position: he does not have the same clarity as Nietzsche, even though he is preoccupied with the same theme, that of an 'aristocratic morality.'

22 Welles makes some lyrical declarations about Falstaff's vital goodness: 'He is goodness; he is the character in whom I believe the most . . . his goodness is like the bread and the wine' (interview, *Cahiers du cinéma*, p. 41; and also Marienstras, op. cit., p. 43).

23 On all these subjects, cf. Michel Serres, *Le système de Leibniz*, PUF, I, pp. 151–74, II, pp. 648–67.

24 Charles Tesson (*Cahiers du cinéma*) analyses depth of field as a factor of disequilibrium, 'off-balance': it is as if a scorpion were filmed head on, 'the important thing is not in front but at the back', to the extent that the image must 'topple over towards a pure clairvoyance'. There is an effect of toppling over in the sequence shot as well as in short montage.

25 Among Welles's projects is *The Dreamers*, inspired by Isak Dinesen: a classical singer who has lost her voice after a painful love affair finds a small boy in the village choir who has exactly the same voice; she gives him lessons, so that the world hears her voice again for three years; a highly erotic relation is formed between the two which pushes the boy to revenge . . . It is a story of traitors and forgers, in the Welles fashion, but also inevitably of vanishing of the person. Isak Dinesen made the heroine say, more or less in the same terms

as Virginia Woolf: 'I will no longer be a person, Marcus, from now on I will always be several.' Welles declares that he shot this scene as one of the *raisons d'être* of the film (interview, *Cahiers du cinéma*, pp. 49 and 58).

26 We follow more or less closely the essential article by Gérard Legrand on *It's All True* (*Positif*, no. 167). But Legrand sees a contradiction between 'will to power' and 'report of illusion'. We see none, will to power being life as power of the false.

27 The great theory of forgers according to Nietzsche appears in Book IV of *Zarathustra*: we find there the man of state, the man of religion, the man of morality, the man of science . . . A power of the false corresponds to each one; they are thus inseparable from each other. And 'the truthful man' was himself the first power of the false, who develops through the others. The artist in turn is a forger, but this is the ultimate power of the false, because he wants metamorphosis instead of 'taking on' a form (form of the True, of the Good, etc.). Will or will to power thus has two extreme degrees, two polar states of life, on one hand will-to-take-over or will-to-dominate, on the other hand the will which is identical to becoming and metamorphosis, 'bestowing virtue'. Nietzsche will be able to call himself creator of truth, from the second point of view, while wholly maintaining his critique of the True. An equally strong opposition between form and metamorphosis, 'form' and 'shape', will be found in Melville (notably in *Pierre; or the ambiguities*; cf. Jaworski's commentary, 'Le désert et l'empire', thesis, University of Paris VII, pp. 566–8).

28 A very clear presentation of these basic conditions will be found in certain authors, all the clearer in that these authors propose to go beyond them. Thus Beckett, on *Film*, says that one must distinguish what the camera OE sees from what the character O sees, 'the perception by OE in the bedroom and the perception by O of the bedroom': 'it is better to avoid the double shot, the superimposition, and to underline the qualitative distinction between the two kinds of images, as far as the final identification of OE and O' (Translators' note; see Volume I, p. 228) (*Comédies et actes divers*, Editions du Minuit, p. 130). Similarly, Godard, in relation to *Two or Three Things I Know about Her*, calls what the camera sees object, what the character sees subject, and adds up the two, $1+2=3$ to arrive at the final identity, $1+2+3=4$, life (*Jean-Luc Godard par Jean-Luc Godard*, pp. 393–6). Similarly, Pasolini distinguishes the double nature of cinema, as much from the point of view of the character as of the film-maker himself: cinema is 'simultaneously extremely subjective and extremely objective', the two elements remaining indissociable to the point of identification (*L'expérience hérétique*, Payot, p. 142).

29 On this point, see Reynold Humphries's detailed analyses, *Fritz Lang américain*, Albatros, notably chs III and IV: on going beyond the objective and subjective, and the crisis of identity ('centrality of vision and of the gaze and confused identities', p. 99).

30 Pasolini, *L'expérience hérétique*, pp. 147–54: 'pseudo-stories written in the language of poetry'. This new cinema of poetry (about 1960, according to Pasolini) devotes itself to 'making the camera felt'; whilst the old cinema of prose could achieve the greatest poetry of content, it none the less remained linked to a *classical* story where the camera was allowed to be strictly forgotten (one wonders if this is a sufficient criteria even so, and where Pasolini would locate authors like Eisenstein or Gance . . .).

31 On the critique of truth and veneration; on the function of story-telling and the manner in which it goes beyond the real and the fictional; and on the role and the justification for 'intercessors': the most important text is Perrault's interview with René Allio, in *Ecritures de Pierre Perrault*, Edilig, pp. 54–6. To this may be added, in the same volume, all of Jean-Daniel Lafond's analysis, 'L'ombre d'un doute', which portrays the cinema of Perrault as an art of the 'feint': the characters 'are fictional without being even so beings of fiction' (pp. 72–3).

32 cf. Jean-André Fieschi's analysis, which shows how, beginning with *Les maîtres fous*, Rouch makes 'the already troubling dislocation which seemed the film's message' undergo 'a second dislocation'. And, increasingly, 'what Rouch films, and is the first to do so, is no longer behaviour or dreams, or subjective discourses, but the indiscernible mixture which links one to the other' (in *Cinéma, théorie, lectures*, pp. 259–61).

33 *Jean-Luc Godard*, p. 220.

34 Pasolini forcefully emphasized that the free indirect story implied, in literature, different 'languages' depending on what social group the characters belonged to. But, oddly, this condition did not seem to him to be realizable in the cinema, where the visual data always introduced a certain tendency to uniformity: if characters 'belong to a different social world, they are mythified and assimilated into the categories of anomaly, neurosis or hypersensitivity' (pp. 146–7, 155). Apparently Pasolini did not see how direct cinema offered a quite different response to this problem of the story.

35 cf. Shirley Clarke, *Cahiers du cinéma*, no. 205, octobre 1968 ('a certain time is required for the character to seize hold of your expectation . . .', p. 25).

36 On *Faces*, cf. Jean-Louis Comolli, *Cahiers du cinéma*, no. 205, p. 38: on the frontier, the impossibility of determining it, and maintaining a 'reserved zone'.

37 Godard, *Introduction à une véritable histoire du cinéma*, Albatros, p. 168, (and p. 262: 'I have always tried for what is called documentary and what is called fiction to be for me the two aspects of a single movement, and it is their connection which produces the true movement').

38 Godard in *Le Monde*, 27 mai 1982, on *Passion*. And, in relation to *First Name Carmen*, he will remind us that the first name is precisely what is before: we must get to the character before he is captured in

myth or legend, and, on Christ, 'What did Joseph and Mary say to each other before having the child?' (Lecture at the Venice Festival, September 1983).

39   In a fine story (*Le baron Bagge*, Ed. du Sorbier), Lennet-Holenia assumes that death does not occur in a moment, but in a space-time located 'between the moment itself', which may last several days. A conception of death quite close to this appears in Godard's films.

7   Thought and Cinema

1   Elie Faure, *Fonction du cinéma*, Médiations, p. 56: 'It is in fact its material automatism which gives rise inside these images to this new universe which it gradually imposes on our intellectual automatism. Thus there appears, in a blinding light, the subordination of the human soul to the tools which it creates, and vice versa. It turns out that there is a constant reversibility between technical and affective nature.' Similarly for Epstein, the automatism of the image or the mechanism of the camera have as correlate an 'automatic subjectivity', able to transform and go beyond the real: *Ecrits sur le cinéma*, Seghers, II, p. 63.

2   cf. Martin Heidegger, *What Is Called Thinking?*, trans. Fred D. Wieck and J. Glenn Gray, New York; Harper & Row, p. 3.

3   Elie Faure nevertheless retains a hope founded on automatism itself: 'true friends of the cinema have only seen in it a worthy instrument of propaganda. Maybe. The pharisees of politics, art, letters and science itself will find in the cinema the most faithful of servants until the day when, through a mechanical reversal of roles, it will enslave them in turn' (op. cit., p. 51, a piece from 1934).

4   All these themes are analysed in Eisenstein, *Film Form*, notably in the chapters, 'The principle of cinema and Japanese culture', 'The fourth dimension of cinema', 'Methods of montage 1929', and especially in the 1935 speech, 'Film form: new problems'.

5   cf. 'La centrifugeuse et le Graal', *La non-indifférente Nature*, Paris: UGE, Volume I.

6   Epstein, *passim*. He often emphasizes metaphor (it is from him that we take the following example, after Apollinaire, 'The hands flutter', I, p. 68).

7   cf. the interview with Jakobson, which introduces many details in this regard: *Cinéma, théories, lectures*. Jean Mitry, on his part, suggests a complex notion: cinema would not proceed by metaphor, but by 'metaphoric expression based on a metonymy' (*Cinématographe*, no. 83, novembre 1982, p. 71).

8   Bonitzer, 'Voici', *Cahiers du cinéma*, no. 273, janvier 1977. Gance and L'Herbier lay equal claim to a metaphorical montage: the scene of the Convention and the storm, in *Napoleon*, the scene of the Stock Market and the sky, in *Money*. With Gance, the technique of

superimpositions which go beyond the possibilities of perception serves to constitute the harmonics of the image.

9 Eisenstein admires Tolstoy (and Zola) for having known how to compose the image so as to integrate into it the way in which the characters themselves feel and think, and in which the author thinks of them: thus the 'criminal' embraces of Anna Karenina and Vronsky. This time, the 'compositional principle' is no longer expressed in an image in echo (a sad nature, a sad light, a sad music for a sad hero . . .), but is expressed directly in the image: Eisenstein, *Film Form*, pp. 155–60. Eisenstein himself, however, does not appear to have achieved images of this kind. He rather proceeds by the first means, resonance or echo. Likewise Renoir, in *La bête humaine*, or in *Partie de campagne*. L'Herbier, by contrast, achieves an intrinsic composition with the amazing images of rape in *L'homme du large*: rape as murder.

10 Bazin, *What Is Cinema?*, Vol. I, pp. 100–7.

11 Eisenstein, *La non-indifférente Nature*, II, pp. 67–9.

12 The theatre and opera came up against the problem: how to avoid reducing the crowd to an anonymous, solid mass, but also to a collection of individual atoms? Piscator, in the theatre, gave crowds an architectural or geometric treatment which would be taken up by expressionist cinema, especially Fritz Lang: as in the rectangular, triangular, or pyramidal arrangements in *Metropolis*, but it is a crowd of slaves, cf. Lotte Eisner, *L'écran démoniaque*, Encyclopédie du cinéma, pp. 119–24. Debussy claimed more for opera: he wanted the sound to be a focus of physical and moving individuations, irreducible to those of its members (Barraqué, *Debussy*, Paris: Seuil, p. 159). This is what Eisenstein realizes in cinema; its condition is that the masses become *subject*.

13 Eisenstein, 'Dickens, Griffith and us' (*Film Form*). He criticizes Griffith for not achieving a truly dialectical 'monism'.

14 Bonitzer presents a broad Hitchcock–Eisenstein comparison notably in view of the close-up: *Le champ aveugle*, Cahiers du cinéma/Gallimard.

15 Serge Daney, *La rampe*, p. 172.

16 Paul Virilio shows how the system of war mobilizes perception as much as arms and actions: thus photo and cinema pass through war, and are coupled together with arms (for example, the machine-gun). There will increasingly be a *mise-en-scène* of the battlefield, to which the enemy replies, not now by camouflage, but by a counter-*mise-en-scène* (simulations, trickery, or giant illuminations of the air defence). But it is the whole of civil life which passes into the mode of the *mise-en-scène*, in the fascist system: 'real power is henceforth shared between the logistics of arms and that of images and sounds'; and, to the very end, Goebbels dreamt of going beyond Hollywood, which was the modern cinema-city in contrast to the ancient theatre-city. Cinema in turn goes beyond itself towards the electronic image, civil as well as military in a military-industrial

complex. cf. *Guerre et cinéma I, Logistique de la perception*, Cahiers du cinéma/Editions de l'Etoile.

17 Artaud, 'La vieillesse précoce du cinéma', ['Old age of the cinema'], *Oeuvres complètes*, Gallimard, III, p. 99 (this piece marks Artaud's break with cinema, 1933).

18 All these themes are developed in Vol. III of Artaud. In regard to the only screenplay of *La coquille et le clergyman*, that was produced (by Germaine Dulac), Artaud says (p. 77) that the specificity of cinema is vibration as 'hidden birth of thought'; it 'can resemble and ally itself with the mechanics of a dream without really being itself a dream'; it is 'the pure work of thought'. Artaud's attitude in relation to Germaine Dulac's writing raises many questions which have been analysed by O. and A. Virmaux, *Les surréalistes et le cinéma*, Seghers. Artaud would constantly point out that this is the first surrealist film, and would reproach Buñuel and Cocteau for restricting themselves to the arbitrariness of dream (pp. 270–2). It seems that what he likewise criticized Germaine Dulac for was having already pulled *La coquille et le clergyman* in the direction of a simple dream.

19 It is in this sense that the philosophic tradition (Spinoza, Leibniz) takes up the spiritual automaton; and also Valéry in M. Teste. Jacques Rivière compares Artaud to Valéry, but this is one of the numerous misinterpretations he makes, in the famous correspondence (Vol. I). Kuriichi Uno has ably shown the radical contrast between Valéry and Artaud in relation to the spiritual automaton: 'Artaud et l'espace des forces', thesis, University of Paris VIII, pp. 15–26.

20 Véronique Tacquin has made a profound study of Dreyer's cinema, pointing to what she calls the Mummy ('Pour une théorie du pathétique cinématographique', thesis, University of Paris VIII). She does not refer to Artaud, but to Maurice Blanchot, who is close to him. Artaud had already introduced the Mummy in some passages of *Bilboquet* (I). Véronique Tacquin's analyses open up a whole cinematographic development of the Mummy theme.

21 'Sexuality, repression and the unconscious have never seemed to me a sufficient explanation of inspiration or of the spirit . . . ' (III, p. 47).

22 Maurice Blanchot, 'Artaud', *Le livre à venir*, Gallimard, p. 59: Artaud inverts 'the terms of movement'; he puts in first place 'dispossession, and not the totality of which this dispossession at first appeared as simple lack. What comes first is not the *fullness* of being, but the crack and the fissure . . . '

23 cf. Heidegger, op. cit., pp. 4–6. '*Most thought-provoking is that we are still not thinking* – not even yet, although the state of the world is becoming constantly more thought-provoking . . . *Most thought-provoking in our thought-provoking time is that we are still not thinking.*'

24 Jean-Louis Schefer, *L'homme ordinaire du cinéma*, Cahiers du cinéma/Gallimard, pp. 113–23.

25 Artaud, *Oeuvres complètes*, Volume III, pp. 22, 76.

26 Drouzy gives a narrowly psychoanalytic interpretation of Dreyer's problems: *Carl Th. Dreyer né Nilsson*, Ed. du Cerf, pp. 266–71.

27 Rossellini, interview, in *La politique des auteurs*, Cahiers du cinéma/ Editions de l'Etoile, pp. 65–8.

28 The reader is referred to the book by Agel and Ayfre, *Le cinéma et le sacré*, Ed. du Cerf, and to the studies on *La passion du Christ comme thème cinématographique*, (*Etudes cinématographiques*).

29 cf. Jean Collet, *Jean-Luc Godard*, Seghers, pp. 26–7.

30 In the history of philosophy, the substitution of belief for knowledge takes place in authors of whom some are still believers, while others carry out an atheistic conversion. Hence the existence of real couples: Pascal–Hume, Kant–Fichte, Kierkegaard–Nietzsche, Lequier–Renouvier. But, even with the believers, belief is not now directed towards another world, it is directed to this world: faith according to Kierkegaard, or even Pascal, restores man and the world to us.

31 cf. Claude Beylie's excellent analysis in *Procès de Jeanne d'Arc* (*Etudes cinématographiques*).

32 Serge Daney, p. 80: 'To what the other says, assertion, declaration, sermon, Godard always replies with what *another* other says. There is always a great unknown in his pedagogy, for the nature of the relation that it enjoys with *good* discourses (those he defends, Maoist discourse, for instance) is undecidable.'

33 Alain Bergala: 'Les ailes d'Icare', *Cahiers du cinéma*, no. 355, janvier 1984, p. 8.

34 Daney shows that, because of the status of discourses in Godard, the only 'good' discourse is the one that can be given or restored to the body: this is the whole story of *Ici et ailleurs*. Hence the necessity to reach things and beings 'before they are named', before all discourse, so that they can produce their own: cf. Venice press conference, on *First Name Carmen*, in *Cinématographe*, no. 95, décembre 1983 (and also Louis Audibert's commentaries, p. 10: 'There is a great freedom in this film which is that of a belief . . . The traces of the world captured in the filmic canvas, offered as a kind of speech, evangelical . . . Finding the world again implies returning this side of codes . . . ').

35 Alexandre Astruc, in Pierre Lherminier's *L'art du cinéma*, Seghers, p. 589: 'The expression of thought is cinema's fundamental problem.'

36 Artaud, *Oeuvres complètes*, Vol. III, p. 76.

37 The theme of the Outside, and its relation to thought, is one of Blanchot's most consistent subjects (notably in *L'entretien infini*). In a homage to Blanchot, Michel Foucault takes up this 'Thought of the outside', giving it a more profound status than any internal foundation or principle: cf. *Critique*, juin 1966. It is in *The Order of Things* (trans. Alan Sheridan, London: Tavistock, 1970) that he analyses, for his own purposes, the relation between thought and an 'unthought' which is crucial to it: pp. 322–38.

38 Drawing on the literary notion of 'focusing' in Genette, François Jost distinguishes three possible types of *ocularizing*: internal, when the camera seems to be in the same place as a character's eye; external, when it seems to come from outside or be autonomous; and 'zero', when it seems to be effaced in favour of what it is showing (*Communications*, no. 38). Resuming this question, Véronique Tacquin, op. cit., attaches a great deal of importance to *zero-ocularizing*: she makes it the characteristic of Dreyer's last films, in so far as they embody the instance of the Neutral. For our part, we think that internal focusing does not just concern a character, but every centre existing in the image; it is, therefore, the case of the action-image in general. The two other cases are not precisely defined as the external and the zero, but apply when the centre has become purely optical, either because it moves into the light source (Welles's depth), or because it moves into the point of view (Dreyer's planitude).

39 Daney, op. cit., p. 174. The importance of Serge Daney's book lies in the fact that it is one of the few to take up the question of cinema-thought relations, which were so common at the beginning of reflection on cinema, but later abandoned because of disenchantment. Daney restores the full weight to it, in relation to contemporary cinema. Jean-Louis Schefer does the same.

40 Everywhere in Rohmer, as in Kierkegaard, choice is posed in view of the 'marriage' which defines the ethical stage (*Contes moraux*). But below this there is the aesthetic stage, and beyond it the religious stage. The latter exhibits a grace, but one which is continually sliding into chance as uncertain point. This was already the case in Bresson. The special number of *Cinématographe* on Rohmer, no. 44, février 1979, analyses this interpenetration of chance and grace very well: cf. articles by Carcassone, Jacques Fieschi, Hélène Bokanovski, and especially Devillers ('It is also chance which is perhaps the secret subject of *My Night with Maud*: metaphysical chance weaves its enigma throughout the narration around Pascal's wager, a theme already initiated by the shot of a work dealing with mathematical probabilities . . . Only Maud, who plays a game of chance, that is, that of the real choice, is exiled in a higher misfortune'). On the difference between the completed series of *Contes moraux* and the series *Comédies et proverbes*, it seems to us that the tales still had a structure of short theorems, while the proverbs increasingly resemble problems.

41 cf. precisely Rohmer's commentaries on Dreyer's *Ordet*: *Cahiers du cinéma*, no. 55, janvier 1956. Véronique Tacquin writes: 'Dreyer represses the external manifestations of the internal lived part of the role . . . Even in the most serious bodily affections of characters, we see neither vertigo nor paroxysms . . . the character who has received the blows without showing it suddenly loses his consistency and collapses like a mass' (Tacquin, op. cit.).

42 'The automatism of real life', excluding thought, intention and feeling is one of the recurrent themes of Bresson's *Notes*, trans.

Jonathan Griffin, London: Quartet, 1986, pp. 15, 21–2, 59, 100. To see how this automatism crucially relates to an outside, cf. p. 22 ('Automatically inspired and inventive models'), pp. 53–4 ('Causes are not in models'), p. 59 ('a mechanism gives rise to the unknown').

43 Before the new wave, Bresson brought this new style to perfection. Marie-Claire Ropars sees its most extreme expression in *Au hasard Balthazar*: 'Chosen as an image of chance, the picturesque thread is none the less insufficient as the basis of extreme dividing into pieces of the story; each of Balthazar's stays with a master itself appears broken into fragments each of which in its brevity seems to be snatched from the void only immediately to fall back into it . . . The function of [the fragmenting style] is to place a barrier between the viewer and the world, which transmits feelings but filters their background.' This is the break with the world specific to modern cinema. cf. *L'écran de la mémoire*, Seuil, pp. 178–80.

44 Maurice Blanchot, *L'entretien infini*, pp. 65, 107–9.

45 On the critique of the notion of 'voice-off', cf. Chateau and Jost, *Nouveau cinéma, nouvelle sémiologie*, p. 31 ff. On the notion of 'sound frame', cf. Dominique Villain, *L'oeil à la caméra*, Cahiers du cinéma/Editions de l'Etoile, ch. 4.

46 Albert Spaier has clearly distinguished the two kinds of arithmetical cut in the theory of the continuous: 'What characterizes all arithmetical cuts is the redistribution of the sets of rational numbers into a lower class and a higher class, that is, into two collections such that any term in the first is smaller than any term in the second. Now each number likewise determines such a redistribution. The only difference is that the *rational number* must always be included either in the lower class or in the higher class of the cut, whilst no *irrational number* forms part of either of the two classes which it separates' (*La pensée et la quantité*, Alcan, p. 158).

47 Chateau and Jost have analysed Robbe-Grillet's cinema as *serial* using different criteria from those proposed by us, ch. 7. Robbe-Grillet had carried out a whole critique of metaphor from a novelistic perspective, exposing the pseudo-unity of man and nature, or the pseudo-link between man and the world: 'Nature, humanism, tragedy', *Snapshots, or Towards a New Novel*.

48 Automata or 'models' according to Bresson are not at all a creation of the author: in contrast to the role of the actor, they have a 'nature', an 'I', which reacts on the author ('They allowing you to act in them, and you allowing them to act in you', p. 23). Bresson's cinema, or, in a different way, Rohmer's is evidently the opposite of direct cinema; but it is an *alternative* to direct cinema.

49 In two crucial pages of *L'expérience hérétique*, pp. 146–7, Pasolini moves, with plenty of precautions, from the idea of internal monologue to that of free indirect discourse. We saw in the first volume that free indirect discourse was a constant theme of Pasolini's, in his literary but also cinematographic reflection: what he calls 'the free indirect subjective'.

50   This goes for the genre of cinema itself. In regard to *Numéro deux*, Daney says: 'Cinema's sole specificity is that of collecting images which are no longer made for it', photo or television (p. 83).

51   Barthélemy Amengual, in *Jean-Luc Godard* (*Etudes cinématographiques*), pp. 117–18: 'There, dance is only accident, or, if you like, only a moment in the heroes' behaviour . . . [Cukor's] *Girls* dance for the viewer. Angelo, Emile and Alfred dance for themselves, the time needed for their plots . . . While the rhythm of dance aims to set up an imaginary temporality on the stage, Godard's cutting never for a moment removes the characters from a concrete time. Hence the constantly derisory aspect of their agitation.'

52   Bouligand, *Le déclin des absolus mathématico-logiques*, Ed. de L'Énseignement supérieur.

53   On Godard's graphic forms, cf. Jacques Fieschi, 'Words in images', *Cinématographe*, no. 21, octobre 1976: 'In the great silent mystery, the phrase in the intertitle arrived to secure the sense. In Godard, this written sense is brought into question and inflected with a new interference.'

54   cf. Jean-Claude Bonnet, 'Le petit théâtre de Jean-Luc Godard', *Cinématographe*, no. 41, novembre 1978. It is not a question in Godard's case of introducing a play or rehearsals into a film (Rivette); for him theatre is inseparable from an improvisation, a 'spontaneous *mise-en-scène*' or a 'theatricalization of the everyday'. Similarly for dance, cf. the above remarks of Amengual.

55   Godard, *Cahiers du cinéma*, no. 146, août 1963.

56   Bakhtin, before Pasolini, is the best theorist of free indirect discourse: see V. N. Volosinov, *Marxism and the Philosophy of Language*, trans. Ladislav Matejka and O. R. Titunik, London: Harvard University Press, 1973. On 'plurilingualism' and the role of genres in the novel, cf. *Esthétique et théorie du roman*, Gallimard, p. 122 ff.

8   Cinema, Body and Brain, Thought

1   This is the neo-realism 'without a bicycle' invented by Antonioni: cf. the texts quoted by Leprohon, *Antonioni*, Seghers, pp. 103, 105, 110. Everything that Blanchot says about tiredness and waiting is particularly applicable to Antonioni (*L'entretien infini*, Preface).

2   On all these aspects of Bene's cinema, cf. the comprehensive analysis by Jean-Paul Manganaro, in *Lumière du cinéma*, no. 9, novembre 1977.

3   Dominique Noguez stresses real time and the elimination of narrativity ('mirror of time . . . relation to time which goes beyond the story'): in *Le cinéma en l'an 2000*, *Revue d'esthétique*, Privat, p. 15.

4   On the ceremonial pole of experimental cinema, cf. Paolo Bertetto, 'L'éidétique et le cérémonial', ibid., pp. 59–61.

5 Brecht, 'Music and gest', *Brecht on Theatre: the development of an aesthetic*, trans. John Willett, London: Eyre Methuen, 1978. Roland Barthes gave an excellent commentary on this piece ('Diderot, Brecht, Eisenstein', in *Image-Music-Text*, trans. Stephen Heath, London: Fontana, 1977, pp. 69–78): the subject of *Mother Courage* may be the Thirty Years War, or the repudiation of war in general, but 'its *gest* is not there', but 'in the blindness of the tradeswoman who thinks herself able to live off war, only, in fact, to die of it' (ibid., p. 76); it is in 'the critical demonstration of the gesture' or 'the co-ordination of gestures'. It is not a ceremony (empty gest), said Brecht, but rather a ceremonializing of 'the most current, the most vulgar and the most banal' attitudes. Barthes clarifies the point: it is the gesture with which the canteen-woman checks the genuineness of the money offered, in Brecht, or, in Eisenstein, 'the excessive flourish with which the bureaucrat in *The General Line* signs his official papers', (ibid., p. 74).

6 Comolli, *Cahiers du cinéma*, no. 205, octobre 1968 (cf. Sylvie Pierre's commentary). Cassavetes himself says that life is not enough: a 'spectacle' is needed, for only the spectacle is creation; but the spectacle must come from living characters, and not vice versa.

7 Yann Lardeau has clearly demonstrated the relation between the new wave and burlesque: 'The relation of the body to the objects which surround it on stage *produces* a series of obstacles which the actor's route comes successively up against', and 'becomes the raw material of cinematographic language'. He says, of *First Name Carmen*: 'the repeated collisions of the a-synchronic bodies propelled towards one another like meteors' (*Cahiers du cinéma*, no. 355, janvier 1984).

8 The very title of Brecht's piece, 'Music and gest', is enough to indicate that the gest must not be only social: being the principal element of theatricalization, it involves all aesthetic components, notably musical ones.

9 cf. two important articles by Jean-Pierre Bamberger, one on *Slow Motion*, the other on *First Name Carmen* (*Libération*, 7 and 8 novembre 1980, 19 janvier 1984). In the first, Bamberger analyses the breaking down [*décomposition*] of movement according to attitudes, but also the composition of melodic lines according to characters, and the corresponding role of music. In the second, he analyses the relation between the body and sound, but also between the musical gesture and the body's attitude: 'How is a relation between the pluckings of violin-strings and those of embracing bodies, between the bow's curve of movement as it goes for the string and the arm which entwines a neck, to be brought into existence?'

10 Or rather it is Alain Philippon who asks Akerman about the limit of her stylization of bodies and postures. To which she replies that, from the beginning, she had a technical mastery which was too perfect, notably in framing. This mastery is not necessarily good: how is the 'seriousness' of stylization to be avoided? Philippon

analyses Akerman's evolution in *Toute une nuit*: cf. *Cahiers du cinéma*, no. 341, novembre 1981, pp. 19–26.

11 Serge Daney, *Cahiers du cinéma*, no. 306, decembre 1979, p. 40: 'We can clearly see that a purely critical, demystifying approach would have failed, by reducing the festival to what it *signifies* or to those who use it, to its meaning or its function . . . The festival [*had to be*] criticized whilst still showing it in its entirety, in its opacity.' And Eustache's own text, 'Pourquoi j'ai refait la Rosière'.

12 Jean Narboni compares *Faux-fuyants* to Gombrowicz's novel, *La pornographie* (*Cahiers du cinéma*, no. 353, novembre 1983, p. 53). For the novel, like the film, presents an adult protagonist who devotes himself to observing the attitudes of young people, attitudes which are at once innocent and imposed, and all the more 'pornographic' for that, and which lead to a catastrophe: 'their hands above their heads touched involuntarily. And they were instantly lowered, violently. For some time they both looked fixedly at their joined hands. And abruptly they fell; it wasn't clear which one had over-balanced the other, you would think that it was their hands which had tipped them over' (*La pornographie*, Julliard, p. 157).

13 Jean Douchet ('Le cinéma autophagique de Philippe Garrel', in *Garrel composé par Gérard Courant*, Studio 43). 'Two sensations by which solitude reveals itself, cold and burning, *Athanor*, for instance, is a film about fire. *La cicatrice intérieure* is a film about fire and ice . . . The idea of the hot, the burning, the feverish, the intense, reinforces the fundamental character of an icy universe.'

14 Noël Burch, *Praxis du cinéma*, Gallimard, pp. 85–6.

15 cf. Alain Philippon (in *Garrel*, Studio 43): 'What is the subject of *La cicatrice intérieure* if not birth and creation? We are there in the world of before the world, in a past or a future, it matters little, undated . . . It is clearly a birth that we have just witnessed, and the Child, in various guises, will later be the carrier of the film's fiction . . . If fire, earth and water are called together in *La cicatrice intérieure* as in the first moments of the universe, it is in the role of *primary* elements of a world to be born, to which speech is to give life.' And Philippe Carcassonne, in a rather guarded article (*Cinématographe*, no. 87, mars 1983) cites *Le bleu des origines* (in black and white): 'It is the colour of genesis, what precedes history and will assuredly survive it; it is the eschatological envelope, not only of cinema, but of any representation from which characters have their sources.'

16 Garrel sometimes alludes to his personal history which is mixed up with his work: 'At the end of *Le berceau de cristal* there is the girl who commits suicide, and somewhere it's as I said in *Marie pour mémoire*, let madness come quickly . . . until the day that it hit me. Until I find sanity again through cinema.' (*Cahiers du cinéma*, no. 287, avril 1978.)

17 Bazin, *What Is cinema?*, Vol. I, pp. 95 ff.

18 Phillipon, 'L'enfant-cinéma', *Cahiers du cinéma*, no. 344, février 1983, p. 29. And, on movement and the body in Garrel, cf. Jean Narboni, 'Le lieu dit', *Cahiers du cinéma*, no. 204, septembre 1968.

19 On this pre-hodological space, space before action, overlapping of perspectives and fluctuation of the soul, cf. Gibert Simondon, *L'individu et sa genèse physico-biologique*, PUF, pp. 233–4.

20 Neurosis is thus not the consequence of the modern world, but rather of our separation from this world, of our lack of adaptation to this world (cf. Leprohon, op. cit., pp. 104–6). The brain, in contrast, is adequate to the modern world, including its possibilities of the expansion of electronic or chemical brains: an encounter occurs between the brain and colour, not that it is enough to paint the world, but because the treatment of colour is an important element in the awareness of the 'new world' (the colour-corrector, the electronic image . . .). In all these respects, Antonioni identifies *Red Desert* as a turning-point in his work: cf. 'Entretien avec Antonioni par Jean-Luc Godard', in *La politique des auteurs*, Cahiers du cinéma/Editions de l'Etoile. A project of Antonioni, 'Technically soft', shows an exhausted man who is on his back dying and looking at 'the sky which becomes ever bluer, this blue becoming pink', Albatros).

21 The reader is referred to Michel Ciment's essential analyses, especially of *Space Odyssey*, and *The Shining*, in his book *Kubrick*, Calmann-Lévy.

22 Bounoure, *Alain Resnais*, Seghers, p. 67 (on *Toute la mémoire du monde*: 'Resnais activates a universe in the image of our brain. What happens in front of his lens is suddenly transformed, and from documentary reality we slide imperceptibly towards a different reality . . . a film set which has been turned round and which returns our own image. Thus the librarian . . . assumes the face of a nervous, neuronic messenger.'

23 cf. interview, cited by Benayoun, *Alain Resnais arpenteur de l'imaginaire*, Stock, p. 177.

24 René Prédal, *Alain Resnais, Etudes cinématographiques*, ch. VIII, cf. Cayrol, 'Pour un romanesque lazaréen, *Corps étrangers*, Paris: UGE.

25 Jean-Claude Bonnet, on *L'amour à mort*, in *Cinématographe*, no. 103, octobre 1984, p. 40. Bonnet underlines the profession of the man and woman: archaeologist of the past, botanist of the future; if the man has gone through death from the inside, the woman is summoned by death from the outside. Ishaghpour said about *Stavisky*: 'Telescoped together are a past which seizes a character, and a future conceived as constitution of his character and as machination which destroys him' (*D'une image à l'autre*, p. 205).

26 Pauline Harvey, 'La danse des atomes et des nébuleuses', in *Dix nouvelles humoristiques par dix auteurs québécois*, Ed. Quinze.

27 Prédal, op. cit., pp. 22–3.

28 cf. The Resnais–Eisenstein parallel according to Ishagpour, op. cit.,
    pp. 190–1.
29 Bergson, *MM*, ch. III.
30 This is very clear in Jakobson (*Langage enfantin et aphasie*, Editions
    de Minuit), who recognizes the two axes while emphasizing the
    associative one. The persistence of the cerebral model in Chomsky
    should also be studied. For the understanding of cinema, the
    question is inescapably raised in semiology inspired by linguistics:
    what is the implicit cerebral model underpinning the cinema–
    language relationship, for instance in Christian Metz? In the
    development of this semiology, François Jost seems to us most
    aware of the problem: his analyses imply a *different* cerebral model,
    although, to our knowledge, he has not dealt directly with this
    problem.
31 Gilbert Simondon has analysed these different points: how the
    process of integration-differentiation refers to a relative *distribution*
    of organic internal and external environments [*milieux*]; how these,
    in turn, refer to 'an absolute interiority and externality', which
    appear in the topological structure of the brain (op. cit., pp. 260–5):
    'the cortex cannot be adequately represented in a Euclidean way').
32 (Translators' note: in English in the original.) This is the problem of
    synapses and of electrical, or chemical, transmission from one
    reason to the other: cf. Jean-Pierre Changeux, *L'homme neuronal*,
    Fayard, pp. 108 ff. The discovery of synapses was enough in itself to
    shatter the idea of a continuous cerebral system, since it laid down
    irreducible points or cuts. But, in the case of synapses with electrical
    transmission, we think that the cut or point may be called 'rational',
    in accord with the mathematical analogy. In contrast, in the case of
    chemical synapses, the point is 'irrational'; the cut is important in
    itself and belongs to neither of the two sets that it separates (in fact,
    in the synaptic gap, vesicles will release discontinuous amounts of
    transmitter substance or 'quanta'). Hence the ever greater impor-
    tance of a factor of uncertainty, or rather half-uncertainty, in the
    neuronal transmission. Steven Rose has underlined this aspect of
    the problem: *Le cerveau conscient*, Seuil, pp. 84–9.
33 cf. Rosenstiehl and Petitot, 'Automate asocial et systèmes acentrés',
    Communications, no. 22, 1974.
34 On the flight of associations, the window and transparency-effects,
    and the efforts of the principal character who goes against the
    current, cf. Téchiné, interviews with Sainderichin and Tesson,
    Cahiers du cinéma, no. 333, mars 1981: in this perspective, the film set
    has a cerebral rather than physical function.
35 cf. 'Entretien avec Jacques Fieschi', *Cinématographe*, no. 31, octobre
    1977: 'I think that cinema is an art of literature . . . My intention was
    to make literal everything that has a metaphorical role in the film', as
    in the cone which is passed on in *Les enfants du placard*. In other
    words, 'infinite interpretation' is not achieved through metaphor or
    associative linkage, but, as we shall see, through break in association,

and relinkage around the literal image. It is this method which brings Jacquot close to Kafka, and allowed his fine adaptation of an episode of *America*. In the history of cinema, the first films inspired by psychoanalysis in contrast worked through metaphor and association.

36 Andrei Bely, *Petersburg* (and Georges Nivat's postscript to the French translation which analyses the conception of the 'cerebral game' in Bely). We borrow the expression 'relinked dividing up' from Raymond Ruyer, who uses it to characterize the famous *Markoff chains*: these are distinguished from both determined linkages and chance distributions; they concern semi-accidental phenomena or mixtures of dependency and uncertainty (*La genèse des formes vivantes*, Flammarion, ch. VII). Ruyer shows how Markoff chains intervene in life, in language, in society, in history, in literature. The example of Bely in this respect would be a particularly clear one. More generally, neuronal chains as we have just defined them, with their synapses and their irrational points, correspond to Markoff's scheme: they are 'partially dependent' successive draughts, semi-accidental linkages, that is, relinkages. The brain seems to us peculiarly subject to a Markovian interpretation (between the neuronal sender and receiver, there are successive, but non-independent, tugs or draughts).

37 The great piece by Eisenstein which examines *Battleship Potemkin* is not a case of applied theory: it is rather the point where practice and theory relaunch each other and find their concrete unity: *La non-indifférente Nature*, Vol. I, 'The organic and the pathetic', pp. 54–72. This text underlines two aspects: the necessity of commensurable relations between whole and parts

$$\frac{OA}{OB} = \frac{OB}{OC} = n$$

as formula of the spiral; the necessity for the points of distribution to be 'rational', and to comply with a connected formula of the golden section, the cut or caesura being the end of one part or the beginning of the other, depending on whether one begins 'from one end of the film or the other' ($n=0.618$). We are concerned here only with the most abstract aspect of Eisenstein's commentary, which is, however, important for its very concrete bearing on the images of *Battleship*. And the practice of false continuity in his later films, for instance in *Ivan the Terrible*, does not call this structure into question.

38 Jean-Pierre Bamberger, on Godard's *Slow Motion*: 'In the framing are the different moments of shooting; the taking of one shot is the framing, the shooting of another shot is the deframing of one shot in relation to the framing of the following one, and the montage is the final reframing . . . Framing is no longer defining a space, but imprinting a time' (*Libération*, 8 novembre 1980).

39   Our analysis is so summary that we can only give a few bibliographical references. (1) On the first two ages, Jean Mitry, *Le cinéma expérimental*, Seghers, ch. V and ch. IX. (2) On the more recent period, Dominique Noguez, *Eloge du cinéma expérimental*, Centre Georges-Pompidou (where studies of the forerunner, McLaren, and of the American underground may be found), *Trente ans de cinéma expérimental en France*, Arcef (especially on lettrism, 'expanded cinema' and Maurice Lemaître), *Une renaissance du cinéma*, Klincksieck. cf. also the article by Bertetto already cited, 'L'éidétique et le cérémonial'. On the procedures of blinking and loops in the American underground, cf. P. A. Sitney, 'Le film structurel', in *Cinéma, théorie, lectures*.

40   For example on democracy, the community and the necessity of a 'leader' in King Vidor's work, cf. *Positif*, no. 163, novembre 1974 (articles by Michel Ciment and Michael Henry).

41   cf. Kafka, *Journal*, 25 December 1911 (and letter to Brod, June 1921); Klee, *On Modern Art*, trans. Paul Findlay, London: Faber, 1966, p. 55. ('We have found parts, but not the whole. We still lack the ultimate power, for: the people are not with us. But we seek a people. We began over there in the Bauhaus. We began there with a community to which each of us gave what he had. More we cannot do.') Carmelo Bene has also said: 'I make popular theatre. Ethnic. But it is the people who are missing' (*Dramaturgie*, p. 113).

42   Roberto Schwarz and his definition of 'tropicalism', *Les Temps modernes*, no. 288, juillet 1970.

43   On Lino Brocka, his use of myth and his cinema of drives, cf. *Cinématographe*, no. 77, avril 1982 (especially the article by Jacques Fieschi, 'Violences').

44   On the critique of myth in Perrault, cf. Guy Gauthier, 'Une écriture du réel', and Suzanne Trudel, 'La quête du royaume, trois hommes, trois paroles, un langage', in *Ecritures de Pierre Perrault*, Edilig. Suzanne Trudel distinguishes three kinds of impasse, genealogical, ethnic and political (p. 63).

45   Jean-Louis Comolli, interview, *Cahiers du cinéma*, no. 333, mars 1982.

46   Yann Lardeau, 'Cinéma des racines, histoires du ghetto', in *Cahiers du cinéma*, no. 340, octobre 1982.

47   cf. Serge Daney, *La rampe*, Cahiers du cinéma/Gallimard, pp. 118–23 (especially the character of the story-teller).

48   On Rocha's critique of myth and the evolution of his work, cf. Barthélemy Amengual, *Le cinéma nôvo brésilien*, *Etudes cinématographiques*, II (p. 57: 'the counter-myth, as one says counter-fire').

49   *Ecritures de Pierre Perrault*: on real characters, and the speech-act as story-telling function, *'flagrant offence of making legend'*, cf. the interview with René Allio (on *La bête lumineuse*, Perrault would say: 'I recently came across an unsuspected country . . . Everything in this apparently quiet country is made into legend as soon as one dares to talk about it.').

9 The Components of the Image

1 Louis Audibert, 'L'ombre du son', *Cinématographe*, no. 48, juillet 1979, pp. 5–6. This review has devoted two important issues, numbers 47 and 48, to the problems of the silent film and the talkie.

2 cf. Sylvie Trosa, no. 47, pp. 14–15: the silent image had an autonomous 'materiality' which filled it with meaning. According to Trosa, L'Herbier was one of the authors of the silent film who lost most with the talkie, despite all his literary taste: 'the visual constructions' which he had the secret of, and which ensured 'the appropriateness of substance and expression', of nature and culture, lose much of their function.

3 It is in the name of the talkie, amongst other reasons, that the Stalinists criticize Eisenstein for having confused history with nature, as we saw in relation to the Soviet congress of 1935.

4 cf. Benveniste's distinction between the level of the 'story' which connects events, and that of the 'speech' which utters or reproduces words: *Problèmes de linguistique générale*, Gallimard, pp. 241–2 (and how speech passes into the indirect style).

5 Balazs observed that sound 'has no image': cinema does not 'represent' it but 'restores' it (*L'esprit du cinéma*, Payot, p. 244). However, it 'emerges from the centre of the visual image', and its elements are distributed in terms of this image: cf. Michel Chion, *La voix au cinéma*, Cahiers du cinéma/Editions de l'Etoile, pp. 13–14. It is in this sense a component of the visual image.

6 This interactionist sociology of communication appears in America with Park and Goffman, in connection with urban phenomena and the problems of information, of circulation of information. Its precursors are Georg Simmel in Germany, and, in a less recognized way, Gabriel Tarde in France. Phenomena such as rumour, newspapers, conversation, and characters such as the socialite, the stroller, the drifter, the marginal, the adventurer feature prominently in it, because they pose the question of sociability rather than society. Isaac Joseph, who has made a big contribution to the exposition of this sociology in France, has written a fine book, *Le passant considérable* (Librairie des Méridiens), in which he studies in particular the 'difficulties in interaction'. In its very modernity, this school seems to us to hold a place in sociology analogous to that of the American comedy in the talking cinema – this is clearly a very important place.

7 Noël Burch, 'De Mabuse à M: le travail de Fritz Lang', in *Cinéma, théorie, lectures*, p. 235.

8 Cicourel, *La sociologie cognitive*, PUF, quoted by Isaac Joseph (who discusses this notion of 'problematic', op. cit., p. 54).

9 It will be asked whether cinema can achieve phenomena of interaction with its own means. But this can only be done in silent films which give up intertitles, and which proceed by aberrant movements. We saw this in Vertov's *Man with a Movie Camera*, where

the gap acts as differential of movements. Or equally in _The Last Laugh_, it is the 'unleashed' camera which makes certain interactions visible.

10 Jean Douchet, in 'Cinéma américain', _Cahiers du cinéma_, no. 150, decembre 1963, pp. 146–7.

11 Gérard Genette's theory concerning the literary story underlines the difference between the questions: 'Who is speaking?' and 'Who is seeing?' (_Figures_, III, p. 203, and _Nouveau discours du récit_, Seuil). This is the inspiration behind François Jost's ideas in _Communications_, no. 38, 1983. Mankiewicz seems to us the best cinematographic example.

12 F. Berthet, in 'La conversation', _Communications_, no. 30, 1979, p. 150.

13* Translators' note: the French word '_mondanité_', which literally means 'worldliness', is also used in the plural with the sense of 'society life' or 'small talk'.

14 Alejo Carpentier, quoted by Mitry (_Esthétique et psychologie du cinéma_, Ed. Universitaires, II, p. 102): 'Conversation has a rhythm, a movement, an absence of sequence in the ideas, with, on the contrary, strange associations, curious reminders, which bear no resemblance to the dialogues that usually fill' novels and plays.

15 Georg Simmel, 'Sociologie de la sociabilité', in _Urbi_, III, 1980 (cf. the way Simmel produces a definition of democracy from this).

16 Claire Parnet, in an unpublished piece, analyses the voice in American cinema, comedies and thrillers.

17 cf. Comolli, _Cahiers du cinéma_, nos 230 and 231, juin–juillet 1972.

18 Michel Chion, op. cit., pp. 36, 44.

19 Alain Philippon, _Cahiers du cinéma_, no. 347, mai 1983, p. 67.

20 Michel Chion, op. cit., p. 72. Bazin wrote a fine passage on the deforming of sound relationships: 'Indistinct sound elements are few ... on the contrary Tati's whole shrewdness consists of destroying clarity by clarity' (_Qu'est-ce que le cinéma?_, Ed. du Cerf, p. 46). And the interview with Tati about sound, _Cahiers du cinéma_, no. 303, septembre 1979.

21 Michel Fano, in _Encyclopaedia Universalis_, 'Cinema (musique de)'. Fano's conception clearly implies the active presence of the musician on the editing-table, his involvement in all sound elements, a musical treatment of non-musical sounds. We shall see that this argument takes on its full range in a new conception of the image.

22 cf. Eisenstein, Pudovkin and Alexandroff, 1928 Manifesto, in Eisenstein, _Film Form_, Appendix A, pp. 257–9. Sylvie Trosa is right to attribute the manifesto's ideas to Pudovkin in particular: Eisenstein, for his part, believes less in the virtues of the out-of-field and sound-off than in the possibility of 'sound-in' to raise the visual image to a new synthesis.

23 Bresson, _Notes_, pp. 50–2. It is clear that Bresson is not only thinking of sound-off: there may be a 'preponderance' of sound-in over the image itself, and, through this, 'neutralization' of the visual image.

On the sound space in Bresson, cf. Henri Agel, *L'espace cinématographique*, Delarge, ch. VII.

24 According to Bonitzer's crucial text, 'there are at least two types of voice-off: which refer to at least two types' of out-of-field: one homogenous with the field, the other heterogeneous and enjoying an irreducible power ('absolutely other and absolutely indeterminate'). cf. *Le regard et la voix*, Paris: UGE pp. 31–3. Michel Chion proposes the notion of '*acousmètre*' to designate the voice whose source is not seen; and he distinguishes the relative *acousmètre* and the 'integral' *acousmètre*, possessing the power of being ubiquitous, omnipotent and all-seeing. However, he relativizes Bonitzer's distinction, because he wants to show how the two aspects have all kinds of connections, and enter into a circuit which does not, however, erase their difference in nature: pp. 26–9, 32.

25 cf. the analysis of Fusco's music in *The Eclipse*, by Emmanuel Decaux, *Cinématographe*, no. 62, novembre 1980 (issue on film music).

26 Balazs, *Le cinéma*, Payot, p. 224: 'The talking film represses programme music.'

27 Eisenstein, *The Film Sense*, London: Faber, 1943, pp. 114–56. Eisenstein thinks that internal correspondence can also apply to the immobile visual image: in this case it is the eye that constitutes the movement corresponding to musical movement (as in the waiting sequence before the attack). He draws a most important consequence from this: the visual image as such becomes readable 'from left to right', or sometimes in a more complex way: 'plastic reading' (pp. 146–9). Thus Eisenstein is the inventor of the notion of readable image. Jean Mitry takes up the question, and devotes himself to a thorough study of the visual image/music correspondence: especially in *Le cinéma expérimental*, Seghers, chs V, IX and X. He begins by challenging all external correspondences, either because the image retains a spatial content which will work only as illustration of the music, or because the image, becoming formal or abstract, presents only arbitrary, reversible and decorative relations which do not really correspond to the musical relations (even in McLaren). He likewise challenges Eisenstein's readable image, and criticizes the waiting sequence, which remains, according to him, at a level of external correspondence (pp. 207–8). On the other hand, he thinks that the sequence with the battle on the ice is more appropriate because it tends to reveal a movement common to the visual and the musical. This is the condition of an internal correspondence, such as Honegger was looking for. But, according to Mitry, the common movement can only be achieved if the visual image is detached from bodies, without, however, becoming abstract or geometrical: the visual image must set in motion a matter, a materiality capable of vibrations and reflections. In this event there will be two corresponding expressions of a single 'univocal whole' (pp. 212–18). Eisenstein only half-achieved this in

the battle on the ice, but Mitry thinks he has almost achieved it in his own attempts, in certain parts of *Images pour Debussy*. He willingly acknowledges, however, that it was under the conditions of an experimental film which had exclusively set itself this task.

28   Nietzsche, *The Birth of Tragedy*, paras 5, 16 and 17.
29   cf. 'Table ronde sur la musique de film', in *Cinématographe*, no. 62.
30   Adorno and Eisler, *Musique de cinéma*, Arche, p. 87. And in the example of the barcarolle, which would apply against Mitry and Eisenstein alike, cf. p. 75. Eisler was often Brecht's collaborator (he is also the musician in Resnais' *Night and Fog*). Even in a Marxist context, it goes without saying that conceptions of music reflect very different influences.
31   Balazs has produced a very fine cinematographic portrait of Greta Garbo (*Le cinéma*, p. 276): the specific feature in Greta Garbo's beauty seems to him to come from the fact that she stands out from every environment, so as to express 'the purity of someone imprisoned inside themself, the internal aristocracy, the shivering sensitivity of the *noli me tangere*'. Balazs does not mention Garbo's voice, but that voice would confirm his analysis: it brings together the variation of an internal whole, beyond psychology, which the movements of the actress in her environment still did not express directly enough.
32* Translators' note: in English in the original.
33   Michel Fano himself, in a very subtle piece (*Cinématographe*, p. 9), says that the two conceptions, his and Jansen's, are equally legitimate. But we think that there is no need to choose and that each can be part of the other, at two different levels.
34   We have defined free indirect discourse as an enunciation forming part of an utterance which depends on a different subject of enunciation: for instance: 'She collects her energy, she will rather suffer torture than lose her virginity.' It is Bakhtin who shows that it is not a matter of a mixed form (*Marxism and the Philosophy of Language*, 3rd part).
35   cf. Eric Rohmer, 'Film and the three levels of discourse, indirect, direct, hyperdirect', *Le goût de la beauté*, Cahiers du cinéma/Editions de l'Etoile, pp. 96–9.
36   Michel Chion, p. 73: 'The Bressonian model talks as one listens: picking up as he can in himself what he has just said, to the extent that he seems to conclude his speech as he goes along uttering it, without giving it the chance to resonate with the partner or the public . . . In *Le diable probablement* no voice is resonant any more.' (cf. Serge Daney, *La rampe*, pp. 135–43. In *Four Nights of a Dreamer*, the flashback takes on a special sense, because it allows the characters to talk all the more as if they were reporting their own words. It will be observed that Dostoevski already endowed his hero with a strange voice ('I began as if I were reading in a book . . . when you speak they say that you are reading in a book').
37   Marion Vidal, *Les contes moraux d'Eric Rohmer*, Lherminier,

pp. 126–8: in *Claire's Knee*, the narrator turns to the woman novelist; 'if she allows Jerome's story, the latter will have won, he will have become a character in a novel, at least comparable to Valmont and Julien Sorel. This is the very principle of story-telling becoming reality [*l'affabulation réalisante*] which allows, through the magic of the verb, the embodiment of an impalpable and in practice non-existent reality.' On what Rohmer calls 'lie' as cinematographic principle, cf. *Le goût de la beauté*, pp. 39–40.

38 Pasolini is even more important here because it is he who introduces the 'free indirect' into cinema, as we have seen. For an analysis of the speech-act in Pasolini, sometimes act of tale, sometimes act of myth, cf. *Pasolini, Etudes cinématographiques* (on myth and the sacred, in *The Gospel according to St Matthew, Oedipus Rex, Theorem, Medea*, Volume I, articles by Maakaroun and Amengual; on the tale and story, in *The Decameron, The Canterbury Tales, The Thousand and One Nights*, Vol. II, articles by Sémolué and Amengual).

39 On this point, as on the cinema of Straub and Huillet as a whole, there are two essential texts, one by Narboni, and one by Daney (*Cahiers du cinéma*, no. 275, avril 1977, and no. 305, novembre 1979). Jean Narboni emphasizes the buryings, lacunae or gaps, the visual image as 'rock', and what he calls 'the places of memory'. Serge Daney entitles his piece 'The Straubian shot', and answers the question by saying 'the shot as tomb' ('the content of the shot is, then, *stricto sensu* what is concealed in it, the corpses under the ground'). It is not a matter of an ancient tomb, but of an archaeology of our time. Daney had already dealt with this theme in another piece entitled 'A tomb for the eye' (*La rampe*, pp. 70–7), where he observes in passing that there is in Straub a fragmentation of bodies which connects them to the earth, 'discrete picking out of the most neutral and least spectacular parts of the body, here an ankle, there a knee'. This would be a reason, though minor, for confirming the comparison with Bresson and with Rohmer. To the texts of Narboni and Daney may be added that of Jean-Claude Biette, analysing the stratigraphic landscapes in *Trop tôt, trop tard* and the role of pan shots (*Cahiers du cinéma*, no. 332, février 1982).

40 cf. Daney, *Cahiers du cinéma*, no. 305, p. 6. And in *Moses and Aaron*, the interview between Straub and Huillet, and Bontemps, Bonitzer and Daney, no. 258, juillet 1975, p. 17.

41 Jean-Claude Bonnet, 'Trois cinéastes du texte', *Cinématographe*, no. 31, octobre 1977, p. 3 (it is Straub himself who spoke of telluric sequence and central fissure).

42 Narboni, *Cahiers du cinéma*, no. 275, p. 9. Pascal Bonitzer had spoken of 'petrified and paralysing inscriptions': 'We are dealing with blocs, say Straub and Huillet ... for instance the graffiti-dedication *Für Holger Meins* over a bloc of shots as epigraph for *Moses and Aaron* is what ended up as the most important thing in the film for the Straubs'. (*Le régard et la voix*, p. 67.)

43 Of course inscriptions in the image (letters, newspaper headlines),

remained frequent in the first stage of the talkie; but they were usually delivered through the voice (for instance, the newspaper-seller's voice). Inscriptions and intertitles have their own importance in modern cinema as in the silent, yet it is in a very different way: modern cinema carries out a 'jamming' of written meaning, as Jacques Fieschi shows, devoting to the question two articles which compare the modern and the silent, 'Mots en images' and 'Cartons, chiffres et lettres', *Cinématographe*, nos 21 and 32, octobre 1976 and novembre 1977.

44   The tectonic or geological power of the pictorial image in Cézanne is not one feature among others, but an overall characteristic transforming the whole, not only in the landscapes, a rock or a mountain outline, but also in the still lifes. It is a new system of visual sensation which contrasts equally with the dematerialized sensation of impressionism, and the projected, hallucinatory sensation of expressionism. It is the 'materialized sensation' cited by Straub with Cézanne as his reference: a film is not thought of as offering or producing sensations for the viewer, but as 'materializing them', achieving a tectonics of sensation. cf. 'Entretien', *Cahiers du cinéma*, no. 305, p. 19.

45   To our knowledge, it is Noël Burch who reinvents the notion of 'reading' of the visual image, by giving it an original meaning quite different from Eisenstein's. He defines it as we saw in the earlier quote and applies it in particular to Ozu: *Pour un observateur lointain*, pp. 175, 179 and particularly 185. And he shows how Ozu, coming to the talkie in 1936 (*The Only Son*), introduces a 'division of labour' or a disjunction between the 'spoken event' and the fixed image 'empty of events': pp. 186–9.

46   Marion Vidal analyses a sequence in Rohmer's *Claire's Knee* which begins with an almost motionless, sculptural and pictorial image and then goes on to a narration which will itself return to the fixed image: 'A to-and-fro between speech and image' (op. cit., p. 128). Vidal shows how in Rohmer speech often creates the event. Similarly, in Resnais' and Robbe-Grillet's *Last Year in Marienbad*, a to-and-fro occurs between the narrative speech which creates the event and the static hotel grounds which assume a mineral or tectonic value, with their different areas, white, grey, black.

47   Burch, op. cit., p. 174: from film continuity, 'there results an effect of hiatus which underlines the disjunctive nature of change of shot, which elaboration of the rules of montage had always concealed'.

48   Marie-Claire Ropars analyses a movement common in Godard's work in this respect: the separation of the 'abstract components' of the image will give way to a recomposition of all their audio-visual support 'in an instant, the absolute', until the components separate again (*Jean-Luc Godard, Etudes cinématographiques*, pp. 20–7).

49   Visual–sound contradictions are numerous in *The Man Who Lies*: the inn is shown full of people whilst the voice presents it as empty; Boris's voice says 'I don't know how long I stayed there . . .' whilst

the image shows him going away. But it is not the contradictions which are of fundamental importance according to Gardies, it is rather the repetitions and permutations which they allow, based on a 'paradigmatic' which sets the visual and sound in motion (*Le cinéma de Robbe-Grillet*, ch. VIII and conclusion). Chateau and Jost expand the notion of paradigm, and bring it to bear on parameters with functions of anticipation and retrogression: hence their discovery of 'telestructures' and an audio-visual code which depends on them (*Nouveau cinéma, nouvelle sémiologie*, ch. VI).

50 Michel Chion shows that the absolute voice-off takes on all the more independence because it ceases to know and see everything, giving up an omnipotence: he cites Marguerite Duras and Bertolucci, but finds a first, remarkable example in Sternberg's *The Saga of Anatahan* (pp. 30–2). On the 'voice-off-off', when a rift is introduced between the visual and sound, cf. Bonitzer, p. 69. More generally, the metamorphoses of voice-off can be followed in the light of the distinctions introduced by Percheron, when he calls 'voice-off-in' the case where 'the speaker is on the screen, but no words come out of his mouth' (*Ça*, no. 2, octobre 1973), and especially in the light of the new topology proposed by Daney (*La rampe*, pp. 144–7).

51 It is Kant who makes the 'autonomy-heautonomy' distinction in another context (cf. *Critique of Judgement*, introduction, section V).

52 Marguerite Duras, *Nathalie Granger*, followed by *La femme du Gange*, Gallimard, pp. 103–4.

53 Balazs, *Le cinéma*, ch. XVI.

54 In the field of linguistics, we do not refer to the analysis of the dimensions of the speech-act, according to Austin and his successors, but to the classification of these acts as 'functions' or 'powers' of language (Malinowski, Firth, Marcel Cohen). The present state of the question can be found in Ducrot and Todorov's *Encyclopaedic Dictionary of the Sciences of Language*, trans. Catherine Porter, Oxford: Blackwell, 1981, pp. 61–7. The threefold distinction we propose, with the interactive, the reflexive and the story-telling, seems to us to be based on cinema but to be perhaps more generally applicable.

55 On the 'deprivation' of language and the 'return to aphasia' cf. Straub and Huillet, interview in relation to *Othon, Cahiers du cinéma*, no. 224, octobre 1970, and Jean Narboni's commentaries, 'La vicariance du pouvoir', which shows how the theatrical scene remains 'involved' in its cinematographic transformation, p. 45. On *Fortini Cani*, Narboni pointed to 'the idea of a text turning against itself when it is read' (*Cahiers du cinéma*, no. 275, p. 13).

56 'The framing here is that of speech' (in *Les films de J-M. Straub et D. Huillet*, Goethe Institut, Paris, p. 55).

57 Straub and Huillet: 'The dialectic between suffering and violence is concealed in the art of Bach himself.' And they emphasize the necessity of showing 'people in the process of making music': 'Each piece of music that we will show will be really performed before the

camera, picked up directly on sound and filmed in a single shot. The core of what will be shown when there is a piece of music is on each occasion how this music is made. It may be that it is introduced by a score, a manuscript or an original printed edition ...' (ibid., pp. 12–14).

58 cf. the detailed analysis of the roles of Moses and Aaron in the interview in *Cahiers du cinéma*, no. 258.

59 On the two moments, their exchange and their circulation in Cézanne, cf. Henri Maldiney, *Regard, parole, espace*, Age d'homme, pp. 184–92. Certain commentators have clearly shown the richness of the two moments in the Straubs, from different perspectives which always lead back to Cézanne: the 'active mixture between two passions, the political and the aesthetic' (Biette, *Cahiers du cinéma*, no. 332); or double composition, of each shot and of the relationship between shots, 'the axis and the air' (Manfred Bland, *Cahiers du cinéma*, no. 305). This latter text gives an analysis of the 'system' in *Della Nube* . . . 'Whilst all that was being filmed, the sun moved from the east towards the west and lit up the people, who are seen still in the same place, from a different angle for each shot . . . And this sun is fire, the fire which goes into the earth and wakes up the earth; it is a sun setting, and a shot in parallel with the plane of the field.' The Straubs often quote Cézanne's dictum: 'Look at the mountain, once it was fire.'

60 *India Song* is one of those films which have led to a great many examinations of the visual-sound relationship: notably Pascal Bonitzer (*Le regard et la voix*, pp. 148–53); Dominique Noguez (*Elogue du cinéma expérimental*, Centre Georges-Pompidou, pp. 141–9); Dionys Mascolo (in *Marguerite Duras*, Albatros, pp. 143–56). This last collection also contains essential articles on *La femme du Gange*, by Joël Farges, Jean-Louis Libois and Catherine Weinzaepflen.

61 Marguerite Duras, *Nathalie Granger*, followed by *La femme du Grange*: when 'the film of the image' and 'the film of voices', without being reharmonized, each independently touches the other at the infinite point which constitutes their 'joining', both 'die', at the same time as their respective sides are crushed (Marguerite Duras locates this point in *La femme du Gange*, op. cit., pp. 183–4; the film continues none the less, as if there were a 'more' or a survival which will be put into the next film, which is in turn double).

62 Youssef Ishaghpour, *D'une image à l'autre*, p. 285 (this formulation is taken from a detailed analysis of Duras's work, pp. 225–98).

63 Marguerite Duras talks about the 'depopulation of space' in *India Song*, and in particular about 'The desertedness of the area in *Son nom de Venise* . . . (*Marguerite Duras*, pp. 20, 94). Ishaghpour analyses this 'abandoning of the habitat' which begins with *La femme du Gange*, pp. 239–40.

64 Viviane Forrester, 'Territoires du cri', in *Marguerite Duras*, pp. 171–3.

65   cf. Nathalie Heinich's analysis on the river-speech complementarity, *Cahiers du cinéma*, no. 307, pp. 45–7.
66   To the question, 'Is the text of Fortini not authoritarian?' Straub replies: 'This language is that of a class in power, but none the less a language of someone who has betrayed this class as much as he could . . .' (*Conférence de presse*, Pesars, 1976; and also 'all the characteristics of peasant wars have something in common with these landscapes').
67   Marguerite Duras put forward the idea, as rather 'the fugitive feeling of a class of violence' in *Nathalie Granger*, pp. 76, 95 (and p. 52 on the commercial traveller's very specific situation). Bonitzer comments on this class of violence in *India Song*, which brings together 'lepers, beggars and vice-consuls': pp. 152–3.
68   Blanchot, *L'entretien infini*, 'Speaking is not seeing', pp. 35–46. This is a constant theme in Blanchot, but the piece that we quote is the most concentrated example. The role that Blanchot assigns to seeing, will be all the better observed, from the other side but in an ambiguous or secondary way.
69   On the practical conception of the sound 'continuum' and the aspects of its novelty, in Fano, cf. especially Gardies, *Le cinéma de Robbe-Grillet*, pp. 85–8. On the treatment of a sound continuum in Godard's *First Name Carmen*, cf. 'Les mouettes du pont d'Austerlitz', an interview with François Musy, *Cahiers du cinéma*, no. 355, janvier 1984. Our problem of sound framing is not directly taken up by these authors, although they move decisively towards the solution. More generally, technical analyses seem to be lagging behind in this respect (apart from Dominique Villain, *L'oeil à la caméra*, who asks the question directly, ch. IV). We believe that a sound framing can be technologically defined by:

1. the *number* of microphones and their qualitative diversity; 2. the filters, corrective or for cutting; 3. the time modulators, with echo or time-lapse (including the Harmonizer); 4. stereo sound, in so far as it ceases to be a positioning in space and becomes the exploration of a sound-density or time-volume. A sound framing can be achieved by home-made means, but only because one would know how to produce effects comparable to those of modern technology. What is important is that the means come into play from the point of the sound recording, and not only in the mixing and montage; the difference, moreover, is increasingly relative. Glenn Gould is furthest ahead, not only in sound montage, but in framing, which he creates with radio (cf. the film *Radio as Music*). Fano's conception should be compared with Gould's. They imply a new conception of music, which derives for Fano from Berg, and for Gould from Schoenberg. According to Gould, and likewise Cage, it is indeed a question of framing, of inventing an active sound-frame for everything that surrounds us auditively, for everything that the environment

puts at our disposition. cf. *The Glenn Gould Reader*, Knopf, New York; and Geoffroy Paysant, *Glenn Gould, un homme du futur*, ch. IX, which is mistaken in its analyses only in privileging the operations of sound-montage at the expense of those of framing.

10 *Conclusions*

1 An excellent general presentation of Guillaume's work in this connection will be found in Alain Rey, *Théories du signe et du sens*, Klincksieck, II, pp. 262–4. Ortigues gives a more detailed analysis in *Le discours et le symbole*, Aubier.

2 On the tendency to eliminate the notion of sign, cf. Ducrot and Todorov, *Encyclopaedic Dictionary of the Sciences of Language*, pp. 349–65. Christian Metz shares this tendency (*Langage et cinéma*, Albatros, p. 146).

3 Jean-Louis Schefer, *L'homme ordinaire du cinéma*, Cahiers du cinéma/ Gallimard.

4 These are the two extreme states of thought, the spiritual automaton of logic, pointed to by Spinoza and Leibniz, and the psychological automaton of psychiatry, studied by Janet.

5 cf. Serge Daney, *La rampe*, 'L'Etat-Syberberg', p. 111 (and p. 172). Daney's analysis is based here on numerous declarations by Syberberg himself. Syberberg takes his cue from Benjamin, but goes further, launching the theme 'Hitler as film-maker'. Benjamin notes only that 'mass production' in the domain of art found its privileged object in 'the reproduction of the masses', grand processions, meetings, sporting gatherings, ultimately war ('The work of art in the era of mechanical reproduction', in *Illuminations*, trans. Harry Zohn, London: Fontana, 1973.

6 Syberberg does not begin like Benjamin from the idea of the reproductive arts, but from the idea of cinema as art of the movement-image: 'for a long time people have begun from the presupposition which let it be understood that to talk about cinema was to talk about movement', mobile image, mobile camera, and montage. He thinks that the culmination of this system is Leni Riefenstahl, and her 'master who was hiding there behind'. 'But it was forgotten that in the cradle of cinema there had also been something else, projection, transparency': another type of image, implying 'slow, controllable movements' capable of bringing contradiction into the system of movement, or of Hitler – film-maker. cf. *Syberberg*, special number of *Cahiers du cinéma*, février 1980, p. 86.

7 cf. Pascal Kane, 'Mabuse et le pouvoir', *Cahiers du cinéma*, no. 309, mars 1980.

8 On not only the technical but the phenomenological differences between the types of image, the reader is particularly referred to the studies of Jean-Paul Fargier in *Cahiers du cinéma* and of Dominique

Belloir in the special number 'Video art explorations'. In an article in *Revue d'esthétique* ('Image puissance image', no. 7, 1984) Edmond Couchot defines certain characteristics of numerical or digital images, which he calls 'immedia', because there is no longer a medium properly speaking. The fundamental idea is that, already in television, there is no space or image either, but only electronic lines: 'the fundamental concept in television is time' (Nam June Paik, interview with Fargier, *Cahiers du cinéma*, no. 299, avril 1979).

9 Sometimes an artist, becoming aware of the death of the will to art in a particular medium, confronts the 'challenge' by a use which is apparently destructive of that medium: one might thus believe in negative goals in art, but it is rather a question of making up lost time, of converting a hostile area to art, with a certain violence, and of turning means against themselves. cf. in regard to television, Wolf Vostell's attitude as analysed by Fargier ('The great trauma', *Cahiers du cinéma*, no. 332, février 1982).

10 Noël Burch, *Pour un observateur lointain*, Cahiers du cinéma/ Gallimard, p. 185.

11 Leo Steinberg ('Other criteria', lecture at the Museum of Modern Art, New York, 1968) was already refusing to define modern painting by the conquest of a pure optical space, and isolated two characteristics which, according to him, were complementary: the loss of reference to the vertical human carriage, and the treatment of the painting as surface of information; for instance, Mondrian, when he metamorphoses the sea and sky more or less into signs, but above all with reference to Rauschenberg. 'The painted surface no longer presents an analogy with a natural visual experience, but becomes related to operational processes . . . The plane of Rauschenberg's painting is the equivalent of consciousness plunged into the city's brain.' In the case of cinema, even for Snow who offers himself a 'fragment of nature in the wild state', nature and the machine 'inter-represent themselves': to the extent that visual determinations are information data 'caught in the machine's operations and passage': 'This is a film as concept where the eye has reached the point of not seeing' (Marie-Christine Questerbert, *Cahiers du cinéma*, no. 296, janvier 1979, pp. 36–7).

12 cf. especially Jean-Claude Bonnet, 'Trois cinéastes du texte', *Cinématographe*, no. 31, octobre 1977.

13 On dissociation or disjunction, cf. the articles by Lardeau and by Comolli and Géré, in relation to *Hitler*, *Cahiers du cinéma*, no. 292, september 1978. For the definition of front-projection, and for the use of puppets, see the texts of Syberberg himself, in *Syberberg*, pp. 52–65. Bonitzer, in *Le champ aveugle*, draws out a whole conception of the complex shot in Syberberg.

14 cf. a crucial passage in Syberberg, *Parsifal*, Cahiers du cinéma/ Gallimard, pp. 46–7.

15 Jean-Pierre Oudart, *Cahiers du cinéma*, no. 294, novembre 1978, pp. 7–9. Syberberg has frequently emphasized his conception of

'documents' and the necessity of constituting a universal video school (*Syberberg*, p. 34); he suggests that the originality of cinema is defined in relation to information, rather than in relation to nature (*Parsifal*, p. 160). Sylvie Trosa and Alain Ménil have both underlined the non-hierarchic and non-causal character of the information system according to Syberberg (*Cinématographe*, no. 40, octobre 1978, p. 74, and no. 78, mai 1982 p. 20).

16 cf. in this connection Daney's commentaries, *La rampe*, pp. 110–11.

17 This is a constant theme of Syberberg's in his great text on irrationalism. 'L'art qui sauve de la misère allemande' in *Change*, no. 37. If there is none the less an ambiguity in Syberberg in relation to Hitler, it is Jean-Claude Biette who has most aptly expressed it: in 'the quantity of pieces of information' chosen, Syberberg emphasizes 'persecution against dead persons to the detriment of persecution of living ones', 'ostracism against Mahler' rather than 'ostracism against Schoenberg' (*Cahiers du cinéma*, no. 305, novembre 1979, p. 47).

18 On myth as irrational story-telling function, and as constitutive relation with a people: 'L'art qui sauve ...' What Syberberg reproaches Hitler for is having stolen the German irrational.

19 Michel Chion analyses the paradox of the playback as it functions in *Parsifal*: synchronization no longer has the object of *making believe*, because the miming body 'apparently remains foreign to the voice it gives itself', whether because it is a girl's face over a man's voice, or because there are two people laying claim to it. The dissociation between the voice heard and the body seen is thus not overcome, but on the contrary strengthened, accentuated. So what is the purpose of synchronization? asks Michel Chion. It becomes part of the creative function of myth. I makes the visible body, not now something imitating the utterance of the voice but something constituting an absolute *receiver* or addressee. 'Through it the image says to the sound: stop floating everywhere and come and live in me; the body opens to welcome the voice.' cf. 'L'aveu', *Cahiers du cinéma*, no. 338, juillet 1982.

20 The question of redemption runs through Syberberg's book on *Parsifal*, on two axes: the source and the addressee (the great head of Wagner and the Parsifal couple), the visual and sound (the 'cephalic landscapes' and the spiritual speech-act). But the Parsifal couple forms no more of a totality than the rest: redemption comes too late, 'the world is dead, all that is left is a frozen and murdered landscape' (interview in *Cinématographe*, no. 78, pp. 13–15).

21 This is what Raymond Ruyer has done philosophically in *La cybernétique et l'origine de l'information*, Flammarion. Taking into account the evolution of the automaton, he asks the question of the source and addressee of information, and constructs a notion of 'framer' which has connections with the problems of cinematographic framing.

22 Paul Schrader has spoken of a 'transcendental style' in certain

cinema-authors. But he uses this word to indicate the sudden arrival of the transcendent, as he thinks he sees it in Ozu, Dreyer, or Bresson (*Transcendental Style in Film: Ozu, Dreyer, Bresson*, extracts in *Cahiers du cinéma*, no. 286, mars 1978). It is thus not the Kantian sense, which in contrast opposes the transcendental and the metaphysical or transcendent.

23 More precisely, crystal-images are connected to the states of the crystal (the four states that we have distinguished), while crystalline signs or hyalosigns are connected to its properties (the three aspects of the exchange).

Glossary

CHRONOSIGN (point and sheet): an image where time ceases to be subordinate to movement and appears for itself.

CRYSTAL-IMAGE OR HYALOSIGN: the uniting of an actual image and a virtual image to the point where they can no longer be distinguished.

DREAM-IMAGE OR ONIROSIGN: an image where a movement of world replaces action

LECTOSIGN: a visual image which must be 'read' as much as seen.

NOOSIGN: an image which goes beyond itself towards something which can only be thought.

OPSIGN: an image which breaks the sensory-motor schema, and where the seen is no longer extended into action.

RECOLLECTION-IMAGE OR MNEMOSIGN: a virtual image which enters into a relationship with the actual image and extends it.

Index